W9-CMZ-440

Readers in
Librarianship and Information Science

Published Readers in the series:

Reader in the

HISTORY OF

BOOKS

and

PRINTING

edited by
PAUL A. WINCKLER

26

Information Handling Services
An Indian Head Company
Englewood, Colorado

**LIBRARY OF CONGRESS CATALOGING
IN PUBLICATION DATA**
Main entry under title:

Reader in the history of books and printing.

   (Readers in librarianship and information science; 26)
   Bibliography: p.
   Includes index.
   1. Books—History—Addresses, essays, lectures.
2. Printing—History—Addresses, essays, lectures.
I. Winckler, Paul A. II. Series.
Z4.R4   001.55'2   78-17260
ISBN 0-910972-78-8

Published by Information Handling Services
P.O. Box 1276
Englewood, Colorado 80150

Printed in the United States of America.

To

ANNE

Contents

IV
THE PRINTED BOOK

Foreword

Unlike many other academic disciplines, librarianship has not yet begun to exploit the contributions of the several disciplines toward the study of its own issues. Yet the literature abounds with material germane to its concerns. Too frequently the task of identifying, correlating, and bringing together material from innumerable sources is burdensome, time consuming or simply impossible. For a field whose stock in trade is organizing knowledge, it is clear that the job of synthesizing the most essential contributions from the elusive sources in which they are contained is overdue. This then is the rationale for the series, *Readers in Library and Information Science*.

The *Readers in Library and Information Science* will include books concerned with various broad aspects of the field's interests. Each volume will be prepared by a recognized student of the topic covered, and the content will embrace material from the many different sources from the traditional literature of librarianship as well as from outside the field in which the most salient contributions have appeared. The objectives of the series will be to bring together in convenient form the key elements required for a current and comprehensive view of the subject matter. In this way it is hoped that the core of knowledge, essential as the intellectual basis for study and understanding, will be drawn into focus and thereby contribute to the furtherance of professional education and professional practice in the field.

Paul Wasserman
Series Editor

Introduction

This book provides a selection of readings on the historical development of books and printing from ancient to modern times as a survey of the evolutionary history of graphic communication through the ages.

This is an ambitious task to be attempted in one volume and necessitates editorial selectivity. Any such selection reflects the editor's viewpoint and my aim has been to include items which are informative, useful, and readable—bringing together a variety of sources for convenience and enjoyment.

The subject of books and printing has interested many authors and scholars who have examined, studied, researched, interpreted, and recorded their findings and observations in a vast literature. From this plethora of materials I have selected those which may provide the reader with a general introduction to the history of books and printing. At the end of each unit is a list of "Additional Readings" for those who are interested in knowing and reading more on the topic. These lists include general material but not items on specific individuals or presses.

Unfortunately, many people who deal with books and media know very little about their origins, historical development, and changes which have been brought about by time and circumstance. A study of these developments can provide insight and add new dimension to our understanding of what has happened and what is happening today. The study of the history of books and printing is, in reality, a survey of the history of civilization as revealed in the recording, preserving, and disseminating of these materials and their use in the transmission of ideas.

This book has been compiled for the pleasure and enlightenment of students, librarians, educators, historians, media specialists, bibliophiles, bookmen, and bookwomen—all who are interested in books and printing. Hopefully each will find this work informative and useful in their understanding and appreciation of one of the greatest developments of civilization—the history of graphic communication.

PAUL A. WINCKLER

Palmer Graduate Library School

I.

OVERVIEW OF

BOOKS AND PRINTING

Part I. OVERVIEW OF BOOKS AND PRINTING

Introduction

"In the beginning was the word"—written communication was the start of recorded history and of civilization. According to Escarpit, "writing enabled the word to conquer time, but the book enabled it to conquer space. The pliant, light-weight supports which, thirty centuries ago, gave the book its various names opened the way to two decisive developments: first, it became possible to copy a long text rapidly and easily; and second, it became possible to transport a considerable number of copies of the text rapidly and easily to any destination." This meant that the message of one age could now be passed on to the next.

The essay "Fiat Lux" by Denys Hay is an appropriate beginning because he presents an introduction which succinctly shows the relationship of books and printing to society and the "impact of printing on the mind of man." The author skillfully presents a panorama of the development of graphic communication, revealing that "the printed page [and the book—Editor] illuminates the mind of man, and defies in so far as anything sublunary can, the corrosive hand of Time."

Hay establishes the theme of this reader—*Vox audita perit, littera scripta manet*— "The spoken word passes away, the written word remains."

Denys Hay

Fiat Lux

I

In principio creavit Deus caelum et terram. These are the first words of the text of the first book to be printed with movable metal type, the great 42-line Bible that came out at Mainz about 1455. In Genesis that beginning was followed by others. Immediately after heaven and earth came light. 'And God said: Let there be light.' On the sixth day God created man in his own image: 'male and female created he them.'

The earliest men and women communicated with each other (it must be supposed) by making noises. Grunts and screams, ejaculations prompted by pain, fear, hunger and desire, the smoother tones of momentary comfort and warmth, these were intelligible in a given situation when eked out by gesture and mime. Groups of men were small and their material equipment was scanty. The family and the tribe responded instinctively to the rhythmical demands of the seasons and met the slow changes in climate and geography with a dogged love of life which made them move their hunting grounds in the face of ice or drought. One can capture still this inarticulate but expressive atmosphere in moments of panic, in grief and in laughter and in the obscure but telling sounds made by babies and lovers.

Yet the passing millennia brought words, and this command of language was probably the most important single instrument which primitive peoples were able to use in the complicated game of survival. Particular noises became attached to particular actions and objects. It became possible to describe absent things and to

SOURCE: Reprinted from John Carter and Percy H. Muir, Compilers and Editors, *Printing and the Mind of Man: A Descriptive Catalogue Illustrating the Impact of Print on the Evolution of Western Civilization During Five Centuries* (New York: Holt, Rinehart and Winston, and London: Cassell and Company, 1967), "Fiat Lux," by Denys Hay, pp. xv to xxxiv, by permission of Percy H. Muir. Copyright © 1967 by John W. Carter and Percy H. Muir.

construct future relationships. The tribe could debate its problems and plan concerted action. The powerful could exert their wills in relatively distant places by
servants carrying messages; and one way of winning and consolidating power was the
exercise of oratory, the construction of arguments, the pronouncement of effective
verbal threats and promises. The leader of men, though tongue-tied himself, might
yet have fluent spokesmen and such men were at hand in the priests. With words
came the magic of words, the power to identify gods and to offer them prayer and
praise. And with words came poetry. The bard who recited the deeds of the heroes of
the tribe and the dynasty passed on his talents and his stories to other bards, as the
priests trained other priests to recite the hallowed incantations. Memories were acute
and tradition strong, for the lines spoken by bard and priest, like the commands borne
by the courier of a king, had to be exactly reproduced. Curiously enough it is more
difficult for people living in advanced societies to recapture this phase of speech than
the earlier phase of sounds and signs. The glimpses one can get of it suggest languages
(there were many of them) of repetitious formulae. For those members of society for
whom words had public importance it must have been like the game 'I packed my bag
and in it I put;' if one forgot one's sequences one was out of the game, perhaps
painfully or utterly out of the game. In a world of speech words could become
shackles.

II

The bondage of words was broken by writing them down. This stage seems to have
been first reached in Mesopotamia between about 4000 and 3000 B.C. From a large
number of conventional pictorial signs marked on clay tablets, symbols for things and
numerals, writing arrived at a point where abstractions could be conveyed. It could
further use the symbols to represent not only things and the actions or abstractions
associated with them, but also phonetic qualities—a step towards the transcription of
actual speech which the Sumerians had evidently reached at the time the earliest
surviving examples of their cuneiform script were made. A little later writing roughly
similar in accomplishment was evolved in the so-called hieroglyphics of Egypt and
the 'characters' of Chinese. Sumerian cuneiform and Egyptian hieroglyphics
perished in the course of time; Chinese has survived, a living fossil, so to speak,
among the great scripts of the world.

    Almost as important as the achievement of pictorial abstractions was the invention
of a purely phonetic alphabet. This is known to have existed in Syria from at least the
sixteenth or fifteenth century B.C. and there is now strong evidence of an alphabetical
script being used in Canaan one or two centuries earlier than that. 'Of all the areas of
the Near East,' writes David Diringer, 'the region of Palestine and Syria provides the
most likely source for the invention of the Alphabet.' The antecedents of 'Northern-
Semitic' may be obscure. It can however be shown that from Canaanite, through
Greek, were to descend the European alphabets, destined to overrun most of the
world.

Writing and literature developed in every part of the globe. They were to have the greatest extension in Europe because there writing was practised in an alphabet composed of a very small number of letters. Latin, which had originally only twenty-one characters (derived from Etruscan and Greek) and the alphabets derived from it (such as modern English with its twenty-six), should be compared with the enormous numbers of characters of Chinese; some 5,000 to 6,000 are regularly used. Moreover the materials used for writing in Europe also changed. From carvings or incisions on wood, stone and clay, and marks on bark, leather and cloth, scribes adopted first of all papyrus and then prepared skins marked with ink. Papyrus, fibre from a marsh plant found in the Nile valley and in the East Mediterranean area, was formed into sheets which could be used separately or glued together lengthways to make a continuous writing surface which was rolled up for storage. In the fourth century A.D. these rolls of papyrus came to be replaced by books made from sheets of vellum or parchment, in which the material was folded and sewn, in much the same manner as a modern book. Papyrus books are found, but the material was less robust and did not lend itself to this format. The paged book made of skins was also easier to handle than a roll on which the columns of writing succeeded each other continuously, and the surface of parchment lent itself to more rapid cursive writing.

The availability of the written word conditioned the whole development of civilization. A new dimension was given to the mind of man: he could afford to forget since he could store his information outside himself. The priest could list his temple-dues, assemble the canon of his scriptures and preserve the details of the liturgy. The prince could have his rights listed and transmit his orders with a new precision and authority. In both religion and politics the written word encouraged larger unities. In place of the fugitive contacts of speech the written word remained: *littera scripta manet*. The seeds of an advanced civilization could thus scatter themselves and the dominant position in the Mediterranean area and the southern half of Europe acquired successively by Greek and then by Latin culture was due principally to writing. These seeds could, moreover, lie dormant for centuries and yet spring to life, as did the literature and learning of the Greeks and Romans in the European Middle Ages and Renaissance.

The literature of the written word was not only religious and political. The bard gave way to the poet and in its turn imaginative prose found a place beside older epic and newer lyric. Men could and did play with their pens, and more subtly than they could play with their tongues: the crude pun and spoonerism could be matched by complicated acrostic and anagram, meaningless until seen in black and white. The simple arithmetic of addition and subtraction could give rise to the abstractions of pure mathematics. Language and literature acquired norms preserved in the certainties of grammar and orthography. The scriptures of religion could have secular parallels, 'classics' as they were later to be called, to which the grammarians turned as models of style.

These changes occurred in all regions where writing developed. They were probably carried furthest and fastest in Christian Europe. The 'third portion of the inhabited world,' peopled by the sons of Japhet, inherited the simplified alphabet of the Graeco-Roman Mediterranean tradition and acquired a religion based on written scriptures, old and new. Christianity was thus pledged to the promotion of reading and writing. Its Bible or book bred other books. Its priests were committed to an educational programme which in the end was to make so many men clerkly that the demand for the written word could not be met by conventional methods. The pressures thus built up in Europe resulted in the invention of printing.

The growth of literacy in the Middle Ages is imperfectly documented. Broadly speaking the education of priests was the main aim of formal instruction until the thirteenth century, and the curriculum was geared to the acquisition of a mastery of Latin, both written and spoken. The grammar school and the university remained throughout the period coloured by this original purpose; but by the later Middle Ages large numbers of laymen were attending both types of institution with no intention of following either a career in the Church or in one of the professions (law and medicine) for which the universities also catered. Secondary schools began to multiply in all European countries in the fourteenth and fifteenth centuries. They were most common in the bigger towns but gradually the gentry also sent their sons to be educated. Laymen in public positions in the tenth or eleventh centuries were usually illiterate. By the fifteenth century a nobleman and his steward could read and write, so could many of the ladies in the landed classes, and so of course could the merchants and shopkeepers in the towns. Doubtless by 1400 the illiterate still formed the large majority of the population, but it is certain that by then the clergy formed a minority of those who could read and write.

This transformation of society was accompanied by a transformation in the character of the book. In the so-called Dark Ages a book was a rarity. Produced in a sheltered corner of culture, a monastery in Ireland or Italy, it was usually connected with the Church and was treated with the reverence accorded to sacred things. With the spread of parishes over Christendom and the rising number of monasteries (in England convents increased from about sixty in the early eleventh century to just over 1,000 at the beginning of the fourteenth century) books ceased to be so precious. They were needed as Bibles and service books; they were needed as grammars to instruct clergy; they were needed for the religious who were transcribing old commentaries and works of devotion and composing new works of their own. Education by the twelfth century was entirely dependent on books. At school and even more at the university 'authors,' prescribed and approved, were read and glossed and considerable numbers of texts were required.

By this time the monasteries, which had earlier been the main centres of book-production in western Europe, could not meet the demand and their monks were, in any case, not particularly involved in the education of the secular community or even of the clergy, except their own monks. Hence the market was supplied by professional scriveners, men who made a career as book-producers. In Barbarian Europe author and scribe were often the same person. By the thirteenth century there began to be a difference between them. In and after the thirteenth century one could rely on there being a bookshop in a university town. Furthermore a big step had been taken to increase production of books, and lower the costs of producing them, by the use of paper. Parchment, it is true, had by the end of the Middle Ages become very fine and light and until the mid-fifteenth century there seems to have been enough of it. But by then the use of paper was widespread. Paper had first entered Europe from China by way of Muslim countries in the twelfth century. By the early fourteenth century rag paper was manufactured on a considerable scale both in Spain and in Italy and from Italy its manufacture spread north of the Alps. This does not mean that by about 1400, with an important manufacture of books (many made of paper), in all essentials the situation as we know it today had been reached. There were big differences and to appreciate the influence of printing one must look carefully at the manuscript book in the last two centuries before Gutenberg's invention.

The handwritten book was a separate unit unlike any other. This is true not only of original works, written *ab initio*. It is almost as true of books of which very large numbers of copies were made, works like the Bible itself, or the dozens of approved authors read by students at school or university. The very greatest care was certainly taken to secure authentic texts. Rules for copyists in the *scriptoria* of monasteries were strict and universities laid down the most stringent regulations for the *stationarii* who supplied texts. Yet the transcribers each wrote a distinct hand, conforming certainly with the accepted style of their time and place but permitting themselves endless variations in the formation of letters and in methods of abbreviating words or shortening them by other conventions, such as suspension of final syllables. Even when a work was copied quire by quire with gatherings of parchment or paper of the same length as the gatherings of the *exemplar* (the *pecia* system), the resulting manuscript was still distinguishable from its exemplar by infinite if subtle or minor variations. If the text of no two books was exactly alike, it can be imagined how much greater differences there were in apparatus—contents, index, glosses. The index in particular tended to be a highly particularized exercise and when found was the work of an owner rather than of a copyist. In such a situation the identification of books was frequently less by the general description afforded by a title, and more often by the precise indications afforded by their opening words (*incipits*) and concluding words (*explicits*) together with the number of the first and last folio. This is how books were usually catalogued in the public libraries which were beginning to be found in universities at the end of the Middle Ages, as in the collections formed earlier by great monasteries and cathedrals.

When books were made by hand errors were thus bound to occur and they naturally had a cumulative effect. In the case of fundamental texts like the Bible repeated efforts at emendment were made and a general correctness was maintained. In service books knowledge of the liturgy secured correct copies. But in a wide range of writing a manuscript book tended to become less authentic the more it was copied. This deterioration was intensified when the main source of supply was no longer the clergy, especially the regular clergy, but lay scriveners. Writing often under great pressure for a steady and known market, the professional scribe was often careless and incompetent. At the same time the handwriting itself became poorer in quality. Though there were splendid manuscripts produced by proud calligraphers in fifteenth-century Italy, and even some noble volumes made in the north of Europe, the average manuscript book of the later Middle Ages was slovenly, unattractive to look at and difficult to read when compared with similar works of the eleventh and twelfth centuries. Writing and reading were, as has been observed already, much commoner by the later date, and familiarity bred contempt.

The book trade existed. It was, however, essentially dealing in well-known works, and it did not have much if any influence on the composition of new books, which entered the dealer's regular stock only when there was a large and certain demand. An author as such (as in the days of Greece and Rome) thus needed to support himself by means other than his pen; he was a monk, a beneficed clerk, a university professor or the familiar protégé of a prince or great man, occasionally an official in the employment of a city. His writing could redound to the honour and prestige of his patron, and occasionally he might be rewarded by some extraneous Maecenas to whom he dedicated a work; but he was in no sense paid for writing. Above all he had no right in his book, no copyright. If it proved popular and began to figure regularly on the stalls of Paris or Cologne, he had no royalties.

In these circumstances publication was effected in one of two ways. The writer could deliberately send a fair copy of his completed manuscript to a friend or patron, usually with a letter of dedication. Or he might lend his work, perhaps in an unfinished state, to a colleague and find later that copies of it were circulating without his prior agreement. Further, the author often dedicated the same work to different patrons, perhaps revising the text to suit them; in this way arose the four main recensions of Froissart's Chronicle. Or he might keep the original manuscript beside him, constantly tinkering with it but allowing portions of it or the whole of it to be transcribed from time to time; this explains the complicated textual history of Thomas à Kempis's De imitatione Christi. Here again a vast range of variables distinguishes copies of the same work. Which is the 'true' text of Froissart or the Imitation of Christ?

If publication was erratic, suppression of manuscript books could be much more systematic. Nothing offers better evidence of the rapid spread of books than the repeated attempts made to stifle the use of some of them. From the early thirteenth century (and there are cases even before that) works by theologians and philosophers were from time to time proscribed by other, more powerfully placed theologians and philosophers. Sometimes such attempts were in vain, as was the hierarchy's condemnation of Aristotle in the schools of Paris in the early thirteenth century; in the next generation a new race of Aristotelians had secured acceptance for his doctrines. Marsilio of Padua and William of Occam encountered papal censure; they and their works survived unscathed. A more concerted attack, in which the popes concerned had the support of most responsible theologians, was made on the teaching of Wycliffe, though he was burned as a heretic only many years after his death. John Huss's writings brought him to the pyre at Constance in 1415. The condemnation of a man carried with it the condemnation of his books and they too were destroyed. Clearly it was easier for bishops and inquisitors to obliterate heretical works when they had just been written and before they had attained a wide circulation, and this in fact happened: many a minor heretic's writings have survived only in the indictment of his crimes. Yet the circulation of books was such that not only did Wycliffe's theology easily move from Oxford to Prague, but the writings of Wycliffe and Huss (wrongly accused of being a disciple of Wycliffe) in large measure survived the official holocaust.

An author might not be able to control the publication of his book or ensure in all cases that it survived unmutilated or at all, and he could not derive an income from it even if it was successful. But by the later Middle Ages he had readers beyond his own immediate circle and, if the work was non-technical and in the vernacular, he had a public in the modern sense of the term. Dante's *Divine Comedy*, Petrarch's lyrics, the *Decameron* of Boccaccio and Chaucer's *Canterbury Tales* were written not to entertain one man or even a court or a coterie but to be enjoyed by all who had the ability to read. The fourteenth- or fifteenth-century author had linguistic difficulties. There was no one French or English or Italian. Significant creative writing in the vernacular did, however, promote the emergence of dominant literary languages as the works of Dante, Petrarch and Boccaccio stimulated the later importance of what might be called 'courtly Tuscan.'

The rising literacy of the fifteenth century was to make many more readers, so many more that the printing press was invented. At that critical moment, what was the intellectual stock of Europe? What books existed for the early printers to print? The list is formidably long. It contains the main writers of classical antiquity, including by 1450 all the main Roman writers save Tacitus, and (in Latin translation as well as in the original) most of Aristotle and some Plato, as well as Homer. From these works there had already stemmed a vast literature of commentary and creation as Roman and Greek ideas mingled with and challenged the most revolutionary corpus of writing inherited from the past—the Hebrew Scriptures and the Christian New Testament. With these Greek, Roman and Hebrew ingredients were mixed the scholarship and science of the Arab world—Rhases, Averroes and the rest. Like their Hellenistic predecessors, medieval scholars and men of letters often channelled their vast reservoirs of ideas into digest, anthologies and *florilegia*. They had developed to a fine art, again repeating the pattern of an older day, the habit of glossing and expounding a text, aided by the conviction that dialectic was a way of approaching the truth and that the written word of an *auctor*, an authority, was at any rate the beginning of wisdom.

The plenitude of ideas generated by medieval books defies simple analysis. One finds in the millennium between the fall of Rome in 410 and the fall of Constantinople in 1453 the expression of practically every imaginable opinion. There are monarchists, republicans, and communists. There are philosophers who bound man and the created world in a net of rational causation and others who denied this legalism in favour of a subjective approach to the mysteries and a pragmatic attitude to the language of metaphysics. There are cynics and mystics, and many who are a bit of both. There are chroniclers and memorialists, and scholars whose computations of chronology formed the basis for such narrators. There are tellers of stories, of lives of the saints and of great men, and there are even a few introspective writers (like Petrarch) who display their souls with pen and ink. And there are poets. The poets in Latin sometimes aped the classical writers they had learned at school—with happy results in a few cases. But they had a better chance when they let their fancy wander, even in Latin, to the rhythmical and rhymed verse of the vernacular as in the goliardic songs, full of a casual gusto and sometimes of a carnal pathos which should have been foreign to the 'clergy' who wrote them.

One important distinction must be made. With few exceptions, writing on serious subjects was in Latin and the vernaculars were the vehicles of written compositions only in what at the time were regarded as frivolous and secular fields. Dante's scholarship, like Petrarch's and Boccaccio's, was in Latin: like theirs his Italian writings were reserved for more popular themes. Latin was the language of cultivated men, understood universally and taught in every part of Christendom. It was the only language which was regularly taught beyond the elementary stage. Italian did not exist: there were a dozen Italians; and so it was with French, German, English and the languages of Spain. In France and England the court and the capital were giving one particular kind of French and English a predominance over the others. By the early fifteenth century there was no similar incipient unity in other parts of Europe save what was being imposed by the great vernacular writers themselves. Yet even in the dialects, as the regional languages would later become, there was a remarkable sharing of cultural trends. Arthurian romance penetrated everywhere, and so did many of the Latin classics, translated into North German or Catalan. The really literate were still the clerks and the men (often laymen now) who had acquired some Latin at a grammar school or university primarily designed for clerks. But for those who were not able to read Latin there was also much to hand. Among the works generally available in a vernacular version by the end of the Middle Ages was the Vulgate Bible.

III

At the entrance to the 1963 Exhibition, there was an enlarged reproduction of the first page of Gutenberg's Bible, on which a spotlight picked out the words *fiat lux*; 'Let there be light.' The vast increase in the accessibility of books which resulted from printing may suitably be illustrated by the example of the Bible itself. The Latin Vulgate had been printed ninety-four times by 1500; vernacular translations were in print for virtually every European language by 1600. By the latter date a press was to be found in nearly every town of any size. Some inventions (the water mill, for example) have taken centuries to be widely adopted and even more have taken several generations. Printing was an exception. It spread at a phenomenal speed from Mainz and by the 1490s each of the major states had one important publishing centre and some had several.

The world of books had been transformed and it is impossible to exaggerate the rapidity of the transformation. It is all too easy to exaggerate the consequences and to credit printing as such with occasioning as rapid a change in the mind of man. When Bacon listed the printing press along with gunpowder and the compass as ushering in the modern world he sadly oversimplified the realities. A closer examination of the first age of printing, from Gutenberg in the 1450s to the early nineteenth century, reveals many and profound continuities with the old manuscript-bound Middle Ages.

The early printed book physically resembled the manuscript book. The latter had been made up of gatherings of parchment or paper, sewn and bound between covers. On a shelf a row of medieval manuscripts does not look different from a row of early printed books. Nor does a manuscript look different from an early printed book when taken off the shelf and opened. The printer aimed his wares at the existing book-buying public and he did his best to provide an article with which his customers were familiar. In the Rhineland Gutenberg had used type designed to look like the best local book hands. In the Low Countries a 'bastard' hand was imitated and this Caxton used for the first works for the English market. In Italy 'humanist' hands, to settle down as 'Italic' and 'Roman,' were being used, especially for the copying of texts in the humanities. These were the models followed by the printers of Rome, Venice, Milan, Naples and Florence; printers were at work at all of these places by the early 1470s. Nor did the first printers venture often to display their capacity for large-scale production. Editions seldom consisted of more than 1,000 copies and 200 seems to have been a common figure. There were technical and financial reasons for this, and not least the difficulty of raising capital to be tied up in large stocks of paper, metal and finished books. Yet the main explanation lay in the dependence of the printer-publisher on a market which was not unlimited. He could rely on a steady sale only of established works like the Bible, Donatus's grammar, prayer books and so on. The bulk of the works printed in the first century of printing were the old works, familiar to the region where the printer was at work. Fairly soon a degree of specialization developed and the volumes produced by some printers established themselves as articles of long-distance commerce and formed the staple of special markets or book fairs, such as the celebrated ones at Frankfurt and Leipzig.

Nor was there any change in the position of the author, who was not paid for the sales of his work on any pro rata basis. Many new books, perhaps most, were printed at the cost of the author or his patron. If the author was becoming well known the printer might share the costs. If the author was famous—Erasmus or Luther, for example—the printer might bear the entire cost and even allow the author some copies to give away. But nothing prevented a popular book being reprinted dozens of times and in dozens of places without the knowledge of the author. Men like Erasmus and Luther could thus make a fortune for a printer; the reverse was not true. It was only in the course of the seventeenth century that authors began to be paid in cash and not until the early eighteenth that they were given big sums of money. Finally, beginning with England, the state gave copyright to the author. By 1800 the process had been more or less completed. Authors could, if successful, live directly from their pens and not indirectly through a proliferation of dedications to rich and powerful men or by enjoying sinecures in Church or State. One of the fundamental characteristics of the first three centuries of printing is that the creative writer, the man of ideas and inspiration, wrote his books because he wished to express himself and not to make money. Erasmus with his well-placed friends was comfortably off, but his enormous output of best sellers, the *Praise of Folly*, the *Adagia*, the *Colloquies*, the long series of volumes of educational and moral works, the massive erudition of his classical and patristic editions, were the product of a man who researched and wrote compulsively and not for cash. Milton did not write *Paradise Lost* for the £5 paid for the manuscript by his publisher (or the further £5 which was to follow if a reprint was needed).

In many respects books and authors were thus not materially affected by printing, save that larger numbers of a work could now be rapidly made. Yet this multiplication of books was itself a very remarkable change. Coinciding, as the invention and spread of printing did, with the further development of the rising literacy which had provoked it, the increasing consumption of books undeniably meant that more persons wanted to read, just as it facilitated their acquiring the ability: a *virtuous* circle had been set up. In the sixteenth and later centuries it became almost impossible for a man to attain positions of wealth or influence if he was illiterate. The well-to-do in every European country knew that to survive here below, and even to spend their money in fashionable ways, education was necessary; the ambitious knew that education opened a well-paved road to success. All gentlemen's sons and the sons of most of the urban bourgeoisie went to grammar school, *lycée* or *gymnasium*. The crofter's son in Scotland who sought his M.A. to become a minister or a dominie, the sons of *contadini* in the Romagna and the Abruzzi who entered religious orders, caused (in the seventeenth and early eighteenth centuries) what would be termed, in the jargon of the modern economist, 'a crisis of overproduction.' The curriculum of secondary education was remarkably similar in all European countries. Roman and Teuton, Roman Catholic and Protestant, were given a lot of Latin grammar and a little Greek. The texts they read furnished their masters with moral aphorisms and the subjects pursued were those which could be illustrated by the ancient classics: the history of antiquity, rhetoric, poetry—in a word, the humanities. Education was literary and mathematics had small part in it. At a level below this children could learn their letters and some arithmetic in the sporadic schools run by a parson or his clerk or by a literate 'dame,' and the craftsman and the merchant picked up their skills, including the ability to read and write, mainly through apprenticeship or its equivalent. The grammar school was, however, the main regular source of education for those who could afford it and it covered the gentry and upper bourgeoisie of Europe with a patina of Latin-based culture.

The books used by the schoolmaster and his pupils, and those written and read by the handful of *literati* and scholars, were also technically improved compared with those of the later Middle Ages. When a volume was printed instead of being copied by hand it became worthwhile to take pains, infinite pains, to get the text right. In the manuscript accuracy was highly desirable but in practice hardly attainable; in print, with careful composition, with careful proofreading, with the *corrigenda* published at once and then incorporated in later reprints, something like perfection seemed in sight and was certainly aimed at by the great printers of the sixteenth century (Aldus, Froben, the Estiennes and others) and by their successors. Further, when there were more books than before it became necessary to identify them precisely and quickly. The title of a book, obscurely found (if at all) in the colophons of manuscripts and early incunables, came to figure prominently at the beginning of the printed work and soon occupied a full preliminary page—an advertisement for the work which followed. The clumsy gloss gradually gave way to the footnote, permitting author and reader to avoid tiresome interruptions of the text by learned references or lengthy asides. The index was perfected and the alphabet took a further big step forward as an instrument of enlightenment and erudition.

Libraries became more plentiful and much bigger. The library of the Sorbonne in the early fourteenth century numbered fewer than 2,000 volumes and at Cambridge in the fifteenth century there were only 500 or so books in the University collection. By the seventeenth century the picture had altered. Princely patrons and great men were competing to establish great public libraries, such as that formed by Cardinal Mazarin with its 40,000 volumes. England lagged behind as far as noble or princely patronage was concerned, but the Bodleian Library at Oxford at this time became a national institution and led the way with its printed catalogues, as the Library of the British Museum, founded in the mid-eighteenth century, still does in the mid-twentieth. More significant, perhaps, was the spread of private libraries. In the course of the sixteenth century the main purchasers of books ceased to be the clergy: between 1557 and 1600 surviving inventories of books in France show that for every collection made by an ecclesiastic (prelate, priest or don) there were more than three made by lawyers and administrators, the lay 'aristocracy' of the *gens de robe*. 'In 1500' (Mr. Sears Jayne tells us in his *Library Catalogues of the English Renaissance*) 'the principal owners of books in England were ecclesiastical institutions. . . By 1640. . . both Universities boasted many fine libraries of thousands of volumes each, there were several private collections of more than a thousand volumes, and there was not a single important ecclesiastical library in the country.' By the early eighteenth century a gentleman's house of any size had a room called the library. With this development went a new system in library management and in bibliographical expertise. Lists of books on a subject basis begin almost with printing. Johann Tritheim, who became abbot of Spanheim (not far from Mainz), published a *Liber de scriptoribus ecclesiasticis* in 1494. In 1545 the Swiss physician and naturalist Conrad Gesner published his *Bibliotheca Universalis* 'or complete catalogue of all writers in Latin, Greek and Hebrew, surviving and perished, old and modern up to the present. . . A new work necessary not only for the formation of public and private libraries but for all students. . . .' The science of bibliography had been established. By the mid-seventeenth century it was relatively easy to find out what books had been published on any topic. The purchaser was already able to turn to catalogues produced regularly by the biggest printing houses. The annual lists of the Frankfurt book fair began in 1564. More or less full lists of books published in France were issued from 1648 to 1654; a similar English catalogue appeared first in 1657. Even more important for the dissemination of information about new books and the ideas in them was the review-journal. This started with the French *Journal des Savants* (1665) which was followed by the *Philosophical Transactions* of the Royal Society of London (1675). By the early eighteenth century this process had been internationalized by translations of such periodicals and by the group of scholars (of whom Pierre Bayle was the most important) who diffused the intellectual novelties circulating in Europe from their asylum in the United Provinces where they published *Nouvelles de la République des lettres* and similar reviews.

One other list of publications was also published from time to time, but with the object of warning readers against the books it named. This was the *Index Librorum Prohibitorum*, issued under papal authority from 1559. The papal inquisitor or, in areas where there was no papal Inquisition (England was one), the local bishop had been responsible in the later Middle Ages for the suppression of heretical and erroneous writings. The printing press made such supervision of books of even greater concern not only to the prelates or the pope, but also to governments. Two generations after Gutenberg Luther roused Germany and a horrified orthodoxy tried to identify the sources of Lutheran doctrine and prevent such influences continuing to be effective; not only were earlier prohibitions of the books of Wycliffe and Huss repeated, but at the same time Erasmus's writings were attacked and condemned. Equally the hierarchy and its theologians attempted to suppress Luther's writings and those of his disciples. At first the attempts at censorship were localized. The centralization of Roman Catholic censorship in the Roman *Index* was effected after the Council of Trent. Frequently issued in revised editions, the *Index* undoubtedly impeded the free circulation of books in countries where there was a vigilant bishop or inquisitor, and it continued to do so for centuries, though signs of increasing tolerance became apparent in the year of grace 1966. But it entirely failed to prevent the books which it condemned from penetrating even areas obedient to Rome. Elsewhere, among Protestants or (later) among *libres penseurs* or 'progressives,' the knowledge that a book was in the *Index* constituted a positive reason for reading it. Nor were princes and town magistrates much more successful in suppressing books which they judged to be seditious or immoral; it should be remembered here that with printing came pornography. There were many attempts at state supervision of unwelcome works. The wary, ingenious and covetous printer defeated them all, though not without occasional danger to himself and not without leaving behind some bibliographical puzzles. It had not been easy to burke a manuscript book. It was impossible to stifle print. In Milton's *Areopagitica* the doctrine of freedom of publication was given canonical form.

The printed book thus differed from the manuscript book by appearing in numbers so large that suppression was in practice impossible, by presenting in general a more reliable text (supported when appropriate by footnotes, indices and other apparatus), by lending itself easily to collection in public and private libraries and to access through bibliographies and periodical reviews. In all these ways printing made book-learning and book-pleasures of other kinds much more accessible. It also promoted changes in style and presentation which caused the printed book to become inherently more attractive, more attractive as a physical object , than earlier manuscripts. It is, of course, true that all through the Middle Ages beautiful books were made by hand, from the glorious manuscripts made in Charlemagne's day down to the glorious manuscripts collected by Guidobaldo Montefeltre at Urbino in the fifteenth century; it was said that he would not tolerate a printed volume in his library.

But the general level of ordinary manuscript books, the workaday tools of teacher or researcher, were unpleasant to look at by the fourteenth and fifteenth centuries. Bibles could be made sufficiently neat and small, but at the price of writing them in a hand so minute as to be almost indecipherable. Early printing, aimed at a mass market, at first copied locally prevailing book hands. This however changed as printers and typographers accustomed themselves to the new medium. Everywhere the trend was away from heavy black pages towards lighter pages, which gave an overall impression of grey. This was achieved mainly by adopting a lettering which was lighter, finer, better spaced and arranged. In this steady transition Italian printers provided in their italic and roman faces a model which was generally followed in Europe, save in Germany and in Slavonic lands. The victory of Italian typography was the last, but by no means the least, stage in the conquest of the rest of Europe by the values and methods evolved in the peninsula during the Renaissance. Associated at first with the texts of Latin classics and the humanists of Italy, these agreeable and economical founts acquired general prestige by being used by the Venetian printer Aldus Manutius. That they were steadily adopted all over Europe is a tribute to the key position of the grammar-school master and his high-born and influential pupils. Even in Germany roman type was used for classical or humanist texts. At the same time books began to be smaller. Great folios still abounded in the seventeenth and eighteenth centuries, but there were more quartos, octavos and duodecimos.

It has been observed earlier that the advent of printing had no immediate effect on the material circumstances of the author. As the printed book slowly evolved and perfected itself, consequences for authorship nevertheless slowly followed.

It is impossible to believe that the writers of the sixteenth and seventeenth centuries did not feel sensuous pleasure at the sight of their work in print, as their twentieth-century successors do. The smell of the paper, the ink and the glue have not (thank heavens) been distilled and bottled in Paris or New York and one can still discriminate between the scent of a woman and the perfume of a new book: yet the ensuing sensations can be of the same invading wholeness. The authors of an earlier day would, it is true, have titivated their noses with vellum and leather, odours which can nowadays only be savoured among the aromatic shelves of a great library where the gold and the calf exude incense, even if it is only saddle-soap and insecticide. They too would view a dozen crisp copies of one of their books with astonished pride: not everyone can father such multiplicity, nor send into the unknown so many heralds and hawkers.

Composition of a book which was to be 'published' in manuscript meant that the writer knew who would read it, at any rate initially. With a printed work publication meant something different. Automatically it was offered to a number, perhaps a very large number, of purchasers and readers with whose background and tastes the author could not be familiar. In the case of some specialized works, for instance in medicine and law, a professional audience could be anticipated. But in more general fields, history, literary criticism, philosophy, natural philosophy and even theology, as well of course as imaginative prose and verse, there was no telling in advance who precisely would be attracted. It is true that the medieval writer was aware that he could often expect ultimately to have unknown readers, but the degree of anonymity in his public to which an author was committed by printing was of a different order. New inducements existed to make one's writing intelligible and its presentation agreeable. Where appropriate, the author must now avoid plunging *in medias res*; he must rather set the scene and provide an introductory summary, explaining himself and his subject. (Compare the preliminary pages of the fourteenth-century Florentine *Chronicle* of Giovanni Villani with the beginning of Machiavelli's *Istorie Fiorentine*, which was designed for publication though it appeared after the author's death.) Moreover an attractively written book was much more likely to be published, for—from the mid-sixteenth century onwards—it was booksellers rather than printers who put up the capital for a new work and they knew, or thought they knew, what the public wanted.

From the sixteenth century there arose one basic change in the public for books which conditioned authorship: Latin gradually ceased to be the only or even the main vehicle for serious writing. It has already been pointed out that the vernaculars were used in the Middle Ages, broadly speaking, only for ephemeral works, even if a later age was to regard the *Romance of the Rose* and the *Divine Comedy* as immortal. This attitude persisted in the first century of printing, but gradually the vernaculars (under the pervasive influence of Latin) acquired a maturity which enabled English, French and the others to carry with confidence and efficiency the most sophisticated thoughts. Prudent and far-sighted men might question whether professional knowledge (in medicine, physical science or theology) should thus be made available on the market-place; certainly there were meaner experts who resented their *arcana* being exposed to the light of common day. But the process was irreversible. Latin scholarship in all subjects was turned into English and French and Castilian, and in the same languages scholars now began to compose. By the end of the seventeenth century Latin was no longer indispensable to the learned *writer*, even though as a *scholar* he still found it indispensable. At the Frankfurt book fair the proportion of Latin to German books was two to one in the decades between 1560 and 1630; by the 1680s more books were for sale in German than in Latin.

In English the appearance of Richard Hooker's *Of the Laws of Ecclesiastical Polity* (1594-97) marks the emancipation of English as an autonomous medium. Fifty years earlier such a book would have been written in Latin or else would have appeared in the clumsy obscurity of what C. S. Lewis called 'drab.' Yet Hooker paid a penalty for his achievement. His remarkable theological work remained virtually unknown to continental scholars. Isaak Walton in his life of Hooker (1664) described how he had been told 'more than forty years past' that the attention of Pope Clement VIII was drawn to the book by 'either Cardinal Allen, or learned Dr Stapleton.' The pope was informed that 'though he [the pope] had lately said he never met with an English book whose writer deserved the name of an author; yet there now appeared a wonder to them, and it would be to his Holiness, if it were in Latin; for a poor obscure English priest had writ four such books of Laws and Church-Polity, and in a style that expressed such a grave and so humble a majesty, with such clear demonstration of reason, that in all their readings they had not met with any that exceeded him.' With this view Clement concurred when Dr. Stapleton read him the first part in an extempore Latin translation.

Across the linguistic frontiers of Europe scholars continued to communicate in Latin even when they ceased to publish in it. One must remember that many original Latin works were being printed until well on in the eighteenth century, and that many writers (Galileo, Descartes and scores more) published works with equal fluency in Latin and a vernacular. Latin remained the normal language for international correspondence between scholars in different countries, only slowly being replaced by Italian and then by French. Translation was also able to diffuse knowledge originally available only in vernacular writing and was undertaken with an increasing care for accuracy. Latin translations were even published of periodicals such as the French *Journal des Savants* and the English *Philosophical Transactions*. Translation was, moreover, facilitated by the nature of vernacular prose and poetry down to the end of the eighteenth century. Heavily influenced everywhere by Latin grammar and syntax, vernacular writers shared a common attitude to style. They had also been brought up on a classical pabulum which ensured that their allusions and points of reference were readily understood everywhere. There was nevertheless now a choice before an educated author, whether to address himself first or mainly to an international audience in Latin or to a national audience in his mother-tongue.

The choice of such a writer was often determined by his purposes. The moralist and above all the church reformer naturally sought to address large numbers. This was not a new situation. Huss preaching in Czech, Bernardino in Italian, were doing what Luther and others were to do in print—going to the masses. Indeed, the sermon-hungry audiences of the fifteenth century often represented the whole population of a town, whereas the printed word immediately reached only those who could read, though they in turn might speak out the message. But the vast quantities of pamphlets issued in Germany (630 have been listed from the years 1520 to 1530) leave no doubt that without the printing press the course of the German Reformation might have been different. Luther's own writings constitute a third of the German books printed in the first four decades of the sixteenth century; his address *To the Christian Nobility of the German Nation* (August 1520) was reprinted thirteen times in two years; *Concerning Christian Liberty* (September 1520) came out eighteen times before 1526; as for his translation of the Bible, Dr. Steinberg summarizes the complicated bibliographical story thus: 'All in all, 430 editions of the whole Bible or parts of it appeared during Luther's lifetime.' Polemical literature was also naturally put to the service of governments. Here again the propagandist had predecessors, as can be seen in the chauvinist pamphleteering provoked by Anglo-French hostilities during the Hundred Years War or by the respect accorded by other courts in Italy to the Florentine scholar-chancellors from Salutati onwards. But the government which sponsored manuscript warfare was trying merely to influence other chanceries and the councillors of princes. Printed polemics were designed to interest large and influential sections of public opinion. Hence the retained men who wrote for kings and ministers from the days of Henry VIII, Francis I and Charles V down to the hacks operating official journalism in the eighteenth century. Hence the 'historiographers royal' who spread from the French court to other countries in the seventeenth century. Hence, too, the counter-government publications of critics and rebels, the object of censorship and persecution, which reached behind the police to the man in the study, if not the man in the street.

Much, perhaps most, of what was printed in the centuries which followed the invention was to be of no lasting interest, save when digested statistically: the mounting number of royal proclamations, the emergence and diffusion of the periodical press, the very numbers of books published themselves. What is of interest is the growing enlargement of the human spirit which is recalled in the pages of this book. By 1600 the whole range of ancient thought was available to the curious, and much of it was accessible in vernacular versions. The main philosophers, scientists and historians of the Middle Ages had been printed, though as yet without the critical care that was beginning to be lavished on the writings of antiquity. And to this inherited knowledge and reflexion the Renaissance added its own contributions, which germinated rapidly and which thus could rival the influence of the works by those established *auctores* of the ancient and medieval periods. The pace of intellectual change quickened and the notion of *auctoritas* was challenged by novelty. The excitement of the new began to act as a leaven. There are no medieval Utopias. From More onwards the world has never been without them, and it was by printed books that moralists, scientists, philosophers and critics of art and literature mapped out fresh paths.

Prior to the French Revolution the audience for serious writing was composed of all educated men and women and learning was, at any rate in principle, undivided. The rigid academic distinctions which were later to impose themselves were absent. Galileo regarded himself not only as a scientist but as a philosopher and a man of letters and he did in fact write good Latin and good Italian. The cultivated public was able to understand, even if it disapproved of, the current advances in natural philosophy and technology, let alone the more familiar subjects of ethics and theology. Difficult some of the ideas were, but good writing and the device of correspondence or dialogue facilitated attractive exposition; when a physicist like Newton was too austere to do this for himself a writer like Fontenelle was available to undertake the necessary *haute vulgarisation*. Even reference books could be idiosyncratic, witty and stylish, as Bayle and Johnson showed. The existence of a wide reading public turned publication itself into a gesture of some significance and the writer, even if unrewarded as such until the eighteenth century, had emerged as a distinct species. And some writers had *genius* 'as opposed' (says the dictionary) 'to *talent.*' Genius in this sense apparently comes into English in 1759.

Printers were responsible not only for issuing books and pamphlets of temporary significance and for works of genius or at least talent. They also published an increasing number of books which, by adding to the conveniences of the scholar and man of affairs, saved his time for more important things. Dictionaries are the most obvious instance of this and the student who had a printed *Thesaurus* should be compared with the medieval scholar who had to make his own or depend on a tatty copy of the *Catholicon*. The published tables of logarithms and other tabulated mathematical and astronomical material not only speeded up scientific calculation but put reliable instruments into the hands of ships' navigators.

Besides the utilities the press encouraged the graces of life. The printing of music disseminated the latest songs and compositions among the gentry who were often still themselves performers. Hand-copied music depended on skills which the amateur could scarcely be expected to possess; the engraved music of the printer provided the equivalent in accurate, legible and convenient form. Engraving also speeded up the knowledge of the pictorial art of distant centres. Long before the young painter or architect had visited Italy he could study the masters in albums and absorb the principles of Palladio. His patron came back from the Grand Tour provided, if he could afford it, with some original canvases but certainly with engravings by Piranesi.

With music and the fine arts the function of printing was, so to say, ancillary. With imaginative literature it had by the seventeenth century become an essential part of composition. Though the bard lingered on in the Balkans and Finland until the twentieth century, though ballads were composed in industrial Britain and in America during the nineteenth, oral literature was in effect displaced by print, and the poetry of the later Renaissance has a quality it could not otherwise have possessed; it was meant to be read, not recited. Read aloud it often was, and so were the prose romances and the elegant essays (of indescribable dullness for the most part), on wet days when hunting was impossible, or by the ladies after dinner while the men sobered up. But it was designed by the writer for the reader. Both saw it silently on a printed page.

IV

With the nineteenth century the pace of communication speeded up, at first with books themselves and later with the invention of other devices. The more rapid production of books was made possible by the perfection of various technical improvements—stereotyping, then mechanical type-setting and machine binding—which enabled steam and other forms of power to be applied to printing so that what had remained for centuries a craft was steadily transformed into an industrial enterprise. Publishers, who had by the end of the eighteenth century become largely separated from the printers who made books and the shopkeepers who sold them, were often now large companies of influential businessmen, keen to supply the widening market for print.

That market increased rapidly. The men who came to power in Europe in the generation after the French Revolution can be described, in a phrase which came to be generally adopted at the time, as middle class. At one end of the spectrum they were promoters of industrialization, of international commerce and banking, and at the other they were middlemen and retailers. Their prescription for the world's woes was the diffusion of their own values as the wealth of the community increased. Those of their critics who deplored the passing of the golden age of an educated *élite* were powerless to resist the march of bourgeois egalitarianism. Their other adversaries, who challenged capitalism and foretold its doom, shared to the full the optimism of the age. Both capitalists and socialists advocated universal literacy to be achieved by compulsory education. They were pushing at an open door. A predominantly agrarian community can dispense with reading and writing: the farmer's education is (or perhaps was) provided through an apprenticeship with nature. The industrial revolution brought in its wake the necessity for a lettered population. In the world of nineteenth-century machinery the illiterate not only went to the wall; they could be dangerous in a big factory and were useless as shop assistants in a big store.

The Revolution in France had led to the enunciation of the principles of free and compulsory education at the primary level, and this was incorporated in the constitution of 1791. On the Continent the early nineteenth century saw the general adoption of state schools for all. In Britain progress was, as usual, much slower, save in Scotland where effective parish schools were already in existence. Yet even in Britain the provision of public schools (as opposed to Public Schools) came hesitantly in the mid-century although, before that, there was an amazing degree of self-improvement: Mechanics' Institutes, the *Penny Cyclopaedia*, and so forth. Nor was self-improvement restricted to the working class. In the early decades of the nineteenth century a big town usually acquired an institution—the one at Newcastle upon Tyne is called the Literary and Philosophical Society—which organized lectures and maintained a library of serious books. At the same time the intelligent reader could now turn to an intelligent journalism, of which the *Edinburgh Review* was the first great example.

The idealization of literacy and the remarkably quick progress which literacy made, at any rate in Western Europe and North America, were further encouraged by more rapid transport. The isolated parts of great countries were penetrated by better roads, by canals and, even more important, by railway lines, which drove first from one big centre to another and then curved through tunnels and over viaducts into mountain and moor. One could now travel through the Apennines, the Massif Central and the Scottish Highlands in hours instead of days. Pockets of traditional life were eliminated. The language (and the books and ideas) of Paris and London began to erode ever more quickly the frontiers, already in retreat, of Catalan, Provençal and Breton, of Welsh and Gaelic. The schoolmasters in highland areas had been trained in the big towns and their pupils were brought up to feel that culture went with capital cities. The demand for books was stimulated by these enlargements of the market. Railways also affected publisher and author by providing tranquil hours of disoccupation. The railway bookstall supplied the necessary distraction. The yellowbacks of early Victorian England, the sophisticated publications of Tauchnitz (designed for the English-speaking visitor to the Continent) and serious magazines like *Blackwood's*, *The Atlantic Monthly* and so on, were direct results of the new world of steam.

'World' is the right word. Just as the railway made for rapid and certain travel on land, so did the steamboat at sea. Here, too, there were *longueurs* to be sweetened by print and here too there were markets to be exploited. The English publisher now had vast English-speaking areas overseas at his disposal—North America, where the population was quickly augmented by immigrants from all over the world, Australia, India and a wide network of smaller colonies where literacy was largely confined to the white administrators, the settlers and missionaries, who did their best to spread a reading knowledge of the Word.

Until the early twentieth century the overseas conquests of English might have been paralleled, though not equalled, by German, French and Spanish. In the event, although Spanish has still a huge currency in South and Central America, English is now unrivalled as a world language, and it is surely not fanciful to foresee the day when it will be universally known. This is a factor which weighs heavily with contemporary publishers and authors and which will undoubtedly weigh much more heavily in years to come.

The scholarship and the science of nineteenth-century Europe were, however, far from being determined by the British. The leadership in letters, the arts and academic subjects had moved at the Renaissance from France to Italy. In the nineteenth century a much more complicated *translatio litterarum* came about. Cultural primacy was shared by Germany and France, and to some extent the division was one between the 'two cultures' about which so much has been written in recent years. The German university recovered first from the doldrums in which higher education had been becalmed and it was in the German university that a new science and a new scholarship emerged in the post-Napoleonic period to set their seal on advanced teaching elsewhere in Europe and in North America. The German professor, with his disciples in a seminar or laboratory, was interested in furthering the knowledge of his subject, not in turning out gentlemen or even men of affairs. France, on the other hand, with romantic literature and later with realism, with the impressionists and the post-impressionists, acted as a magnet for poets, novelists and painters. There were, of course, great French scientists; Darwin was an Englishman educated in Scotland. But the pacemaking in nineteenth century history, philology, physics and chemistry was by Germans and there is no British Stendhal or Flaubert, no Spanish or Italian Cézanne. The decision to exclude from the 1963 Exhibition works of imaginative literature (though some squeezed themselves in) means that this French monopoly is not reflected in this book. But it is noticeable that, of the scholarly works which were published in the century and a half after 1800, a third are from German-speaking Europe, mostly from Germany itself.

As for the attitudes to books themselves which developed by 1900, one finds a curious contradiction. On the one hand old books are cherished with care, and on the other new books are generally regarded as expendable. The collecting of books, which had originally been restricted to incunables and editions of celebrated authors, has been enlarged in the last two generations to cover every variety of printing and every type of writer. Bibliographical expertise has increased and a tender concern watches for minute variants. This, reflected in sale-room prices, has led to the amassing of collections by men who regard books as an investment rather than as reading matter, and among the connoisseurs and the Ph.D. students it has given enormous prestige to libraries lucky enough to possess or acquire numbers of rarities. The days are over when the Bodleian Library could eject its first folio of Shakespeare when the third edition was printed in 1664.

At the same time the paperback, starting slowly in the early decades of this century, has now taken over much of the market in books. The strident display at a shop like Brentano's Basement in New York is totally different from the quiet of even the pre-Second World War bookshops and this brittle assertiveness seems to be the pattern for the future. Who does not see his local bookshop being slowly engulfed by the lava from the paperback volcanoes? The issue of a serious work in paper covers apparently for many readers confers on it the hallmark of the classical. Such books do not last physically; they are as flesh, all too easily assimilated to the lascivious-seeming works of fiction which are sold beside them. The reader buys the solid product as an instrument of entertainment or ambitious self-improvement. My own shelves are clogged with the detritus of thirty years of casual buying of paperbacks on all sorts of subjects, kept because I am an old-fashioned book-keeper and these belong to the genus *book*; but not kept in my study. Yet there, too, I have paperbacks—some of them, it is true, are in French and Italian (for publishers of serious and even expensive books in continental countries still tend to assume that their readers will have them bound) but some of them are editions of important works of scholarship in English which one might hunt for too long in a bound edition.

The multiplication of books in our own day is only one aspect of the changes which have recently occurred in communications. Far more important has been the advance of radio—first sound and then television. Like printing, radio is a technical innovation which has spread with extraordinary rapidity. And it represents a further stage not only in the diffusion of news and knowledge, but in the scope of political and cultural organization. Writing, it will be remembered, enabled government to increase in range and efficiency, and printing furthered the process. With radio the reach of political power is in principle almost boundless in our small universe. If the nineteenth century experienced a quickening pace in the penetration of more isolated areas by the central culture of bigger countries, radio is in a fair way to obliterating entirely the locally rooted community and the values that went with it.

It is, of course, conceivable that radio might replace the world of books. If this were to happen man might find himself back again in square two—not square one, that environment of gesture and emotive sound, but the next stage, the use of speech without writing. The invulnerability of the book must certainly not be taken for granted. Man has been reading now for something like six thousand years, a short enough space in the whole span of his development. He has been speaking for a far longer period than that and even before he spoke he had developed those activities of feeding and fighting and making love which still give him his deepest satisfactions. Reading and writing are relatively recent accomplishments and for that reason may suffer: 'last in, first out,' as they say. There are, indeed, forces within scholarship itself which militate against the book. Advances in some of the sciences mean that a book on the subject is out of date almost as soon as it is printed. The biologist, the physicist and the medical researcher depend on periodical literature to keep in touch with their fields of interest. Even that is less satisfactory to them than direct contact and so they turn to the spoken word at congresses, conferences and colloquies. In the old humanist arts' subjects, where tradition might seem most deeply entrenched, the language laboratory is making otiose the familiar grammars and texts. Will radio, the acceleration of scientific discovery and new techniques of instruction mean that the book as we have known it will pass away?

Littera scripta manet: let us give the adage in its entirety—*Vox audita perit, littera scripta manet.* 'The spoken word passes away, the written word remains.' It is appropriate that the tag seems to have appeared first in one of the earliest printed books, Caxton's *Mirrour of the World* (1481). It is surely inconceivable that the impresarios of the future will succeed entirely in persuading the creators, the makers, to consign their inspiration to the ether, to be bounced about between the earth and the Heaviside Layer until the waves peter out in inaudible murmurs. Authors are not like children, content to see their beautiful pebbles flung into the pool of eternity. The student and the scholar, at any rate in many fields of human learning, will also want a measure of continuity. They will want shoulders to stand on as they peer at the past and future, and will not want to revert to the age when memory counted for everything. Equally the endless varieties of individual research and enjoyment could never be adequately reflected in the choices broadcast by Public Authority or Private Enterprise, however enlightened. Perhaps some day it may be possible to devise ways of recapturing the flying words and images of the past. Until that happens there will be no substitute for print and the book will remain the only way by which one age can speak to another.

This essay is entitled 'Let there be light.' This may seem a paradoxical way of describing printer's ink and the art of putting it on paper which was discovered by Gutenberg five hundred years ago: it is the dark letters we look at, not the white paper. But it may be justified. The printed page illuminates the mind of man and defies, in so far as anything sublunary can, the corrosive hand of Time.

OVERVIEW OF BOOKS AND PRINTING

Additional Readings

Binns, Norman A. *An Introduction to Historical Bibliography.* 2d ed. London: Association of Assistant Librarians, 1962.

Esdaile, Arundell. *Esdaile's Manual of Bibliography.* 4th rev. ed. by Roy Stokes. New York: Barnes and Noble, 1967.

Innis, Harold A. *The Bias of Communication.* Toronto: University of Toronto Press, 1951.

Labarre, Albert. *Histoire du Livre.* Paris: Presses Universitaires de France, 1970.

Lehmann-Haupt, Hellmut. *The Life of the Book.* New York: Abelard-Schuman, 1957.

Levarie, Norma. *The Art and History of Books.* New York: Heineman, 1968.

Vervleit, Hendrik D.L. *The Book Through Five Thousand Years.* London and New York: Phaidon, 1972. (Distributed in the United States by Praeger.)

II.

THE MATERIALS OF
BOOKS AND PRINTING

Part II. THE MATERIALS OF BOOKS AND PRINTING

Introduction

In order to fully understand the historical evolution of books and printing it is important to have some idea of the materials used and the techniques and processes involved in their production, as well as a knowledge of their history. A look into the method of producing clay tablets, papyrus, parchment, vellum, and paper is essential for full comprehension of the limitations which the medium places on the message. A study of the alphabet, writing, and typography explains the next stage of development—the impressed, written, or printed text. When the material has been so produced there is the need to preserve it in some functional and convenient format. From this evolved the development of the variations of covers or bindings for preservation, storage, and retrieval. The final touch is the ornamentation and/or decoration used to visually embellish or explain the text. All these elements fuse into the physical book in which the limitations of materials and processes determines the final product—the medium is truly the message.

Throughout history the materials of books and printing involved the skill and talent of a variety of craftsmen, technicians, artists, papyrus-makers, papermakers, book-binders, scribes, typographers, book designers, illuminators, rubricators, illustrators, and graphic artists—all involved in producing books. Their main task was to transmit the ideas and message of author to reader in an unobtrusive manner.

This unit covers a wide variety of readings intended to familiarize the reader with some of the basic concepts and methods of book production of the ancient, medieval, and modern world. At best this coverage is superficial, serving as introductory information. Each is a major area on which much has been written.

The surfaces for writing and printing are described in the essays by Falconer Madan and Adèle M. Smith. These authors briefly discuss the various materials used in book production by ancient peoples, as well as the manufacture and use of papyrus, parchment, vellum, and paper.

Material on the alphabet, writing, and typography reveals the impact of these major developments on civilization. James Breasted in *The Conquest of Civilization* stated: "The invention of writing and of a convenient system of records. . . has had greater influence in uplifting the human race than any other intellectual achievement in the career of man." This idea is developed by Douglas C. McMurtrie, who traces the alphabet back to its beginning. David Diringer studies the development of writing as the "counterpart of speech." Warren Chappell is interested in letter forms and the evolution of the book hands of the written documents. Handwriting was the forerunner of printing and movable type the extension of writing. Stanley Morison and Holbrook Jackson provide a summary review of type faces from Gutenberg to Goudy with relevant illustrations.

The need to provide a method of keeping the pages of a book together developed into the art and craft of the bookbinder. The codex lent itself to hard-covered boards to hold the parchment pages and this format continued with the use of paper. J. S. Hewitt-Bates traces the history of bookbinding, showing how it is "essentially linked with that of writing; as the nature of the materials and forms used determined the method of preservation." John P. Harthan not only examines the history of bookbinding but also the evolution of the decoration of the binding with various materials and designs.

The concluding unit by Harry G. Aldis, which has been revised by John Carter and E. A. Crutchley, briefly traces the highlights of the history and techniques of book illustration. Other aspects of book illustration and illumination will be studied in the unit on the hand-produced book of the ancient and medieval world.

In this section the "Additional Readings" are especially helpful, providing more detailed and in-depth information on this most extensive topic—the materials of books and printing.

Falconer Madan

Materials for Writing
and
Forms of Books

A. MATERIALS.

Probably the earliest efforts of the human race to record its thoughts and history were by scratching with some hard instrument on stone. The permanence of the result has always made stone or metal a favourite substance to receive engraving for sepulchral tablets, for official records, such as State decrees, and for honorary inscriptions. Among obvious examples are the drawings of prehistoric man on the walls of caves, the Ten Commandments graven on stone, the Nicene Creed cut in silver by Pope Leo III's order to fix the absolute form decreed by the second General Council, the Parian Chronicle, the Rosetta Stone, and tombs of all ages. It is on stone almost alone that we find in the early classical days of Rome the pure capital forms of letters, as on the tombs of the Scipios. And as material tends to act on style, and as curves are harder to grave than straight lines, writing on stone tends to discard the one and to encourage the other, so that we find in such inscriptions a decided preference for angular forms of letters.

But another very early material for writing was the wood or bark of trees. It was common, soft, and fairly durable. Three of our common terms are derived from the custom of cutting or scratching on wooden boards or bark, the Latin *liber* (a book,

SOURCE: Reprinted from Falconer Madan, *Books in Manuscript*, (London: Kegan Paul, Trench, Trübner and Company Ltd., 1893), Chapter II, "Materials for Writing, and Forms of Books," pp. 5-17. (Also appeared as a second revised edition, 1927 and Reprint-New York: Haskell House Publishers Ltd., 1968.)

properly the bark of a tree, whence such words as *library, libretto*), the Latin *codex* (or *caudex*, a tree-stump, then sawn boards, then a book, now narrowed to a manuscript book; compare *codicil*, a diminutive form), and perhaps the Teutonic word which appears in German as *Buch* and in English as *book*, meaning originally a beech tree and beechen boards.

Next we come to the substance which has given us much of the terminology of books. A common reed, chiefly found in Egypt, and known to the Greeks as πάπυρος (*papūros*), and to the Romans as *papyrus*, was discovered to be, when properly prepared, a facile and cheap material for writing. The inner rind was cut lengthways into thin strips (βύβλοι *bubloi*), and laid in order; on this were glued, with the help of rich Nile water or other substance, another set of slips laid on the former transversely. This cross-formed substance, properly pressed, hammered and dried, presented a smooth but soft receptive surface for ink, and was most extensively used in classical times until parchment competed with it, or, more accurately, till the export of papyrus began to fail. The papyrus, however, was not used in the form of our books, but as a long roll, with the writing in broad columns placed thus, the writing being represented by a wavy line:

Birt, in his *Antike Buchwesen* (1882), has shown that there was a normal length of about thirty-eight letters in each line, but the length of the entire roll might be anything up to 150 feet. Lately it has been discovered that there is a face and a back to papyri, a right and a wrong side for writing. In the British Museum there is a papyrus roll containing, in Greek, the funeral oration of Hyperides on Leosthenes, B.C. 323; on the other side of this is a horoscope of a person born in A.D. 95. Naturally, for some time it was believed that the horoscope was casually inscribed on the back of the Hyperides; but a closer examination has proved that the horoscope is on the face of the papyrus, and the Hyperides perhaps a school exercise accidentally entered on the back. So that A.D. 95 is not the *terminus ad quem* of the date, but the *terminus a quo*.

Unfortunately, of all possible materials for permanent record, papyrus is among the worst. Even when first written on, it must have seemed ominous that a heavy stroke was wont to pierce and scratch the smooth surface, so much so that in all papyrus records the writing is of necessity light, and hardly distinguishable into up and down strokes. This foreshadowed the time when, on the complete drying of the substance in course of years, the residuum would be fragile, friable, and almost as brittle as dead leaves. Every papyrus that comes into a library should therefore be at once placed between two sheets of glass, to prevent, as far as possible, all further disintegration.

The terms used in connexion with writing in Greek, Latin and English are chiefly derived from the rolls of papyrus. Let us begin with two words which have had an interesting history. Our 'paper' is derived from the Greek πάπυρος; (papūros; in Latin, papyrus), explained above as the name of an Egyptian reed. Thence it came to mean the papyrus as prepared to receive writing. How then has paper, which has always been made out of rags, usurped the name without taking over the material? Simply because the term came to signify whatever substance was commonly employed for writing; so when papyrus was disused (the latest date of its systematic use is the eleventh century), a material formed of rags was beginning to be in fashion, and carried on, so to speak, the term. The Latin charta (paper) has had a partly similar history, for when first found it is applied to papyrus as distinguished from parchment. Still more interesting is the word Bible. βύβλοι (bubloi) was the Greek term for the strips of the inner bark of papyrus. Then the book formed of papyrus began to be called βίβλος (biblos) and βιβλίον (biblion, a diminutive form). The Romans took across the second word, but chiefly used it in the plural, biblia, which came later to be regarded as a feminine singular, as if its genitive were bibliæ and not bibliorum. Lastly, the word became specially and exclusively applied to The Book, the Bible, and as such has passed into English. Other terms which recall the days of papyrus are volume (Latin, volumen, 'a thing rolled up,' from volvo, I roll; corresponding to the Greek χύλινδρος, kulindros), the long stretch of papyrus rolled up for putting away; the Latin term evolvere, to unroll, in the sense of 'to read' a book; and the common word explicit, equivalent to 'the end,' but properly meaning 'unrolled,' 'explicitus,' the end of the roll having been reached. So, too, the custom of writing on parchment with three or even four columns to a single page, as may be seen in our most ancient Greek MSS. of the New Testament, is probably a survival of the parallel columns of writing found on papyrus.

We next come to the most satisfactory material ever discovered for purposes of writing and illumination, tough enough for preservation to immemorial time, hard enough to bear thick strokes of pen or brush without the surface giving way, and yet fine enough for the most delicate ornamentation. Parchment is the prepared skin of animals, especially of the sheep and calf; the finer quality derived from the calf being properly vellum; and if from the skin of the calf's intestines, uterine vellum, the whitest and thinnest kind known, and used chiefly for elaborate miniatures. Parchment has neither the fragile surface of papyrus nor the coarseness of mediæval paper, and has therefore long enjoyed the favour of writers. Its only disadvantages in mediæval times were its comparative costliness and its thickness and weight, but neither of these was a formidable obstacle to its use. The name of this substance contains its history. In the first half of the second century before Christ, Eumenes II, King of Pergamum, found himself debarred, through some jealousy of the Ptolemies, from obtaining a sufficient supply of papyrus from Egypt. From necessity he had recourse to an ancient custom of preparing skins for the reception of writing, by washing, dressing and rubbing them smooth; probably adding some new appliances, by which his process became so famous that the material itself was called Περγαμηνή; in Latin, Pergamēna, 'stuff prepared at Pergamum,' whence the English word *parchment*. Both parchment and paper have had less effect than stone or papyrus on styles of writing, because both are adapted to receive almost any stroke of the pen. They have rather allowed styles to develop themselves naturally, and are specially favourable to the flowing curves which are as easy as they are graceful in human penmanship.

Paper has for long been the common substance for miscellaneous purposes of ordinary writing, and has at all times been formed exclusively from rags (chiefly of linen), reduced to a pulp, poured out on a frame in a thin watery sheet, and gradually dried and given consistence by the action of heat. It has been a popular belief, found in every book till 1886 (now entirely disproved, but probably destined to die hard), that the common yellowish thick paper, with rough fibrous edge, found especially in Greek MSS. till the fifteenth century, was paper of quite another sort, and made of cotton (*charta bombȳcina*, bombyx being usually silk, but also used of any fine fibre such as cotton). The microscope has at last conclusively shown that these two papers are simply two different kinds of ordinary linen-rag paper.

A few facts about the dates at which papyrus, parchment and paper are found may be inserted here. The use of papyrus in Egypt is of great antiquity, and the bulk of the earliest Greek and Latin writings we possess are on papyrus; in the case of Greek of the third century B.C., in Latin of the first century A.D. It was freely exported to Greece and Rome, and, though it gave way before parchment, it was not till the tenth century A.D. that in Egypt itself its use was abandoned. Practically in about A.D. 935 its fabrication ceased, although for Pontifical Bulls it was invariably used till A.D. 1022, and occasionally till 1050. Parchment has also been used from the earliest times; and its use was revived, as we have seen, in the second century before Christ, and lasted till the invention of printing, after which it was reserved for sumptuous editions, and for legal and other records. Paper was first manufactured (outside China) at Samarkand in Turkestan in about A.D. 750; and even in Spain, where first it obtained a footing in Europe (in the tenth century), it was imported from the East, not being manufactured in the West till the twelfth century; but from that time its use spread rapidly. In England there was a paper-mill at Hertford shortly before 1470, owned by one John Tate; but no book was printed on English paper till 1495, when Bartholomæus Glanville's *De proprietatibus rerum* was issued on native paper. Watermarks in paper are entirely a Western invention, found first towards the end of the thirteenth century, and never found at all in Oriental paper.

Besides stone, papyrus, parchment, and paper, the materials used for writing, though numerous, are rather curious than important. Tablets of wood, hinged like a book and covered with wax, on which letters were scratched by a small pointed metal rod (*stilus*, whence our words *style, stiletto*, etc.), were common at Rome in classical and later times, and are believed to have suggested the form of our ordinary books. For private accounts and notes these wax tablets are said to have been quite common in Western Europe until the time of printing. Various metals, especially lead, have been made use of to bear writing; and also bones (in prehistoric times), clay inscribed when soft and then baked (as in Assyria), potsherds (*ostraka*), and the like.

B. FORMS OF BOOKS.

We now come to the forms of books—the way in which they are made up. In the case of papyrus, as has already been observed, we almost always find the roll-form. This long strip was, of course, rolled round a stick or two sticks (one at each end) when not in use, very much as a wall-map is at the present day. With parchment the case has been different. Though in classical times in Rome, so far as can be judged, the roll-form was still in ordinary use even when parchment was the material, and though, in the form of court-rolls, pedigrees, and many legal kinds of record, we are still familiar with the appearance of a roll, the tendency of writers on parchment has been to establish and perpetuate the form of book best known at the present day, in which pages are turned over by the reader, and not membranes unrolled.

The normal formation of a parchment book in the Middle Ages was this: four pieces of parchment, each roughly about 10 inches high and 18 inches broad, were taken and were folded once across, so that each piece formed four pages (two leaves) of what we should call a quarto volume. These pieces were then fitted one inside another, so that the first piece formed the 1st and 8th leaves, the second the 2nd and 7th, the third the 3rd and 6th, and the fourth the two middle leaves of a complete section of eight leaves or sixteen pages, termed technically in Latin a *quaternio*, because made of four (*quatuor*) pieces of parchment. When a sufficient number of quaternions were thus formed to contain the projected book, they were sent in to the scribe for writing on, and eventually bound. Many variations of form, both smaller and larger than quarto, are found, and often more or fewer pieces than four make up the section.

Paper was essentially different from parchment, in that it could be made of larger size and folded smaller; whereas the cost of skins was almost prohibitive, if very large and fine pieces were required. As a fact, paper has almost always been used in book and not roll-form. The normal formation of paper-books has been this: a piece about 12 inches high by 16 inches wide was regarded as a standard size. This was folded across along the dotted line *a b*, and if this singly-folded sheet was regarded as the basis of a section, and the whole book was made up of a set of these sections, it was called a folio book (fig. 1); if, however, the singly-folded sheet was folded *again* across the dotted line *c d*, and *this* was treated as a section (containing four leaves or eight pages), the book made up of such sections was called a quarto (fig. 2). Once more, if the doubly-folded sheet was again folded along the dotted line *e f*, and this trebly-folded sheet was treated as a section (containing eight leaves or sixteen pages), the book was called an octavo (fig. 3). The methods of folding the sheet so as to produce a duodecimo, a 16mo, etc., and the use of half-sheets to form sections, are matters which concern printing rather than writing. But it should be clearly understood that, whereas we now mean by a folio a tall narrow book, by a quarto a shorter broad book, and by an octavo a short narrow book, judging by *size* and *shape*; in the earlier days of paper, these terms indicated, *not* size or even shape, but form, that is to say, the way in which the sheets of paper were folded up to form sections, and that it is only owing to the fact that a certain size of paper was generally adopted as a standard that the terms came to have their modern signification. So true is this, that some early folios are quite small, and many quartos larger or smaller than what we call quarto. But there is one infallible test of a true folio, quarto, or octavo. Observe the diamond on the figures and the lines drawn across them. The diamond represents the *watermark*, a trade design (such as a jug, an unicorn, a pair of scissors, etc.) inserted by the maker in every sheet, and the lines are 'chain-lines,' the marks where the wire frame supported the half liquid paper-sheet as it gathered consistency by being dried. The position of the watermark and the direction of the chain-lines were fortunately invariable, and therefore (as may be easily seen by a paper model) every true folio has the watermark in the centre of a page and the chain-lines perpendicular; every quarto has the watermark in the centre of the back, not easy to see, and the lines horizontal; and every octavo has a watermark at the top of the back at the inner edge, and the lines perpendicular.

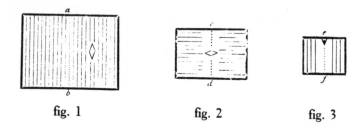

fig. 1   fig. 2   fig. 3

C. INSTRUMENTS AND INK

On this subject few words are necessary. For hard substances and for wax and clay, a graving pen or pointed metal rod is necessary; for papyrus, parchment and paper, a pen. Pens have till modern times always been of one of two kinds, either made of a reed (*calamus, arundo*, a reed-pen), or made of a quill, usually from a bird's feather (*penna*, a quill-pen). The latter appears to be the later in invention, but is found as early as the sixth century of our era.

Ink (*atramentum*) has hardly varied in composition from the earliest times, having been always formed in one of two ways: either, as was the common practice in classical times, by a mixture of soot with gum and water, which produces a black lustrous ink, but is without much difficulty removed with a sponge; or by galls (gallic acid) with sulphate of iron and gum, which is the modern method, though also so ancient as to be found on the Herculanean rolls. At Pompeii ink of this kind was found still liquid after seventeen centuries of quiescence. The chief coloured inks known to antiquity were red, purple, green, and yellow: gold and silver solutions were sometimes used, especially when the parchment had been stained purple to enhance the effect.

So far we have been concerned with passive substances prepared and presented to the scribe, to become instinct with life when the message of the author is consigned to the expectant page.

Adèle M. Smith

Materials Used by Ancient Peoples Papyrus Parchment and Vellum Paper

MATERIALS USED BY ANCIENT PEOPLES

The chief substances which have been used as writing materials are stone, clay, bark, leaves, skins of animals, metal, potsherds, wood, linen, papyrus, parchment, wax, and paper.

It is probable that the primitive races first wrote on rocks with some sharp-pointed instrument, to delineate familiar objects or to convey information to passers-by. The Eskimo of Alaska, at the present day, cut characters upon the smooth sides of their ivory drill-bows with sharp pieces of iron or steel. They thus graphically depict their hunting expeditions and various social and religious practices. The prairie tribes of Indians, also, incise characters upon the shoulder-blades of the buffalo and other large animals, when they are on the hunt, to inform members of their band of the course of travel.

When men were able to give fuller expression to their ideas, instead of making inscriptions on rocks, they wrote on tablets of soft stone with a pointed tool, called a stilus, made of iron or other metal. The pen used by the early Hebrews was probably such an instrument. In some instances the stilus was pointed with diamonds, as mentioned in Jeremiah xvii, 1.

SOURCE: Reprinted from Adèle M. Smith, *Printing and Writing Materials: Their Evolution* (Philadelphia: published by the author, 1901), "Writing Materials," Chapter I, "Materials Used by Ancient Peoples," pp. 123-130, Chapter II, "Papyrus," pp. 131-137, Chapter III, "Parchment and Vellum," pp. 138-141, Chapter IV, "Paper," pp. 142-162. Copyright 1900 by Adèle M. Smith. All rights reserved.

Wooden tablets were used at an ancient date. Sometimes the inscriptions were made upon the bare wood; in other cases, the tablets were coated with some kind of composition, the writing being scratched upon the surface with a pointed implement. The Egyptians employed tablets covered with a glazed composition, upon which they wrote with ink. Wooden tablets containing the names of the dead have been found with mummies.

Lead was employed in very early times. Pliny states that the public acts of the most remote nations were recorded in leaden books. Tablets of lead have been discovered which contain petitions to oracles, and in some cases the answers; charms and incantations were also inscribed on leaves of this metal. These leaden plates were often so thin that they might easily have been rolled up. For literary purposes, lead was employed to some extent in the middle ages in Northern Italy. Bronze was a material used in both Greece and Rome, on which to engrave laws, treaties, and other solemn documents.

In Babylonia and Assyria, tablets were made of soft clay; after receiving impressions, they were dried in the sun or baked in ovens. The scribe, who held an important position, was always provided with slabs of fine plastic clay, sufficiently moist to take an impression easily, but also sufficiently firm to prevent the inscriptions from becoming blurred or effaced. The writing, of course, was done with the stilus.

The Greeks and Romans used wooden and ivory tablets covered with a thin layer of wax; the instrument was still the stilus, made of metal, bone, or ivory. The tablets were sometimes fastened together with wire. They were employed for memoranda, accounts, school exercises, correspondence, literary composition, and legal documents. The stilus was sharpened at one end for the purpose of writing, and was left blunt at the other, to make erasures when necessary. Wax tablets continued to be used to a limited extent in Europe until the fourteenth or fifteenth century.

In Egypt inscribed potsherds have been found in great numbers. The inscriptions are sometimes scratched with a pointed instrument; generally, however, they are written in ink with a reed. In Greece this material seems to have been used only on rare occasions or from necessity. Such inscribed fragments have received the name of *ostraka*, a term which we associate with the ostracism practised by the Athenians, in which the votes were recorded on pieces of broken vessels. In Egypt the ostraka were generally receipts for taxes or letters or orders to officials.

Graffiti, or wall-scribblings, abounded in nearly all places under Roman domination. They have been discovered in the ancient cities of Italy, but in the greatest numbers at Pompeii. The scribblings and rude drawings are generally scratched with a sharp instrument or scrawled with red chalk or charcoal, and were evidently traced by idle loungers or triflers; inscriptions of a more serious nature were drawn with a brush. We find doggerel and amatory verses, caricatures, quotations from the poets, idle words, names to which opprobrious epithets were attached, pasquinades, and satirical remarks; among the tracings of a serious import were notices of household events, advertisements and announcements of games, appeals to the public, prayers, and invocations to the martyrs. These inscriptions disclose the current life of the people, afford material for the study of the Roman cursive writing, and are often of historical and archeological importance.

The Egyptians covered with inscriptions the stone walls of their buildings,—their palaces, temples, monuments, the walls and ceilings of subterranean passages, and even the interiors of their tombs. The history of the nation was thus written in hieroglyphics, and on stone walls and tablets kings recorded their exploits, their campaigns into distant lands, their victories, and their triumphant returns.

In the earliest ages of their history the Hebrews, in common with other primitive peoples, engraved the record of their important events upon stone; they also wrote with the stilus on rough tablets of wood, earthenware, or bone; at a later period they employed the skins of animals. The Law was written in golden characters on skins in the form of a scroll. Leather is still used by the Jews for their synagogue rolls. Parchment was also employed by the Hebrews as a writing surface.

Among other materials used by primitive peoples to receive writing, besides the skins of animals, the most common were the bark of trees, and leaves, principally those of the palm. The Latin word for bark, *liber*, came to mean also book. Linen cloth was employed as a writing surface by the ancient Egyptians, also by the Romans for certain rituals in their history. The Ojibwa Indians of North America still make records on birch-bark, and own scrolls which they say have been in their possession for centuries. The Indians have also painted on skins of animals, but of recent years they have employed muslin and canvas as a writing surface. The Oriental traveler, Mr. F. Jagor, observed in India and elsewhere the use of birch-bark and palm and similar leaves to receive writing. The characters are usually inscribed with a finely-pointed instrument of steel or other hard substance, after which a composition of grease and powdered charcoal is rubbed into the indentations.

With ink the writing implement was the calamus, or reed, sharpened and split like the pens of the present day. The reed pen was employed for writing upon papyrus or parchment. This instrument was made from the tubular stalks of grasses growing in marshy lands and from the hollow joints of the bamboo. The calamus is the true ancient representative of the modern pen. In Greece and Rome the reeds in common use were obtained from Egypt, but persons of wealth often wrote with a silver calamus. Some of the ancient reed pens are still preserved; one found in a papyrus at Herculaneum is now kept at Naples. The natives of Persia and of some neighboring countries still employ the reed, as the metal pen is not adapted to their mode of writing. The Japanese and Chinese use a hair pencil or small brush.

The ink of the ancients was made from the black fluid of the cuttle-fish, or of lampblack or charcoal and gum. The thick inks were applied with a brush; for the reed a thinner ink was made of gall-nuts and sulphate of iron. Red and blue inks were employed for titles and initial letters. The ancient inks were thicker and more durable than those of the present day. The writing on the ancient Egyptian papyri is legible even now after the lapse of several thousand years.

Gold and silver have both been employed as writing fluids. Manuscripts of purple-stained vellum were written in gold, and ordinary white vellum was also so inscribed, particularly during the reigns of the Carlovingian kings of the ninth and tenth centuries. The practice of gold writing survived until the thirteenth century, after which date only a few isolated examples are to be found. Silver would produce little effect on a white ground; its use as a writing fluid therefore ceased with the disuse of stained vellum.

PAPYRUS

The *Cyperus Papyrus* of Linnæus was a plant extensively cultivated in ancient times in the Delta of Egypt. It is now extinct in Lower Egypt, but is found in Nubia and Abyssinia. It is said to grow also in Western Asia and in Sicily.

One of its ancient names was P-apu, from which the Greek title *papyrus* was derived. The Greeks called it also *byblos* and *deltos*. Its Hebrew name was *gomé*, a word resembling the Coptic *gom*, or "volume." In modern Arabic its name is *berdi*. In hieroglyphic writing the papyrus plant is used as the symbol of Lower Egypt.

On the ancient Egyptian monuments, the papyrus is represented as a plant about 10 feet in height. Theophrastus gives the first accurate description of it, and says that it grew in shallows of about 3 feet or less, its main root, which lay horizontally, being of the thickness of a man's wrist and 10 cubits in length. From this main root, smaller roots extended down into the mud; the stem of the plant rose to the height of 6 feet or more above the water, being triangular in form with a tufted head of numerous drooping spikelets.

The papyrus plant was used for many purposes, both useful and ornamental. Of the tufted head, garlands were made for the shrines of the gods. Its roots were dried for fuel and its pith was boiled and eaten. Of the stem, were made sandals, boxes, boats, sails, mats, cloth, cords, and writing material. In sculptures of the period of the fourth dynasty,[1] workmen are represented in the act of building a boat of stalks cut from a neighboring plantation of papyrus. Isaiah probably refers to boats of this kind when he speaks of 'vessels of bulrushes upon the waters' (xviii., 2).

The widespread use of papyrus as an ancient writing surface is attested by early writers and by numerous documents and sculptures; the material was employed in Egypt at a remote period. The names of the plant, given above, were applied to the writing material, which by the Greeks was called also *charta*. Papyrus rolls are represented in the sculptures of Egyptian temples, and numerous examples of the rolls themselves are still in existence. The dry atmosphere of Egypt has been peculiarly favorable to the preservation of these documents; in many instances they remain untouched by decay, and are as fresh as when first written.

Pliny's account of the manufacture of the writing material from papyrus refers to the process followed in his time, but it is probable that the same general method of treatment had been practiced for many centuries. The stem was cut into longitudinal strips, those from the centre being, of course, the broadest and therefore the most valuable. The strips were laid on a board, side by side, until the desired width was obtained; across the layer thus formed another layer of shorter strips was laid at right angles. The two layers were soaked, Pliny says, in water of the Nile. It is supposed that they were joined either by the juice of the plant or by a thin gum. The layers were then pressed and dried in the sun. Any inequalities in the surface were removed by the use of ivory or a smooth shell. Newly-made papyrus was white, or brownish white, and flexible, but the papyri which have been preserved until the present day have become of a light or dark brown color and so brittle as to break at the touch. The sheets varied from 4 or 5 inches to nearly 18 inches in width; the usual width was about 8 inches. Any required length could be obtained by fastening a number of sheets together, end to end. The sheets were put together in the order of their quality, the best sheet on the outside of the roll and the worst sheets in the centre. They were thus arranged, not for the purpose of concealing the bad material, but that the strongest sheets should be placed where there was most wear and tear. Besides, if the entire roll should not be needed, the poorest sheets could be better spared and easily cut off. The papyrus roll, as a rule, was written on one side only, and was fastened to a wooden rod or roller, around which it was wound.

The rolls were of various lengths. A fairly full copy of the ritual of the dead, the whole or a part of which was buried with every person of consequence from the eighteenth dynasty[2] to the Roman period, required a roll 15 inches wide and from 80 to 90 feet long. The Harris papyrus, in the British Museum, is the longest known, having a length of 133 feet. The most ancient of the papyri now extant is the Prisse papyrus, so called from the name of its former owner, and is preserved at Paris. It is supposed to date from about 2400 B.C., or earlier, and contains a work composed during the reign of a king of the fifth dynasty.[3] The papyri of Egypt have usually been found in tombs, or in the hands, or wrapped with the bodies, of mummies. Besides the ritual of the dead, which is most frequently the subject, and religious rolls, there are civil and literary documents, in the hieratic style of writing, and the demotic or enchorial papyri, relating generally to sales of property.

The discovery of papyri containing works of classical Greek authors, begun about the middle of the nineteenth century, has resulted in a great gain to literature. There were brought to light four or five quite complete orations of Hyperides, an orator who before had been known only by name. Additions were made to the works of Euripides and Alcman, and early manuscripts were found of parts of Homer, Plato, Thucydides, Demosthenes, and Isocrates. In the great discovery of 1891, of more than 160 ancient mummies in a subterranean passage at Deïr el Bahari, near Thebes, many Egyptian papyri were given to the world. These contained the usual ritual passages and extracts from the Book of the Dead. In the same year the British Museum obtained from Egypt papyrus rolls containing almost the whole of a lost work of Aristotle on the Constitution of Athens. There were four of these rolls, the longest 7 feet, the shortest 3 feet in length. They date from about the end of the first century A.D.

It has been thought that the early Chaldeans had a knowledge of papyrus paper, and either made it themselves or had it brought from Egypt, but if they possessed papyrus writings they have entirely disappeared. Egypt was the true home of this plant, where paper was manufactured from it at least 2000 years B.C. It was for a long time an article of export and in great demand. It is supposed that the manufacture of papyrus in Egypt ceased about the middle of the tenth century.

Papyrus was used among the early Greeks but it did not come into general use until after the time of Alexander the Great, when it was exported from the ports of Egypt. It is not known when papyrus was first used in Italy, but under the Empire there was a great demand for it. It was then employed not only for making books, but for domestic purposes, correspondence, and legal documents. It is said that during the reign of Tiberius the failure of the papyrus crop almost caused a riot. Although the plant was cultivated in Italy, the staple was doubtless imported from Alexandria. It is thought by some that papyrus paper was never manufactured from the native plant anywhere except in Egypt.

Papyrus continued to be employed to some extent as a writing material in Europe until the tenth century; by the twelfth century it had entirely disappeared. Its use for books ceased sooner than for documents. During the later period of its use in book-making, it was no longer made in rolls but was cut into square pages and bound like a modern book. To the square form of book, the name *codex* was given.

PARCHMENT AND VELLUM

The skins of animals were employed as a writing surface at a very early period. The word parchment is derived from *Pergamum*, the name of a city in Mysia, where it is said the material was first used. The story as told by Pliny is that Eumenes II, King of Pergamum (B.C. 197-159?), wishing his library to rival that of the Pharaohs at Alexandria, was forced to develop the manufacture of parchment in consequence of the prohibition of the exportation of papyrus from Egypt through the jealousy of Ptolemy Epiphanes. Papyrus was used as a writing surface in Italy as late as the tenth century, but parchment was also employed. From the tenth century until the fourteenth, when paper became generally known, parchment was the ordinary writing material. It was the influence of the Christian Church that eventually caused vellum to supersede papyrus as a writing surface. Because of its durability, it was used for new volumes, also to replace damaged works on papyrus. When Constantine desired copies of the Scriptures for his new churches, he ordered the manuscripts to be inscribed on vellum.

During the middle ages, vellum dyed purple, or other brilliant color, was used for valuable manuscripts, such as the Gospels, the Psalter, and important Codices. The entire surface of leaves of this material was sometimes gilded, but this mode of decoration must have proved too expensive to be very generally employed.

Parchment[4] is skin so prepared that both sides can be written upon. Ordinary parchment is made chiefly from sheepskin and sometimes from those of the goat. Fine parchment, or vellum, is prepared from the skins of calves, kids, and dead-born lambs. A coarse variety used for drumheads, tambourines, etc., is made from the skins of goats, calves, and wolves; for battledores the skins of asses are employed; for bookbinders' use parchment is sometimes manufactured from pigskin. Sheepskins are often split so as to produce two sheets of parchment. The Eskimos make this material from the entrails of seals, and manufacture from it blankets and clothing. The skin of the fur-seal is sometimes converted into parchment, which is used for making cases for holding valuable papers or other articles.

With some slight differences, all the skins are prepared in the same way. They are first soaked in water and then in milk of lime for the purpose of removing the hair. They are shaved, washed, and gone over with a sharp knife to remove superfluous parts. The skins are then stretched on a stout wooden frame, called a *herse*, and dried in the air. The finer varieties are dusted with chalk and rubbed with pumice-stone. Parchment intended for the use of bookbinders is planed, in order to produce a rough surface capable of being dyed or written upon.

Vegetable parchment, or parchment paper, is made by dipping ordinary unsized paper for a few seconds in dilute sulphuric acid and immediately removing all traces of the acid. Paper thus acted upon undergoes a remarkable change; it becomes translucent, horny, and parchment-like, and acquires about five times the strength of ordinary paper. It is impervious to water, but becomes soft and flaccid when dipped into it; it is not affected by boiling water. The same effect is produced by subjecting paper to a solution of chloride of zinc.

Stout varieties of vegetable parchment have been employed for book-covers and as a writing surface for deeds; its chief use, however, is for covers of vessels, such as preserve-jars and bottles. Thin sheets of it are employed for tracing plans and charts.

Parchment for printing purposes is imported into the United States from Europe and is sold in rolls of sixty skins. It is made in Hanover, at Augsburg, Breslau, Dantzic, and Nuremberg, and in Holland, England, and France.

PAPER

The earliest material which resembled the paper of the present day was made from the Egyptian papyrus. From the Egyptian word *P-apu* were derived the Greek and Latin terms *papyrus*, and from these all similar writing material has been named.

The Chinese seem to have had a knowledge of the art of making paper many centuries before the material was introduced into Western Asia and Europe. At a very remote period they made paper of sprouts of bamboo, of Chinese grass, and of the bast of a special mulberry-tree. Fang Mi-Chih, author of an encyclopedia, states that at first the Chinese wrote on bamboo boards; but that for a long time, both before and after the Christian era, the usual writing material was paper made of silk waste. The manufacture of paper from fibrous matter and from the wool of the cotton-plant, reduced to a pulp, has been traced back by some writers to the second century B.C. The invention of paper made of vegetable fibre is attributed to the statesman Ts'ai Lun. It is said that in 105 A.D. he had succeeded in making paper of bark, of hemp, of rags, and of old fish-nets.

By the Chinese the art was made known to the Hindus, the Persians, and the Arabs. A paper manufactory was established at Samarkand in the latter part of the sixth or early in the seventh century of the Christian era. The Arabs conquered this city in 704 A.D., and there learned the use of the material. From this time paper became available for the rest of the world. At Bagdad its manufacture was carried on from about 795 A.D. until the fifteenth century. The art was practised also in Damascus, Egypt, and the North of Africa. From the large quantities made at Damascus, paper received the name of *charta Damascena*, a term by which it was generally known in Europe in the middle ages; the titles *charta* and *papyrus* were transferred to it from the Egyptian writing material; cotton paper was called also during the middle ages *charta bombycina, gossypina, cuttunea, xylina, Damascena,* and *serica.*

Paper was probably introduced into Greece through trade with Asia, and thence carried to other countries in Europe. It seems not to have been used very extensively in Greece before the middle of the thirteenth century.

The first paper manufactured in Europe was made by the Moors in Spain. In 1154 there was a paper-mill at Jativa; factories were also established at Valencia and Toledo. The Arabs introduced paper-making into Sicily; from Sicily it passed over into Italy, where there is evidence, in the city of Genoa, of a trade in this material as early as 1235. In Germany the first factories seem to have been established between Cologne and Mainz towards the end of the thirteenth century, and in Mainz itself about the year 1320. Mills were started also at Nuremberg, Ratisbon, and Augsburg. Paper was introduced from Spain into France, where it is said to have been manufactured in the district of Hérault as early as 1189. The Netherlands and England first obtained their supply from France and Burgundy. It is believed that the first paper-maker in England was a person named Tate, who is said to have had a mill in operation in Hertford early in the sixteenth century. Very little is known of the manufacture of the material in that country, however, until about the middle of the sixteenth century, when there was a paper-mill at Dartford.

In America paper was first manufactured by William Bradford, the printer, in 1690, at Germantown, near Philadelphia. Having discovered a paper-maker among the immigrants to the colony, with the help of some of his neighbors, he started a paper-factory, which was operated by the Rittenhouse family for several generations.

The paper first manufactured in Europe was made from the cotton-plant; rags were afterwards mixed with the raw material or substituted for it.

Many early Arabic manuscripts on paper, dating from the ninth century, are still in existence. Among the earliest dated documents is the *Gharîbu 'l-Hadîth*, written in the year 866 A.D. This is a treatise on the rare and curious words found in the sayings of Mohammed and his companions, and is preserved in the University Library of Leyden. The oldest dated Arabic manuscript on paper in the British Museum is of the year 960, and is a treatise by an Arabian physician on the nourishment of the different members of the body. In the Bodleian Library (Oxford), is preserved a manuscript of a grammatical work of 974. As this was written at Samarkand, the paper was probably made at that seat of early Arab manufacture.

Of the documents on cotton paper written in Europe, the oldest is the deed of King Roger of Sicily, of the year 1102; other deeds of Sicilian kings of the twelfth century are recorded. The oldest known imperial deed on paper is a charter of Frederick II to the nuns of Goess in Styria, of the year 1228, now kept at Vienna. This emperor, however, in 1231, forbade the use of paper for official documents, which he desired inscribed on vellum. The British Museum possesses astronomical treatises written on paper, in an Italian hand of the first half of the thirteenth century. Examples of Spanish-made paper are the letters addressed from Castile to Edward I of England, in 1279 and subsequent years.

Manufacture of paper

At first, paper, both ancient and modern, was made entirely by hand. In 1799 a paper-machine was invented by Louis Robert, a clerk employed by the Messrs. Didot of the celebrated Essonnes mills near Paris, and this caused a great development of the industry. The manufacture was introduced into England, through the agency of the Messrs. Fourdrinier, and the first paper-machine in that country was erected in 1804, at Frogmoor Mill, near Boxmoor, Herts. Henry and Sealy Fourdrinier, of London, bought the English patents, and so perfected the machine that it has since been given the name of Fourdrinier. In America the first steam paper-mill was started at Pittsburg, in 1816. The first cylinder machine for the manufacture of paper was designed by Thomas Gilpin, and was employed by him, in 1817, in his mills on the Brandywine. Since 1820 paper made by machinery has supplanted hand-made paper, except fine grades used for special purposes.

The staples, or the materials, from which writing and printing papers are made are wood-pulp, rags, and esparto.[5] The staple of wrapping-paper is old ropes and jute. The finest writing and printing-papers, whether made by hand or machinery, are manufactured from linen and cotton rags. A great part of paper-making material is a by-product obtained from the refuse of other manufactures, such as waste paper, rags, old rope, old bagging, etc. At the present day paper is put to so many uses that rags cannot be procured in sufficient quantities, hence the greater amount of even white paper is now made from wood-fibre. Paper can be made of almost any vegetable fibre, but those fibres are strongest which are most completely interlaced. The woods generally used are the poplar, pine, spruce, and hemlock.

The idea of making paper from wood-pulp arose in the early part of the nineteenth century. Various patents were granted, but it was not until about 1855 that wood began to take the place of rags for book and newspaper work. A distinction must be made between wood-pulp and wood fibre: the pulp is produced by mechanical means, or by grinding; the fibre by chemical treatment, or by a process which separates from the wood all resinous and gummy substances, and leaves what is called *cellulose*, or fibre divested of all incrusting matter. Wood-pulp generally receives an admixture of wood-fibre to give it strength.

The manufacture of paper really begins with the first step required to prepare the stock. In making wood-pulp, the bark and knots are first separated from the wood. The wood is then cut into convenient lengths and put into a machine termed a wood-pulp grinder, which tears off the fibres. To produce wood, or chemical, fibre, the wood is cut into chips, dusted, and then boiled in an alkaline or acid solution in a vessel known as a digester. The chemicals separate the gummy or resinous substances from the fibre which, when washed and bleached, is almost pure cellulose. It is soft and of considerable strength.

Esparto, or Spanish grass, is cleaned and sorted by hand, and is afterwards boiled in an alkaline solution. Jute, hemp, and waste paper are all treated in about the same way, being boiled in alkaline solutions. Cotton and linen rags are passed first through threshers, then through cutters, and are afterwards boiled in a solution of caustic soda.

After the preparation of the staple, the making of it into pulp and the manufacture of the pulp into paper are about the same whether rags or other varieties of stock are employed. The process of the preparation of the pulp, whether for machine or for hand-made paper is substantially the same, but in making paper by machinery each operation is performed on a larger scale.

In making paper by machinery, the rags are first put into a thresher or dusting-machine. After they have passed through this, women sort them by hand, and remove all extraneous substances, such as buttons, hooks and eyes, bone, india-rubber, leather, and pieces of metal, at the same time loosening all hems and knots. The rags are then cut into small pieces, either by hand or machinery; for the common qualities of paper, machine-cutting is used. When the rags are cut by hand, the sorter stands at a long table, to which scythe-blades are attached; the back of the blade is towards the sorter, who draws the cloth against the edge. The rags are again dusted and sent to openings in the floor of the room, underneath which are brought the mouths of large boilers called rotaries. The boilers contain a solution of soda ash, caustic soda, or lime in water. The mouths of the rotaries are closed, steam is introduced, and the rags are boiled under pressure for several hours; by this treatment all fatty, glutinous, or coloring substances are separated from the pure fibre. Afterwards, the rags are drained and taken to the washing-and-beating engines. They are sometimes washed in one engine and beaten in another, sometimes both operations are performed in the same machine. This engine is an oblong shallow tub or vat. The rags are placed in it, with a sufficient quantity of water, and are brought by power under the action of two sets of knives, by which they are subdivided. The water in the washing cylinders is constantly changing, thus affording a continual supply of fresh water and the carrying off of the dirty fluid. The rags are thus treated from three to five hours, at the end of which time they are sufficiently cleansed. They are now known as *half-stuff*.

The next step is bleaching. A solution of chloride of lime and some sulphuric acid are added to the half-stuff, which is emptied into a chest or drainer. Here the bleaching is finished. The pulp is then washed to free it from the chemical products adhering to it, and for this purpose it is again put into the engine or tub, the roller with knives being raised to avoid cutting the fibre. The stock is now beaten to the desired fineness and sent to the stuff-chest. This completes the preparation of the pulp.

From the stuff-chest the pulp is pumped into a regulating-box, or supply-box. The stuff is sent to the Fourdrinier machine through a pipe containing a rapidly-flowing stream of water. After passing through the preliminary parts of the machine, the pulp is deposited upon a wire-cloth, which is a huge belt, having both a forward and a lateral motion. The pulp is laid upon this belt evenly, and is still in a liquid condition;

the water oozes out through the bottom into a depression below. The constant vibration of the wire-cloth, by means of a shake attachment, throws some of the fibres across the machine, while the motion or travel of the belt causes the lay of the fibre in the other direction. Endless rubber-bands, called deckles, extend on each side on top of the wire; these prevent the pulp from spreading beyond the edges of the wire, and also determine the width of the paper. The deckles continue about two-thirds of the distance of the run of the belt; by that time the paper is formed, but is not sufficiently compact. A cylindrical frame covered with wire-cloth, known as the dandy-roll, passes over the paper and presses the fibres more closely together. Upon the dandy-roll are frequently placed letters, monograms, or other signs, which may be seen in the finished paper when held up to the light. To produce these marks in the paper, some of the wires are made to project a little more than usual, or other wires are fastened over them, the paper thereby being made thinner in such places. These letters or signs are produced also by depressing the wires where a mark is desired, thus causing the paper in those places to be thicker.

The web then passes over the suction-boxes, and just as it leaves the wire-cloth it passes under the couch-rolls, after which moisture is expelled by two sets of rollers. The remaining moisture is driven out by heat. So far, no heat has been employed.

The paper is now sent to the driers, a series of iron cylinders of large diameter, heated by steam. Accompanied by a belt of duck, it passes over and under the cylinders, becoming drier and more solid as it approaches the end of the machine. The web then passes into a tub of animal sizing. If the paper is to be "loft-dried," it is cut into sheets and taken to the loft, where it is hung on poles. The cheaper varieties remain there two days, the finer grades a week. "Machine-dried" paper passes from the size-tub into a mechanical drier, without being cut into sheets.

The Fourdrinier machine, above described, has been improved in all its details, but in theory its construction is about the same as when invented by Robert. This machine was first employed in the United States about 1827 at Springfield, Massachusetts.

On the Cylinder machine no lateral motion is given to the wire-cloth; the paper therefore felts in but one direction. Paper made on the Cylinder machine is stronger in the direction of its length than that made by the Fourdrinier, but is weaker in its breadth. This machine is used in the United States for the manufacture of hanging papers, wrapping papers, and straw and binders' boards.

To receive a finish, all papers pass through a "stack" of calenders, which consists of a series of polished iron rollers, mounted one above the other. Paper which goes but once through the calenders is given the name of "machine-finish." Loft-dried paper is calendered in single sheets; machine-dried in the roll.

To supercalender paper, it is passed between a series of rollers called supercalenders; some of these are made of chilled iron, others of sheets of paper or of compressed disks of cotton.

Sizing is given to paper for the purpose of removing its porous and absorbent character, so that when written upon the ink will not spread. Vegetable sizing is put into the engines; animal sizing is given on the machine, by passing the web through a trough containing a solution of gelatine.

To fill up the pores or interstices, paper is loaded with some other substance. This not only gives the paper a finer surface but also makes it heavier. Kaolin or china clay is the loading material for ordinary paper; for the finer grades, sulphate of lime or pearl hardening is used. The clay is made into a thin cream and is put into the pulp while the latter is in the beating-engine.

When paper first comes from the machine, little ridges or hollows are found on its surface, resembling those on the rind of an orange. To make the paper smoother, it is surface-coated with some white substance, and the most delicate half-tones can then be printed upon it. In surfaced papers the mixture is applied by brushes, and the paper is calendered by steel rollers to the degree of finish desired. The oftener the paper passes through the rollers, the higher will be the finish. Some papers are brushed to a finish instead of being put through the rollers.

It is not possible to make from the raw materials absolutely white paper, as the web always inclines either to blue or yellow. Paper is therefore shaded slightly towards a buff or bluish tint. This is generally accomplished by putting a coloring substance, which dissolves very slowly, into the pulp in the engine.

As has been stated above, the preparation of the pulp, whether for hand- or machine-made paper, is substantially the same. The old stamps or beaters have been superseded by the Hollander or beating-engine which is still in use. In making paper by hand, the pulp is carried to the working-vat, a vessel either of wood or stone, about 5 feet square and 4 feet deep, with a flaring top. In the vat the pulp is mixed with water and is heated by means of a steam-pipe. The mould for making the paper is a wooden frame, with bars about an inch and a half apart, flush with one edge of the frame. Parallel wires, about fifteen or twenty to the inch, are laid upon these bars, lengthwise of the frame. A movable frame, called a deckle, fits upon the mould, the two forming a shallow tray, with a wire bottom like a sieve. Paper made in such a mould is known as "wove" paper. When small wires placed close together, with coarser wires running across them at equidistant intervals, form the bottom of the mould, in place of the wire-cloth used as the bottom for wove paper, the paper made in such a mould takes the impression of all these wires. It is then given the name of "laid" paper.

The mould or wire-frame on which the pulp is formed is raised where the water-mark, or trademark, is desired. The sheet in that part is thereby made thinner than in other places, and the design remains impressed in each sheet.

The workman dips the mould into the vat containing the fluid pulp, and takes up a sufficient quantity to form a sheet of paper. Great dexterity is needed to make a perfect sheet, and to follow this with other perfect sheets, all of even weight; this depends on the skill of eye and hand acquired by experience. The vatman gives the mould an oscillating motion, to cause the intermixture of the fibres necessary to secure uniformity of texture. Gradually the water drains through, the pulp solidifies and assumes a peculiar shiny appearance, which indicates the completion of the first step of the process. The deckle is then taken off, and the mould is sent to a workman known as the "coucher," who deposits the sheet upon a piece of felt. Another piece of felt is placed upon the paper, and this process is continued until the pile contains six or eight quires. The pile is then subjected to great pressure. A workman known as the "layer" separates the pieces of felt and the paper. The sheets are again pressed to remove, so far as possible, the felt-marks and the moisture, and are then hung in a loft to dry. When dry, the paper is sized. Sizing is made of some material containing a great deal of gelatine, such as sheeps' feet or pieces of skin cut off by curriers before the hides are tanned. These materials are boiled to a jelly and strained, and a small quantity of alum is added. The sheets are spread out in a tub containing the sizing diluted with water. Care is taken that the sheets shall be equally moistened. After sizing, the paper is again pressed and slowly dried. Women take out the knots and imperfections with small knives, and separate the perfect from the imperfect sheets. After being again pressed, the paper is finished and counted into reams. These reams when pressed and tied up are ready to be sent to the warehouse. There is but one mill in the United States which produces hand-made paper [as of 1901. Editor], that of the L. L. Brown Paper Company at Adams, Massachusetts. In the vat-mills of Europe, after the preparation of the pulp by machinery, paper is made by hand in about the same way as in this country. In some towns the same process has been employed for several centuries. In a number of the ancient mills at Amalfi, Italy, the rags are still beaten by hammers.

Deckle-edge is the name given to papers which are rough on the outer edges. In making paper by hand, the pulp is shaken in a sieve, and the sides therefore are uneven. When paper first issues from the machine, it is rough on the outer edges, next to the deckles, and is afterwards trimmed. Deckle-edged machine paper, however, can be made in narrow strips of any desired width. This is done by putting in a number of deckle-straps on the wire-cloth, so as to give the true deckle. The edge thus formed is more feathery than that of regular hand-made paper; it occurs on two sides instead of four.

Classes of paper.

Paper may be divided into four general classes: printing-paper (book and newspaper), writing-paper, wrapping- or packing-paper, and special or miscellaneous papers. Printing papers include the following:

Machine-finish—A paper with an unglazed surface, having passed but once through the calenders.

Wove—A paper which receives no other impression than that made by the weave of the wire-cloth and the dandy-roll.

Laid—When made by hand, a paper which takes the impression of both the small and the coarse wires which form the bottom of the mould. In machine-made paper, the equidistant parallel lines are produced by a series of wires which pass around the exterior of the dandy-roll.

Calendered—A paper which receives a surface by being passed through a series of polished iron rollers, known as calenders. This operation makes the paper even and also gives it a gloss.

Supercalendered—A paper which receives a still higher finish by being subjected to the action of supercalenders, which are a series of rollers, some made of chilled iron, others of sheets of paper or of compressed disks of cotton.

Coated—A paper which has received a coating of a white substance, such as china clay, or gypsum, sulphate of barytes, etc.

Coated and supercalendered papers are used for first-class magazines and for illustrated books, as they take the impression of a plate better than many other papers.

Enameled papers are coated with a colored substance which adds both to their weight and thickness. They are used for covers.

Deckle-edged papers are rough on the outer edges. They are made both by hand and machinery.

Plate paper—Paper which has passed between highly polished metal plates or heavy rollers that give a powerful pressure. Plate paper is a high grade of book stock, and has the same finish on both sides. It takes well the impression of printer's ink, and receives the most delicate lines of half-tones.

Copperplate paper is unsized paper, unfinished on one side and calendered on the other.

Writing-paper has a smooth surface, as it is made with a sizing or glue. Without the sizing, the ink would penetrate the paper and render each line of the writing too thick. It sometimes has the same name, but not always the same size, as printing-papers.

Among writing papers are:

Bond—A fine stock of paper, usually uncalendered and very strong.

Linen—A paper made from the same stock as bond, but laid and usually of a rougher finish.

Ledger—The finest qualities of writing-paper large in size. Ledger-paper is very strong and has good erasing qualities.

The fine varieties of writing-papers are, of course, made of linen rags.

Some of the special papers are used just as they come from the mill; others are prepared for special purposes by manufacturers known as converters. These products may be divided into special papers and converted papers. Among special papers may be mentioned blotting, copying, India, Japan, manifold, parchment, rice, sand, safety, silver, sponge, and tracing paper; among converted papers are carbolic acid, carbon, emery, glass, gold or gilt, oiled, photographic, satin, silver, and test paper. Coated paper, safety paper, and tracing paper are sometimes subjected to treatment by converters.

NOTES

[1] From about 3998-3721 B.C.
[2] From about 1587-1328 B.C.
[3] From about 3721-3503 B.C.
[4] In modern times the term parchment has given place to that of vellum. The true vellum is made from calf-skin or from the skins of kids or dead-born lambs, but the name is now applied to a medieval skin book of any kind. The use of the word parchment is generally restricted to sheepskin or a skin on which law deeds or other formal writings are engrossed.
[5] Esparto is the name of two or three species of grass found in Southern Europe and Northern Africa.

Douglas C. McMurtrie

The Origin of
the Alphabet

Almost from their very beginnings, systems of writing tended to become phonetic—
that is, capable of representing the sounds of spoken languages. But if writing was to
become truly useful to mankind, it was necessary that the complicated systems of
phonograms be simplified so that the art of writing could be acquired and used by the
ordinary man. The process of simplification has resulted in the relatively small group
of written and printed characters which make up what we today call the alphabet.

We use the letters of our alphabet every day with the utmost ease and unconcern,
taking them almost as much for granted as the air we breathe. We do not realize that
each of these letters is at our service today only as the result of a long and laboriously
slow process of evolution in the age-old art of writing. The centuries during which
mankind learned to write alphabetically are now telescoped into a few years of school
life, from the primary school youngster awkwardly tracing his first ABC's to the
grammar-school child who can (sometimes) make more or less legible letters.

What is our alphabet? It is a set of symbols, seemingly of quite arbitrary form,
which we use to represent the elemental sounds of our spoken language. It is perfectly
obvious to all who use it—and especially to those who use it for writing the English
language—that the alphabet as we know it is at best only a makeshift as a means of
representing spoken sounds. But mankind, curiously enough, has a way of getting
along nicely with makeshifts. The alphabet, as nearly as we can judge, has been in
process of development for about four thousand years and is still far from a perfect

SOURCE: Reprinted from Douglas C. McMurtrie, *The Book: The Story of Printing and
Bookmaking,* Third revised edition. (New York: Oxford University Press, c1943), Chapter II,
"The Origin of the Alphabet," pp. 20-39, by permission of the publisher. Copyright 1943 by
Douglas C. McMurtrie; renewed 1971 by Helen M. Hogsdon.

implement. In fact, a perfect, truly phonetic alphabet, except as invented by scholars for the scientific study of human speech, seems to be impossible of realization. For our letters have now become so imbedded in usage that it is almost hopeless to try to dislodge or change them.

But, imperfect though it is, where did this alphabet originate? For an answer to this question, as with our inquiry about the beginnings of writing, we must go back to remote antiquity. And even from the evidence to be found there we can make no more than shrewd conjectures. An enormous amount of study has been devoted to the subject, but scholars still disagree widely on many important details. We have a very good clue, however, in the very word "alphabet," to guide us at the start of our search. For the word "alphabet" is nothing more than the names of the first two letters, *alpha, beta,* in the alphabet of the ancient Greeks. Following up this clue—first noting that many letters in the ancient Greek alphabet had true *names,* such as *alpha, beta, gamma, delta, iota, kappa, lambda,* and so on—we are next impressed by the fact that the letters of the Semitic alphabets (ancient Phoenician, ancient and modern Hebrew, Arabic, and others) also had names, and that the Semitic names (in Hebrew *aleph, beth, gimel, daleth, yod, kaph, lamed,* and so on) have a striking similarity to the Greek names. The conclusion seems inescapable that the ancient Greeks got the names of their letters, at least, from a Semitic source.

But it seems unlikely that the Greeks could have taken the names alone, without the characters to which the names belonged. The names unquestionably had some meaning for the Semites who first used them, but they were meaningless to the Greeks, who could not even pronounce them correctly. To those Greeks of a very ancient day who first learned to use the alphabet, the strange-sounding and meaningless names must have been identified with the separate letters which some strange-speaking foreigners taught them.

In pursuing the search for the land from which the letters first came to Greece, scholars have made careful studies of ancient inscriptions. In Phoenician inscriptions there have been found abundant evidences of a system of alphabetic characters. Most of these characters have been clearly identified as the prototypes, if not as the actual models, of letters with the same phonetic values as those in very ancient Greek inscriptions. Greek tradition, also, credits the Phoenicians with being the "inventors" of writing. The accumulated evidence is convincing that at some remote time the inhabitants of various parts of the Greek world acquired the alphabet through contacts with the seafaring Phoenicians.

We are speaking now of the Greek alphabet which became in time the ancestor of the Roman alphabet and thus of ours. The progenitors or predecessors of the ancient Greeks, on the coast of Asia Minor, on the islands of the Aegean Sea, and on the Greek mainland, have left evidences of a system of writing possibly derived from the linear script of prehistoric Crete. But when the alphabet as we know it first made its beginnings in ancient Greece, all knowledge of that earlier script seems to have been wiped out completely, except perhaps on one or two of the islands and a few localities in Asia Minor. On the island of Cyprus a local syllabary remained in use until the sixth century B.C. And Lycia and Lydia in Asia Minor also had ancient syllabaries.

But these were so exceptional that it truly may be said that from the Phoenicians the Greek world learned all over again the art of writing.

We now confront the critical question: how and when did the Phoenician alphabet come into being? In their search for an answer to this question, scholars have long been groping in a realm of historical obscurity. Monuments of vast age have been found, bearing inscriptions in Phoenician characters. But these characters are already wholly alphabetic, with apparently no trace of ideographic phonograms in them. Without an ideographic ancestry, how did they originate? Did some brilliantly inspired Phoenician, once upon a time, just "make them up"? Such an explanation makes too great a demand upon credulity. But where are the ancestors of these twenty-two Phoenician letters to be found?

The first serious attempt at an answer to this question was made in 1859, when Emmanuel de Rougé, a French scholar, presented before the French Academy a memoir in which he sought to show that each one of the known Phoenician characters was derived from a corresponding character in the Egyptian hieratic writing. For many years this answer to the question was generally accepted as final and conclusive. But the work of later scholars, based upon more recently discovered inscriptions, in characters more archaic than any to which de Rougé had access, so thoroughly discredited the Frenchman's theory that the question again became an open one.

Sir Arthur Evans in 1895 advanced the suggestion that the Cretan pictographs and the later Cretan linear characters lay behind the Phoenician alphabet. It is not out of the question, of course, that Cretan refugees, fleeing from the catastrophe which overwhelmed their civilization about 1200 B.C., found their way to Palestine with their peculiar script. But the Cretan characters at best are only imperfectly understood, and until more is known of them the suggestion of a connection between them and the Phoenician alphabet must remain only a suggestion.

In general appearance the Phoenician characters can be compared with some of the characters found in the Cretan script or in the scripts of prehistoric Cyprus or Asia Minor. But nowhere are appearances more deceitful than in tracing the descent of the letters in a primitive alphabet. Religious and governmental conservatism fixed the forms of the Egyptian hieroglyphic characters and to a large extent those of the Mesopotamian cuneiform writing. Thus the characters on the very latest Egyptian monuments are practically identical with the same characters as found on the very earliest. But when alphabetic writing made its start, conservative forces had no control over it. Writing became purely utilitarian, the tool of traders and men of business who refused to be bothered with the complications of the older systems. Those who used the primitive alphabets did so with perfect liberty—not to say license—to do with them as they saw fit. The forms of the letters were fluid, so to speak, and changed from place to place and from time to time all through the ages as they spread from Phoenicia through Greece to ancient Rome and from Rome throughout Europe, until the invention of printing fixed them in their present almost unalterable forms.

Thus we find the ancestor of the letter A, for example, lying on either side, standing on its apex, or canted at all possible angles, and with its crossbar across its feet, tangent to its point, or crossing anywhere between. In some archaic Greek inscriptions the characters for M and for S can barely be differentiated. If these mutations and variations are found in inscriptions that can be read, in which the values of the letters are accurately known, how uncertain must it be on the basis of appearance alone, to identify characters in unknown scripts with the known letters of primitive alphabets!

Other possible sources of the Phoenician alphabet have been sought in the characters developed by the ancient Hittites of Asia Minor and in the linear script of the Akkadians, Sumerians, and earliest Babylonians in Mesopotamia. A Hittite origin cannot be intelligently discussed as yet, since next to nothing is known of the meanings of the Hittite characters. A Babylonian origin seems much more plausible. The Phoenicians, according to tradition, had migrated from the region of the Persian Gulf in the third pre-Christian millennium, just as Abraham had led the ancient Hebrews out of Chaldea to Canaan at about the same time. The linear Babylonian script had not been entirely displaced by the cuneiform writing at the traditional time of the Phoenician migration, and it is interesting to speculate that the emigrants may have taken a knowledge of writing with them. At a much later time, about 1400 B.C., it is known from Egyptian records that Babylonian was the language of diplomacy and officialdom in international communications. Babylonian and its script must have been known in Palestine and among the Phoenicians, at least in official circles. But no conclusion can be drawn from this fact as to the language and script (if any) used by the Phoenician populace for internal communication. French was for many years the diplomatic and "polite" language of Europe, but its use in this way did not perceptibly affect the vernaculars of the different European nations.

Of all the ancient cultures which hemmed in that little strip of seacoast inhabited by the Phoenician people and from which they may have derived their alphabet, none remains to be considered—unless we should find that in some bygone time there was an ancient culture south of the Phoenicians and between them and Egypt. When we turn in this direction, we are getting "warm," as children say. For in quite recent years there has been found evidence of just such a culture, though a quite primitive one, between Phoenicia and Egypt and, what is more, inscriptions which offer a most intriguing clue to the origin of the Phoenician alphabet.

On the Sinai Peninsula, the wedge-shaped land mass which juts into the Red Sea southeast of the Isthmus of Suez, Sir Flinders Petrie, the famous English Egyptologist, discovered in 1904 and 1905 some stone objects inscribed with characters which seemed to be alphabetic. In all, about fifteen such inscriptions have been found, containing in all about 225 characters, of which about thirty are highly problematical because of the wearing away of the soft sandstone in which they were cut. About twenty-five distinctly different forms have been sorted out. Unfortunately, the inscriptions are all quite short, and very few identical groups of characters (that is, identical words) recur. But there is one group of four characters which recurs several times, and these have been quite conclusively identified by Alan H. Gardiner, another English scholar, as B'LT, spelling the name of the primitive Semitic goddess Ba'alat, who was identified with the Egyptian goddess Hathor.

This was enough to make it reasonably clear that the characters were truly alphabetic and also that the language of the inscriptions was Semitic. Many scholars have busied themselves with the problems of deciphering and interpreting the inscriptions, with varying results. In 1931, Martin Sprengling, an accomplished Arabist, published what seem to be highly satisfactory interpretations of the inscriptions. As Sprengling reads them, they are mostly votive in character and are inscribed on objects that a primitive Semitic people, working in the mines of the Sinai region, used as offerings to the tribal goddess.

Sinaitic Inscription, about 1800 B.C.

The accompanying illustration shows in outline drawing (after Sprengling) the inscription on one of these Sinaitic stones. Sprengling translates the characters thus: "The gift of Benshemish, sculptor of Upwawet, beloved of Ba'alat." Upwawet was the name of the Egyptian deity whose statue, possibly the one carved by Benshemish, is sketched at the right of the inscription. The name of the goddess is spelled with the four characters, interpreted as B'LT, below the crack in the left-hand column, reading downward.

For the probable date of the origin of these inscriptions Sprengling refers us to James H. Breasted's *History of Egypt*: "While operations in the mines of Sinai had been resumed as early as the reign of Sesostris I, . . . it remained for Amenemhet III to develop the equipment of the stations on the peninsula, so that they might become more permanent than the mere camp of an expedition while working the mines for a few months. . . . Amenemhet III made the station at Sarbut el-Khadem a well equipped colony for the exploitation of the mineral wealth of the mountains." Details of this account by Breasted, supplemented by extracts from his *Ancient Records*, include the mention of a stele set up by an Egyptian official, barracks for the workmen, fortifications against the marauding tribes of the desert, a temple of the local Hathor, mine shafts each under the charge of a native foreman after whom it was named—all of which fits in with the tentative translations of the inscriptions as made by Sprengling.

Amenemhet III reigned in Egypt from 1849 to 1801 B.C. It seems almost certain, therefore, that the Sinai inscriptions date from the last half of the nineteenth pre-Christian century, when the Sinai mines were being worked by crews of local Semitic natives under the direction of Egyptian officials. Not long after this date the Egyptian Empire suffered reverses which caused the mines to be abandoned.

How did an alphabet come into being under such circumstances? Before attempting an answer to this question, we must recall that the Egyptian system of writing at that time was already well on its way toward becoming alphabetic. It had reached the point of identifying some of its ideographic characters with the initial sounds of the spoken words which corresponded to those characters. But it never reached the point of assigning one character to the function of representing one sound; for each sound it preferred to have a wide range of characters from which to choose. What happened in Sinai, we may imagine, was the reduction of this complicated formula to its simplest terms—only one character for each sound.

The method by which this came about might be compared with what the electricians call "induction." As an electric current passing through a coil of wire somehow causes an independent current to flow through another wire which moves in the field of this coil, so the influence of the Egyptians in Sinai set in motion an impulse to write among those ancient Semites. One may suppose that some Egyptian scribe connected with the management of the Sinai mines lightened the tedium of his exile in that desolate place by "teaching" an intelligent native foreman the rudiments of writing. This foreman, or perhaps several foremen, could use these rudiments in keeping simple records, thus no doubt saving some labor for Egyptian clerks. The few characters which the natives learned were written for them, no doubt, with the Egyptian pen brush on papyrus. They may have been in the cursive, hieratic form, or they may have been in the more easily identified form of the hieroglyphic pictographs. But when the Semites came to using them on stone, as they saw their Egyptian masters doing, some modification and simplification of the forms were doubtless necessary. Still, some of the characters as they stand can be quite easily identified with Egyptian characters, although, it is important to note, they were not used with the same phonetic values as in Egyptian, but with phonetic values derived from the *Semitic* words for the objects which the Egyptian symbols represented.

The system of writing which thus developed was a bare skeleton of some two dozen consonantal characters. How condescendingly the Egyptians may have smiled at the pathetic efforts of those natives to write with an equipment so pitifully meager! But those efforts were the beginnings of the alphabet—one of the mightiest implements of power now at man's command. Those primitive natives of Sinai were intelligent enough to grasp the principle of alphabetic writing that their Egyptian superiors were much too learned to perceive. They discovered the advantage of having a few characters which could be used in innumerable combinations over a system of innumerable characters to serve the same purpose.

From Sinai this primitive alphabet seems to have been carried on currents of migration and trade southeastward into what is now Arabia and northward into Palestine. The two branches became markedly differentiated, but the northern branch may well have been the progenitor of the earliest Phoenician alphabet.

Even if this latest theory as to the origin of the Phoenician alphabet is not completely established in all details, it is at least the most credible theory thus far advanced. No doubt the Phoenicians may have modified their alphabet under influences from other sources, but the Sinaitic origin of its beginnings seems to be quite satisfactorily established.

The earliest known inscription in which the Phoenician alphabet appears dates from an era about six hundred years after the probable date of the Sinaitic inscriptions. Six centuries allow plenty of time for experimentation with alphabetic writing and afford plenty of opportunity for other systems of writing—Cretan, Hittite, Babylonian, Egyptian—to contribute whatever they had to offer for its improvement. The Phoenicians were a practical people. In business and trade they had contacts everywhere. It is not at all unlikely that they borrowed letter forms from other peoples; but if they did so, they modified the borrowed forms and adapted them to their own uses. But it is important to keep in mind that what persisted throughout those six centuries was the tradition of the *function* of the letters rather than of their *form*. Through all possible changes or even substitutions of forms, the function of that little group of symbols for the sounds of human speech remained essentially unchanged. The principle of writing alphabetically survived among a few Semitic peoples occupying a relatively unimportant geographical area, while mighty nations such as Assyria and Egypt continued their cumbersome methods of writing with hundreds and hundreds of symbols.

And it does not seem likely that alphabetic writing, after its principle had once been discovered, fell entirely into disuse and had to be discovered anew. Durable objects bearing clearly alphabetic inscriptions may be lacking—but the users of the alphabet, the ancestors of the Phoenicians, were not builders. They were not pre-possessed, as the ancient Egyptians so evidently were, with the idea of projecting themselves into the future by means of imperishable monuments inscribed with records of their deeds. They were concerned with practical day-to-day affairs, and their notes and records of these were made on perishable materials. Even though the Babylonian language and script came to be used in official and diplomatic correspondence, we may quite reasonably suppose that in their own private affairs the Phoenicians used their own alphabet, just as they used their own language.

The earliest known Phoenician inscription shows the alphabet in a mature and well-developed state, which gives the impression that it had been in use for a considerable time. This inscription was found in 1923, by a French archaeological expedition, on the sarcophagus of a Phoenician king of Byblos named Ahiram. Scholars have determined that the tomb and the sarcophagus date from the middle of the thirteenth century B.C., in the time of Rameses II, king of Egypt. Byblos (the Gebal of the Old Testament) was then under strong Egyptian influence.

Portion of the Ahiram Inscription of about 1250 B.C.

In the inscription, of which a portion of the first line is here reproduced, the son of the deceased king dedicated the tomb with a curse on any person who should dare to violate it. It is read from right to left. The alphabet, as in the case of the Sinaitic inscriptions, is still almost purely consonantal, with no letters for true vowel sounds. Weathering of the stone has obliterated a few letters in the name of the king's son, but following the break the letters shown in the reproduction, reading leftward, are TB'AL BN ACHRM MLK GBL, or, . . . *tbaal ben Ahiram melek Gebal*— ". . . tbaal son of Ahiram king of Gebal." With an effort of the imagination the reader may be able to recognize ancestors of A, H, L, and T; perhaps of R and M. It should be noted that the occasional short vertical strokes are not letters but indications of divisions between words or word groups.

Phoenician Inscription on a Bronze Bowl, about 950 B.C.

A fragment of a bronze bowl found at the site of a Phoenician colony or outpost on the island of Cyprus carries an inscription which has been interpreted as referring to that Phoenician King Hiram who was the friend of King Solomon. If that interpretation is correct, the fragment dates from about the middle of the tenth pre-Christian century, and the inscription on it is the next earliest known use of the Phoenician alphabet. An outline drawing of this interesting relic appears here. The inscription reads leftward, so that the letters must be reversed before any possible resemblance to our letters can be recognized. The primitive forms of K, M, and N are fairly easy to distinguish. But the letter that at first sight looks like K is really A, lying on its side and with its crossbar at or near the angle. And the letter that resembles W is an archaic letter with a value similar to that of S.

This Cypriote bowl has also been ascribed to the time of another Hiram, king of

Sidon, in which case its date is about two hundred years later, or in the eighth century B.C., and the next earliest known inscription in the Semitic alphabet would then be the famous Moabite stone now in the Louvre at Paris. This monument was found in 1868 by a missionary in the vicinity of the Dead Sea. As soon as the local Arabs saw that it was of some interest or value to the Christian intruders, they tried to destroy it by heating it in a fire and then pouring water over it, thus splitting it into scores of pieces. Fortunately, "squeezes" had already been made of the inscription, so that it was possible to restore the stone in part to its original condition.

The inscription on the Moabite stone is the record made by Mesha, king of Moab, of the rebellion of his people against Jehoram, king of Israel, some time between 896 and 884 B.C. As was the case with conflicting *communiqués* from the opposing forces in the late war, the story of the rebellion as told by Mesha differs considerably from the account of it in the second Book of Kings in the Old Testament. Of more immediate interest to us, however, is the fact that the letters of the inscription show recognizable resemblances to those of our own alphabet. Below are shown the letters of the Moabite stone (but reversed, to face rightward, in the direction in which we read), with our modern equivalents under them.

There is still much controversy as to the date when the Phoenician alphabet found its way into Greece. Rhys Carpenter had no sooner made it clear, by an excellent line of observation and reasoning in an article published in 1933, that the Greeks could not have received the alphabet much earlier than 700 B.C., than Mrs. Agnes Newhall Stillwell showed, by an inscription on a vase fragment found at Corinth, that "by the period 775-750 B.C. writing must have already become a permanent feature of Greek civilization." Carpenter then pointed out that the evidence of this vase fragment was inconclusive by itself. If we were to "split the difference" and say that alphabetic writing was probably introduced into the Greek world between 800 and 700 B.C., we should be reasonably safe—at any rate until some inscriptions come to light which are much more archaic than any yet found.

A B CD E F Z H Th I K L M N S O P Ts Q R Sh T

The Alphabet of the Moabite Stone.
(Reversed, so as to read from left to right.)

It would seem that the Phoenicians, in their active commercial exploitation of the Mediterranean region, were in contact with the Greek-speaking peoples, particularly in Asia Minor and the islands of the eastern Mediterranean, for an indefinitely long time, and that it was possibly in Rhodes or in Cyprus that their alphabet was first adapted so that it might be used efficiently for writing the Greek language. The Phoenicians had colonies, or trading posts, in Melos, Rhodes, and other Aegean islands as early as the thirteenth century B.C., and somewhat later at Thasos, Samothrace, Corinth, and other points. Writing first took root in some of the islands. Herodotus, the first Greek historian, tells of the coming of Cadmus, the legendary hero, with a company of followers whom he brought from Phoenicia, and of how Cadmus first stopped at Thera, an island in the Aegean Sea, and later settled in Boeotia, on the mainland, where he introduced the art of writing to Greece.

Primitive Greek Writing
from the Island of Thera.

An Ancient Greek Inscription from Attica.

Cadmus in Greek legend has been explained as the personification of the forces of a foreign culture which profoundly affected ancient Greek life. It may be significant that what seems to be the most archaic form of the Greek alphabet has been found in inscriptions from the island of Thera. The letters of these inscriptions are described as being almost pure Phoenician and in the earliest cases are written leftward, as the Phoenicians wrote. The Thera inscriptions have been ascribed to about the ninth or eighth century B.C. The earliest surviving Phoenician inscriptions, as has been noted, date from about the same period.

Corinthian Vase Inscription, Thought to Date about 750 B.C.

But even with the alphabet safely on Greek soil at about 800 B.C., we find difficulty in recognizing our familiar letters in the characters at first used by the Greeks. Here are shown drawings of some very early inscriptions from Thera, from Attica, and from Corinth, and especially a few lines from the famous inscription in which were published, about 650 B.C., some of the laws of the ancient Cretan city of Gortyna. From a casual inspection of these specimens it would seem that the Greeks, in their first struggles with alphabetic writing, were somewhat like our primary-school children. They apparently felt quite at liberty to write as they pleased, with the characters sideways, hindside before, or upside down, and in a delightful variety of forms. To them, it would seem, a letter was a letter, no matter in what position it was written or carved. The Gortyna inscription, however, is a striking illustration of how Greek genius, even at a very early date, was able to bring order into confusion and create proportion and beauty.

Lines from the Gortyna Inscription, about 650 B.C.

But Gortyna was a shining exception for its time. Elsewhere for another century or so the Greek use of the alphabet was quite notably "free style." The creative spirit of the Greeks was at work in making the alphabet over to suit their own purposes. They introduced two important innovations: they fixed for all the western world the convention of writing from left to right, and they adapted some of the Phoenician letters to the representation of vowel sounds.

Whether writing is done from left to right or from right to left is more or less a matter of convention, fixed by age-old usage. The Phoenicians wrote leftward. The first experiment of the Greeks was in writing alternate lines in opposite directions. In the Gortyna inscription, for example, the first line shown in the illustration reads leftward, the second rightward, and so on alternately. This forward-and-backward method of writing the Greeks called *boustrophedon*, meaning literally "ox-turn-like," the term having reference to the movement of the animal pulling a plow up one furrow and down the next. In boustrophedon writing the letters in alternate lines are reversed as in so-called mirror writing, so as to make them face in the direction of the reading.

The earliest Greeks wrote leftward, boustrophedon, and rightward, but finally settled upon the rightward direction. We write and read from left to right, and our letters face the way they do, because the Greeks of about twenty-five centuries ago decided to have it so. On the other hand, the Semitic alphabets, such as Hebrew and Arabic, are still written in the direction preferred by their Phoenician ancestor—from right to left.

The Phoenician alphabet as first introduced into Greece was almost purely consonantal. The vowel sounds, unless we except certain voiceless breathings, were mostly taken for granted. It was somewhat as if our writing were restricted to such groups of consonants as *bldg*, *mfgr*, and the like, which we know how to expand to their fullness of sounds when they are read. This method of writing only the consonants was more or less suitable to the characteristic word structure of the Semitic languages. Classical Hebrew is still written and printed this way. To simplify matters for students or learners, the proper vowel sounds are indicated in Hebrew by means of a system of diacritical marks, or points, written or printed under or over the consonants.

But the ancient Greeks found this lack of vowel signs an inconvenience in writing their language, in which a variety of vowel sounds played an important part in inflections. At a very early date, therefore, they adapted some of the Phoenician characters for obscure or voiceless breathings to represent some of the Greek vowels. The earliest inscriptions from Thera show five true vowel signs in use. Later on, the Greeks introduced some additional characters to represent other vowel sounds, and also cleverly combined vowel signs in pairs to form diphthongs such as *ai, ei, oi, ou,* and so on.

The Greeks likewise created, or derived from non-Phoenician sources, a few characters to represent certain consonantal sounds peculiar to their language, such as *ks, ps, ph,* and *ch.* But the addition of the vowel signs was the outstanding contribution of Greek genius to the alphabet as we know it.

In different parts of ancient Greece the alphabet developed along somewhat different lines. For the Greeks, although of one race and speaking different dialects of the same language, were far from being a unit politically or culturally. They were divided into a number of groups, each of small geographical extent, but with marked individualities—so marked, in fact, that the different groups found it hard to get along with one another. It is not surprising, therefore, that no uniform use of the alphabet was established among them until a relatively late date. Almost every Greek state had its own alphabet, at least ten of which can be distinguished by the shapes or functions of the letters.

But disregarding many local variations, we can distinguish two main lines of evolution in the alphabet as the Greeks used it. These resulted in what may be called the eastern alphabet and the western alphabet. The eastern, the earlier of the two, came to be the alphabet of the Ionian branch of the Greek race, at first on the islands of the Aegean Sea and in the many Greek cities on the coast of Asia Minor, later reaching the Greek mainland. It became the alphabet of ancient Athens after the Peloponnesian War, displacing an earlier Attic form. With hardly any change since about 400 B.C. it has been revived as the alphabet of modern Greece, and some of its letters, with only minor changes, have found their way into the alphabets of Bulgaria, Serbia, Russia, and other Slavic nations.

The eastern Greek alphabet, even in its modern form, has a number of characters which cannot be recognized without some study as having anything in common with our letters for the same sounds, although they actually have a common ancestry. But its outstanding characteristic, from the point of view of the history of the alphabet, is its use of two letters, identical in form and origin with letters of our alphabet, but having entirely different functions. These are H and X. The form of H was derived from the Semitic letter *cheth,* a heavily aspirated breathing. In the earliest Greek inscriptions H was used for an aspirate, but in early times the Ionian division of the race settled upon the use of H as a vowel, with a value something like that of *a* in "cane" or of *e* in "they." The X was an added character, not in the Phoenician alphabet, which the eastern Greeks used for a sound like that of *ch* in the Scotch word "loch."

The western Greek alphabet is of importance to us because it passed into Italy and there became the ancestor of the alphabet that we use. Most of its characters were the same as those of the eastern alphabet, although some of the letters had quite decidedly changed their shape and posture. But the outstanding difference was in the functions of H and X. In the west the letter H was used in its original value of a strong aspirate, and X was used for the sound of ks—just as we use those letters today. For the long vowel that the eastern alphabet represented with H, the western used the diphthong ei and for the sound of ch it used the letter which the eastern Greeks used for ps.

Among the Ionians the characters for F and Q were dropped quite early, as the sounds they represented disappeared in speech. In the west they were retained long enough to be transported to Italy, although they were later dropped by the western Greeks also.

We have traced our alphabet back to its beginnings in the desert of Sinai (if that was indeed its place of origin) and have seen it planted and taking firm root in ancient Greece. Before we go on to its later history in western Europe, we may digress long enough to notice quite briefly some of its distant relatives of the same ancestry. For the Phoenician alphabet spread not only westward through the islands to Greece. It also grew prolifically eastward.

Before the Babylonian Captivity the Jewish people used the Phoenician alphabet in its pure form, as is attested by Hebrew inscriptions and coins. Towards the end of the seventh century B.C. an offshoot of the Phoenician alphabet began to come to the fore in the Aramaean alphabet of ancient Syria. As the commercial supremacy of Phoenicia fell before the onslaughts of the Babylonians, ending with the destruction of Tyre by Nebuchadrezzar, the Aramaean alphabet spread in influence. It was used by the Jews during their captivity by the waters of Babylon, and also by the civilian population of Assyria and Babylonia, becoming a powerful competitor of the ancient cuneiform.

After the Captivity the Jews brought the Aramaean alphabet with them to Jerusalem, where it developed into the old Hebrew script of the second and first centuries B.C. From this, but many centuries later, there came the "square" Hebrew which is commonly in use today. The Yiddish alphabet is a modification of the Hebrew.

In another direction the Aramaean alphabet spread through Syria where, through a long series of changes, it became the Syriac of the early Christian centuries and eventually appeared, quite unrecognizable, in the swinging curves of the modern Arabic. A curious side issue of the ancient Aramaean, while it was still quite close to the Phoenician, was the Samaritan, which seems to have adhered to the Phoenician tradition while the Aramaean was being transformed in Babylonia.

David Diringer

"Introduction"—
Writing

Literally and closely defined, writing is the graphic counterpart of speech, the 'fixing' of spoken language in a permanent or semi-permanent form, or, in the words of a French scholar, *'une représentation visuelle et durable du langage, qui le rend transportable et conservable.'* By means of it, language is made capable of transcending the ordinary conditions of time and space. By means of it, a Babylonian merchant, ensuring himself against legal difficulties, could record the precise details of a transaction on a tablet of wet clay, subsequently baked (unaware, of course, that it would survive to find a place in the British Museum); a complete copy of Quintilian could survive, buried in rubbish and dust at the monastery of St. Gall, to be found by Poggio Bracciolini; and, to take another example very much at random, Matthew Arnold was able to record the precise series of thoughts and feelings known as *Culture and Anarchy.*

IMPORTANCE OF WRITING

Writing, as even these scattered examples indicate, is at one time the most universal and the most elusive of things. It has escaped formal study in most universities, yet every scholarly discipline touches upon it at some point, and often in matters of considerable importance. Like sunlight and the air we breathe, it is so 'common,' so

SOURCE: Reprinted from David Diringer, *Writing* (New York: Frederick A. Praeger, Inc., 1962), "Introduction," pp. 13-24, by permission of Praeger Publications, Inc., and Thames and Hudson, Ltd. Copyright © 1962 by David Diringer.

'ordinary' and so 'understood' a thing that often it is not understood at all; and the study of its history and development has suffered as a result.

Without writing, culture, which has been defined as 'a communicable intelligence,' would not exist (except, perhaps, in a form so rudimentary as to be virtually unrecognisable). Law, religion, trade, poetry, philosophy, history—all those human activities which depend upon a degree of permanence and transmission—would be, not impossible, but incalculably restricted. The possibilities inherent in oral transmission are far wider than was conceived a century or two ago, but, in comparison with the worlds opened up by the use of writing, they are bounded by fixed and absolute limits.

Nor is this importance simply a matter of scholarly hindsight. Writing was held in such esteem and awe by most ancient peoples that its invention was frequently attributed to divinities or folk-heroes. The ancient Egyptians assigned it alternatively to Thoth and Isis; the Babylonians to Nebo, son of Marduk, who was also the god of man's destiny; the Greeks to Hermes and other of the Olympians. An ancient Jewish tradition considered Moses the inventor of the Hebrew script. And many other peoples, including the Chinese, the Indians, and the pre-Columbian inhabitants of Mexico and Central America, also believed in its divine origin.

We can with justice, therefore, speak of writing as so uniquely useful and powerful a craft that to call it an 'instrument' is implicitly to understate. At a time when the distinction between subjective and objective was less clear-cut than it is today, it seemed to most men a magic power: a connotation which continued to cling to it even in the West until comparatively recent times.

WRITING VERSUS LANGUAGE

As our initial definition indicates, writing presupposes the existence of spoken language. Indeed, mankind lived for an enormous period without writing of any kind, and there is no doubt that articulate speech was in use during this time. What degree of complexity it attained cannot be proven, but it must have been sufficient to cover the considerable range of activity which characterises even a pre-urban society, nomadic or settled. For thousands of years languages developed, changed and disappeared, following into extinction the peoples who spoke them, leaving behind no scrap or fragment for scholars to puzzle over or laymen to romanticise. No comparable disappearance can be cited: flint, pottery and bone can be buried, scattered or broken, and yet survive; anthropologists and archaeologists can reconstruct prehistoric villages, and even, to some extent, the habits of the men who lived in them; but the languages of those men are irrecoverably lost, and with the languages their religions, their thoughts, their myths. The evidence of burials and figurines must always remain, to a good extent, conjectural.

ORIGINS OF WRITING

At some point in the comparatively recent past, within those few thousand years which have seen the real intellectual development of mankind, writing, in the sense that we understand the word today, had its origins. An analysis of first causes here is an extraordinarily difficult and touchy affair, much like analysing the 'causes' of a war or revolution: in each case those present when the phenomenon has its birth have usually little or no concern with posterity, and posterity must, in consequence, tread warily. What can be said with certainty is that there is no evidence to prove that any *complete system* of writing was employed before the middle of the fourth millennium B.C. Representational cave-paintings and carvings on small objects have been found from as early a period as the Upper Palaeolithic (some 20,000 years or more B.C.), as well as circles and other symbols, full of variety and distinction. Some of these were apparently used as property marks, or for similar purposes. But they are not in any way complete (that is, established and systematic) forms of writing, nor can any connection be traced between them and the ancient systems we know. The ultimate roots of the latter are in every case matters of conjecture.

We can perhaps say that all forms of graphic inscription, however crude or refined, have their roots in the central and universal human need to *communicate* and *express*. Nevertheless, a clear distinction must be made, if our subject is to be rendered at all practicable, between what we shall henceforth call *embryo-writing* and *writing proper*. The prehistoric painting and sculpture which we find from the Upper Palaeolithic onwards was partly an attempt at expression and communication, and partly, as we shall see, a kind of sympathetic magic (it is impossible to separate completely the two functions). Such forms have continued to spring up well into historic times, and long after the appearance even of alphabetic writing. But most of these devices, ancient and modern, are isolated, arbitrary and unsystematic in the way that they 'fix' language and ideas, and have little to do with the systematic and (in the fullest sense of the word) *conscious* writing which we find for the first time in the fourth millennium B.C.

This is not to say that everything before that time must be neglected: on the contrary, anything which throws light upon man's earliest attempts at expression and communication, however distant it may be from the study of actual scripts, cannot but assist our understanding of writing and its development, and cannot but be worthy of examination. Even the evidence of modern anthropology should not be neglected when, in examining recent or contemporary 'primitive' communities and peoples, it gives us new insights into the workings of many rudimentary forms of communication. But a line must be drawn, and we should not, in reacting against oversimplified ideas about 'primitive' and 'rude' stages of civilisation, go to the opposite extreme, and lump together in the category of 'writing' every form of graphic expression used by man.

Writing, as we understand it, is a conscious activity, intricately and inseparably bound up with the development, comparatively recent, of man's conscious intellect. The establishment or stabilisation of a written script—cuneiform, or Chinese, or Hittite hieroglyphic—implies a degree of consciousness towards language so much larger than that of, say, Palaeolithic man, as to amount to a difference in kind.

DEVELOPMENT AND SPREAD OF SCRIPTS

At the risk of seeming paradoxical, a word must now be said about the 'progressive' fallacy, of which so much has been written in other contexts. It is a fallacy inherent not only in modern liberal habits of thought, but, alas, in the very structure of our language, and most of all in the language and methodology of modern scholarship. Some would banish the word *progress* itself to the hinterlands: but *development* and *evolution* remain behind to plague them, with their tinge of something very similar. Difficulties such as these—above all, the assumption that all change is necessarily 'progressive'—are especially inherent in our present subject. A very helpful picto-graphic diagram, carelessly used or interpreted, can give the impression of a vast river of script churning purposefully and irrevocably towards the modern alphabet. Such misunderstandings must be anticipated now if we are to be free to use a good many common verbs, and to introduce any concept of progress.

The struggle for survival is the principal condition for the existence of a script, as for so many other things; and *on the whole,* barring severe interference of any kind, a script will 'evolve' in the direction of simplicity and utility (which, in the case of writing not intended for mere physical impressiveness, is *ipso facto* an improvement), and the fittest scripts will survive: the scripts which are most useful and adaptable, and which best meet the needs of the men who use them. Yet, in the course of history, how much 'severe interference' there has been! The invasion of a land by a foreign people may have untold consequences in obliterating a native script, introducing a new one, or in making the invaders literate for the first time. Sometimes the use of a particular script for ritual and religious purposes—as, say, in the Rabbinic, Samaritan and Coptic transmission of Biblical texts—effectually removes it from ordinary forms of competition and use, ensuring that it will survive at least as long as those who revere it. The movement of religious conversion has often introduced a script into use throughout vast land-areas to which it may perhaps have penetrated without such 'severe interference,' but only at an immensely slower pace: and good examples of this are the transmissions of the Arabic alphabet to all the lands from Spain to Indonesia.

Moreover, there have been cases in which, without any external interference being visible, a script did not move towards greater utility and simplicity but developed in a quite contrary direction. Thus, Chinese writing, which has been in a kind of linguistic straitjacket since its time of origin, has today some tens of thousands of symbols, of which 3,000 to 5,000 are actually employed by Chinese scholars. The Egyptian hieroglyphic script, in the course of its several thousand years of existence, became progressively more cluttered with auxiliary signs which, though their intent had at one time been to ensure a correct reading of various words, were now inserted quite uselessly and redundantly (though they were undoubtedly very decorative!). And other, similar examples could be cited. So that there are many factors, aside from the ideal usefulness of a script, which determine its development, spread and survival.

In addition to all this, we must keep in mind that the most rudimentary forms of communication are not always earlier in time than systematic scripts: a fact which the methodology of our subject often obscures. Indeed, such rudimentary forms have continued to spring up—and, in their own ways, to develop—long after the appearance of alphabetic writing, and some remain in use to this day. From here it is only a short step to saying that various kinds of writing often develop contemporaneously in different or even in the same parts of the world, and that at any point in history a cross-section of the writings in use would reveal a very vast panorama, with little in it of the false clarity of retrospect. From an imaginary vantage point in the stratosphere we would, without any previous knowledge, be hard put to tell which script was doomed to rapid oblivion, which to a steady and prolonged but not very spectacular existence, and which to a sudden acceleration of fortune. Above all, we would see little of the 'inevitability' which a survey of the sort may seem to suggest.

All this is preliminary and cautionary. It is in no way a throwing-up of the hands, or a denial that we can ever point to a straightforward example of progress in the history of writing. Such examples there have in fact been. As we have already implied, the appearance of systematic scripts, of which cuneiform was (so far as we know) the first, represented an immense stride forward in the history of mankind, more profound in its own way than the discovery of fire or the wheel: for while the latter have facilitated man's control over his physical environment, writing has been the foundation for the development of his consciousness and his intellect, his comprehension of himself and the world about him, and, in the very widest sense possible, of his critical spirit—indeed, of all that we today regard as his unique heritage and his *raison d'être*. Only the most recalcitrant and quixotic of intuitionists could find in all this a Bad Thing.

ALPHABETIC WRITING

A second, more specific, and perhaps more dramatic example of progress is the development of alphabetic writing. The Alphabet almost certainly had its origin at a single point in history, and in a specific, if hitherto uncertain, place in the Near East, probably in Palestine or Syria. It was, historically, the last major form of writing to appear, and it is the most highly developed, the most convenient, and the most easily adaptable system of writing ever invented. From its point and time of origin it moved on to become the basis for all Semitic, Indian, Greek, Latin, Slavonic and modern Western scripts, as well as of several others we shall have occasion to mention later. It moved on, that is, towards what has been called the 'triumph' or 'conquest' of the Alphabet: phrases somewhat too military for so great a benefaction to mankind. Here, too, keeping in mind the qualifications and reservations just made, the concept of progress is integral to our subject.

And lastly, many examples could be cited of scripts which *have* moved in the direction of greater usefulness and utility during their 'lifetimes': most often in a slow, sometimes millennia-long evolution at the hands of countless generations of scribes; sometimes in a single conscious leap, as in the establishment of Persian cuneiform or the Turkish (Latin) alphabet.

WRITING AS A FIELD OF STUDY

We may, for the moment, broaden out the definition with which we began this introduction, and take writing to mean the conveyance of ideas or sounds by marks on some suitable medium ranging from stone to wood, clay, metal, leather, linen, parchment, paper and wax (a definition which would include embryo-writing as well). Although, as we have mentioned, the history of writing as such is not studied in most universities, it does form the principal basis for two other important branches of research: and since the real prevalence of extant documents written on such surfaces as paper and parchment is chronologically later in time than the prevalence of inscriptions in harder materials, the division between these two falls quite naturally into what we know as *epigraphy* and *palaeography*.

Epigraphy, ordinarily subdivided into such specialities as Greek epigraphy, Latin epigraphy and Hebrew epigraphy, is the study which deals principally with ancient inscriptions cut, engraved or moulded on such materials as stone, metal and clay. Such study includes the problems of decipherment and interpretation. Palaeography, which is subdivided in a parallel fashion into specialities like Greek, Latin and Hebrew palaeography, deals principally with writing which is painted or traced on to soft materials such as paper, parchment, papyrus, linen and wax, using such tools as a stylus, brush, reed or pen. Once again, decipherment and interpretation of texts are an integral part of the discipline.

The study of palaeography has been and is of the greatest practical importance for textual criticism of all kinds, for classical philology, for ancient and medieval history, and for other branches of historical science. The study of epigraphy, on the other hand, has revolutionised our knowledge of the ancient world, and has led to the rediscovery and reconstruction of entire civilisations.

The fragmented study of writing is grounded at least partly, therefore, in these differences between materials. Certain branches of the study, however, form parts of other departments of learning. Hieroglyphic, hieratic and demotic writing (the three ancient Egyptian scripts) are ordinarily comprehended in the general discipline of Egyptology, cuneiform in Assyriology, 'primitive' writing in anthropology and ethnology, and so forth. Philology and glottology—studies of language—may also deal with writing, when and if the latter is relevant to the issue at hand (as it very frequently is). Graphology, 'the science of writing', is more concerned with the subject from the biological and psychological points of view than in terms of its history.

CLASSIFICATION OF SCRIPTS

Used by and sometimes cutting across these various fields are a number of classifications which attempt to group different writings according to their nature, and according to the stage of development which each has attained. Some of these classifications are very useful, but all must be taken with caution: they are matters of convenience, not hard-and-fast lines of demarcation. The categories (all of which have to do with true writing, not embryo-writing) are:

Pictography or *picture-writing*.

This is the most rudimentary stage of true writing. It is the first important step beyond embryo-writing in that it is no longer restricted to the recording of single, disconnected images, but is capable of representing the sequential stages or ideas of a simple narrative. The action is recorded by a series of more or less straightforwardly representational pictures or sketches, each one of which is called a *pictogram*. Picture-writings can be expressed orally in any language without alteration of content, since the pictures do not stand for specific sounds. Intrinsic phonetism (from Greek *phonê*, 'voice') is still absent: though each of the objects or things represented did of course have an oral name of some kind among those who did the drawings. Pictography of various kinds was used by many prehistoric peoples, including those of Egypt, Mesopotamia, Phoenicia, Crete, Spain, southern France, China, America, and Africa. They have continued to be used in modern times by inhabitants of Central Africa, Southeast Asia, Siberia and elsewhere.

Ideographic writing.

In appearance a highly-developed kind of picture-writing, ideographic writing is really very much more: it is in fact the first step in rendering a script capable of conveying abstractions, subtleties and multiple associations. The pictograms now, as before, can represent simply the things they show, but may connote as well the underlying ideas or conceptions with which those things are bound up. Thus, whereas in simple pictography a circle might represent the sun, in ideographic writing it might also stand for heat, light, a god associated with the sun, or the word 'day.' In addition, an animal might be ideographically depicted, not by a complete representation, but by a sketch of the head alone: a part calls up the complex whole. The individual symbols are called *ideograms*, and they show a striking similarity in many rudimentary scripts otherwise separated in time and space. 'Pure' ideographic writing has been found among the indigenous inhabitants of North America, Central America, Africa, Polynesia and Australia, as well as among the Yukaghirs of northeastern Siberia. In dealing with ideographic writing, we still do not generally have to do with *complete systems* of writing.

Analytic transitional scripts.

The writings of the ancient Mesopotamians, Egyptians, Cretans and Hittites have frequently and incorrectly been called 'ideographic.' In fact, though they may very well have been ideographic in their origins, the very earliest examples known to us of each of these scripts are already only partly ideographic, having a phonetic element as well: the two forms being combined in various ways. For lack of a better term, these forms of writing have been labelled 'transitional,' in that they stand somewhere between pure ideographic and pure phonetic writing. It should be remembered, however, that some of these systems of writing lasted for three thousand years or more, and that they can be regarded as 'transitional' only within the broadest of historical perspectives. The word 'analytic' simply indicates a script whose basic units (however these are represented) are *words*.

Phonetic scripts.

In 'pure' ideographic writing, there is still no connection between the depicted symbol and the spoken name for it: the symbols can be read with equal facility in any language. In phonetic writing we have, for the first time, the graphic counterpart of speech. Each element in such a system of writing corresponds to a sound or sounds in the language which is being represented. A direct and inseparable relationship has therefore been set up between written and spoken language: the former can only be explained or read through a knowledge of the latter. The single signs used in phonetic writing may be of any shape, and there need be no connection between the external form of the symbol and the sound it represents.

This brings us to the last great division of our subject: for phonetic writing (if it is in a 'pure' form, and not simply an element in a transitional script) may be either syllabic or alphabetic. Syllabic forms of writing (or *syllabaries*) are ultimately based upon the fact that the smallest unit into which any spoken word or series of sounds can be subdivided is the syllable. The idea of using single symbols to represent syllables seems to have arisen at various times in many parts of the world, though few scripts ever managed to shed completely the ideograms of an earlier stage and so to become 'pure' syllabaries. A flexible method of writing, far less cumbersome and far more exact than ideograms, a syllabary can nevertheless be an unwieldy system when in a particular language syllables contain more than one or two consonants. Thus, although it would be a simple matter to represent syllabically a word like *fa-mi-ly*, the word 'strength' would have to be written *se-te-re-ne-ge-the*, and, since each syllable would be represented by some single differentiated sign, the total number of symbols in the script would still be comparatively large.

Alphabetic writing.

Though technically a subdivision of phonetic writing, alphabetic writing has within the past three thousand years assumed such importance as to deserve a category of its own. The enormous advantages implicit in using letters to represent single sounds (rather than ideas or even syllables) are obvious, and need no prolonged restatement here. With its 22 or 24 or 26 signs, the Alphabet is the most flexible and useful method of writing ever invented, and, from its origins in the Near East, has become the nearly universal basis for the scripts employed by civilised peoples, passing from language to language with a minimum of difficulty. No other system of writing has had so extensive, so intricate and so interesting a history.

Warren Chappell

The Alphabet

The letter forms we use stem from lapidary Roman capitals—incised with a chisel—
that came to full flower early in the Christian Era. The classic model is the inscription
on the column erected in Rome about A.D. 114 by the Emperor Trajan in a Latin
alphabet of twenty letters of Greek origin, plus G, Y, and Z. The letters U, W, and J,
added to the Latin alphabet centuries after the Trajan capitals, brought the total
number up to our present twenty-six characters. U and W are outgrowths of the V
form. The letter J, which appeared last, is an alternate form of I.

The symbols that compose our alphabet are phonograms; they are phonetic rather
than pictorial; they stand for sounds rather than objects. In fact, they have reached an
advanced stage of simplification, where they represent elementary sounds in a
progressive change from signs as syllables and, previously, signs as words. Before
phonograms, there were ideograms, a more primitive alphabet, with symbols standing for either objects or concepts.

While paleography, the study of ancient writing, is both fascinating and rewarding,
too deep a probe into the past here will only confuse. To understand the development
of the Latin alphabet up to the invention of type, it is enough to know that the Romans
derived their alphabet from the Greeks. They in turn borrowed from the Phoenicians.
Letters of the Greek and Phoenician (Semitic) alphabets are closely related in names,
forms, and order. For instance, *alpha* and *beta*, the names of the first and second
letters in the Greek alphabet, are derived from the Semitic *aleph* and *beth*.

By the ninth century B.C. the Greeks had learned to write. First, they carried their
lines from right to left. Then for a time a method called *Boustrophedon* was used, in
which lines were alternated right to left, then left to right. Finally, the line flowed
from left to right, as it does today.

SOURCE: Reprinted from Warren Chappell, A *Short History of the Printed Word* (New York:
Alfred A. Knopf, 1970), Chapter II, "The Alphabet," pp. 20-37, by permission of the
publisher. Copyright © 1970 by the New York Times.

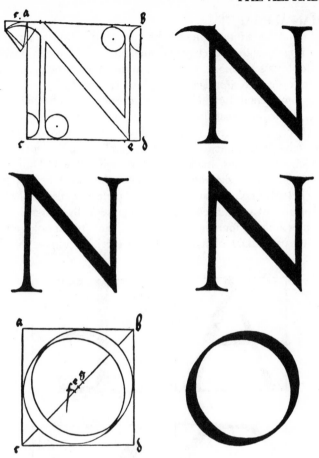

Albrecht Dürer. *Unterweysung der Messung.*

Latin manuscripts go back to the first century A.D., and it is well to understand, from the beginning, that the physical act of writing will play an ever-increasing part in the development of letter forms. The tools used to produce letters have always been formidable forces in developing their character, shape and rhythm.

Littera scripta manet

Geofroy Tory. *Bâtarde,* based on his *Champfleury.*

THE ROMAN ALPHABET

Earlier, I stressed my strong belief in the sculptural nature of type. Here, I call attention to the fact that the archetypes for our written and printed alphabets were a set of carved letters. This is echoed, of course, in the original method of type-making, where written forms were translated, sculpturally, into steel.

The great monumental Roman letters can be thought of as having simple geometric bones, so fleshed-out that the straights and curves relate organically. A letter should seem to be of one piece, not a sum of parts. The round forms bespeak circles and parts of circles. But despite many efforts to develop formulae for the construction of the alphabet, such as those made by Luca Pacioli, Albrecht Dürer, and Geofroy Tory, no set of rules can be slavishly held to. The subtleties of the great Roman forms have always eluded the compass and square. The perfect expression of a letter remains in the mind of an artist as a pure concept of form, essentially abstract in nature. Just as a draftsman uses a model for a figure drawing, a letter artist should respond through memory and the particular tool in his hand to the special requirements of his design.

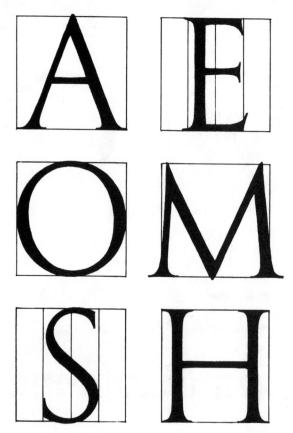

Trajan capitals set against square fields to demonstrate the proportions and rhythms of roman.

There are several ways of reaching a general understanding of the basic nature of roman. One logical and rewarding way is to think of the forms as a series of geometrical variations on a theme of square, circle, and triangle, which, when set together, will become a frieze of contracting and expanding spatial interruptions. This breathing quality is the very essence of the inscriptional concept, and is responsible for the liveliness as well as the nobility of the great classic carvings. Almost every letter shape carries its contained space, which in type is called the *counter*, and which is related, in composition, to the separations between letters. This inner space is not only vital to the color of a form—its black-and-white value—but is also an integral part of it.

If, in visualizing roman, one thinks of the shapes in relationship to square fields, proportion can be more dramatically understood in a structural way, and the variations from narrow S to wide M become clear as skeletal archetypes. This is perhaps better shown than described. Here, several letters based on the Trajan capitals are set against square fields, which are subdivided in the cases of the narrow E and S to show their forms against half the field. The thick-and-thin characteristics of these examples indicate their development from written forms produced with a wide-edged tool. In Pompeii, which was destroyed in the first century A.D., there are examples of mural writing made with a flat brush. This would be an obvious way of laying in an inscription to be incised in stone. Thus the antiquity of the flat-edged instrument is established in shaping the appearance of Western alphabets. The centuries between the Emperor Trajan and Gutenberg will be dominated by calligraphy, written with reeds and quills sharpened to a wedge-shaped point.

AMELIORATIONS OF ROMAN

LITTERA SCRIPTA MANET

Square capitals.

The more formal written alphabet of this early Roman period was known as square capitals (*capitalis quadrata*). These capitals were used for important works from the second century into about the fifth century, and their proportions had much in common with the lapidary capitals. The principal differences lay in their strong contrasts of thicks and thins, and the pen-derived serifs of the square capitals. A serif is a terminal device, functionally employed to strengthen lines which otherwise would tend to fall away optically. This is especially true of incised lines. By using a chisel in such a way that the finishing cuts were wider, a craftsman produced a strong terminal with a bracketed appearance. Performing a similar function for type, serifs continue to be seen on the majority of faces in general use. They derive more often from the example of the chisel than of the pen.

ATVENVSASCANIOPL
INRIGATETFOTVMGR
IDALIAELVCOSVBIM
FLORIBVSETDVLCIA

Square capitals.

Square capitals are not easy to write, and this limited their wide usage. The story of writing can be told in terms of the search for simpler forms, requiring fewer strokes and pen lifts and providing their own beat or rhythm to such an extent that spacing for color and legibility could be more easily controlled.

LITTERA SCRIPTA MANET

Rustic capitals.

Such an amelioration is expressed in the rustic capitals (*capitalis rustica*) of the same period, roughly, as the square capitals. These rustic letters anticipate an ever-recurring tendency to condense, usually to save space. Such economy was indicated when the material to write on was rare and costly vellum. By holding a flat-nibbed pen or wedge-shaped brush at an acute angle, the writer thins the verticals to a point where they become little more than a recurring beat, against which the round and diagonal strokes make their pattern and the horizontals provide their accent. Much could be learned from these early forms that would be of value in designing a condensed type face for use in newspaper headlines. Forms essentially full and round cannot be accommodated to narrow usage simply by squeezing them together. The color-clotting in the joints of many headline faces could be avoided by designs stemming from naturally condensed forms.

QUIDPRIMUMDISERIAQUAERARCC
CARTHAGOAUIANTIQU:.ITYROSIIA
SERAIUISTIMORIENSIADIAIMIADI
IDIAIAMBASSIRODOLORADQ IADLI

Rustic capitals.

Littera Scripta Manet

Uncials.

By the fourth century, there developed a style of writing that had as its chief characteristic the rounding off of certain angles and joints. This style, called *uncials*, carried into the eighth century. Rounded forms were used chiefly to increase speed, since the curves reduced the number of strokes necessary to shape the letters. They flow directly and easily from a quill or reed, and therefore have a natural authority, in addition to aiding legibility. The style affected the forms of A, D, E, H, M, U, and Q.

Uncials.

As noted, earlier angular pen-written joints are hard to keep clear and open. Since they are prone to filling up and darkening in color, they can be spotty in the mass.

littera scripta manet

Semi-uncials.

Up to this point, Roman letters have stood between two hypothetical horizontal lines. Early in the sixth century, the *half-uncial*, or *semi-uncial*, came into use. This marked a change to a true variant on capitals, and was the beginning of what we think of as lower case. Instead of two lines enclosing the forms, four lines are implied in the half-uncials; ascending and descending elements were introduced. This new variation provided an alphabet that was easier to write and could have great intrinsic beauty as well—witness the Irish and English versions of the half-uncial. A notable change in the curves of these alphabets was caused by the manner in which the pen was held, horizontal to the line, as opposed to the strongly slanted position used for writing rustic capitals. Half-uncials belong to the seventh, eighth, and ninth centuries.

Semi-uncials.

On the Continent, the calligraphic hands of this general period had degenerated, especially in comparison to the work being done in England and Ireland. Under the influence of a corrupted Roman cursive, best described as a running script, Europe's book hands had suffered. There had been no unifying force to fill the vacuum caused by the dissolution of the Roman Empire, and it was only natural that all means of expression fell victim to provincialism.

THE CAROLINE MINUSCULE

The Caroline minuscules.

Such was the state of calligraphy when Charlemagne came to power in 768. By decree, in the year 789, he ordered a revision of the books of the Church. His plans do not seem to have envisioned textual revision; instead, he wanted the most beautiful and accurate copies made of the finest existing manuscripts. Success for such an undertaking called for the development of a standard model hand that could be practiced throughout the Emperor's domains. The result was the beautiful Caroline minuscule, a true small letter, with definite classic ancestry, but employing a four-line system. Credit for the alphabet is given to Alcuin of York, Abbot of St. Martin's, Tours, from 796 to 804.

The Caroline minuscules.

The spread of this letter was rapid, not only in France but in all of western Europe, where it was dominant for many years. Introduced into England in the tenth century, it was generally adopted there after the Norman Conquest. The Caroline minuscule is the true ancestor of our lower-case printing type. The forms are simple, clear, and handsome, rounded and relatively wide. The alphabet tends to avoid cursive forms and excessive ligatures, especially those that would change its character, and it keeps the letters independent of one another. Those curved forms that spring from straight stems have an organic relation to the source, much as a growing leaf does in nature. All of these considerations have a strong bearing on the making of a workable, movable cast type for printing.

In addition to looking like lower case, the Caroline minuscule was used in the same way. Majuscules, or capitals (often built up with more than a single pen stroke), started a sentence that continued in minuscules. Improvement in the organization of the text, through better punctuation as well as sentence and paragraph arrangements, is also credited to this thoroughly constructive period. The flourishing centuries of manuscript production during the Caroline influence did much more than establish a fresh start on a common writing hand. It is generally conceded that without the appearance of the Caroline reform, coupled with the scholarly enterprise of the period, there would have been serious losses in the quality of the texts which reached the Renaissance. In most instances, it appears, the preferred texts were those preserved in manuscripts of the ninth and tenth centuries.

Despite the wide appeal and use of the Caroline minuscule, its uniformity and high standards could not be maintained. Inevitably, national characteristics and experience were impressed upon the original models to such an extent that numerous hands resulted. The large divisions were essentially geographical, that is, north and south. Thus the writing in France, the Low Countries, and England showed some kinship, at least for a time, and Italy, Spain, and southern France shared certain common characteristics of style.

POST-CAROLINE HANDS

Littera fcripta manet

Textur of Gutenberg's time.

By the eleventh century, there was a general tendency toward smaller and more condensed letters. Again, this was certainly due, in part, to a desire to economize on parchment as well as on time. However, compression of forms for style's sake is one thing; quite another is the development of a more measured system of spacing by using an alphabet of greater homogeneity. The calligrapher managed, in first reducing the full round forms and then finally eliminating them, to acquire a completely different rhythm. Roman capitals have been described as having a breathing rhythm; the gothic lower case has the pattern of a picket fence. To some degree, the achievement of even color throughout the page was partly mechanical, due to the regular beat of the verticals and the evenness of the counters. The diagonal couplings and footings of the letters gave them a pointed effect, but they also served as terminal accents, similar in function to serifs. This so-called gothic script underwent numerous transitional forms. It was known in fourteenth-century Germany as *Textur*, in France as *lettre de forme*, and in England as *black letter*. It was a *lettre de forme* of the following century that served as a model for the type used in Gutenberg's 42-line Bible and in the Mainz Psalter.

Black letter. Fourteenth-century breviary.

Southward, in Italy and Spain, there was strong resistance to the harsh, acute angles of northern contemporaries. There, a rounder "gothic," called *Rotunda*, was

Rotunda based on Cresci models.

developed. It was as rich in color as the black letter, but its style was reminiscent of a classic roman heritage, especially as expressed in the Caroline minuscule. In general, the "gothic" scripts are considered to be variations on the Caroline even when the modifications seem extreme.

HUMANISTIC SCRIPT AND CHANCERY CURSIVE

Scrittura umanistica.

Rotunda was not the only attempt to resist the northern gothic style. There was also the neo-Caroline letter, a Renaissance roman hand, known as *scrittura umanistica*, which most directly relates our present lower-case type to the earlier Caroline minuscule. In the fifteenth century, the Renaissance had rekindled enthusiasm for classic culture and calligraphers sought pre-gothic models for their transcriptions of classical texts. The result of their efforts was not merely a resurrection of ninth-century writing. For their new, written capitals they used the early lapidary letters as models.

The humanistic script was a more compressed letter than its Caroline predecessor, but it was significantly rounder than the northern gothics it was destined to supplant. Early manuscripts in this script (late fourteenth, early fifteenth centuries) tended to be labored and unsteady. The period when the first great examples of printing were being produced witnessed the perfecting of the hand.

Scrittura umanistica.

From the standpoint of the scribe, the gothics had many advantages, especially in ease of writing. In addition, there is the essential authority of black letter that derives from its being a lower-case alphabet, devised to solve basic writing problems. This cannot be said of the majuscules developed to fit with the gothics.

With roman the situation is reversed: the capitals have the authority and the lower case is a series of improvisations. The elegance achieved by the use of long ascenders and descenders can so reduce the middle, or x, height of roman lower case that the type face appears small. This is especially noticed where space limitations require a high letter count to the line. Despite all calligraphic shortcomings, however, the eventual precedence of roman must have played a significant and happy part in preventing the re-emergence of numerous and confusing national hands.

Fairly early in the history of printing, *cancellaresca*, an offspring of the *scrittura umanistica*, was translated into types, the first italic. Although first used chiefly to save space, in time it became the basic typographic tool for accent.

Cancellaresca

Cancellaresca. Chancery script.

Of all the semi-formal hands developed over the years of the emerging Latin alphabet, *cancellaresca*, or chancery script (so-called because of its use by papal secretaries), is unquestionably the most beautiful. It has some general interest today because of the efforts that have been made, especially in the last half century, to revive it for correspondence.

Littera scripta manet

Chancery script, early sixteenth century.

Chancery cursive was an outgrowth of the neo-Caroline hand, written with greater speed. The tendency was toward a slope, but slanting was not obligatory. The cursive quality was built into the letters. First, the forms were more compressed than *scrittura umanistica*, and, as in the case of black letter, the rhythmic beat of nearly even strokes and spaces created a characteristic pattern. Round forms became elliptical, approaching a parallelogram. Roman capitals were used, but they were small in relationship to the over-all height of the four-line system.

THE FINAL FLOWERING OF CALLIGRAPHY

EℓƐℰee

The development of written hands from the time of the square capitals to the *scrittura umanistica*.

This chapter began with the statement that today's letter forms stem from the great Roman capitals of more than eighteen centuries ago. With the perfecting of the humanistic script in the fifteenth century, the esthetics of type design had come full circle and classic forms were again firmly established as ideal archetypes. Finally, the various expressions of the alphabet could be divided into three classes: formal, semi-formal, and epistolary, which, rendered into the type faces we know, are recognized as capitals, lower case, and italic.

In many places, notably Florence, the coming of printing was strongly resisted. Scribes understandably set themselves against such an economic threat and their patrons were often equally contemptuous of what they considered the crude and vulgar imitations of good manuscripts.

In *The Civilization of the Renaissance in Italy*, Jakob Burckhardt gives an interesting picture of the libraries and the copyists at the time of the *incunabula*, those first printed books:

> The library of Urbino, now in the Vatican, was wholly the work of the great Frederick of Montefiltro. As a boy he had begun to collect; in after years he kept thirty or forty scrittori employed in various places, and spent in the course of time no less than 30,000 ducats on the collection. It was systematically extended and completed, chiefly by the help of Vespasiano, and his account of it forms an ideal picture of a library of the Renaissance. At Urbino there were catalogues of the libraries of the Vatican, of St. Mark at Florence, of the Visconti at Pavia, and even of the library at Oxford. It was noted with pride that in richness and completeness none could rival Urbino. Theology and the Middle Ages were perhaps most fully represented. There was a complete Thomas Aquinas, a complete Albertus Magnus, a complete Bonaventura. The collection, however, was a many-sided one, and included every work in medicine which was then to be had. Among the 'moderns' the great writers of the 14th century, Dante and Boccaccio, with their complete works occupied first place. Then followed twenty-five select humanists, invariably with both their Latin and Italian writings, and with all their translations. Among the Greek manuscripts the fathers of the church far outnumbered the rest; yet in the list of classics we find all the works of Sophocles, all of Pindar, all of Menander. The last must have quickly disappeared from Urbino, else the philologist would have soon edited it.
>
> We have, further, a good deal of information as to the way in which manuscripts and libraries were multiplied. The purchase of an ancient manuscript, which contained a rare, or the only complete, or the only existing text of an old writer, was naturally a lucky accident of which we need take no further account. Among the professional copyists, those who understood Greek took the highest place, and it was they especially who bore the name of 'scrittori.' Their number was always limited, and the pay they received very large. The rest, simply called 'copisti,' were partly mere clerks who made their living by such works, partly school masters and needy men of learning, who desired an addition to their incomes. The copyists at Rome in the time of Nicholas V were mostly Germans and Frenchmen—'barbarians,' as the Italian humanists called them, probably men who were in search of favors at the papal court, and who kept themselves alive meanwhile by this means. When Cosimo de' Medici was in a hurry to form a library for his favorite foundation, the Bardia below Fiesole, he sent for Vespasiano, and received from him the advice to give up all thoughts of purchasing books, since those that were worth getting could not be had easily, but rather to make use of the copyists; whereupon Cosimo bargained to pay him so much a day, and Vespasiano, with fifty-five writers under him, delivered 200 volumes in twenty-two months.
>
> The material used to write on when the work was by great or wealthy people was always parchment; the binding, both in the Vatican and at Urbino, was a uniform crimson velvet with silver clasps. Where there was so much care to show honor to the contents of a book by the beauty of its outward form, it is intelligible that the sudden appearance of printed books was greeted at first with anything but favor. Frederick of Urbino 'would have been ashamed to own a printed book.'

Stanley Morison and
Holbrook Jackson

The History of
Printing Types

Handwriting is of course the forerunner of printing. The livelihood of the first printers depended upon their being able to reproduce by movable types a fair imitation of the manuscript books of their generation and locality. Hence it is that Gutenberg of Mainz in Germany (who it is generally held invented printing with movable types in 1448 or 1450), cut gothic letters. In Germany these letters have held their own until the present century. In France, Italy, and the Latin countries generally, the roman letter was much used by the scribes in later Renaissance times. The gothic letter had therefore a short life everywhere but in the Netherlands, Germany, and England. In 1465 appeared an edition of Lactantius printed at Subiaco in a letter more roman than gothic in spirit. Semi-roman letters were also cut by Gunther Zainer at Augsberg in 1475, but in 1469 John of Spira, a printer at Venice, brought out the first pure roman letter. Next year Jenson followed with an almost identical type. This letter completely defeated the gothic in Italy. Aldus, also of Venice, followed in 1494 with a type founded upon Jenson, and in 1501 astonished the world with the first italic letter. It was Geofroy Tory, artist, scholar, and painter, who achieved for France a victory over the black letter. Tory, who was born at Bourges in 1480, associated himself with the printer Simon de Colines about the year 1520. In 1524 they published in partnership a magnificent *Horace*, in which was used an elegant roman letter. We cannot aver that these characters were actually cut by Claude Garamond, but their feeling is very similar to those known to have been cut by Tory's famous workmen some years before 1540. Jenson headed the Venetian type family with his own creation and to

---

SOURCE: Reprinted from Stanley Morison and Holbrook Jackson, *A Brief Survey of Printing History and Practice* (New York: Alfred A. Knopf, 1923), "The History of Printing Types," pp. 47-64.

Garamond belongs the similar honour of inventing the second great type family—the *old face*. The difference between the V*enetian* and the *old face* is mainly a matter of serif formation. The Garamond letter at once commended itself to printers generally, and in a short time became the model type of Europe. Though a little roman letter of the Venetian family was introduced into England by Pynson in 1509, gothic type was in complete possession until 1572, when John Day cut a series of types. These were copied from a letter made in 1565 for Plantin of Antwerp by Robert Granjon, the illustrious Lyonnese cutter, himself an ardent admirer of Garamond. Day's was the first roman type made in England. The repressive decrees of the Star Chamber, however, successfully forced typefounders, and many printers, out of existence. Elizabethan and Jacobean printers were obliged to secure their type from abroad. Their purchases consisted for the most part of Dutch adaptations of Garamond's letter. In this connection we may note the admirable types cut by such Dutch craftsmen as Christoffel Van Dijck and Dirck Voskens, whose work formed a large part of Bishop Fell's extensive purchases on behalf of the Oxford University Press in 1672. French founders also adhered very closely to the type of Garamond. His pupil Guillaume La Bé, and the latter's family, continued the typefounding business of Garamond. In 1640 Louis XIV, at the initiative of Richelieu, inauguarated a Royal Printing House. From the times of François I, who appointed Geofroy Tory "printer to the king," a like privilege was conferred upon outstanding members of the craft in Paris, but was a mere title or patent. To the new Royal Printing House, situated in the Louvre, came, as a matter of course, large supplies of the Garamond letter, but in 1693 the royal punch-cutter, Philippe Grandjean, created a new face—"Romain du roi." This letter displays a marked difference in the treatment of the serif and a great neatness in cutting and regularity of alignment. It is not too much to say that the "Romain du roi" was the first "*modern*" type. For the first time Grandjean employed the flat double serif at the head and tail of the "ascending" and "descending" letters. Louis Luce, royal punch-cutter under Louis XV, also drew further away from the *old face* of Garamond, and produced in 1740 the first condensed or narrow-bodied letter. The new fashion was now well set. Pierre-Simon Fournier, who purchased in 1736 the Le Bé foundry, which was established in 1552, cut several romans and italics in the new spirit, and he was the first to employ the term "modern" in respect to type design. To Fournier printing is indebted for the invention of a vast collection of ornaments, vignettes, fleurons, and a number of decorated types. These were derived from the florid characters affected by the master engravers of the eighteenth-century France, e.g., Le Veau, Simonet, Fessard, and Chenu, who engraved on copper the designs of Nicolas Cochin, Moreau-le-jeune, Gravelot, Boucher, and others. Thus were evolved certain *caractères de fantaisie* which, reproduced and marketed by Fournier, became for a few years a veritable rage. The family of Enschedé, owners of the oldest (and to-day the largest) Dutch foundry, were quick at imitation, and these letters even found their way into the backwater of British printing, and more recently into modern Germany. As a recent revival of the Peignot foundry of Paris has led to their reintroduction, it is worthwhile remarking that in discriminating hands these types may still be used where it is desired to suggest an atmosphere or to provoke an antiquarian interest. England was in the meantime muddling along with the help of

Dutch matrices. The advent of William Caslon I in 1720 at last raised English reputation to a high position in the art. The Caslon old face is based upon the best Dutch letters, themselves dependent upon Garamond. Caslon was too late, however, for immediate success, except locally. The fashion for the modern cut letter was only too well set. The attempts of John Baskerville and Andrew Wilson also failed to reinstate the old faces. The former's magnificent press work, however, was appreciated and produced a famous exponent in G. B. Bodoni. By means of the Baskerville methods in press work, i.e., large margins, wide spacing, and careful machining on the one hand, and a supply of imitations of Fournier's types on the other, Bodoni successfully captured an enormous reputation, the works of Walpole even being printed on his presses. This was more than the successors to Caslon's business could stand. The Bodoni types were therefore reproduced, adapted, and debased by various English and other foundries. In 1812, at the Royal Printing House, Paris, where the modern types had been originated, Firmin Didot produced a letter more finished in cutting, though less condensed, than either Fournier's or Bodoni's. These types had at first no great success. The thirst for novelty had led Thorne of London to cut the first bold face letters, and these were at once much favoured. Thorne was even commissioned to cut a bold face for the Royal Printing House itself. In 1818 Jacquemin cut a face for the same house, and the Didot foundry evolved a variety of fat-faced letters based upon Thorne's. In 1820 William Pickering, the eminent London publisher, endeavoured, by redrawing several of the old French borders and headpieces, to rescue English printing from the cold Bodoni and heavy Thorne influence, but he was compelled to use *modern* types. His printer, Corrall, was hardly a good second to him, and it was not until the accession of the younger Whittingham to his uncle's printing business at Chiswick that Pickering secured a suitable colleague. Their revival of the *old face* is too well known a story to justify a repetition here. At least it must be said that the Pickering-Whittingham combination became an important influence upon English domestic printing, greater perhaps than that of William Morris, whose work was and is interesting mainly to the speculator. For the past twenty years or so initiative in fine type design has passed to America. Mr. Bruce Rogers has designed for private use the Centaur type and the Montaigne types. Of these the first is of French inspiration, while the second is predominantly Venetian. The American Typefounders Company are reviving such historic types as Garamond and Jenson while Mr. F. W. Goudy has created two or three faces and adapted several others of established position. In spite of the activity of modern typefounders the future of fine letter design is none too secure. There are, and always will be, a vast array of bad novelties to embarrass the choice of the printer. Unfortunately, too, even when the printer knows better the customer does not. The constant imitation and adaptation of the ancients, however lively and good as a beginning, threatens to be carried to a palsied end. In the absence of creative genius the old mines are being worked, and there is great danger of their being soon worked out. There is but one remedy for the general bad taste exhibited by many printers and their customers. The real antidote for bad type designing is not to be found in the reproduction of ancient models, however good, but lies in the evolution of a school of beautiful writing. It was this existence of a tradition of beautiful writing that made it possible for Jenson and Garamond to design their admirable creations. In our own generation Mr. Edward Johnston has effected a remarkable renaissance of calligraphy. It is noticeable that, while his teaching has secured an extraordinary change in formal handwriting, the pupils for the most part, unlike their master, rarely use any other than the somewhat heavy quill-written roman. Mr. Johnston's triumph over Shelley, Bland, Bickham, and the other "elegant round hand" copperplate calligraphers is complete. Is it too much to ask that he will supply the present generation with a series of new copybooks in which will be taught a variety of hands? Who will lead us back to the great sixteenth-century masters, Palatino of Rome, Tagliente of Venice, Yçiar of Saragosa, and Beauchesne of Paris? Only then shall we be able to evolve letters and types original as well as beautiful. In Germany the zeal of Fraulein Anna Simons, and in Austria the efforts of Prof. Rudolph Larisch in popularizing Mr. Johnston's teaching have had remarkable results, as the letters of Herrn Ehmcke, Tiemann, and Rud. Koch testify. That all these types are not in every respect satisfactory is perhaps true, but at least they represent a living craftsmanship rather than the mere revival of dead men's work.

Gothic Letter

Gutenberg's first type, 1455

Gutenberg's second type

The earliest Dutch type, 1460

Semi-Roman

Poetę uero cū ſáréc boc ſeculū malis oībus
ūc.ne laboꝛ ac maloꝛ méores aię reuerd

Sweynheyn & Pannartz, Subiaco, 1465

Dér Samuel als er das ſchön
ein tiger tier/begerte er des blûte

Gunther Zainer, Augsburg, 1475

Types of this form were used
By William Caxton in his
'Dictes and Sayings of the
Philosophers' printed at West-
minster in the year 1477

William Caxton, 1477

Roman (Venetian)

These three lines are composed in a
modern facsimile of Jenson's roman
letter first cast at Venice in 1470 A.D.

Jenson, Venice, 1470

Italic

P·V.M.Buolia. Georgia Aeneida quam emenda
ta, et qua forma damus, uidetis. caetera, quae Poe
ta exerandi fui gratia compofuit, et obfcaena, quae ei
dem adfcribuntur, non cenfuimus digna enchiridio.
Eft animus dare pofthac usdem formulis optimos
quofque authores· Valete.

. Aldus, Venice, 1501

These lines are set in the italic of a recently-cut letter
whose form, in many respects, closely follows the
Aldine italic. It differs from the latter in that its
capitals are also inclined. This consistency was developed by Claude Garamond, who was the first to
attempt to harmonize roman and italic, and thus to
fit them for companion use upon the same page

10 point Goudy Italic

Old Style or Old Face

This is the Garamond type, the first of what are now known as old faces. Cut during the years 1520-30

(Set in the American Typefounders Co. facsimilie)

Claude Garamond, Paris, about 1520-30

rationem, fed hoc fatis
multò abfurdius effe ei
artem non tenet, quàm
infano, quàm ebrius.
Jn aliis fpeЄandum,

Cut by Robert Granjon of Lyons for Chr. Plantin, of Antwerp, 1565

Tardius aliquanto moleftiufque cum O.
G I O aЄta res eft. Is enim recua fcripferat,
landis, Zelandifque atque Burgundis P
Єtum defignaret quando fe hifce prefeЄtu
h i j k l m n o p q f s t v u w A B C D E F
A B C D E F G H I K L M N O P Q STVUX

Æadem, is admonenti Gubernatrici ut
Amftelodamo,non modo non a paruerit, fed
Miffuma Gubernatrice Turrium a fecret
urbe Protinus abfcendere,non Exaudito R
A A B C D E F G H J I K L M M

The Dutch Old Face, Chr. Van Dijck, 1660

Punches for these types were purchased
for the *University Press* at Oxford by
Dr. John Fell about the year 1672. They
were cut by Dutch artists of whom the
most prominent was Dirck Voskens of
Amsterdam

Fell

William Caslon, *the first great Eng-lish typefounder*, cut his old face series during the years 1720-26 Caslon old face remains one of the finest available letters

The English Old Face, 1720

John Baskerville

Baskerville, 1750

Modern Face

d'*Imprimerie des affignats* & fut placé sous l diate du Gouvernement.

En 1792, l'Imprimerie du Louvre devin *exécutive*. Malgré l'activité que déployait ne pouvait suffire à la publication des l tionnaires dont le nombre allait chaque j

The first modern face, cut by Philippe Grandjean, royal punch-cutter, Paris, 1693

Mais, dans la pratique, il s'en faut que cet ar façon intégrale. Bon nombre des impressions imputable au budget de l'État», sont confiées imprimeries secondaires dont je rappellerai la 1° L'imprimerie du *Journal officiel;*

The first condensed letter, cut by Louis Luce, royal punch-cutter, Paris, 1740

G. B. BODONI (1740–1813), was not,
as is generally supposed, a great innovator.
His letters display a considerable likeness
to those of Fournier (1712–1768) and Luce.
Bodoni, however, increased the contrast between the thick and thin lines of the letter.
Bodoni cut these types about the year 1785

Bodoni, Parma, 1785

Grammaire de la langue serbo-croate
FEUVRIER. – 1904, in-8° raisin.
Je signalerai enfin le *Corpus scrip*
orientalium, sous la direction de M
I. GUIDI, H. HYVERNAT, B. CARRA DE

Ambroise Firmin Didot, Paris, 1812

Oui, Madame, à la Vérité
Rendons cet hommage

Jules Didot, Paris, 1819

NEne

The Didot culmination of the "mechanically-perfect" letter. Note
the extreme thick and thin lines

**In the year 1483 no
more than FOUR
Printing Presses**

The English "fat face," originated in 1810 by Robert Thorne

Decorated Types

MFN *LP*

ABCDEF

FOURNIER

ABCD

Fournier - le - jeune,
who succeeded to the
Le Bé foundry, ap-
plied himself with
great industry to the
cutting of decorated
characters of very var-
ious merit

Fournier-le-jeune, Paris, 1746

SCHRIFTSTELLER

A modern German revival of a Fournier decorated type

ABCDEFGHIJ
JKLMNOPQR
ABCDEFGHIJK

Scottish versions of Fournier's decorated types, cut by Wilson,
Glasgow, 1820

Modern Revivals of Old Faces

ABDEFGHJKSW

Old roman capitals cut at Lyons in 1820 and revived by Beaudoire
(Paris, 1850)

FORUM IS A GRACEFUL LETTER
FOUNDED ON THE BEAUTIFUL
SHAPES EVOLVED BY THE STONE
CUTTERS OF ANCIENT ROME

Classical roman capitals, by F. W. Goudy, 1913

ABCDEFGHIJKL
MNOPQRST 1234

The "Hadriano" type, designed by F. W. Goudy, based upon
third-century inscription letters (1920)

Nicolas COCHIN

An original type of 18th-century spirit, cut by Peignot (Paris, 1915)

MOREAU-le-jeune

Recent French revival of an 18th-century face (cut in 1915)

A Recent Successful "Modern" Face

Mr. Goudy designed this beautiful letter in 1921. It is
named the "Goudy Modern."
There is also a companion white
letter named "Goudy Open"

J.S. Hewitt-Bates

A Short History of Bookbinding

The History of Bookbinding is essentially linked with that of writing; as the nature of the materials and forms used determined the method of preservation. Possibly the earliest writing was that scratched or chiselled on rocks and stone pillars or tablets. Later clay was used for the purpose; stamps were made by which it was impressed, and then submitted to the action of the sun or fire to harden, then tablets of slate, lead, wood, bone, skins of animals, ivory, and even plates of gold were used. Palm leaves were perhaps the earliest pliable material used for writing purposes. Evidence is not wanting that many of these writings have been preserved, as many specimens are in our museums today.

The word 'book' is probably derived from the same root as 'beech', Anglo-Saxon 'boc', German 'buch', Dutch 'beuke', the bark of this tree having been anciently used for writing in most of the northern countries of Europe.

The Greek names 'byblos' or 'biblion' are derived from the Egyptian papyrus, and the Latin word 'liber' from the same source.

An event of the greatest importance in the history of writing and bookbinding was the invention of papyrus by the Egyptians about 4000 B.C. Great skill was displayed in the preparation of this material for writing purposes. It was made from the stem of the papyrus plant, a kind of reed that grew in the marshes in Egypt. The outer concentric layers of the stalk were first separated into thin sheets by means of a needle; two or more sheets were then laid on one another crosswise, covered with a thin paste, rolled or beaten to weld the fibres together, and dried in the sun. The sheets thus

SOURCE: Reprinted from J.S. Hewitt-Bates, Bookbinding, Eighth revised edition (Leicester: The Dryad Press, 1967), Chapter I, "A Short History of Bookbinding," pp. 1-10, by permission of the publisher. All rights reserved.

obtained were afterwards coated over with a preparation that gave them an even surface and made them pliant and flexible.

By joining the sheets thus formed, rolls of any length could be obtained, and frequently twenty or more were employed for a single manuscript.

Pens of reed were used for writing. Such pens are still in common use throughout the East. The ink was made from lamp-black, burnt ivory, charcoal, sepia, etc.; the particles being ground very fine and suspended in gum water.

At first the writing was in short lines across the rolls; at each end a roller would be attached, and the reader would unroll and roll as he read. Sometimes the writing was in long lines the length of the roll; later in columns across the roll. There is no doubt that the writing in columns suggested folding as being more convenient to read and for storage. This form led to the sewing of the back folds together, as is still done in China and Japan. The first step in bookbinding was thus evolved. The oldest manuscript known written in this form is the 'Papyrus Prisse', in the Louvre at Paris, consisting of eighteen pages in Egyptian hieratic writing, ascribed to about 2500 B.C. The rolls were often put for further protection into cylindrical cases, called 'Capsa' or 'Scrinium', frequently made of beech wood and stored in 'The House of Rolls'. The Romans called the roll 'volumen', hence our word—volume.

A still nearer approach to modern binding was made by the Romans in their 'pugillaria', or table books. They consisted of from two to eight leaves made of ivory, wood or metal, with raised edges, and covered with wax to take the impression of the stylus. They were connected at the back by rings or thongs of leather. These pugillaria, much more than the rolls, suggested a cover, which at first was of sheep or other skin; afterwards boards were attached.

With the introduction of parchment both writing and bookbinding were much advanced. Successive experiments in the manufacture of skins for writing purposes led to the invention of vellum and parchment. This discovery is attributed to the prohibition of the exportation of papyrus from Egypt, by one of the Ptolemys, in order to throw an obstacle in the way of Eumenes, King of Pergamus, who endeavoured to rival him in the magnificence of his library. Thus, left without material for writing on, we find that Eumenes invented a method of cleaning skins on both sides; before they could only be written on one.

The word 'parchment' is said to be derived from Pergamentum, a city in Asia Minor, where the sheep skins were first prepared about the year 190 B.C. Vellum treated in the same way as parchment is made from calf skin.

At first the parchment was written on as were the papyrus rolls, but later Eumenes adopted the method of writing on separate leaves on both sides; hence the folded form came into use. The sheets were folded once, and gatherings of four or more folded sheets were made, so that stitches through the fold at the back would hold all the sheets together, and each leaf could be conveniently turned over.

Very soon the obvious plan of fixing several of these gatherings, or sections, together by fastening the threads at the back round a strong strip of leather or vellum was adopted. This early plan of 'sewing' is today used in the case of best bound books; it is known as 'flexible' sewing, and has never been improved upon.

When the method of sewing sections together in this way became known, it was found that the projecting bands at the back needed protection, so that when the book was sewn, strips of leather were fastened all over the back. It was also found that the parchment leaves were apt to curl, and to counteract this tendency wooden boards were put on each side, the loose ends of the bands were laced into the boards and the protecting strip of leather at the back was drawn over the boards far enough to cover the lacing-in of the bands. So we get what is now termed 'quarter-binding'.

The tendency of wood to warp and crack led to the use of sheets of papyrus or parchment pasted together and heavily pressed—this formed a strong and tough material, which when dry would not crack, shrink or warp.

To the East we must look for the most marked advance in the art of bookbinding.

Recent research and discoveries have proved that the Copts, an intelligent and cultured Christian race, direct descendants of the Ancient Egyptians, were well advanced in the art of writing and bookbinding in the second century of our era. The newly discovered Bible texts of papyri from Egypt assigned to the second century are all written in Codex form—i.e. in sections like modern books. This form was used by the Christians at a time when pagans still adhered to the roll.

Later we come to the massive books which were carried in the public processions of the Byzantine Emperors in the fifth century; doubtless these mighty records of the nation's laws and sacred manuscripts impressed the populace with awe and added to the dignity of the sovereign ruler. The bindings of these splendid volumes were in red, blue or yellow leather, and thin golden rods were placed across the back.

In the sixth century these 'Byzantine Coatings', as they were called, were decorated by the silversmith—the binder was only allowed to sew the leaves together and fasten them into the wooden boards. In this state they were passed on to the silversmith, who covered them with beaten gold and silver, into which jewels and precious stones were introduced.

A century or two later we find that the monks were almost the only 'literati'. They wrote chiefly upon subjects of religion, and bestowed great pains upon the internal and external decoration of their books. They not only transcribed and bound books, but they prepared the parchment for their manuscripts, and the leather for the binding.

An interesting example of monastic writing and binding in the seventh century is that of a book, usually known as St. Cuthbert's Gospel. It is one of the earliest known examples of the semi-uncial style of writing in Britain and, if the binding is contemporary, the earliest known decorated leather binding in Europe. It was found in St. Cuthbert's coffin in 1105 and is now in the library of Stonyhurst College.

'It was written by Eadfrid, bishop of Durham, and Ethelwold, his successor, executed the illuminations and capitals, with infinite labour and elegance, Bilfred, a monk of Durham, is said to have covered the book and adorned it with gold and silver plates set with precious stones.' These particulars are related by Aldred, the Saxon glossator, on the fly-leaves at the end of St. John's Gospel. The vellum fly-leaves of the book, however, were added at a much later date, and have caused some doubts as to the early date of the present binding.

Many curious tales are related concerning this book: amongst others, Turgot gravely asserts that when the monks of Lindisfarne were removing from thence, to avoid the depredations of the Danes, the vessel wherein they were embarked oversetting, this book which they were transporting with them fell.into the sea. Through the merits of St. Cuthbert, the sea ebbing much further than usual, it was found upon the sands, about three miles from the shore, without having received any injury from the water.

The present binding of this volume is in red leather, either russia or goat skin. In the centre of the front cover is a repoussé Celtic design; above and below are small oblong panels filled with interlaced work executed with a style, and coloured with yellow paint. As to the date of this binding there are different opinions, some assigning it to as early as the seventh century, others the twelfth.

Mr. Douglas Cockerell, an authority on ancient bindings, writes of this volume:

The early date is not universally admitted, mainly because it is difficult to believe that a binding could have survived the known vicissitudes of St. Cuthbert's coffin without damage.

'However, as the manuscript itself shows no serious signs of damage, we may, I think, suppose that the conditions that have led to the preservation of the manuscript have preserved the binding. The little book probably had a stout leather outer case, and it may well have been preserved and carefully cherished as a holy relic apart from the coffin, and only have been placed in the outer coffin for convenience of transport.

'The ornament is such as we might expect to be produced under the Lindisfarne tradition, and nothing we know of at all like it was produced in the twelfth century, when it has been suggested the book might have been rebound.

A detailed history of this book is given, as it shows that all the essential features of good binding were practised in England at that early date.

In the eighth and ninth centuries bookbinding as an elaborate art is said to have made great progress in the age of Charlemagne, when Italian artists and craftsmen were employed. It is unfortunate that none of these bindings have been preserved, as an examination of them might have assisted us in forming a more accurate idea of the progress of the art in this period.

Then the art was neglected for several centuries, owing to the plunder and pillage that overran Europe, and books were destroyed to secure the jewels and metals with which they were covered.

In the twelfth century it is claimed that England was still ahead of all European nations as regards binding. Winchester, London, Durham and other monasteries had each their school of binding. Their books were covered with stag-hide, calf, and pig skin, and were tooled with numbers of small engraved blocks in the Gothic style.

This method of forcibly impressing from metal stamps in blind-tooling had a sobering effect on the bookbinder's art—the elaborate work of the silversmith gradually gave way to this more legitimate means of decoration by the actual binder himself.

The method of making blind impressions from engraved metal dies is claimed by Mr. Weale to be of English origin, and may have led to the invention of printing. In the light of modern research, however, it has been discovered that the Copts were familiar with 'blind-tooling', either by heated tools or with punches, before the sixth century.

Although the majority of medieval leather bindings are decorated with engraved metal stamps, contemporary with these there were produced a number of remarkable bindings, the decoration of which was worked with a blunt, pointed tool or cut into the surface of the leather. (This method was much the same as now used on our modern embossed leatherwork.) Generally the design is impressed on the surface of the leather and the background stippled, making the pattern stand out in apparent relief.

The majority of such bindings are of German and Austrian origin, but there are also specimens from Italy and England in the British Museum.

In the Middle Ages many bindings were brought from the East by the Crusaders, which no doubt helped to mould the destinies of bookbinding.

Towards 1465 the Saracenic patterns on Venetian books began to be sprinkled with gold dots. This innovation gradually sealed the fate of blind-tooling.

The invention of printing by Gutenberg in 1438 entirely changed the character of bookbinding. As a rule wooden boards, clasps, and gold ornaments were laid aside and leather and parchments became of ordinary use. The printer at first was his own binder, but as books increased in number, bookbinding became a separate trade, and as a consequence of men applying themselves to one craft, the art improved so much that in the fifteenth and sixteenth centuries some of the finest specimens of bookbinding were executed.

About the year 1470 gold tooling by means of engraved stamps (as used at the present time) was introduced into Venice, and under the patronage of Maioli and Grolier a new and beautiful method of decorating books came into fashion. Their designs were, of course, influenced by the then dominant style of decoration, namely the Renaissance: while Byzantine in its original elements, it also has a mixture of Venetian and Norman ornament. It reasserted the aesthetic principle, and attained its highest pitch of excellence in the sixteenth century. It is little wonder that this style gained such favour with designers of the period. Its influence was so powerful that the old and somewhat dull Gothic work of Western Europe was speedily extinguished in the efforts of the bookbinder to imitate the Italian work.

The chief characteristics of the Grolier bindings are their interlaced geometrical framework, at first somewhat stiff; later he adopted the mosaic style of painting or inlaying the strapwork and filling in the spaces with graceful scroll work terminating in small outlined leaves and sprigs of conventional form, shaded with closely worked crosslines, i.e. azured. Grolier is said to have been the first collector to have his books lettered on the back; he also had the generous motto 'Io Grolierii et Amicorum' lettered on the side.

From Italy the art of bookbinding passed into France, where during the sixteenth century it was brought to great perfection.

Of the early French binders the Eve family, Du Sueil, Le Gascon, Derome, occupy the first rank, each having a characteristic style.

In England at this period much good work was done by Thomas Berthelet, Royal binder to Henry VIII; he it was who first introduced gold tooling into this country.

Chained books were common objects enough from the time of the Reformation onward, and a chained book implied a solid and heavy binding. What an old writer says makes the meaning of the chained book apparent:

> The thievish desposition of some that enter into libraries to learn no good there, hath made it necessary to secure the innocent books, even the Sacred volumes themselves, with chains—which were better deserved by those persons, who have too much learning to be hanged, and too little to be honest.

Bookbinding shared in the general advance of the fine arts in England during the reign of Queen Elizabeth I, and the bindings of the Queen's books are superior, both as regards beauty of design and finish of workmanship, to those of her predecessors. Elizabeth was very fond of embroidered book-covers, some of which she worked with her own hands.

Charles and Samuel Mearne, binders to Charles II, did much to raise the artistic side of the craft in this country. They invented the 'Cottage' style of decoration. Many of their bindings have the fore-edge painted, under the gilt, in such a way that the work is invisible when the book is shut, and only shows when the leaves are fanned out.

Towards the end of the eighteenth century bookbinding in England was decoratively at a low level, when Roger Payne, a native of Windsor, came to London and set up as a bookbinder. He adopted a style peculiarly his own, and was the first English binder who endeavoured to make his ornaments appropriate to the character of the book on which he put them. He knew the secret that elemental forms combine best: dots, gouges, simple little circles, a crescent, and one or two sprigs of flowers made up the whole of his stock. But their marvellous combinations under the old craftsman's hand are the admiration of all who admire good bookbinding in the English-speaking world. He drank much and lived recklessly; but notwithstanding his irregular habits, his name ought to be respected for the work he executed. His sewing is as good now as when it left his hands more than a century ago; his backs are flexible, and his forwarding excellent. His tools, original in form, were both designed and cut by himself. His favourite leathers were russia and straight-grained morocco, which he decorated chiefly with corners and borders, and the field studded with gold dots. Even though the French school influenced him at the commencement of his career, when he became a master of his art he stood alone, original and unique.

It may be observed here, that as the mechanical aids to the art grew in number, taste declined. After Payne's time we see little else than reproduction of the great models, with often an extremely injudicious combination of different styles. The modern binder, in imitating some old master, is not able to reproduce the spirit of the original—he only betrays his own lack of invention, and his copy remains, for all his labours, the mechanical production of today.

Recent years have witnessed a marked revival in the interest in the art of bookbinding, due largely to the influence of the private presses, the most famous of these being the Kelmscott Press, founded by William Morris, the Ashendene Press and the Doves Press. Other well-known presses were the Vale, Essex House, the Eragny, the Cuala, the Golden Cockerell and the Gregynog. All achieved high standards, both in printing and book production.

T. J. Cobden-Sanderson, who was closely associated with William Morris, helped to bring back the art of bookbinding to its first principles, and their treatment showed a scholarly appreciation of ancient methods. Douglas Cockerell, who was a pupil of Cobden-Sanderson, maintained this revival and the fine standard of binding is even now being continued by his son Sidney.

During the period between the two world wars a new impetus was given to bookbinding design by Franz Weisse in Germany and Pierre Legrain in France. Legrain designed bindings for the collector Jacques Doucet, which incorporated motifs associated with the contemporary cubist and abstract movements in art, and had great influence on French binding. The bindings were executed by leading Paris binders.

In 1951 the Hampstead Guild of Scribes was formed by a collection of book binders, bookbinding teachers and amateurs. Four or five years later, it was re-named the Guild of Contemporary Bookbinders, as interest in the scribes waned.

The Guild has been responsible for keeping alive book design, especially in the modern and contemporary idiom. A notable milestone in the history of the Guild was reached in 1955, when members' work was exhibited at the annual exhibition of the National Book League held in London. Members include William F. Matthews, Roger Powell, Peter Waters, Bernard Middleton, J. Clements, Edgar Mansfield, Lawrence Town and F. Austin.

In 1946 Paul Bonet, who was recognised as the inheritor of the Legrain style, instigated the formation of the Société de la Reliure Originale. Although the Guild of Contemporary Bookbinders was not connected with this continental movement, they served the same purpose. In other words, the Société de la Reliure Originale was preserving book design as well as keeping up with modern trends on the continent. It is almost entirely due to these two movements that book design still maintains such a high standard today.

John P. Harthan

"Introduction—
The Development of
Bookbinding Design"

In the ancient world books existed only in the form of tablets or rolls of varying length with no pagination or means of ready reference to the text. The need for a simpler form of record led to the development of the Codex, or book form as we know it today, in which the text is written on separate sheets, secured between two boards and bound together at the back. The earliest codices were versions of the Gospels written on papyrus sheets in the monasteries of the Coptic Church in Egypt during the first six centuries A.D. Because of the lack of suitable wood for boards a cover had to be made of layers of papyrus stuck together. This was covered in leather and provided with thongs of the same material used to fasten the book into a kind of parcel. The leather binding was variously decorated with blind tooling (i.e. without gilding), incised lines or pierced, appliqué designs having a central panel filled with a diamond or circular pattern. Of these earliest Coptic bindings only fragments survive, but specimens of the 9th-11th centuries show a variety of pattern and decorative motif drawn from the fund of Hellenistic ornament which was the common legacy of the Roman Empire to the mediaeval world.

Islamic bookbinding had its origin in this highly skilled leathercraft of Christian Syria and Egypt. The Mohammedan invaders of the 7th century absorbed the craftsmanship and binding methods of the conquered territories, carrying Egyptian skill in leatherwork along North Africa to Europe by way of Sicily and Spain. The

SOURCE: Reprinted from John P. Harthan, *Bookbindings*, Second revised edition (London: Her Majesty's Stationery Office, 1961), Chapter 1, "Introduction—The Development of Bookbinding Design," pp. 7-19, by permission of the Victoria and Albert Museum. © Crown Copyright 1961.

technique of Near Eastern binding came to differ radically, both in forwarding and finishing, from that of mediaeval Europe. Instead of massive, stoutly fastened boards, the oriental bookcover was conceived as a light, wallet-shaped leather casing with a pasteboard foundation. The gatherings of text, lightly sewn, were first fixed at the back to a somewhat wider strip of fabric by means of strong gum; this in turn was glued to the inner spine, much as in a modern publishers' binding. The finishing process differed also both in lay-out and ornament. The most characteristic pattern was symmetrical about a central medallion of circular or almond shape, having leaf-like pendants and cornerpieces in the form of a quadrant of the medallion. In keeping with the puritanical character of the Mohammedan religion, the ornament prevalent throughout almost the entire Islamic world until the later Middle Ages was of an austerely abstract type, consisting of interlacing bands, knotwork, intricate geometrical arabesques and the various Arabic scripts.

With the opening of the 15th century, artistic leadership of the Islamic world passed from Egypt and Syria to Persia, chiefly as a result of renewed contact with China. The ancient, severe method of blind-tooling, apt enough for the decoration of religious books, was discarded in favour of delicate techniques agreeable to the splendours, luxury and refined sensuousness of courtly life. Craftsmen at Herat, the capital city of the Timurid dynasty, developed the techniques of exquisite filigree leather and gilded, cut-paper work on a deep-blue painted ground, commonly used to decorate the doublures of bindings. All-over patterns stamped from large metal blocks, designs embossed in thin leather by means of matrices of tough camel-hide, landscapes with animals in cut and painted leather, floral arabesques, lotus blossoms, cloud ribbons, coloured and gilded motifs drawn from Greco-Roman, Sassanian and Chinese ornament, combined to produce artistic masterpieces unrivalled in the history of bookbinding.

A further development of the 15th-century binders of Herat was the technique of miniature painting on papier-mâché boards under lacquer varnish, which was to enjoy such wide popularity in the 16th and 17th centuries at Tabriz and Isphahan under the Safawid dynasty. The Persian styles were transplanted to Northern India in the 16th, and to Turkey in the 17th century. There they received no significant additions, but shared eventually in the common artistic and economic decay which overtook the entire Near Eastern civilisation during the 18th and 19th centuries.

In Christian Europe the Church's connection with book production remained unbroken. As the papyrus plant did not grow outside Egypt, manuscripts of the gospel books and psalters required for church services were written on vellum sheets made from animal skins and covered with wooden boards. A heavy binding of wooden boards, fastened by clasps, was necessary to keep the vellum from buckling. The sacred books were then elaborately decorated with sculptured ivory panels, metalwork and jewellery; in the 12th and 13th centuries enamel plaques were also used. Such richness of ornament was intended as an act of piety rather than decoration and was generally limited to the Gospels and other liturgical works to be displayed on altar or lectern with reliquaries, plate and other monastic treasures.

Leather was used from a very early date in the West as well as in the East and became the principal material for hand bookbinding. Two techniques were used for its decoration: incised lines, deepened and extended after cutting with a bone or wooden point, known as *cuir ciselé*, and cold stamping with small metal dies in the damped leather. The decorative scheme, which in both techniques was executed in 'blind', followed two basic layouts derived from Coptic bindings, one constructed of rectangular panels and the other built on diagonal divisions. The diagonal pattern, found on Carolingian bindings from the German and Swiss monasteries of Fulda, Freising, and St. Gall, reappears in Germany during the 15th century. In France and England the rectangular scheme, perhaps influenced by Coptic examples brought back from the Crusades, was adopted for the decoration of a group of 12th-century bindings made for the monasteries of Paris, Durham, Winchester, London and elsewhere. All these bindings are decorated with rows of repeated impressions from small, finely cut metal stamps, probably the work of sealmakers. The stamps are of most varied shapes and depict fabulous beasts, human figures and purely ornamental motifs such as rosettes and stars.

In the 15th century new techniques in book production and distribution were evolved to meet the needs of the increasing number of literate persons resulting from the expansion of the monastic system, the rise of the universities, especially Paris, and, most important of all, from the invention in Germany about 1450 of the art of printing from moveable types. During this period the booktrade was organised on a commercial basis. Printers established themselves in all the great commercial cities, particularly of the Rhine and the Netherlands, and thence exported books in unbound sheets for sale in the university towns where stationers and booksellers often maintained their own binderies. These early trade bindings, sometimes bearing the names or initials of the binder or bookseller, while marking the close of exclusive monastic patronage, for many years perpetuated monastic styles of binding. In the 15th century particularly there was a revival of the repeat decoration with small, blind stamps characteristic of 'monastic' bindings of the 12th century. During this period attention was given also to the ornamental possibilities of the protective metal studs and cornerpieces frequently affixed to large and heavy books.

As manuscripts and printed books became more numerous the demand for decorative bindings by private individuals also increased. To meet the commercial opportunity the laborious process of stamping by hand with small dies was superseded by the use of large panel stamps of iron or brass, which were impressed on the leather in a single operation by means of a handpress. The technique of finishing was further mechanised towards the end of the 15th century by the introduction of the roll, a cylindrical tool which by rotation impressed an entire ribbon of repeating pattern. These panel stamps and rolls, depicting in blind tooling mainly religious and allegorical figures frequently adapted from woodcut illustrations, were specially popular in the northern countries, North France, the Netherlands, Germany and England, and marked the close of the mediaeval period of European bookbinding.

The introduction of gold tooling into Italy was the last and most important development in the technique of European bookbinding during the 15th century. Over-all gilding of stamped leather by the application of liquid gold with a brush had long been practised by Islamic craftsmen, especially in Persia; in Egypt and North Africa, where linear decoration was more usual, designs done in blind were picked out by liquid gilding. Both these methods were being used by oriental craftsmen settled in Venice during the mid-15th century. Yet a third, radically different, method, that of gold-tooling done by impressing gold leaf with a heated tool on the leather, was known in Morocco as early as 1256 and in Persia by the mid-14th century. This technical innovation of the Moslem world reached Italy by two routes; through Venice shortly after 1450, and by way of Naples about 1475. In North Italy the source of Islamic techniques was the Middle East, with which Venice had trading relations; in the south, the gold-tooled bindings of Naples are in the North African tradition, and probably derive from the Moorish leatherworkers of the Spanish kingdom of Aragon, whose book-loving dynasty were also, between 1443-1495, rulers in Naples. The earliest European gold-tooled leather binding yet identified is on a manuscript of Strabo's 'Geographia' (now in the Bibliothèque Rochegude, Albi) written at Padua in 1459 for presentation to king René of Anjou.[1]

The influence of Islamic bookcraft on Italian binding was strongest at Venice, the centre of the booktrade in Italy during the later Renaissance; it was thence that decorative patterns and motifs characteristic of oriental bindings, together with the technical processes of gold tooling, entered the general repertory of the European gilder's and binder's craft. Interlaced cable-work and sunken, almond-shaped panels appear commonly on Italian bindings. Gold tooling was at first used in moderation, often in conjunction with blind. The so-called Aldine bindings which are to be found all over northern Italy have simple geometrical patterns of strapwork, or are decorated with rectangular panels of gold fillets having the title or author's name stamped in the middle. The somewhat severe effect is relieved by the use of stylised arabesques and a little trefoil leaf, often called the 'Aldine fleuron', placed in the angles, sides or at the outer corners of the central rectangle.

The humanist preoccupation with classical antiquity, the inspiration of much Italian Renaissance decorative experiment, found expression in bookbinding through the use of intaglio stamps impressed direct into the leather, giving the appearance of an antique cameo. The most widely-known of these 'cameo' stamps are those found on bindings formerly attributed to Demetrio Canevari (1559-1625), physician to Urban VII, but now thought to have been made for a member of the Farnese family, either Pier Luigi (1503-47) or his son Ottavio (d. 1586).

Italian pre-eminence in the art of bookbinding did not survive the troubled political conditions which marked the first quarter of the 16th century, culminating in the sack of Rome by Imperial troops in 1527. The exploitation and development of gold tooling was taken over by the French who became acquainted with the art during the Italian wars of Louis XII and Francis I. Milan, at this time under French occupation, was the centre whence the new style of gold tooling was transmitted to France. A small number of gold-tooled books survive from a court bindery active between 1507-19 which may have been established at Blois, a frequent royal residence at this period. But it was not until towards the middle of the century, and in particular during the years 1535-65, that Parisian binderies began the large-scale production of gold-tooled bindings which in decorative effect, beauty of design and skill in execution

[1] See article by A. R. A. Hobson, *Two Renaissance Bindings*, in *The Book Collector*, vol 7, no. 3 (1958).

remain among the highest achievements of the binder's art. Recent research has established that the finest of these bindings came from the workshop of Claude de Picques (c. 1510-75), also known as the 'atelier au trèfle' from its extensive use of a shamrock or trefoil tool. Claude de Picques was closely connected with the court, holding the post of royal binder to Henry II and his successors as well as to his widow Catherine de' Medici. This patronage by royal and other bibliophiles, combined with the use of high quality morocco leather which was imported from the East as an indirect consequence of the Franco-Turkish alliance, probably explains the sudden appearance in Parisian binderies of gilders or 'doreurs' of high technical ability, capable of translating the most elaborate arabesque designs from contemporary pattern books into designs for book covers. The theory that gilding or 'finishing' was a craft separate from ordinary binding has been abandoned. Such a division of labour was recognised by an ordinance of 1581 and became customary in the 17th century but documentary evidence survives to show that in the mid-16th century forwarding and finishing were both carried out in the same workshop.

The sequence of French styles in the 16th century can be followed in the bindings made for Jean Grolier, Vicomte d'Aguisy (1479-1565), Treasurer in 1510 of the Duchy of Milan, and from 1547-65 Treasurer-General of France. These Parisian bindings mostly date from 1520-40 after Grolier's return to France, with a later group about 1555. Simple geometrical strapwork designs with fleurons at the corners of the central panel developed in the later bindings into elaborate curvilinear interlacings combined with arabesques sometimes enclosed in roll-produced borders. The leaves of the arabesques were usually made with azured tools, i.e. hatched with parallel lines, suggestive of the conventional technique for rendering the heraldic tincture. The strap or ribbon work was also emphasised by colour, usually black or red. The later Grolier bindings in which the whole side of the book was covered by a mass of foliage and interlacings anticipated the 'fanfare' style of the end of the century.

In the Royal bindings made for Henri II (1547-59) linear decoration is enriched by coats of arms, initials and emblematical devices, the latter connected with Henri's mistress Diane de Poitiers. Interlaced initials, HD for Henri and Diane, and HC for Henri and Catherine de' Medici, his wife, appear on many of these bindings, with three crescent moons interlocked, an allusion to the huntress Diana. Another group of bindings dating from 1550-60 belonged to the collector 'Maiolus', the latinised name of Thomas Mahieu, secretary to Catherine de' Medici. The 'atelier au trèfle' which supplied bindings to Grolier and Henri II is probably the source also of these fine Maioli bindings, though the decoration tends to be richer with punched and gilded backgrounds showing a surface of sprinkled dots as a foil for coloured interlacings and arabesques.

The new styles developed in the latter part of the 16th century are known by specific names: 'Lyonese', so-called because it appeared on many books printed at Lyons, with polychromatic effects achieved by painting, lacquering and enamelling the geometrical strapwork; 'Semis', in which the cover is powdered with repeated impressions of little tools pricked out in horizontal, vertical and diagonal rows; 'Centre-and-Corner', which carried on the Islamic use of sunken panels, and 'Fanfare', the most splendid of all. The origin of fanfare style is in the combination of acanthus leaves and strapwork found both on Italian and Grolier bindings, but at the end of the 16th century it underwent a transformation. The tools became smaller and the strapwork reduced with geometrical precision to a complicated system of oval and circular compartments usually based on the figure 8. The blank spaces between these whorls of strapwork were tooled with sprays of olive, bay or laurel branches and a profusion of ornamental tools such as winged volutes, fleurons and slender coils of arabesque. The only space left blank was an oval compartment in the centre destined for a coat of arms. The back of the book was often without bands and decorated with a continuous spray of foliage. The epithet 'fanfare' is not contemporary but dates only from 1829 when the French Restoration binder Thouvenin revived the style for the decoration of a book entitled *Fanfares et corvés abbadesques* (published in 1613), which he rebound for the bibliophile Charles Nodier.

Fanfare bindings are frequently attributed to Nicolas and Clovis Eve, father and son, who held the official post of Royal Binder, in succession to Claude de Picques, between 1579-1634. Though not invented by the Eves the fanfare style became a favourite design for luxury bindings during the first half of the period. Two other styles were in vogue during the Eves' long career: bindings decorated with an all-over design of small, leafy ovals filled with various devices, and semis bindings of alternate fleurs-de-lys and the crowned letter H or L, referring respectively to Henry IV (1589-1610) and Louis XIII (1610-43), whose arms often appear in the centre of the cover surrounded by the collars of the Orders of St. Michael and St. Esprit.

In England, the Netherlands and Germany the old technique of panel stamps on blind tooled bindings survived long into the 16th century with a concession to contemporary taste in the use of Renaissance ornament, medallions and figures. One of the first English binders to use gold tooling worked for Thomas Berthelet, printer to Henry VIII, Edward VI and Mary I; he was described in 1543 as binding 'after the facion of Venice'. The bindings in the Grolieresque style made for the collector Thomas Wotton (1521-87) have been variously ascribed to France and England; a Paris provenance seems the more probable in view of their technical accomplishment and similarity to French models. Elizabethan bindings are mostly based on the 'centre-and-corner' pattern with frequent borrowings from Venetian and Islamic ornament. The interest of such bindings lies in the correspondence of the contours of the centre sunken panel with the four corner-pieces, the neatness of execution and the use of gold stippled backgrounds or arabesques to bring lightness into a somewhat formal design.

German 16th-century bindings are characterised by roll-stamped motifs drawn from textile and Gothic floral ornament, cameos, and portrait panel stamps, often of Luther and other Reformers, impressed on pigskin, a hard, white leather. Gilding was introduced at Dresden by Jacob Krause, court binder to the Saxon Elector Friedrich August between 1566-85. With gold tooling came Renaissance decoration in the Franco-Italian style. The tooling of these Saxon bindings is heavier than that of their French prototypes, but richly impressive, with frequent use of the initials FAHZS—for Friedrich August Herzog Zu Sachsen or other members of the dynasty—and the ducal arms.

In the 17th century the most important innovations in binding styles continued to originate in France. Fanfare bindings were increasingly combined with roll-produced borders which were edged with a line of repeating pattern taken from lace designs similar to those used for cuffs and collars in contemporary costume. The influence of lace and embroidery patterns on binding tools is far more direct in the 17th than in the 18th century, the period usually associated with bindings 'à la dentelle'.

Another decorative motif which made its appearance soon after 1600 was the fan. A design modelled on a partly opened fan filled the corners of a rectangular panel, while two fans, placed back to back, produced a circular ornament or wheel to fill the centre. It is thought that the fan style, a variant on the 16th-century 'centre-and-corner' pattern, was an Italian innovation. Its use in France was restricted, but in Italy, Germany, Spain and Sweden the fan was a popular motif throughout the 17th century and survived in Scotland as an almost national style into the 18th century.

About 1635 the tooling on fanfare bindings began to be executed 'au pointillé', with dotted instead of solid lines and curves, a development perhaps of the 16th-century practice of gauffering gilded book edges with designs and arabesques picked out in dots. Foliage decoration became smaller and was gradually replaced by less naturalistic ornaments, similar to fleurons used in typography. The filigree effect of gilded, pointillé decoration as a background for the ribbon interlacings or fillet scaffolding of a fanfare binding was enhanced by the use of red morocco which in the 17th century largely superseded brown calf. Pointillé bindings are often, though inaccurately, associated with the eponymous binder known as 'le Gascon' who was working in 1622, several years before the style became general. The creators of the finest pointillé bindings have not been identified; a number of them incorporated a profile head into the design, a device also found on two of the three bindings signed by Florimond Badier, a rare instance of a 17th-century French binder signing his work. Le Gascon's influence was rather in the direction of a simplified style with fillet frames and large fleurons at the angles, the central space usually filled by an armorial, represented by the bindings wrongly attributed to the 18th-century binder Du Seuil. At the end of the 17th century plain bindings with little ornament or gilding, except in the doublures, became, most unexpectedly, the fashionable style for Louis XIV's court. The sumptuous, heavy Louis Quatorze decorative style is not reflected in contemporary French bindings, which were known, on account of their austerity, as 'Jansenist' bindings and were much favoured by Mme de Maintenon, the king's second wife.

In England the somewhat stereotyped 'centre-and-corner' pattern continued in fashion during the reign of James I and Charles I, varied by the occasional use of panel stamps, blocked in gold, for smaller books. During this period bindings embroidered with flowers or animal designs in coloured silks and gold or silver thread became popular. These bindings, the work of professional embroiderers, are among the most charming examples of English 17th-century art. In Cambridge a group of binders active between c. 1610-50 produced modest, restrained work in brown calf, white leather and vellum often found on the covers of congratulatory verses issued by the University on royal occasions. The bindery at Little Gidding, Huntingdonshire, a religious community established by Nicholas Ferrar in 1626, was an off-shoot of this

Cambridge school. After 1660 a number of more elaborate mosaic inlaid bindings were made for presentation to royalty and other important personages for which the Cambridge binder John Houlden may have been responsible.

The second half of the century saw the development of the most elaborate bindings ever made in England. In general character they showed the influence of contemporary Dutch ornament rather than that of the 'Jansenist' bindings in fashion at Versailles despite the current French influence on English costume and social manners. Many bindings of this period are associated with the name of Samuel Mearne, Royal Binder to Charles II, whose activities also included publishing, printing and bookselling. In his early years Mearne served an apprenticeship to a bookbinder, Jeremy Arnold; later he probably only supervised the work of the bindery attached to his business where a number of craftsmen, including the Dutch binder Suckerman, were employed. 'Mearne binding' is a term often applied to any showy Restoration binding, though the accuracy of such attributions has been much disputed. No elaborate binding from Mearne's workshop, as distinct from the series of plain red morocco bindings with Charles II's cypher supplied to the royal library, has yet been conclusively identified, but the history of this bindery and its products is not yet fully documented.

The most characteristic feature of Restoration bindings is the gilt or painted ornament placed at top and bottom of the covers in the form of a roof or gable. This local variant of the central rectangular panel is known as the 'Cottage' style and persisted until the middle of the 18th century, particularly on almanacks and prayerbooks. Pointillé technique was used as in France with emphasis on naturalistic patterns formed of leaves, sprays of bay, various kinds of flowers including the tulip and sweet sultan, and bunches of grapes. Two other tools were also very common; a small double-handled vase and a miniature scroll aptly described as the drawer-handle, though probably deriving from the Ionic capital. In applying these motifs great use was made of different coloured leathers pared very thinly and pasted down on the leather covering the book. 'Onlay' rather than 'inlay' is the correct description of this technique. In less ambitious examples a polychrome effect was obtained by staining the flowers, leaves and strapwork.

A new pattern was exploited in England in the first quarter of the 18th century by Elkanah Settle, poet laureate to the City of London, whose bindery was occupied between 1704-23 in producing presentation books for noble patrons. Settle reverted to the rectangular central panel as a frame for elaborate armorial shields built up out of large, clumsily applied, tools surrounded by florid mantling. The decorative motif was supplied by cherub-heads of the familiar type found on monuments and tombstones throughout the country. In more dignified taste were the 'Harleian' bindings made by Thomas Elliot for Robert and Edward Harley, the first and second Earls of Oxford, with broad borders, made up of one or more rolls, and well defined lozenges or central ornaments. In Scotland the panel was filled either by a wheel or by a vertical stem down the middle of the cover with branches sprouting at regular intervals. Irish bindings were decorated with diamond shaped lozenges of inlaid white paper or leather. A group of bindings was also executed in the 'Chippendale' or 'Chinese' style, some having the signature of James Bate, a stationer of Cornhill,

London, with chinoiserie flowers, birds and pagodas inspired by oriental chinaware.

Towards the end of the century the influence of the classical movement became apparent in the application to book decoration of motifs familiar on Wedgwood pottery and on Sheraton and Hepplewhite furniture. The bindery of Edwards of Halifax, a firm founded by William Edwards and continued by his sons James, John, and Thomas, was responsible for several innovations in decorative bindings. The Edwards family invented concealed fore-edge painting under gold (visible only when the leaves are splayed out), introduced the technique, patented in 1785, of using transparent vellum with underpainting in colour and monochrome, and produced many so-called 'Etruscan' bindings in calf stained to imitate the terracotta shades of Greek and Etruscan vases. The neatly designed vellum bindings of the Edwards firm with their delicate gilt borders of various designs—vine or ivy tendrils, Greek frets, and the very common roll of alternate bars and circles, derived from the Doric entablature—matched the elegance of the age and found imitators both at home and abroad.

The leading figure at the end of the 18th century was Roger Payne (1739-97), a superlative craftsman who carried out all the binding processes himself, including the cutting of his tools. The distinction of his designs and tooling and the attention he gave to the backs as well as to the covers of his books brought him many commissions from bibliophiles and book collectors. The most notable series of bindings which Payne executed were those belonging to the Rev. Mordaunt Cracherode for whom he designed and cut one of the finest armorial stamps ever used in bookbinding. A group of German binders, headed by Baumgarten who arrived in 1770, was also active in London during this period. Payne's reputation has tended to obscure the contribution of these immigrant craftsmen to the revival of fine binding in England.

French binding in the 18th century reaffirmed the creative originality of Parisian craftsmen who introduced two new styles, the so-called 'lace' and 'mosaic' bindings. In the former the lace-like border of the 17th century was enlarged until it became the most important single element in the design, often leaving space only for an armorial shield in the centre of the cover. The edges were no longer straight but tooled in a wavy pattern giving a lacy effect currently described as 'à la dentelle', but showing a greater resemblance to contemporary metalwork in furniture mounts, balconies and ornamental gateways. Of the binders working in this style the most notable were the Derome family and Pierre-Paul Dubuisson. The latter, appointed binder to Louis XV in 1758, was a heraldic designer and gilder rather than a bookbinder who, to meet the demand for 'lace' bindings, made use of bronze plaques instead of separate tools.

Mosaic bindings represent perhaps the most luxurious style of book decoration attempted in modern times. The technique, used by Padeloup le Jeune and Le Monnier, was a development of inlaid leather bindings, but resembled marquetry rather than mosaic, with large pieces of citron-yellow, red and green leather combined in massive *compartiments* to form elaborate scroll and floral shapes. The boldness with which this exuberant technique is used has a marked baroque character contrasted with the rococo intricacy of 'lace' bindings.

In the reign of Louis XVI (1774-92) there was a return to more sober bindings inspired, for the first time, by English models. Fashionable anglophilia had already substituted 'le jardin anglais' for the formal parterres and vistas of Le Nôtre; English bindings of tasteful simplicity now became the accepted mode in the last years of the old monarchy. The Revolution, rejecting anything which savoured of the *ancien régime*, confirmed this trend. During the Directoire and Empire periods Bradel, Tessier, the elder Bozerian and other binders confined elaborate tooling mainly to the backs of books, using borders of palmettos, lyres, chain-patterns or Egyptian motifs, alone or with geometrical fillet patterns, for the covers. Under Napoleon there was a partial return to ostentatious bindings executed in embroidery with metal threads and spangled ornament. Such bindings were also popular in Germany and eastern Europe where metal filigree, tortoiseshell and other materials outside the traditional leather had long been used.

The restoration of the monarchy in 1814 introduced a further period of eclecticism with much borrowing of ornamental motifs from the Middle Ages, the Renaissance and later epochs. In this period the exclusive use of gold tooling on leather bindings came to an end. Blind stamping in low relief, little used since the end of the Middle Ages, was revived as a characteristic feature of Romantic bindings, including those in the 'cathedral' style, simulating Gothic architecture, which became fashionable in both France and England around 1820. The increasing frequency with which binders signed their work provides for the first time a long list of names. Among the most notable who worked in France were Simier, Thouvenin, Vogel, Trautz and Kieffer; in England Staggemeier, Hering, Lewis and Bedford were active in the first half of the century.

The general adoption in England during the eighteen forties of two technical innovations changed the whole status of binding craft. The first was the use of cloth instead of leather, a practice begun by the publisher William Pickering in the eighteen twenties; the second, the new technique of trade bindings whereby covers and printed sheets were prepared independently by machinery and glued together instead of being sewn by hand in traditional binding technique. An increased demand for books, following the educational and social reforms of the 19th century, was met by the exploitation of these cheap publishers' bindings. A distinction between 'fine' and 'trade' bindings resulted which for a time accentuated the decline in this branch of leathercraft. Only at the end of the century as a result of the movement initiated by William Morris and Charles Ricketts was binding craft revived by Cobden Sanderson, Morris's pupil, Sarah Prideaux and Douglas Cockerell in England, and by Marius Michel in France. A remarkable group of 20th-century English bindings, issuing from a private press, are those designed by various artists and bound by George Fisher at the Gregynog Press in Montgomeryshire. The influence of these craftsmen has greatly improved the standard of publishers' bindings in England designed by professional artists, such as Paul Nash and Barnett Freedman, making use of new techniques in lithographic and other processes of reproduction.

On the Continent during the period between the two world wars there was a remarkable revival of binding led in Germany by Franz Weisse, of Hamburg, and in France by Pierre Legrain, a Parisian cabinet-maker by training, who began designing book covers for the collector Jacques Doucet in the years 1917-19. Legrain introduced into binding design the contemporary idioms of cubist and abstract art, an innovation which has revitalised French bookbinding. His work is being continued by Paul Bonet, the present leader of the French school, whose bindings, characterised by a *bravura* sense of colour and great originality in design, reaffirm once more Parisian supremacy in what Comte de Laborde described as 'un art tout français'.

Harry G. Aldis
Revised by *John Carter* and *E.A. Crutchley*

Illustrations

Until recent times the chief methods of producing illustrations for printed books were woodcutting, metal engraving, etching and lithography. But during the last fifty years the province of every one of these arts has been invaded by photography; and the various processes by which illustrations in black-and-white and in colour are now produced are bewilderingly numerous. All these methods, whether handicraft or mechanical, may be divided into three groups distinguished by the·nature of the surface of the block or plate from which the picture is printed. In the first of these the design is in relief, like type, and, in printing, it is impressed into the paper. To this group belong woodcuts, wood engravings, and some of the modern mechanical processes such as zinc etchings and half-tone blocks. In the second group the lines composing the picture are sunk below the surface of the plate, and, in printing, the paper is pressed into these lines, so that the picture is in low relief upon the surface of the paper. By this, the *intaglio* method, are produced copper-plate and steel engravings, and certain of the photographic processes such as photogravure. The third group comprises pictures printed from flat surfaces, and includes lithographs and, again with the aid of photography, collotypes.

Although the printing of pictures from wood-blocks preceded the invention of typography, the printer of books in movable type did not at first make use of the art of the engraver—or woodcutter, as the maker of early woodcuts should perhaps be called—to illustrate the printed book. In fact, in its beginnings, the printed book had more affinity with a manuscript than with either the woodcut picture or the block-

SOURCE: Reprinted from Harry G. Aldis, *The Printed Book*, Second edition. Revised and brought up-to-date by John Carter and E.A. Crutchley (Cambridge: At the University Press, 1941), Chapter VIII, "Illustrations," pp. 75-96, by permission of the publisher. All rights reserved.

book, and it was to the illuminator that the early printer naturally turned for the decoration and illustration of his productions.

It was not long, however, before the printer perceived that the woodcutter's art might with advantage be utilized for the adornment of his books; and that not only for decoration in the shape of initial letters, borders and other ornamental adjuncts, but also for pictures which would elucidate the text or add to the attractiveness of popular works. These woodcuts consisted of a flat block of wood upon which the design was drawn and the surface of the wood afterwards cut away so as to leave the lines of the drawing in relief. Occasionally soft metal was used in place of wood. The height of the block being adjusted to that of the type, the picture or ornament could be printed in one and the same operation as the page of text.

The first printer to make use of illustrations was Albrecht Pfister of Bamberg, who about 1461-1462 issued several popular German books containing woodcuts. But the history of illustrated books does not properly commence until some ten years later when pictures begin to make their appearance in books printed at Augsburg, where there existed a guild of craftsmen who cut blocks for printing playing-cards and pictures of saints, for both of which there was at that time a large demand. Ulm, another important centre of woodcutting, followed the lead of Augsburg, and the practice soon spread: Nuremberg, Cologne, Strasbourg and Mainz being among the chief German towns which produced illustrated books in the fifteenth century.

Copyright was as little recognized in pictorial art as in the world of letters, and a successful illustrated book was quickly copied or imitated, generally in other towns than that of its origin. The *Aesop*, printed by Johann Zainer at Ulm and containing two hundred woodcuts, was followed by half a score of other German editions, most of which were frankly copies; and the popular *Narrenschiff (Ship of Fools)* of Sebastian Brant, first published at Basel by Johann Bergmann von Olpe in 1494, with over one hundred illustrations, was paid the compliment of being reprinted in three other towns in the same year. Sometimes the pirated cuts were mere slavish imitations of the originals, perhaps copied by pasting one of the original pictures on the wood-block, in which case the copy would appear in a reversed form in the new book and so betray its origin. But the object was easy reproduction of pictures rather than fraudulent imitation, and details were freely paraphrased. Copies by a poor craftsman would show a distinct inferiority to the originals; but in the hands of a capable artist the new version might be a great improvement both in the handling of the subject and in technical execution.

The illustrations in Breydenbach's *Peregrinationes in Montem Syon* (Mainz, 1486) show a marked advance upon previous efforts in the art of woodcutting. The book also possesses a modern touch in that the illustrator, Erhard Reuwich, joined the pilgrimage as special artist to the expedition; and since the page of animals 'veraciter depicta sicut vidimus in terra sancta' includes a salamander, a unicorn and a baboon leading a camel, it is clear that the special correspondent of the fifteenth century would have little to learn from his modern descendants. Shortly after this two of the most notable illustrated German books made their appearance at Nuremberg from the office of Anton Koberger: the *Schatzbehalter* of 1491, and Hartmann Schedel's *Liber Chronicarum* of 1493. Michael Wohlgemuth was the artist responsible for the cuts in both. The latter, usually called the *Nuremberg Chronicle*, and perhaps the best-known illustrated book of the fifteenth century, has elbowed its way to the front by wide circulation, sheer bulk and a blustering profusion of woodcuts, many of the portraits being repeated over and over again for different persons.[1] The *Schatzbehal-ter*, with its full-page pictures, each with a story to tell, is really the more attractive book. An edition of the *Apocalypse* with full-page woodcuts by Albrecht Dürer appeared in Nuremberg in 1498.

Italy was somewhat later in adopting illustrations. The *Meditationes* of Turrecremata, printed at Rome by Ulrich Han in 1467, is believed to be the first Italian book in which woodcuts occur; but much better work may be seen in the eighty-two cuts which illustrate the edition of the *De re militari* of Valturius printed at Verona in 1472. Erhard Ratdolt, who printed at Venice from 1476 to 1485, is celebrated for his beautiful borders and initial letters; and a few books with pictures appeared both at Venice and other towns during that period. The use of woodcuts did not, however, become common in Italian books until about 1490, in which year Lucantonio Giunta published at Venice the first illustrated edition of Malermi's Italian version of the Bible. Some of the cuts in this book—there are nearly four hundred of them—were adaptations from the German Bible printed at Cologne by Heinrich Quentell some ten years earlier.

Illustration from *Hypnerotomachia Poliphili* (Venice, 1499)

[1]   An enumeration of the cuts shows that the book contains 1809 pictures printed from 645 different blocks. See A. W. Pollard, *Fine Books* (1912), p. 117.

The most remarkable Italian illustrated book of the fifteenth century was the *Hypnerotomachia Poliphili* of Francesco Colonna, which Aldus, who was not given to the use of pictures, printed for Leonardo Crassus in 1499. This fine folio in its rich array of graceful and well-executed woodcuts is a striking contrast to the little Savonarola tracts and *Rappresentazioni*, or miracle-plays, which form the most characteristic illustrated productions of the Florentine press. These popular booklets, with their charming little woodcuts generally surrounded by a border having a white design on a black ground, had a vogue which lasted from 1490 to the middle of the sixteenth century.

In Paris, a stronghold of the trade in manuscripts, the printing press ousted the scribe less easily; and it was here, more than in most other places, that the printed book kept touch with the art of the illuminator. This is specially observable in the *Horae*, or Books of Hours, of which innumerable editions were printed in France between 1486 and the middle of the sixteenth century. In these books nearly every page is surrounded by an elaborate border, generally made up of small pictures enclosed by intertwining foliage or other decorative framework. The subjects may be either Old Testament types, biblical scenes, histories of saints, the dance of death, or even rural scenes and daily occupations. The small pictures were frequently on separate blocks, and so lent themselves to an almost infinite variety of combinations. Besides the borders, a larger picture, occupying nearly the whole page, was placed at the beginning of the several sections of the work, each of which had its appropriate subject. Many copies were printed on vellum, and the borders and pictures were often gilded and coloured in the style of manuscripts by an illuminator, who, when occasion demanded or fancy prompted, would overlay the printed ornament or picture with some entirely different design.

Some of the best of these books of private prayers are among the editions printed at Paris by Philippe Pigouchet for Simon Vostre during the twenty years from about 1490. Other prominent printers and publishers of them were Jean du Pré, Thielman Kerver, Gilles Hardouyn and Antoine Vérard. The last of these was one of the greatest of the early French publishers, and his numerous books are freely illustrated with cuts both new and old. In the *Horae* (1525) of the artist-printer Geofroy Tory the tradition of manuscript decoration is no longer dominant and the ornamentation is in full Renaissance style.

Several books printed in the Low Countries in the fifteenth century were finely illustrated in wood, and Colard Mansion, with whom Caxton worked in Bruges, experimented with engravings in copper, though without much success. The early English press is not remarkable for its illustrations or its decorative qualities. Such pictures and ornaments as were used were mostly either imported from the continent or derived their inspiration from foreign originals. The first English books in which woodcuts occur are *The Mirrour of the World* and the third edition of the *Parvus et Magnus Cato*, both of which were printed by Caxton about 1481. Caxton used illustrations in several other books, notably the second edition of the *Canterbury Tales*, in which the designs were at least of English origin, the *Fables of Esope* (1484), turned into English by Caxton himself and illustrated by one hundred and six pictures, and the *Golden Legend*, the largest and most ambitious of all his books.

Page of a *Horae* (Paris, 1498)

Wynkyn de Worde used woodcuts more freely than Caxton, but he seems to have valued them rather as adding to the saleability of the book than as illustrating the text. Among the more prominent of his illustrated books are the fine folio edition of the *De proprietatibus rerum* of Bartholomaeus Anglicus and the *Morte d'Arthur* of 1498. Several of his small quartos have woodcuts, and he also printed a *Sarum Primer* with borders to every page and a number of small cuts. Pynson, like Caxton and de Worde, also issued a pictorial edition of the *Canterbury Tales*, but his illustrated books are better represented by the 1494 edition of Lydgate's *Falle of Princes* and the *Kalendar of Shephardes* of 1506, though it may be noted that the cuts in both are of French origin. The woodcuts, upwards of one hundred, in Barclay's English version of the *Ship of Fools*, which Pynson printed in 1509, are copies of those in the original Basel edition of 1494; sixty years later they were resuscitated for the edition which John Cawood published in 1570.

In the sixteenth century the talents of the foremost artists found expression in the printed book, and the illustrations of that period still rank with the best ever produced. Dürer, the greatest of these artists, served an apprenticeship to Wohlgemuth in his native town of Nuremberg. Hans Burgkmair, his contemporary, was of the celebrated art centre at Augsburg, as was also Hans Holbein, whose chief work, however, was done at Basel; while Lucas Cranach made his home at Wittenberg. Jost Amman, best known by his clever delineations of trades and occupations in Schopper's *Panoplia* (Frankfort, 1568), belongs to the second half of the century; and at the end of it Theodore de Bry and his sons were bringing out at Frankfort their wonderful series of illustrated travel books. Some of these artists, notably Holbein, also designed book decorations in the form of initial letters and the beautiful borders which are characteristic of sixteenth-century title-pages. In the latter part of his career Pynson frequently placed his title-pages within ornamental borders, of which he possessed some good designs, and this feature also appears in the books issued in 1521 by John Siberch, the first Cambridge printer, who was brought over by Erasmus from the continent. From this date bordered title-pages become increasingly common in English books, though illustrations were by no means freely used. Foxe's *Book of Martyrs* (1563) was one of the most popular illustrated books of the time, and John Day, who printed it, also brought out *A Booke of Christian Prayers*, commonly called Queen Elizabeth's Prayer Book. This book, which has a pictorial border to each page after the manner of the French *Horae*, is a curious revival and the only English representative of that style.

The sixteenth century saw the woodcut at its best, but by the middle of the century a rival craft was beginning to assert itself. The art of metal engraving had occasionally been used for the illustration of books as early as the fifteenth century, but its sporadic employment hardly threatened the early supremacy of the woodcut, which held its own, aided, no doubt, by the fact that it could be printed with the text. But copperplate engraving, which appealed to the artist-engraver as a more sympathetic vehicle for rendering half-tones and shadow, steadily won its way, so that by the end of the sixteenth century it had nearly displaced the woodcut, which then practically disappears for the next two hundred years.

The effect of the use of metal engraving for book illustration was more than a mere change in the method of producing the pictures. It involved changed relations between text and illustrations, and resulted in a loss of homogeneity in the printed book. Metal engravings belong to the intaglio group of processes, and, since they require a different kind of printing machine, cannot be printed at the same time as the letterpress. Consequently, it will be found that the illustrated book of the seventeenth and eighteenth centuries possesses certain new features.

Sometimes, and more particularly in the case of fine books, the engravings were printed in blank spaces left for that purpose in the page of text, or were printed on thin paper and pasted into their places on the page. But since it was less trouble to print the engravings apart from the letterpress, they were usually worked on separate sheets of paper which were afterwards inserted between the leaves of the book or gathered together at the end of the volume. In this form, familiarly known as 'plates', the illustrations are no longer an integral part of the printed book. This practice was further encouraged by the circumstance that the inferior paper which had come into general use was unsuitable for the printing of line engravings. The woodcut border to the title-page also disappears, and instead the book is 'adorn'd' with an engraved title-page in which the brief title of the work is more or less lost in an elaborate design, frequently consisting of architectural features or heavy draperies in combination with allegorical figures and other 'properties' deemed appropriate to the subject of the book. An engraved portrait of the author was an obviously suitable *vis-à-vis* to the engraved title-page.

Engraved title-page: Bacon's *Instauratio Magna* (London, 1620)

An early success in English intaglio illustration was Thomas Geminus's pirated edition of Vesalius's *Anatomy*, published in 1545 and containing several engraved plates by Flemish artists, as well as a fine engraved title-page. Among other English books illustrated with metal engravings Sir John Harington's version of *Orlando Furioso* (1591), containing forty-six full-page pictures, is one of the best examples of that period. During the seventeenth century pictorial illustrations were used very sparingly in this country, and the popular engravers, among whom were Elstracke, Marshall, Faithorne and Hollar, were largely occupied upon title-pages and portraits. The same was true of the continent, Poussin's fine frontispieces to the books of the Paris Imprimerie Royale (founded by Cardinal Richelieu in 1640) being outstanding successes. Exceptions were a number of atlases, notably those of the Netherlander Blaeu, and a few books with etched plates of a descriptive character, such as those of Jacques Callot. In the eighteenth century, engraved illustration reached in France a perfection of taste and a technical virtuosity which have perhaps never been surpassed in any age or country. The work of Oudry or Fragonard, the *Fermiers Généraux* La Fontaine or the Boucher Molière, epitomize the exquisite magnificence of a justly celebrated civilization.

England, at that time, produced nothing comparable: the plates of Gravelot and his kind being largely derivative, and the native genius of Hogarth hardly extending its influence, until the end of the century, beyond the domains of the print market. In another direction activity in antiquarian, architectural, and topographical research resulted in the production of many large volumes on these subjects illustrated with fine engraved plates. In the latter part of the century Thomas Stothard, a prolific book illustrator of inventive fancy, was busy with plates for *Robinson Crusoe, Clarissa Harlowe, Tristram Shandy* and many other English classics, while illustrated children's books found a vogue in many countries. William Blake, in his very individual style, produced some of the most ambitious and beautiful of all book illustrations. He developed a technique of engraving the whole book, text as well as pictures, on metal relief blocks, a reversion in principle to the block-book of the fifteenth century.

Woodcuts had continued to be used occasionally in chap-books and other forms of popular literature; but, as they were generally either battered and hard-worn veterans of an earlier age or debased copies of old cuts, they contributed nothing to the survival of the art, which remained under a cloud until its revival at the hands of Thomas Bewick, whose cuts for Gay's *Fables* (1779), the Poems of Goldsmith and *General History of Quadrupeds* (1790) mark a new era in book illustration. The fresh life which the genius of Bewick and his followers infused into their art was more in the nature of a new development than a mere revival. New methods and principles were introduced, and henceforth we speak of the craft as 'wood engraving' in place of the old term 'woodcutting'. The great technical skill and delicacy of effect which the wood engravers attained brought their art once more into favour and inspired a distinctively English school of illustration.

In the nineteenth century the use of illustrations in books of every kind greatly increased. Although wood engraving was the principal process employed, all the other methods of pictorial reproduction continued in use, their number being augmented early in the century by the introduction of lithography. This new process, in which the design is either drawn upon or transferred to the face of a specially prepared stone which forms the printing surface, was discovered by a German, Aloys Senefelder, at the very end of the eighteenth century—the most important development in printing since the invention of movable type. For over a hundred years, however, it found little place in book-printing, if we except oriental works, in which it served to reproduce the writing and ornamentation of scribes, and musical scores, where it proved cheaper than the relief or intaglio methods, if somewhat inferior to the latter in the beauty of its results.

The first quarter of the nineteenth century was the golden age of those coloured aquatint illustrations inseparably connected with the name of the publisher Rudolph Ackermann. Primarily a print merchant, Ackermann commissioned such artists as Pugin and Rowlandson for the production of descriptive illustrated books on Oxford, Cambridge, London and the like, which have enjoyed as great a reputation in our day as in their own. Nor were others slow to follow his example and in a few instances to rival his success.

With McLean, a fellow print dealer, Ackermann was also prominent in another, and a peculiarly English, department of illustration—the sporting book. The lively drawings of Herring, Sartorius and Wolstenholme were mainly confined to the magazines; but *Jorrocks' Jaunts* and *The Life of John Mytton* displayed in book form the extraordinary talent of Henry Alken for making riders look 'Meltonian' and every horse a thoroughbred as fast as the wind.

The art of caricature was ably sustained by the satirical activities of Dighton, Woodward, Gillray and Rowlandson—the last one of the greatest of all English artists. His *Tours of Dr Syntax* were immensely successful and begat numerous imitations in a genre where the text was subordinated to—in fact usually written merely to accompany—the plates. The medium of these caricaturists was the line engraving, with colouring added by hand; but the tradition was developed, on less exaggerated lines, by George Cruikshank, Seymour and H. K. Browne, illustrators of Dickens, and others working in black and white. John Leech, however, on whose shoulders the Surtees novels rode to fame, returned in the fifties to the earlier technique, which had indeed remained constant in the sporting book field.

Steel engraving was used with early and conspicuous success by that neglected artist John Martin, whose illustrations for *Paradise Lost* (1827) and the Bible almost rivalled the fabulous popularity of his prints. This medium was also characteristic of the many Annuals, Keepsakes, Books of Beauty and the like which flourished expensively in the second quarter of the century. Their quality was fine and their manner so much to the taste of the age that many other volumes equally deserved the comment made on the illustrated edition of Samuel Rogers's *Italy*, that it 'would have been dished without the plates'.

Soon after 1830 the field for wood engraving was enlarged by the use of illustrations in weekly journals, and additional importance was given to this movement by the founding of the *Illustrated London News* in 1842. Books had their full share of this expansion. The mid-Victorians showed equal relish for the stirring scenes of Sir John Gilbert and the rural beauties of Birket Foster as rendered in wood by the brothers Dalziel; while the drawings of John Tenniel are familiar, from his felicitous association with Lewis Carroll, to every child in England and many in other countries. The middle years of the century, however, are best known for the work of the not too homogeneous group of illustrators in wood commonly identified with 'the Sixties'.

Distinguished among these extremely prolific designers were Rossetti, John Everett Millais, Frederick Walker and Arthur Boyd Houghton, and although much of their work appeared in such periodicals as *Good Words, Once a Week* and *The Cornhill,* they also illustrated a great number of contemporary books and provided the *raison d'être* for an even greater number of reprints and selections, many of a poetical or sentimental character. The unfashionable style of much of this outburst of illustration must not, however, be allowed to obscure the very high standard of craftsmanship almost universally displayed, nor the commanding brilliance of a great many of the designs themselves. The *English Illustrated Magazine,* founded in 1883, was a brave effort to revive the cause of wood engraving, and a good deal of delicate and beautiful work is to be found in its earlier volumes, as also in America in the *Century, Scribner's* and *Harper's* magazines. But the day of the wood engraving for ordinary trade books was done.

No other country equalled the volume of England's output of illustrated books in this century, though Russia produced a body of highly interesting material and France had eminent artists at work; among them Delacroix (an early and successful exponent of lithography), Daumier, Gavarni, Doré, Manet and Toulouse-Lautrec. The United States produced little that was original during the first half of the century, but in the second half the illustrated magazines began to provide that effective stimulus which they continue to exert today. Then, in the seventies, came the practical development of line engraving by photo-mechanical methods, and in 1880 the half-tone plate was perfected simultaneously by Meisenbach in England, Petit in France, and Horgan and Ives in America. Book and magazine illustration deteriorated sadly. It was not merely that the results of these methods were inferior, but their facility led to shoddiness of the worst sort. Exceptions, of course, there were: among them the pretty coloured work of Randolph Caldecott, Kate Greenaway and Walter Crane. Nor must the popular Cranford Series be forgotten, with its legitimate off-shoots and numerous imitators. The gifts of Hugh Thomson and his school in black-and-white illustration were considerable, and they were skilfully adapted to the new processes.

Aubrey Beardsley, however, was the first to exploit to the full the artistic possibilities of mechanical line engraving, and the reproduction of his drawings in several works of Oscar Wilde, in *The Yellow Book* and elsewhere among John Lane's publications, show the masterly use he made of it. At the same time, Ricketts and Morris were, each in his own way, rebelling against the encroachments of industrialism and rescuing the wood engraving at least for use in the 'fine' book field.

When we come to the books of our own century, it is difficult to select those which are outstanding in the field of illustration. All the processes, old and new, are employed, and a notable and welcome trend is the effort to blend text and pictures harmoniously. Photo-lithography, by which type and illustrations can be laid down together (usually on metal plates which have replaced the stone surface), afford special facilities for this, and in some cases, particularly children's books, the text is actually reproduced from handwriting. Even the unlovely 'art paper' plate bids fair to be ousted by the progress made, especially in America, in the printing of half-tone blocks on antique paper.

Copper-plate engraving is not common in modern books, though in the hands of J. E. Laboureur it has given us some of the loveliest illustrated books of recent times, such as Rémy de Gourmont's novel *Le Songe d'une Femme*. Laboureur, a disciple of Toulouse-Lautrec, is hardly less successful with his lithographs and wood-blocks—witness such a little masterpiece as the *Chansons Madécasses*—and his breakaway from the heavy French woodcut style, frequently balanced by equally overweighted type, brought a breath of fresh air into the art of the book in that country. It is in

Illustration in line by Aubrey Beardsley

England that the wood engraving is most successfully exploited today, and of the many artists at work in this medium Eric Gill and Robert Gibbings may be picked out for their skill in combining illustration with decoration of the text and in harmonizing the 'colour' of the two constituents, type and blocks.

Auto-lithography, by which the artist works directly on to the stone, has been used in England recently more for the jackets of books than their inside, while photo-lithography and photogravure are still mainly confined to commercial printing. The latter process has, however, been used with great success in the books of reproductions, many of them emanating from Vienna. Collotype, the most sensitive of all photographic methods, is used for the plates in many English and American books where the extra expense as compared with half-tone blocks can be afforded. Its best use, often in colour, was found in Germany until a few years ago, but it has since, for various reasons, lost its popularity there.

Before we leave the subject of illustration, a brief description of the various processes may be acceptable to the reader. We have already seen that there are three kinds of surface from which an image may be reproduced—relief, intaglio, and surface or planographic. Instances of the first are woodcuts and mechanical line and half-tone blocks; of the second, copper and steel plate engravings; of the third, lithography and collotype. Photography may be applied to them all. Even with woodcuts it is not uncommon for a photograph to be printed on to the wood for the engraver to follow with his tool.

The relief method of printing illustrations is precisely the same as is used for printing from type; the raised parts of the block receive a cover of ink which is transferred to the paper. Mechanical line blocks are made by printing a negative on to a zinc plate coated with a thin film of sensitized albumen, which is then covered with a layer of ink. Where light has passed through the negative, that is, in the black parts of the picture, the albumen is fixed. Where light has been obstructed the albumen can be washed away with water, and the ink with it. The zinc plate is next dipped in a succession of nitric acid baths, where the parts unprotected by the ink are etched away. We are left with a reproduction of the original image standing in relief, reversed of course, so that it bears the same relation to the picture printed from it as a photographic negative does to its positive.

It is obvious that in printing from a relief block those portions of the face of the block which come in contact with the paper will produce corresponding solid marks on the paper, whether they be lines, dots, or larger portions of the surface. Since the marks thus made must be solid black, or one tone of colour if a coloured ink is used, tints and shades cannot be rendered by this method; though the effect is approximately attained in wood engraving by the use of lines graduated in thickness and distance from each other so as to produce the simulation of tint. The problem of reproducing pictures composed of tints and light-and-shade (and not of lines) was solved by the invention of the half-tone process. This is similar to that of making line etchings, but, in taking the photograph for transfer to the metal plate, a glass screen, closely ruled with fine lines at right angles to each other, is interposed between the negative and the picture. The result of this is that the image on the negative is broken up into small dots which vary in size and density according to the amount of light reflected through the ruled screen by the different parts of the picture. The face of the plate and the resultant reproduction thus consist of a mass of minute dots which are not separately visible to the eye but by their varying texture give the effect of the tones of the original. This construction may readily be seen by examining one of these illustrations with a magnifying lens. In the lighter parts of the picture it will be noticed that the dots are small and distinctly separated by the white ground between them. In the middle tones the black and white are more nearly even, while in the shadows the texture becomes white dots on a black ground. In some of the work used in newspaper illustration, where a coarser 'screen' is used, this effect may be detected without the aid of a lens.

From the earliest days of book illustration colour has been popular. Copies of books in which the illustrations have been coloured are of common occurrence in all periods, and generally this addition is contemporary work. Sometimes this was done by or for the owner, but in many cases books were issued by the publisher with the illustrations either plain or coloured. Initial letters printed in colour occur as early as Fust and Schoeffer's *Psalter* of 1457; and in the *Book of St. Albans*, printed at St. Albans in 1486, the heraldic shields are printed in colours. But until the eighteenth century little attempt was made to print illustrations in colours, and most of the colouring was done by hand.

During the eighteenth century, however, a number of processes were evolved for colour printing: notable among the experimenters being Le Blon and his pupils d'Agoty and Lasinio. Some copies of Blake's engraved books show a colour-printed base. And in the lavish illustrated books of the Ackermann type the groundwork and paler tints were printed, preparatory to the detail colour being added by hand. This aquatinting was developed by J. C. Lewis from the earlier technique of Le Prince. Later came Savage and Congreve, followed by the enormously prolific and successful George Baxter; while colour lithography came of age about 1840 with the work of Day and Haghe.

The three-colour process is based on the discoveries of Newton, worked out by Clerk Maxwell in the middle of the nineteenth century and quickly adapted to printing technique. Three blocks, representing the primary colours, are employed. The negatives for these are taken through filters of coloured glass or glass cells containing coloured liquid, in addition to the ruled screen. Each of these light filters allows only certain colours to pass through to the negative and stops the passage of all others. The colours of the original are thus automatically dissected and grouped in three categories representing approximately the yellows, the reds, and the blues, each of which is contained on a separate negative. Of the three process-blocks made from these negatives that representing the yellow tones is printed first in yellow ink, over this impression the red block is next printed, and finally the blue. The various colours and tints of the resultant picture are formed by the combination of these three colours printed over each other and varying in proportion according to the density of the printing surface of the respective blocks. The use of the right amount of colour and degree of pressure in printing are important factors in the success of the operation. It is also essential that the register should be absolutely accurate, that is to say, the three impressions must follow each other in exactly the same place on the paper, or the result will be the blurred effect occasionally seen in cheap prints.

The very opposite of relief printing is the intaglio or gravure method, and for this reason it cannot be used with type on letter-press machines. The ink is taken, not from the raised parts of the plate, but from those that are sunk. After the ink has been applied the plate is wiped, so that there is no ink left on the surface. The hand method of preparing these plates, being slow and expensive, is now rare, and has given way to photographic means. The plates are prepared in much the same way as relief blocks, an acid-resist protecting the necessary parts, in this case those which are not to be reproduced. There is no screen, but a grain is necessary so that the etched parts will hold the ink, and this is discernible under a glass.

Of the surface methods, lithography (stone-drawing) was discovered, as we have seen, at the end of the eighteenth century, and after a temporary decline it has now become increasingly popular. In this process the image is laid down on a specially prepared stone of porous quality, in a medium (such as a fatty chalk) which has an affinity for varnish ink but will reject water. The surface of the stone is damped and then swept by inked rollers; the damp parts of the stone reject the ink, but where it has remained dry, that is, over the image, the ink takes and is transferred to paper laid upon it. The image can be laid down either direct or from a transfer; and the process has been adapted to metal plates on which a fatty acid is held by a fine grain, obtained by rocking the plate with powdered glass. Photo-lithography is often used for reprinting books of which no type or plates are available, and various methods have also been developed by which plates are prepared direct from letter matrices, so eliminating all use of metal type.

Collotype is carried out in much the same way as photo-lithography except that instead of stone or metal a gelatine surface is used. It is the most faithful reproduction of all, and also the most expensive. As with lithography and gravure, a grain appears in the reproduction and can be detected under a magnifying glass; and as these three grains, and the half-tone screen, are all different, we have here a method of recognizing the process used for any work.

THE MATERIALS OF BOOKS AND PRINTING

Additional Readings

GENERAL WORKS

Arnold, Edmund C. *Ink on Paper 2: A Handbook of the Graphic Arts.* New York: Harper and Row, 1972.

Brewer, Roy. *An Approach to Print: A Basic Guide to the Printing Processes.* London: Blandford Press, 1971.

Craig, James. *Production for the Graphic Designer.* New York: Watson-Guptill Publications, 1974.

Harrop, Dorothy A. *Modern Book Production.* Hamden: Archon Books, 1968.

Jennett, Sean. *The Making of Books.* 5th ed. London: Faber and Faber, 1973.

Karch, R. Randolph. *Graphic Arts Procedures—Basic.* 4th ed. Chicago: American Technical Society, 1970.

Lee, Marshall. *Bookmaking: The Illustrated Guide to Design and Production.* New York: R. R. Bowker, 1965.

McLean, Ruari. *Modern Book Design from William Morris to the Present Day.* London: Faber and Faber, 1958.

Moran, James. *Printing Presses: History and Development from the Fifteenth Century to Modern Times.* Berkeley: University of California Press, 1973.

Turnbull, Arthur T., and Baird, Russell N. *The Graphics of Communication: Typography—Layout—Design.* 3d ed. New York: Holt, Rinehart and Winston, 1975.

Williamson, Hugh. *Methods of Book Design: The Practice of an Industrial Craft.* 2nd ed. London: Oxford University Press, 1966.

Wilson, Adrian. *The Design of Books.* New York: Reinhold, 1967.

SURFACES FOR WRITING AND PRINTING

Blum, André. *On the Origin of Paper.* New York: R. R. Bowker, 1934.

Clapperton, R. H. *The Paper-Making Machine: Its Invention, Evolution, and Development.* Oxford: Pergamon Press, 1967.

Day, Frederick T. *An Introduction to Paper: Its Manufacture and Use.* London: Newnes, 1963.

Hardman, H., and Cole, E. J. *Paper-Making Practice.* Manchester: Manchester University Press, 1960.

Higham, Robert R. A. *A Handbook of Papermaking.* London: Oxford University Press, 1963.

Hunter, Dard. *Papermaking: The History and Technique of an Ancient Craft.* 2d ed. New York: A. A. Knopf, 1947.

_____. *Papermaking in Pioneer America.* Philadelphia: University of Pennsylvania Press, 1952.

_____. *Papermaking Through Eighteen Centuries.* New York: William E. Rudge, 1930. Reprint, New York: Burt Franklin, 1970.

Library of Congress. *Papermaking Art and Craft.* Washington, D.C.: Library of Congress, 1968.

Mason, John. *Paper Making as an Artistic Craft.* London: Faber and Faber, 1959.

Norris, F. H. *Paper and Paper Making.* London: Oxford University Press, 1952.

O'Casey, I. and Maney, A. S. *The Nature and Making of Papyrus.* Barkston Ash: The Elmete Press, 1973.

Reed, Ronald. *The Nature and Making of Parchment.* Leeds: The Elmete Press, 1975.

Surtermeister, Edwin. *The Story of Papermaking.* Boston: S. D. Warren, 1954.

THE ALPHABET, WRITING, AND TYPOGRAPHY

Anderson, D. M. *The Art of Written Forms: The Theory and Practice of Calligraphy.* New York: Holt, Rinehart and Winston, 1969.

Biggs, John R. *An Approach to Type.* 2d ed. London: Blandford Press, 1961.

Clodd, Edward. *The Story of the Alphabet.* Rev. ed. New York: D. Appleton-Century Company, Inc., 1938. Reprint, Detroit: Gale, 1970.

Denham, Frank. *The Shaping of Our Alphabet: A Study of Changing Type Styles.* New York: A. A. Knopf, 1955.

Diringer, David. *The Alphabet: A Key to the History of Mankind.* 2 vols. 3d ed. London: Hutchinson, 1968.

Dowding, Geoffrey. *An Introduction to the History of Printing Types.* London: Wace and Company, 1961.

Fairbank, Alfred. *The Story of Handwriting: Origins and Development.* New York: Watson-Guptill, 1970.

Gelb, I. J. *A Study of Writing.* Rev. ed. Chicago: University of Chicago Press, 1963.

Hutchins, R. S. *The Western Heritage of Type Design.* London: Cory, Adams, and Mackay, 1963.

Irwin, Keith H. *The Romance of Writing From Egyptian Hieroglyphics to Modern Letters, Numbers, and Signs.* New York: Viking, 1956.

Johnson, A. F. *Type Designs: Their History and Development.* 3d ed. London: Andre Deutsch, 1966.

Lawson, Alexander S. *Printing Types: An Introduction.* Boston: Beacon Press, 1971.

Lowe, E. A. *Handwriting: Our Medieval Legacy.* Rome: Edizioni di Storia e Letteratura, 1969.

Mercer; S. A. B. *The Origin of Writing and Our Alphabet.* London: Luzac and Company, 1959.

Moorhouse, A. C. *The Triumph of the Alphabet: A History of Writing.* New York: Schuman, 1953.

Morison, Stanley and Day, Kenneth, eds. *The Typographic Book, 1450-1935.* Chicago: University of Chicago Press, 1963.

Ogg, Oscar. *The 26 Letters.* 3d ed. New York: Crowell, 1971.

Peacey, Howard. *The Meaning of the Alphabet.* Los Angeles: Murray and Gee, 1949.

Simon, Herbert. *Introduction to Printing: The Craft of Letterpress.* London: Faber and Faber, 1968.

Simon, Oliver. *Introduction to Typography.* 2d ed. Baltimore: Penguin Books, 1963.

Sutton, James and Bartram, Alan. *An Atlas of Typeforms.* New York: Hastings House, 1968.

Taylor, Isaac. *The History of the Alphabet: An Account of the Origin and Development of Letters.* 2 vols. New Edition. London: Edward Arnold, 1899.

Tschichold, Jan. *An Illustrated History of Writing and Lettering.* New York: Columbia University Press, 1948.

Tsien, Tsuen-Hsuin. *Written on Bamboo and Silk: The Beginnings of Chinese Books and Inscriptions.* Chicago: University of Chicago Press, 1962.

Updike, Daniel Berkeley. *Printing Types: Their History, Forms, and Use–A Study in Survivals.* 2 vols. 3d ed. Cambridge: The Belknap Press of Harvard University Press, 1962.

BOOKBINDING

Cockerell, Douglas. *Bookbinding, and the Care of Books.* 5th ed. London: Pitman, 1953.

Comparato, Frank E. *Books for the Millions: A History of the Men Whose Methods and Machines Packaged the Printed Word.* Harrisburg: The Stackpole Company, 1971.

Darley, Lionel S. *Introduction to Bookbinding.* London: Faber and Faber, 1965.

Diehl, Edith. *Bookbinding: Its Background and Technique.* 2 vols. New York: Rinehart and Company, 1946.

The History of Bookbinding, 525-1950 A.D. An Exhibition Held at the Baltimore Museum of Art, November 12, 1957 to January 12, 1958. Baltimore: Walters Art Gallery, 1957.

Lehmann-Haupt, Hellmut. *Bookbinding in America: Three Essays.* Rev. ed. New York: R. R. Bowker, 1967.

Town, Laurence. *Bookbinding by Hand for Students and Craftsmen.* 2d ed. London: Faber and Faber, 1963.

Vaughan, Alex. J. *Modern Bookbinding.* New ed. London: Charles Skilton, 1960.

BOOK ILLUSTRATION

Bland, David. *The Illustration of Books.* 3d ed. London: Faber and Faber, 1962.

Cleaver, James. *A History of Graphic Art.* New York: Philosophical Library, 1963.

George, Dorothy. *Hogarth to Cruickshank: Social Change in Graphic Satire.* New York: Walker, 1967.

Gutlein, Frank and Dorothy. *The Bite of the Print: Satire and Irony in Woodcuts, Engravings, Etchings, Lithographs, and Serigraphs.* New York: Clarkson N. Potter, 1963.

Hind, Arthur M. *A History of Engraving and Etching.* Boston: Houghton Mifflin 1923. Reprint, New York: Dover, 1963.

————*An Introduction to a History of Woodcut.* Boston: Houghton Mifflin, 1935. Reprint, New York: Dover, 1963. 2 vols.

Jussim, Estelle. *Visual Communication and the Graphic Arts: Photographic Technologies in the Nineteenth Century.* New York: R. R. Bowker, 1974.

Klemin, Diana. *The Illustrated Book: Its Art and Craft.* New York: Clarkson N. Potter, 1970.

Lewis, John. *The Twentieth Century Book: Its Illustration and Design.* New York: Reinhold, 1967.

Mayor, A. Hyatt. *Prints and People: A Social History of Printed Pictures.* New York: Metropolitan Museum of Art, 1971.

Pitz, Henry C. *Illustrating Children's Books: History, Technique, Production.* New York: Watson-Guptill Publications, 1963.

Reed, Walt, ed. *The Illustrator in America, 1900-1960.* New York: Reinhold, 1966.

Salamon, F. *The History of Prints and Printmaking from Drürer to Picasso.* New York: American Heritage Press, 1972.

Shikes, Ralph E. *The Indignant Eye: The Artist as Social Critic in Prints and Drawings from the Fifteenth Century to Picasso.* Boston: Beacon Press, 1969.

Simon, Howard. *500 Years of Art and Illustration.* Cleveland: World Publishing Company, 1942.

Slythe, P. Margaret. *The Art of Illustration, 1750-1900.* London: The Library Association, 1970.

Weitenkampf, Frank. *The Illustrated Book.* Cambridge: Harvard University Press, 1938.

Weitzmann, Kurt. *Illustration in Roll and Codex: A Study of the Origin and Method of Text Illustration.* (Second printing with addenda). Princeton: Princeton University Press, 1970.

III.

THE HAND-PRODUCED BOOK

Part III. THE HAND-PRODUCED BOOK

Introduction

From the clay tablets of ancient time to Gutenberg's invention of printing with movable type around 1450, all books were produced by hand.

The earliest medium for recording facts and keeping records was the clay tablet of Sumer, Assyria, and Babylonia into which was impressed wedge-shaped or cuneiform writing. At the same time, in the land along the Nile, the papyrus rolls of ancient Egypt became the dominant form of the book in that region where the scribe, with pen or brush, wrote the hieroglyphics of the priests and people. The papyrus rolls continued into Greece and Rome where the books of that time were also recorded on this fragile material. The codex evolved around 400 A.D., becoming the dominant book form of the Christian era. Parchment and vellum were used as the material on which the medieval scribe, with pen and ink, copied the text and others added the ornamentation and decoration with burnished gold and colors in their "desire to beautify the object of devotion."

Recorded history goes back 5,000 years, and of that time 4,500 years was dominated by the clay tablet, papyrus roll, and vellum codex of the ancient and medieval world. The hand-produced book flourished longer than any other form of graphic communication and has recorded and preserved our religion, philosophy, literature, music, art, science, politics, and thought as a tribute to the ingenuity and skill of the many individuals who took part in its time-consuming and laborious production.

This unit begins with a discussion of the illumination of classical manuscripts by John A. Herbert, who "describes the development of the illuminator's art." John W. Bradley briefly looks at a few of the earliest illuminations of Greece and Rome.

The "Introduction" to David Diringer's *The Illuminated Book* defines book illumination, examining the elements which influenced it. David Bland presents an in-depth analysis of the medieval illuminated manuscript of Western Europe from the seventh century A.D. to 1550 A.D. with the end of the manuscript period. The concluding essay is the examination by Hellmut Lehmann-Haupt of the transition from the medieval manuscript to the printed book. He shows that early book printing was not so much a tentative step in a new art but a "rendering of existing forms and conventions in a new medium."

With Gutenberg's invention printing soon spread rapidly over all of Western Europe and eventually throughout the world. The medieval period was at an end, but there still remained the surviving records of the splendor, brilliance, and beauty of this millenium in their illuminated manuscripts "which are a delight even to us of the atomic age."

John A. Herbert

The Illumination of
Classical Manuscripts

The opening chapter of a complete history of illuminated manuscripts, in the widest sense of the term, ought no doubt to be devoted to Egyptian papyri. Many of these were richly adorned with coloured illustrations; and specimens of this art survive dating back to the fifteenth century B.C., such as the famous *Book of the Dead* made for Ani, now in the British Museum. But the present work is less ambitious: only illuminations on vellum come within its scope, and only such of these, for the most part, as are of European origin. In one respect, however, we must extend the definition of illuminated manuscripts. Strictly speaking, the term is only applicable to manuscripts which are illustrated or ornamented in colours; some writers would even restrict it to those in which the precious metals too are used—which are "lit up" by gold or silver foil. But paintings and outline-drawings are so intimately connected (at all events, as applied to the embellishment of vellum manuscripts) that the latter can hardly be excluded from an attempt to describe the development of the illuminator's art.

Tradition assigns the invention of vellum to Eumenes II, king of Pergamum, B.C. 197-158, though the skins of animals, more or less specially prepared as writing material, had undoubtedly been used in Egypt long before his time. But the earliest definite reference to an illuminated manuscript on vellum occurs in Martial's Epigrams, written towards the end of the first century of the Christian era. Among other inscriptions for gifts of various kinds is one for a Virgil on vellum, having a portrait of the poet for a frontispiece.

SOURCE: Reprinted from John A. Herbert, *Illuminated Manuscripts* (London: Methuen and Company, 1911) (Reprint - New York: Burt Franklin, 1958), Chapter I, "The Illumination of Classical Manuscripts," pp. 1-13, by permission of Associated Book Publishers Ltd.

Vergilius in membranis
Quam brevis inmensum cepit membrana Maronem!
Ipsius et vultus prima tabella gerit.

This gift-book has not survived to our days. It is interesting, however, to find that one of the few extant remains of classical book-illustration is a Virgil[1] containing the poet's portrait; not indeed on the first page, but on more than one of those which follow.

The distich just quoted proves that the art of miniature was practised in Martial's time. No specimens survive, however, which can be assigned to an earlier date than the fourth century; in fact, only three illuminated manuscripts of the classical period are now known to exist—the two Virgils in the Vatican and the Iliad at Milan. These are precious both for their rarity, and also as an indication of the style of much work which has now vanished; for the Iliad and the smaller Virgil show by the fully developed manner of their paintings that they are less the casual beginnings, than the last products, of an art. It seems unlikely, however, that this art had ever attained great proportions or enjoyed general popularity. No doubt there were many classical illuminated manuscripts (as there were many manuscripts of all kinds) which have perished, both separately and in the wholesale destruction of great libraries such as those of Alexandria, Constantinople, and Rome. But we may fairly assume that no greater proportion of these were destroyed than of other kinds. Indeed, books with paintings, being always more costly than plainly written copies, would be guarded more carefully, and we might therefore expect more of them to survive, relatively to the total number executed. The Ambrosian Iliad, for instance, was preserved purely for the sake of its pictures, all the plain leaves having long ago disappeared. But we find that whilst numerous codices of classical texts exist, in a more or less complete state, written in the fourth and fifth centuries, if not earlier, only the three above mentioned show any trace of illumination.

It may seem strange that the masterpieces of Greek and Roman literature, with their wealth of material, and with the numerous models afforded by paintings and sculptures of the best periods of Greek art, should not have produced a large and influential school of book-illustration. But illumination is an art which appeals chiefly to the class of mind that enjoys detailed beauty, small refinements, exquisite finish. The genius of Roman art was quite other than this. It was an art of display which expressed itself chiefly in statuary, architecture, mural paintings; the ornamentation of great surfaces of the house and street. It raised triumphal arches and splendid tombs, but did not trouble itself much about the enrichment of books for private pleasure. The illuminated Homer or Virgil was always the fancy of an individual, never the necessity of the library.

One sort of book, however—the Calendar—seems to have been illustrated with paintings from a very early period, if we may accept the available evidence, which is rather of a second-hand kind, coming mainly, in fact, from a seventeenth century copy of a ninth century manuscript, which is supposed in its turn to have been copied from a fourth century original, now lost. This copy, now in the Barberini Library at Rome,[2] was made for that accurate and unprejudiced antiquary Peiresc, who showed a patience and common sense, in his dealings with antiquity, far beyond the average of his own, or even of a later, day. It bears many evidences of authenticity, as well as some indication of the copyist's desire to "improve upon" his original. In a word, we have fairly good reason for believing the fourth century original to have been illustrated, and that in much the same way as the later copies, so far as the subjects are concerned; but it would be rash to draw any inference from the existing pictures as to the style of execution or even the details of composition, of the lost archetype.[3]

The work in question is generally known as the *Calendar of the Sons of Constantine*, and its date is fixed, by the "Natales Caesarum" and other chronological notes, at the year 354 A.D. It purports to have been executed, probably at Rome, by Furius Dionysius Filocalus for a patron named Valentine. The drawings with which it is illustrated represent the cities of Rome, Alexandria, Constantinople, and Trier, personified in true classic fashion as female figures—Trier as an Amazon leading a captive barbarian; the planets, the sun and moon, the months, the signs of the zodiac. There are also portraits of Constantius II and Constantius Gallus Caesar. The figures of the months are specially interesting as the forerunners of the delightful Calendar-pictures prefixed to the Psalters and Books of Hours of the Middle Ages. They are generally nude or half-draped youths, and symbolize, more or less directly, the occupations proper to the various seasons. Thus March is a shepherd-boy, pointing upwards to a swallow; October, with a basket of fruit, is taking a hare from a trap. These month-pictures exist, not only in the copies made for Peiresc, but also in a fifteenth century MS. at Vienna, from which Strzygowski has published five (January, April to July) to make good the deficiencies of the Barberini MS. The Vienna pictures are rectangular, without any ornamental framing; but those in Peiresc's copy are placed in decorated frames, with a pediment surmounted by a lunette addition, decorated with debased classical patterns, such as the Greek scroll, cable, egg-and-dog-tooth, very carelessly executed. Unless these are the tasteful addition of the ninth century copyist—a not improbable hypothesis—we have here the only evidence that classical illuminators ornamented, as well as illustrated, their books. The miniatures in the classical texts which we shall next consider are pictorial only; it is not until the sixth century that we meet with other instances of the use of decorative borders and conventional ornament.

Of the three classical manuscripts to which we have already referred, by far the best is the smaller of the two Virgils in the Vatican.[4] Its pictures are not all of equal merit, but the best are painted in so mature a manner, with so dexterous a technique, as to make one feel very sure that we have in them the only surviving work of a large and developed school of illumination. It has been very carefully studied by M. Pierre de Nolhac,[5] and published in photographic facsimile by the authorities of the Vatican Library.[6] In its present fragmentary state it consists of seventy-five leaves, containing parts of the Georgics and of the Aeneid; about one-fifth or one-sixth, perhaps, of the original manuscript. Nothing is known of its history until the fifteenth century, when it was at Naples, in the possession of Gioviano Pontano. In tracing its subsequent adventures, M. de Nolhac has shown that it must have been seen by Raphael, who was inspired by more than one of its designs. The text is written throughout by one hand, in rustic capitals, a kind of script notoriously difficult to date with any confidence. The best judges concur, however, in assigning it on palaeographical grounds to the fourth century; and the fine execution of the earlier miniatures, the really classical pose and style of the figures, point to this rather than to a later date, when the artistic decadence consequent on the barbarian invasions was far advanced.

The book has now fifty miniatures, six occupying the full page, the remainder from half to two-thirds of a page. Each is enclosed in a rectangular frame of red, black, and white bands, the red decorated with gilt lozenges. There are nine illustrations of the Georgics, and forty-one of the Aeneid. In these paintings M. de Nolhac finds the work of three separate artists, of the same school and period, but of very different degrees of merit. To the best of the three (A) he assigns the Georgics series, pictures 1-9; to the worst (B), pictures 10-25; the remainder he gives to a third artist (C), inferior to A, but better than B. Sig. Venturi[7] agrees in attributing the first nine pictures to A, but would also credit him with thirteen of the C series (26-32, 40-4, 46); and he is disposed to assign seven of the B series (11, 15, 16, 18, 20, 22, 24) and three of the C series (35, 38, 45) to a fourth artist. It would be presumptuous to attempt to judge between these two distinguished critics. Provisionally, however, M. de Nolhac's hypothesis may be accepted as at least highly probable.

The illustrator of the Georgics was evidently a painter of great skill and taste. His pastoral pictures show something of that sense of the idyllic in country life which is peculiar to the cultured dweller in cities. His figures, too, are well posed, graceful, in good proportion; the animals natural and full of movement. The freedom and sense of space in these little pictures are truly artistic. They are painted with the direct touch of a person accustomed to work in a ductile medium. The colours are thick; many of the miniatures have suffered through this, the thickest layers having flaked off. There is no trace of preliminary outline-drawing. The soft handling of the draperies is very different from the crisp, hard manner of the Byzantine painters. The artist, too, is something of a naturalist. Not content with telling a story, he also composes a credible scene. His backgrounds have recess, his trees are not mere symbols; he even has some idea of perspective, both aerial and linear. As for his personages, slight and graceful in type, they seem to stand midway between the wall-paintings of Pompeii and those late-classical mosaics of Ravenna (Tomb of Galla Placidia and Baptistery of the Orthodox), which show a suppleness and sense of movement not yet crushed by the formalism and part-spiritual, part-decorative aims of Byzantine art.

Many of these excellences, however, belong to the individual artist, not to his school. The first sixteen of the Aeneid illustrations, be they by one hand or two, show a sad falling-off. Good modelling and composition vanish; so does delicacy in sense of colour. The artist (assuming him to be but one—in any case, the main characteristics are the same throughout) illustrates his subject, often with a certain vigour, but does not make a picture out of it. Often he loses all sense of proportion, tiny buildings being combined with figures twice their height. There is no hint of perspective; the painting in general is coarse and careless, and the attempts at facial expression merely grotesque. Perhaps the seven miniatures assigned by Sig. Venturi to a different hand are a trifle worse than some of the others; but all are bad, especially when compared with the charming pictures which precede them.

A marked improvement begins with Picture 26, and is sustained, more or less completely, to the end of the volume. The modelling and colouring become decidedly better; and in some of the pictures, such as the Death of Dido, there is a distinct effort to represent emotion. Individual figures and buildings are well done, but the artist lacks the power of successful combination. The miniature of Latinus receiving the Trojan envoys, however, is a really charming picture. The late-classical temple in the forest is painted with great delicacy, while the contrast between the cold, severe architecture and the deeps of the woods has not only been felt, but is communicated to the spectator.

The colour throughout the manuscript is deep, rich, and harmonious; and the first and third hands show considerable understanding of gradation, e.g. in the Boat-race scene, where the sea gradually changes from a dark tint in the foreground to pale green in the distance. The highlights of draperies and accessories are touched with gold. The flesh-tints are always brick-red, and recall (says M. de Nolhac) those of the Pompeian wall-paintings. Foliage is a dark green, in parts nearly black; but the second artist, in his careless hurry, sometimes uses blue. Otherwise, all three painters seem be have practically used the same paint-box, only distributing their tints with varying degrees of skill.

After the Vatican Virgil it seems natural to mention the fragments of the Iliad, now in the Ambrosian Library at Milan;[8] for the two manuscripts have much in common. The Iliad fragments consist of fifty-two separate leaves of vellum, containing fifty-eight miniatures, all the full width of the page, but of various heights. These are mostly on only one side of the leaf, the other side having portions of the text, in uncial writing of the fifth century; and it is evident that the book in its original state was a complete Iliad, profusely illustrated, comprising (according to Ceriani's estimate) 386 leaves with about 240 miniatures. What survives has evidently been preserved solely for its artistic interest: not only have the leaves been cut down as far as possible without encroaching on the pictures, but the text on the verso pages was covered, until Mai's time, with a paper backing, which was apparently put there as early as the thirteenth century.

Most of the miniatures are so stained and worn that it is difficult to judge of their original appearance. A largeness and freedom of manner, however, are evident, suggestive rather of mural painting than of illumination. Fine juxtaposition of mass is aimed at, rather than subtlety of line. It seems not improbable that the designs may have been copied from frescoes or other large paintings of the Augustan age, since lost. The style of the best is certainly Graeco-Roman, but the work is most unequal, some of the compositions being full of dignity, whilst others, weak, scattered, and lacking in proportion, seem to proceed from a different and very inferior school. Here, perhaps, antique models failed the artist. Many childish devices appear, such as making the slain in battle-pieces only half the size of the living, and the ridiculous—perhaps only symbolic—representation of Troy as a tiny walled space containing half a dozen soldiers. On the other hand, there are many charming single figures, especially Thetis, the winged Night, Apollo with his garland, sprig, and lyre, and the river-god Scamander; some of the battle-scenes, too, are full of life and vigour. There does not seem to be, even in the best pictures, anything like the fine artistic feeling and finished execution of the best miniatures in the Vatican Virgil; but the average merit of the book is perhaps higher. The pictures are enclosed in plain banded frames of red and blue. The favourite tints are white, blue, green, and purple, with a preponderance of red; no gold is used, its place being taken by a bright yellow. Some of the outlines are in pale ink; two of the pictures have landscape backgrounds, in the rest the backgrounds are plain. The coloured nimbi worn by the gods—Zeus purple, Aphrodite green, the others blue—are not without interest for the student of Christian iconography.

From these two books, which retain in an enfeebled form something of the grand and gracious manner of Graeco-Roman art, how great is the drop to our third and last classical manuscript! This is the larger illustrated Virgil[9] of the Vatican Library, numbered Cod. Vat. lat. 3867 and called the "Codex Romanus." Thanks to similarity of subject, age, and place, it has been persistently confused, even by those who should know better, with the probably older and certainly infinitely superior Cod. Vat. lat. 3225 described above—the Vatican Virgil par excellence. The Codex Romanus is a large, coarsely executed manuscript, whose exceeding ugliness has even caused some critics to suggest that it was decorated as a sort of artistic joke for the amusement of a Roman schoolboy! As the text, however, is as debased as the illustration, it would seem that its imperfections are the result of ignorance, not of a strained sense of humour. Expert opinion is divided as to its age: the form of writing—rustic capitals of an early type—has led the editors of the Palaeographical Society[10] to assign it provisionally to the first half of the fourth century, or possibly the closing years of the third; while other critics, judging by the corruptness of the text and the crudeness of the paintings, would relegate it to the sixth century or even later. The Vatican editors review the rival opinions carefully in their learned preface; their own judgment is that the manuscript is not later than the sixth century, nor earlier than the end of the fourth. The book certainly seems to belong to a period when the classical style had become a dead tradition, not a living force. This is strikingly apparent when one compares the feeble portraits of Virgil, which occur on three of the earlier pages, with their indubitable though distant prototype, the superb mosaic-portrait of Virgil sitting between Clio and Melpomene, recently found at Susa and published by the Foundation Eugène Piot.[11] But the shortcomings of the manuscript may perhaps be indications, not of late date, but of provincial origin. Inscriptions at the beginning and end show that in the thirteenth and fourteenth centuries it belonged to the abbey of S. Denis near Paris; and its editors suggest that it may possibly have been there from the eighth century onwards. In that case it might be presumed, without gross improbability, to represent a praiseworthy effort on the part of a Gaulish scribe and artist for the delectation of some wealthy patron; and to have visited Italy for the first time when it made its way, between 1455 and 1475, into the Papal Library.

Unlike its more comely neighbour and the Milan Iliad, the Codex Romanus is nearly complete; it consists of 309 leaves of very fine vellum, containing nearly the whole of the Eclogues, Georgics, and Aeneid. There are nineteen miniatures, many of them full-page, all of them full width of the text, mostly enclosed in rough banded borders of red and gold. The first seven (including the three portraits of the poet) illustrate the Eclogues, the next two the Georgics, and the last ten the Aeneid. The drawing is rough throughout, and the colouring harsh. The Virgil-portrait, which is twice repeated with practically no variation, and some of the scenes in the Aeneid were doubtless copied—as well as the painter could—from classical models. These were not necessarily miniatures; the patron's house may well have been adorned, like that at Susa, with a series of mosaics illustrating the Aeneid. In the rest, where the painter probably had nothing but his own imagination to guide him, the designs are childish, grotesque, and monotonous, particularly in the pastoral pictures. It is perhaps worth noting that the nimbus here occurs, not only—as in the Ambrosian Iliad—as an attribute of the gods in council, but also on the heads of Aeneas and others when sitting in state, whether for consultation or feasting.

On the whole, the Codex Romanus is of little use for the study of classical illuminations; and its chance survival has done injustice to their memory. It is on the Ambrosian Iliad and the Vatican Virgil that our ideas of Roman miniature must be based; and perhaps also on a further series of books which, though not dating from such early times, seem to have preserved the ancient traditions with great fidelity. These are the illustrated copies of the Comedies of Terence, many of which have survived to us from the ninth and later centuries;[12] they seem to have enjoyed a great and unique popularity during the Dark Ages, and indeed right down to the twelfth century. Though differing considerably in age, they are much alike in style. A more or less fixed tradition for their illustration had evidently been early set up, probably in classical· times; and since there are few more absolute despots than an established iconography, this tradition was never disobeyed.

By far the best of these manuscripts is No. 3868 in the Vatican Library. It is of the ninth century; and its finely painted miniatures have been said to make nearly all other illuminated copies of the Latin classics look squalid in comparison.[13] Of the remainder, perhaps the Paris MS. 7899, also ninth century, deserves the leading place. The Ambrosian MS. H. 75 inf., tenth century, is imperfect; it is copiously illustrated with rough but very expressive outline-drawings, tinted in blue and brown, of figures—the *dramatis personae* of the plays—sometimes with suggestions of a building, but with no attempt at background or illusion. Complete manuscripts usually have a portrait of Terence at the beginning, supported by two actors in comic masks. After this come the Comedies, with numerous sketches of the male and female performers gesticulating and pointing at one another in violent and apparently angry conversation. The men are nearly always masked; the ladies have streaming hair, and their attitudes and expressions are full of excitement. At the beginning of each play is a sketch of the faces of the characters, arranged in tiers, often looking out from the front of a theatre, but sometimes simply enclosed in a rectangular frame.

With the Terence codices our meagre supply of classical manuscripts comes to an end. There is an Iliad[14] in St. Mark's Library at Venice, of the tenth or eleventh century, but its few marginal drawings and full-page pictures are aesthetically negligible. The same may be said of the drawings of constellations which occur in manuscripts of Cicero's Aratea. An Aeneid was illuminated in 1198 by the monk Giovanni Alighieri, in gold and colours, and was preserved down to 1782 in the Carmelites' library at Ferrara;[15] but this was probably an isolated exception. The medieval Church, mother of the medieval arts, turned the art of the miniaturist to more pious uses than the illustration of pagan texts. Not until the fourteenth century was far advanced does the supply of illuminated classics recommence. Then, and still more in the following century, when the Renaissance had brought Greek and Latin literature into fashion again, we get a superb series of illustrated codices by Italian and French artists; but these, being classical only in subject, will be best treated along with other works of their school and date.

NOTES

1 Cod. Vat. lat. 3867.
2 Published by J. Strzygowski, *Die Calenderbilder des Chronographen vom Jahre* 354, Berlin, 1888 (Jahrbuch des k. deutschen archäol. Instituts, Ergänzungsheft i.).
3 The danger is well exemplified by a thirteenth century copy (Paris, Bibl. Nat., nouv. acq. lat. 1359) of an eleventh century chronicle of the abbey of S. Martin des Champs (Brit. Mus., Add. 11662). The miniatures in the copy correspond exactly with the drawings in the original as to subject and position in the text; but there the resemblance ceases. The later illustrator, with the sound instincts which characterized his time, made no pretence of imitating the crude designs of his predecessor. See M. Prou in the *Revue de l'art chrétien*, 1890, pp.122-8. On the other hand, some of the drawings in Harl. 603 (eleventh century), are almost exact reproductions of those in the ninth century Utrecht Psalter.
4 Cod. Vat. lat. 3225, sometimes called "Schedae Vaticanae," but more generally known as "the Vatican Virgil"; the larger and artistically inferior Virgil, Cod. Vat. lat. 3867, being styled "Codex Romanus."
5 In *Notices et Extraits*, xxxv, pt. ii, 1897, pp. 683-791.
6 *Fragmenta et Picturae Vergiliana Codicis Vaticani* 3225, Rome, 1899 (vol. i. of *Codices e Vaticanis selecti phototypice expressi*).
7 *Storia dell' Arte Italiana*, i., 1901, pp. 312-26.
8 *Homeri Iliadis pictae fragmenta Ambrosiana phototypice edita*, with preface by A. M. Ceriani, Milan, 1905. See too *Pal. Soc.*, i. 39, 40, 50, 51. The engravings published by Mai in 1819 and 1835 are not exact enough to be satisfactory for study, but his descriptions (which Ceriani reprints) are invaluable.
9 *Picturae . . . Cod. Vat.* 3867, Rome, 1902 (vol. ii. of *Codices e Vaticanis selecti phototypice expressi*).
10 Series i, pl. 113-14, and introd. p. vii.
11 *Mon. et Mém.*, iv, 1897, p. xx, pp. 233-44.
12 *Terentius. Cod. Ambros. H. 75 inf. phototypice editus*, ed. Bethe, Leyden 1903 (vol. viii of De Vries, *Codices Graeci et Latini*); with ninety-one reproductions from other Terence MSS. and printed books.
13 *Ibid.*, col. 10.
14 *Homeri Ilias cum scholiis Cod. Ven. A. Marcianus* 454, ed. D. Comparetti, Leyden, 1901 (De Vries, *Codd. Gr. et Lat.*, vol. vi).
15 See Brit Mus., Add. MS. 22347, ff. 69, 73b: J. W. Bradley, *Dict. of Miniaturists*, i, 1887, p. 22.

John W. Bradley

Greek and Roman Illumination

The earliest recorded miniature painter was a lady named Lala of Cyzicus in the days of Augustus Caesar, days when Cyzicus was to Rome what Brussels is to Paris, or Brighton to London. All her work, as far as we know, has perished. It was portraiture on ivory, probably much the same as we see in the miniature portraiture of the present day.

But this was not illumination. The kind of painting employed in the two Vatican Vergils was, however, something approaching it. These two precious volumes contain relics of Pagan art, but it is the very art which was the basis and prototype of so-called Christian art of those earliest examples found in the catacombs and in the first liturgical books of Christian times.

The more ancient of the two Vergils referred to, No. 3225, which Labarte (2nd ed., ii. 158) thinks to be a century older than the other, Sir M. D. Wyatt considered as containing "some of the best and most interesting specimens of ancient painting which have come down to us. The design is free and the colours applied with good effect, the whole presenting classical art in the period of decline, but before its final debasement." Whereas in the second MS., No. 3867, the style, though still classical, is greatly debased, and probably, in addition to this, by no means among the best work of its time. It is described as rough, inaccurate, and harsh. The method is of the kind called *gouache, i.e.* the colours are applied thickly in successive couches or layers, probably by means of white of egg diluted with fig-tree sap, and finished in the high lights with touches of gold (Palaeograph. Soc., pl. 114, 117). This finishing with touches of gold brings the work within the range of illumination. There is, indeed,

SOURCE: Reprinted from John W. Bradley, *Illuminated Manuscripts* (Chicago: A. C. McClurg and Company, 1909), Chapter IV, "Greek and Roman Illumination," pp. 19-23.

wanting the additional ornamentation of the initial letter which would bring it fully into the class of mediaeval work; but, such as it is, it may fairly claim to be suggestive of the future art. Indeed, certain points in the MS. 3225—viz. that Zeus is always red and Venus fair, that certain costumes and colours of drapery are specially appropriated—would lead to the supposition that even then there existed a code of rules like those of the Byzantine Guide, and that therefore the art owed its origin to the Greeks.

Between this MS. and the first known Christian book work there may have been many that have now perished, and which, had they remained, would have marked the transition more gradually. But even as they stand there is no appreciable difference between the earliest monuments of Christian art and those of the period which preceded them. Nor shall we find any break, any distinct start on new principles. It is one continuous series of processes—the gradual change of methods growing out of experience alone—not owing to any change of religion or the adoption of a new set of theological opinions. Of course we shall find that for a very long time the preponderance of illuminated MSS. will be towards liturgical works; and we shall also find that where the contents of the MS. are the same the subjects taken for illustration are also selected according to some fixed and well-known set of rules.

The first example of a Christian illuminated MS. is one containing portions of the Book of Genesis in Greek preserved in the Imperial Library at Vienna. It is a mere fragment, only twenty-six leaves of purple vellum—that is, bearing the imperial stain—yet it contains eighty-eight pictures. We call them miniatures, but we must remember that by "miniator" a Roman bookseller would not understand what we call a miniaturist; and, as we have said, the word "illuminator" was not then known.

This Vienna Genesis is not introduced among illuminated books, therefore, because of its miniatures—pictures we prefer to call them—but because the text is nearly all written in *gold* and *silver* letters. The pictures, according to the Greek manner, are placed in little square frames. They were executed, no doubt, by a professional painter, not without technical skill and not hampered by monastic restrictions. The symbolism which underlies all early art is here shown in the allegorical figures which are introduced to interpret the scene. We see the same thing in the catacombs. Being a relic of great importance, this Genesis codex has been often described and examples given of its pictures. Of course, in a little manual like the present we cannot pretend to exhibit the literature of our subject. We can scarcely do more than refer the reader to a single source. In this case perhaps we cannot do better than send the inquirer to the Victoria and Albert Museum at South Kensington.

If we select another MS. of this early period it is the one which may be said to be the oldest existing MS. in which the ornamentation is worthy of as much notice as the pictures. We refer to the Collection of Treatises by Greek physicians on plants, fishing, the chase, and kindred matters in the same library as the Genesis fragment. It goes under the name of "Dioscorides," who was one of the authors, and dates from the beginning of the *sixth* century. The Genesis is a century older. Engravings from the Dioscorides are given in Labarte's *Arts industriels*, etc., pl. 78, and in Louandre's *Arts somptuaires*, etc., i., pl. 2, 3.

Enough has been said on these earlier centuries to show quite clearly the character of the art known as Early Christian. It is simply a continuation of such art as had existed from classical times, and had, in fact, passed from the Greeks, who were artists, to the Romans, who were rarely better than imitators. It is carried on to the period when it again is nourished by Greek ideas in the Later Empire, and once more attains distinction in the splendid revival of art under the Emperor Justinian.

Note

Julius Capitolinus, in his Life of the exquisite Emperor Maximin, junior, mentions that the emperor's mother[1] made him a present of a copy of the poems of Homer, written in golden letters on purple[2] vellum. This is the earliest recorded instance of such a book in Christian times. Its date would be about 235 A.D.

[1]   Quaedam parens sua.
[2]   Purpureos libros.

David Diringer

"Introduction"
The Illuminated Book:
Its History and Production

ILLUMINATION

Medieval Illuminators (or 'Miniators')

The Medieval mind delighted in the ornate and colourful; to this the books of the period bear ample witness. Besides the mere copyists of manuscripts, there were in the Middle Ages artists—monks and others—called in Latin *illuminatores*, or 'illuminators', whose profession was to embellish or ornament manuscripts by painting and drawing. Illumination, of course, added much charm. No wonder that this art—expressing itself in coloured illustrations, known as 'miniatures', decorated lettering, and ornamentation in gold (or, rarely, in silver) and brilliant colours—was much practised in the Middle Ages.

While the coloured illustrations and the designs were based largely on the art of the painter, the embellishment of the initials and of the lettering in general was based mainly on the art of the penman, the scribe, or the calligrapher. However, illumination of manuscripts as a form of art cannot be said to be an exclusive and direct development of the art of writing. Indeed if we disregard illustrations of the text, which cannot be considered true illumination, until the early Middle Ages the

SOURCE: Reprinted from David Diringer, *The Illuminated Book: Its History and Production*, Revised edition, (New York: Frederick A. Praeger, Inc., c1967), "Introduction," pp. 21-26, by permission of the publisher and Faber and Faber Ltd. Copyright © 1967 by David Diringer.

written pages were simple and unadorned. In the earliest Middle Ages, even when parchment was dyed purple and the writing was in gold and silver, it was still unadorned. In the course of time, however, there appeared enlarged initial letters and calligraphic ornaments. Still later we see whole title-pages, and especially the *Canon-tables* of the Gospels, richly ornamented.

As mentioned in *The Hand-produced Book*, it was for the illuminators to do their part when the copyists had finished, and we frequently find in manuscripts blanks left for the illuminators which were never filled in.

What is Book-illumination?

Book-illumination, or illumination of manuscripts, or simply, book-painting, is the art of embellishing vellum-manuscript books by painted pictures and/or ornamented letters and geometric designs, in gold and colours, particularly on the borders of the pages. It is a medieval art *par excellence*, and even the term 'illuminated manuscript' seems to be a medieval one meaning a manuscript which is 'lighted up' with coloured decoration.

The English terms 'to illuminate' and 'illuminators' (from the Latin and Italian verb *illuminare*, 'to throw light upon', 'light up', 'brighten') have replaced the old forms—used as far back as the thirteenth century—'to enlumine', also *enlumyne* or *enlomyne*, and *enlumineurs*, derived from Old French *enluminer* and Late Latin *inlūmināre*.

The word 'miniatures' is commonly used for the individual pictures of the illuminated codices, but it would not be exact to consider 'miniature painting' as a synonym for 'illumination'. Miniatures may be executed without the use of gold or silver while illuminations may not. Although there are illuminated miniatures—*i.e.*, pictures finished with touches of gold to represent the lights—many miniatures are not 'illuminations'.

According to some scholars, the words *miniature*—from the Latin *minium*, or red paint (red ochre or red lead), and *miniare*, 'to colour with *minium*'—and *vermilion*, are of the same root; among the Romans, incidentally, bright red was the chief colour of 'illuminated' letters, the pigments used being either sulphide or mercury (or 'vermilion') or, particularly, a lead oxide (now called 'red lead'). 'Miniare' was originally applied to a picture in an 'illuminated' manuscript, but later to the highly specialized art of painting manuscripts. It is only of late years that the word 'miniature' has been used in the restricted sense as applied to a small portrait. This usage of the term is due to its accidental confusion by the French writers with the French word *mignon* and the Latin *minus*.

The term 'miniator' used as a synonym for 'illuminator' is not exact. The Romans used this word for penmen, who applied the *minium* (to mark the initial letters, or titles of sections of the MS., or rubrics), but it was never used for painters of MS. illustrations or portraits.

The art of illuminating begins—as the American leading authority, C. R. Morey, writes—with the end of antiquity, rising, so to speak, from the very ruins of antique culture, and dies with the development of printing, which may be considered the definitive symptom of the modern age. The greatest Italian poet, Dante Alighieri (1265-1321), in the eleventh canto of the *Purgatorio* (verses 80-81), speaks of the perfection of illumination as

> *quell' arte*
> *Ch' alluminar chiamata è in Parisi*
> ('the art which in Paris is called illuminating').

Jean, Sire de Joinville (c. 1224-1317), in his *Histoire de Saint Louis*, likens the deeds of Louis IX to a scribe *qui a fait son livre l'enlumine d'or et d'azur.* Chaucer (c. 1340-1400) writes *Kalendeeres enlumyned ben they.*

Illumination reached its highest degree of perfection in the fourteenth and fifteenth centuries. It survived the introduction of printing by over a century and was especially applied to devotional books intended for use by semi-literate people.

As a class—writes Canon F. Harrison—they are usually spoken of as 'illuminated manuscripts' because, owing to their lovely colours of gold (in the form of gold-leaf) and silver, and all the colours of the rainbow, their ornamentation and their small pictures illuminate or 'light up' the grey of the parchment and the black of the ink. And F. Madan wrote: Even the red rubrics, the plain alternate blue and red letters common in headlines in the fourteenth century, relieve the eye; but when the capital letters are floriated, when the margins are filled with leaf-and-branch work, and when every few pages exhibit a delicately painted miniature, some scene from the artist's own experience—a market-place, it may be. . . or some banquet at the court of Burgundy in the fifteenth century, . . . or, again, a religious scene rivalling in effect and minuteness of detail the greater pictures of Italian artists—then, indeed, we feel that the accessories have invested the written page with a beauty and attractiveness beyond the powers of a scribe alone.

'Book-illustration' and 'Book-illumination'

Illumination in the full sense of the word—as just mentioned—originated in the early Middle Ages, perhaps in the sixth century A.D. If, however, we take the aims of illumination to be beautifying books and gratifying those who take pleasure in beautiful books, the art would appear to have evolved from the ancient methods of illustrating books, one of the most conservative fields in all the fine arts. Indeed, the desire that books should be made attractive is of great antiquity; we can trace its progress as far back as the twentieth century B.C., when the Egyptians were decorating their funeral rolls in the most gorgeous colours.

The methods of making books attractive are, of course, numerous and varied. Illumination is but one, though a particularly important one. While it may not always be easy to preserve a clear distinction between 'illumination' and 'illustration', one would be safe in assuming that the latter is but a part of the former, which would include the use of gold and/or silver, rich colouring, decorative lettering, and any forms of ornamentation which have no connection whatever with the contents of the text. Mere pictures or ornamental letters elegantly drawn in attractive colours do not constitute illumination (though, as said, they do form an essential part in its composition)—the page of an illuminated book has to be 'lighted up' with bright colours and burnished gold or silver foil. *Perfect illumination*—writes John W. Bradley—*must contain both colours and metals.*

On the other hand, manuscript paintings and outline-drawings are so intimately connected that the early history of book-illustration can hardly be excluded from a history of book-illumination. The main purpose of 'illumination'—as distinct from 'illustration'—is, however, 'the desire to beautify the object of devotion rather than to clarify its contents' (C. R. Morey).

Illustrated book-production of pre-Columbian America—as well as, generally speaking, of the ancient Far East—has been treated, though very briefly, in *The Hand-produced Book*.

To sum up, while the art of 'illustration' was practised early in Egypt, the other aspects of illumination, including pure decoration and ornamentation of the initials and of the script in general, would seem to have begun only in the Middle Ages.

Elements which Influenced Book-illumination

The traditions of Egyptian art—and particularly of Hellenistic art, which was centered mainly in Alexandria and some cities of Asia Minor—had a great influence on the origin and development of illumination in Eastern Christianity, where, naturally, local elements played an important part in its formation.

Medieval art, it is to be remembered, was mainly Christian. Its main purpose, indeed, was to decorate the churches, great and small, which were then being built in great numbers in towns, castles and monasteries. If art may be said to be the materialized expression of man's delight in beauty, medieval art was mainly the expression of religious aspirations in terms of beauty. Indeed, it is a characteristic tendency of the medieval mind to express its faith in emotional form, to sing a hymn rather than to recite a creed. This is true of sculpture, and even more of painting in all its main aspects—frescoes, panel-paintings, mosaics, and illumination of manuscripts.

Iconography, or representation of sacred images, was a main feature of the medieval art of painting, and, at least until the thirteenth century, the individual form of expression used by the artist played very little part in comparison with conventional forms, which were nearly always symbolic. Though generally very primitive from the artistic point of view, the conventional style, by making the products appear more solemn and their contents more sure, emphasized their symbolic and religious meanings. This style is particularly evident in Byzantine, Eastern Christian, and perceptible in all the illumination produced before the period of the thirteenth-fourteenth centuries. Hiberno-Saxon elements, Carolingian art, the renaissance of Classical traditions, Persian, and other influences, contributed to the transformation of the 'primitive' style into the superb art of Renaissance illumination, which, however, may be considered a branch of pure art rather than of book-production.

In conclusion, between the artistic man in ancient Egypt and his brother in the modern West there exists—in this field—one long chain of more or less successful achievements in the direction of mutual understanding. We shall travel through ages and across a great part of the globe, and we shall see how various peoples in the far past or in times nearer to us, in the East—the Near East, the Middle East, and the Far East—and in the West, have played important parts in the development of this branch of human craving for beauty. Indeed, the illuminated book reflects the channels through which the art of painting of ancient Egypt, of the Graeco-Roman world, of the ancient peoples of Asia, and of the medieval peoples of Europe developed into the modern art of the Renaissance. But it also reflects the channels through which ancient thought and learning, literary cravings and scientific achievements, the ancient Egyptian longing to placate the gods of the Underworld, and particularly the medieval monk's desire to please God, the medieval romantic troubadour's aim to please a lady, and the Renaissance artist's endeavour to please the bibliophiles, combined to create masterpieces which are a delight even to us of the atomic age.

Book-painting compared with Panel-painting

On the surface book-painting and panel-painting appear to be closely connected. It might therefore seem reasonable to suppose that the great masters in the one field should have been great masters in the other field as well. As a matter of fact, relatively few artists practised both arts, and great masters who excelled in both book-painting and panel-painting were very few. We shall understand the reason for this if we realize that the miniature has an essential character of its own, that it is not a panel-painting on a reduced scale.

Up to a point the development of the two arts ran parallel—the most perfect kinship is apparent during the Gothic period. Gothic art—minute, refined, delicate—was specially suited to the limitations under which the illuminator worked, and it produced the most perfect realization of the aims and ideal proper to his art. But as soon as the aesthetic equilibrium of Gothic illumination broke down, book-painting, to use Dr. Paecht's words, no longer belonged to the leading arts, notwithstanding the production of masterpieces such as the *Most Rich Hours* or the *Sforza Hours*.

Writing of Flanders, which in the fifteenth century was the leading centre in book-illumination, Paecht has pointed out that with the formation in the fifteenth century of the naturalistic art in painting, book-painting soon found itself in an inferior position. The new artistic creed—he writes—demanded that pictorial conception should be based exclusively on the subjective experience of the human eye and the picture plane be treated as imaginary space. To the self-contained picture—continues Paecht—the addition of spatial depth brought a higher degree of compositional unity. For the picture as an element of book-decoration, however, the conquest of the third dimension was a dubious gain. With the transformation of a section or the whole of a book-page into imaginary space a heavy strain was put on the artistic organization of the illuminated book. Paecht concludes thus: There was now the script, inviting the reader's eye to a movement over and along the flat expanse of the page. Then the picture suggesting to the spectator a recession of depth behind the surface of the page and finally a border decoration whose function seemed to be that of reconciling the conflicting claims of reader and spectator.

The essential difference between book-painting and panel-painting is immediately evident. Panel-paintings are displayed, and can be visited simultaneously by a considerable number of people. Books, on the other hand, lend themselves but poorly to public exhibition: they would deteriorate rapidly under the appreciative but uninformed turning of the pages by the crowd. In general, illuminations are contained in volumes belonging to private or public collections, and are available to a few qualified readers, who study and consult them individually. Indeed, the mission of the book is a personal one: it addresses the reader privately and as his mood dictates; this is the great charm, the great power of the book; it has ever been so, since the most ancient times. When—in exceptional cases only—illuminated books are exhibited to the general public, they are in glass cases and only one or two pages are shown. Book-paintings are evidently far more delicate and fragile than panel-paintings, so the non-qualified visitor must *imagine* the endless majestically superb or graciously whimsical diversity of the illuminated pages which are not exhibited, and the soft touch of the velvety smooth vellum of the whole codex.

Finally, panel-paintings should preferably be studied from a certain distance, while miniatures have to be examined at a very close range. Similarly, in medieval times panel-painting was for the congregations of people, while book-painting was for the few rich devout who loved books and could afford them.

At the same time, it should be borne in mind that illuminated books sometimes contain pictures which are independent paintings rather than miniatures. The easy interchange between the separate paintings and the book-paintings is particularly evident in the last stage of the flourishing Flemish school of illumination, *i.e.* in the early sixteenth century. Indeed, there was then an increasing tendency to introduce into the pages of books what are essentially independent paintings—without connection with the text of the book. Some 'miniatures', which belong to illuminated books, were originally intended not as book illustrations but as independent pictures to be mounted in a frame. In the strict sense of the term, these pictures—which have often been cut out and preserved as individual paintings—are not 'miniatures'. An excellent example of such work is a very fine Annunciation (measuring 6⅞ by 5½ in.), preserved in the Robert Lehman Collection, New York City.

David Bland

Medieval Illumination in the West

By the seventh century the Church, which had been the first to exploit the invention of the codex, had almost a monopoly of book production, and until the middle of the thirteenth century books were nearly all written in the religious houses. Whether they were always decorated there is a different matter and although it seems probable that, to begin with, they were, it is known for certain that later they were sent away for illumination, or it was done by visiting freelance artists. In these early days it was Gospel Books that were most frequently decorated but later we find secular books competing with sacred. In fact there was no competition, because our distinction between sacred and profane was not valid then. The use of classical models or styles, which often seems such a strange feature of Biblical illumination, simply means that for those fortunate beings everything in heaven and earth was a single order. As Swarzenski says: 'However great the importance of the book as the chief vehicle and agent of literary, artistic and iconographical traditions may have been for the Middle Ages, its evaluation and its unique position lie in its consecrated character. It elucidates the Christian myth that Christ is represented with a book in His hands; no other religion has given any of its gods this attribute.'

With this belief it is not surprising that they saw nothing incongruous in putting all their skill and lavishness into the decoration of sacred texts; anything less must have seemed wrong. The magnificent books of the Northumbrian School were far different in this respect from the fifteenth-century *Books of Hours*. The former were made for

SOURCE: Reprinted from David Bland, A *History of Book Illustration*, Second revised edition (Berkeley and Los Angeles: University of California Press, 1969), Chapter II, "Medieval Illumination in the West," pp. 40-83, by permission of the publisher and Faber and Faber, Ltd. Copyright © 1958, 1969 by David Bland.

the service of God and their aesthetic appeal was incidental; the latter were made for the eye of some princely patron to whom the text must have been merely an excuse for the pictures.[1] For the Middle Ages the word was of far greater importance than the picture, and this attitude persists after the introduction of printing. Even though the miniature had by then emancipated itself and the book painting was almost independent of the text yet the printed illustration, in the block books for instance, is only there, one feels, to attract the illiterate.

The technical processes of illumination lasted with very little alteration from classical times down to the time of the Carolingian Renaissance. After the tenth century we notice the same fault which was apparent in the Vienna *Genesis* and indeed in the Egyptian *Book of the Dead*; the more beautiful the illumination the less accurate the text. In other words the scribes were becoming mere copyists while the illuminators were becoming painters. Middleton quotes a few amusing comments written at the ends of later manuscripts by the scribes which reflect not only the tediousness of the task but also the loss of a sense of divine duty; e.g. 'Scribere qui nescit, nullam putat esse laborem' (He who knows not how to write thinks it no labour) or 'Vinum scriptori reddatur de meliori' (Let wine of the best be given to the writer) or—significantly from a French monk—'Detur pro pena sciptori pulchra puella.'

At the beginning of our period there was the chaos and unsettlement that came in the train of the barbarian invasions of the Graeco-Roman Empire. Books could always be written and read in the most troublous times but the decoration of books was one of the first luxuries to be dispensed with when times were unpropitious. In the same way the copying of books was a mechanical task that did not require much skill or even a high degree of literacy. But the copying of illustrations was a very different matter and so an illustrated book when copied often became an unillustrated one. Fortunately, however, there remained a corner of the Western world to which neither Roman nor barbarian invaders had penetrated; and it was in Ireland that the illuminated book revived when everywhere else except in Northumbria it was at its worst. And from here it went with the Irish missionaries to Scotland and Northern England, to France and to Switzerland.

After St. Patrick's mission in the fifth century Irish missionaries went to Iona and from there evangelized Scotland, but when they reached Northern England they found in Northumbria religious communities newly established by missionaries from Europe. The clash of ideas and styles seems to have been amazingly fruitful, and it was from Northumbria that the greatest books of the seventh century came. The missionaries from Europe had brought with them Italian books illustrated with miniatures in the classical style. But it was some time before the naturalism of this art had effect. The native genius, whether Irish or Northumbrian, was for pattern. And in the *Book of Durrow* (c. 670) which is one of the earliest books to survive from this period there are, for one solitary human figure, and that not very convincing, many whole pages of pure pattern—a thing unheard of in the south where ornament was only used to mark the beginning and end of a chapter or to frame a miniature.

This type of pattern is sometimes called Irish and the *Book of Durrow* itself was for long thought to have been written in Ireland. It is now believed to have come from England though probably written and decorated by Irishmen. The discovery of Anglo-Saxon treasure at Sutton Hoo in 1938 not only revealed the excellence of seventh-century Anglo-Saxon jewellery design, it also provided many striking points of similarity between that design and the decoration of the *Book of Durrow*. In England as well as Ireland the goldsmiths worked side by side with the illuminators in the same monastery and sometimes indeed both arts were practised by the same monk, who thus became the decorator of the inside and the outside of the book. This reminds us of the unity of the arts in those days. There was none of our modern division into major and minor arts, and the metal-worker was as highly esteemed as the painter. And while many of their stock designs were undoubtedly Irish in origin, many of them also had a classical ancestry. It has been pointed out that several of the spiral patterns found in Irish manuscripts are almost identical with forms in gold ornaments of the Greek Mycenean period 'showing the remarkable sameness of invention in the human mind at a certain stage of development, whatever the time or place may be.' Oriental influences also are seen in some patterns, no doubt derived from Eastern carpets and textiles which were now being imported for ecclesiastical use. Françoise Henry has drawn attention to similarities between the ornament in the *Book of Durrow* and Coptic and Syrian illumination; and she thinks that the Irish monks may have had Oriental models before them. But they never followed the rigid symmetry of the Moslem pattern-makers.

The original Celtic contribution was not so much the patterns themselves as the use of those patterns, particularly in the decoration of the initial. The importance of the initial in Western illumination can be traced back to sixth-century Italy; and in some of these early manuscripts it often dominates the whole page. Occasionally it is subservient to the miniature when the latter is placed above it, but more often the initial has pride of place at the top of the page; and it retained its importance for about 600 years after which it dwindled in size; but even then its tail or its branches often formed a border to envelop the text.

St. Aidan came from Iona and founded the Abbey of Lindisfarne in 635 and for the next hundred years Northumbria was pre-eminent in the art of book illustration as it was to be again more than a thousand years later in Bewick's lifetime. The clash of Irish and classical influences was echoed in the rivalry between the Celtic and Roman churches which was resolved at the Synod of Whitby (664) in favour of Rome. Thereafter, although Irish script continued to be used, classicism increased, helped by the many illuminated manuscripts and paintings that monks like Benedict Biscop brought with them from Rome. The *Lindisfarne Gospels* is the monument of this period and fortunately this great book has come down to us in wonderful condition in spite of falling into the sea during an invasion by Vikings. It dates from about 710 and was written in a fine black ink, much superior to the brownish ink used in contemporary Continental manuscripts. We have the names of the three monks who produced it, Eadfrith the scribe and illuminator,[2] Aethelwold and Bilfrith the binders. It is with the work of Eadfrith that we are here concerned and the most striking thing about it is the combination of the Byzantine figures of the evangelists with the wonderful pages of Celtic ornament. Irish illuminators seemed to be incapable of drawing the human figure and even in the later *Book of Kells* it is subordinated to pattern as if it was metal-work, and is almost unrecognizable. In the *Lindisfarne Gospels* classical and Byzantine influences are so strong that the book has been called one of the earliest links between Oriental and Occidental art. The use here of gold which is never found in contemporary Irish books must also have been revolutionary.

The *Book of Kells* is now generally agreed to have been written towards the end of the eighth century and there is little doubt that it originated in Ireland. It is remarkable for the intricacy of its decoration which must be seen to be believed. Westwood calculated 158 interlacements in the space of a square inch and pointed out that all can be followed, none breaking off or leading to an impossible knot. The general effect of all this ingenuity however is often far from beautiful. The shapes of the letters are hopelessly obscured and some of the colour combinations are frankly hideous. It seems likely that several artists worked on the book, some good and some bad. There is nothing of the frozen perfection of Lindisfarne here but instead an immense vigour, and a demonstration of the somewhat perverse Irish delight in complication for its own sake which we find also for instance in the work of James Joyce. It is significant, too, that the text is far less perfect than in the *Lindisfarne Gospels*. The book represents the peak of Irish achievement however and none of the later manuscripts can come near it. Most of these later books, the ninth-century *Gospels of MacDurnan* for instance, were not intended to compete with the large altar books and were smaller and more portable. In them illustration naturally played a smaller part.

Meanwhile, Bede whose learning had shed so much lustre on Northumbria had died and his mantle fell on Alcuin who lived in York. But learning was not confined to the north of England, although the greatest illuminated books were produced there at this time. It was a West Saxon, Boniface, who became Archbishop of Mainz and founded the Abbey of Fulda which became the centre of German learning. Already St. Gall in Switzerland and Luxeuil in Burgundy, founded by Irish missionaries, had produced many manuscripts of the Irish type, and these three monasteries had a great deal to do with the Carolingian Renaissance. In 768 Charlemagne was elected King of the Franks and soon after he summoned Alcuin from England to supervise the revision of church books. Perhaps too Alcuin was behind the reformation of handwriting which Charlemagne instituted after he had become Emperor of the West in 800. So it will be seen how great was Britain's part in this Renaissance.

Under the Merovingian Dynasty which preceded the Carolingian, Frankish and Lombardic illumination was decorative rather than illustrative, and what remains, e.g. the *Orosius* at Laon, is not very impressive in quality. Initials are fantastic, colouring is crude and the human figure is seldom attempted. The eighth-century *Sacramentary of Gellone* from the south of France has however a certain barbaric splendour. And we find the products of this native school continuing side by side with the more ambitious Carolingian works. Against this background Charlemagne set out deliberately to revive the spirit of the Roman Empire, the result being that most Carolingian illumination is imitative. The Ada school owed most to the late Latin style, the Franco-Saxon to Ireland and that of Tours went back to an earlier classical period than Ada. Only the later Rheims contribution was wholly original.

To begin with, however, the effect of the Carolingian Renaissance on illustration was utilitarian. It sought to teach, to clarify a text, and it naturally looked to the south, the home of illustration, rather than to the north, the home of decoration. As time goes on Carolingian books became increasingly elaborate and there are Byzantine touches in the gold lettering and purple vellum of such manuscripts as the *Evangeliarum of Charlemagne* which was written (*c.* 781) for the Emperor by a monk called Godescalc, and the *Ada Gospel Book* of about the same date with its elaborate purple-stained pages, produced for Charlemagne's sister. The *Harley Golden Gospels* in the British Museum (*c.* 800) which is all inscribed in gold, provides a very early example of an ornamental title-page. Gospel Books were still the commonest type of manuscript just as they were in Byzantium but the Evangelists are now shown as youthful idealized types instead of the old men of Byzantine manuscripts. The general treatment of figures is flat (though there are occasional attempts at modelling) and the outlines seem to have been drawn first in red paint. Then the spaces were filled in with washes of colour mixed with a medium which gave a very glossy surface. Drapery was represented by lines drawn on top of the wash. And in some manuscripts a very splendid effect was achieved by the use of silver to contrast with gold.

Side by side with these rigid conventional portraits which owe so much to Byzantine art, there are also occasional miniatures which lean more to the Roman style in their illustrative tendencies. Although in the best manuscripts like the *Aachen Gospels* the figure drawing is light and brilliant, in most it is still clumsy; but generally the backgrounds make some attempt at naturalism. 'The old contrast between Greek realistic and Latin abstract art, between art aiming at a sympathetic representation of the outside world and art based on purely conceptual design presents itself in a new form as a contrast between the exuberant expression of human emotion and the purely impersonal ornamental display,' says Kitzinger. Towards the end of the Carolingian period we find a mixture rather than a synthesis of the two.

Carolingian illumination reached its highest point in the ninth century during the reigns of Lothair and Charles the Bald. Decoration still surpasses figure drawing (the old Irish patterned figures are still to be found) but subjects for miniatures are becoming more varied. Now besides portraits of the Evangelists we find frontispieces showing Kings; there is for instance a Metz Gospel Book in Paris with a portrait of King Lothair. The Benedictine monasteries at Paris, St. Denis, Rheims, Tours and Metz are the chief centres of book production during this period.

Ascribed to the School of Tours during this century are the two earliest complete illustrated Bibles to have survived, the *Grandval* and *Vivian* Bibles. Weitzmann thinks that the miniatures are made up of several cycles, since it is unlikely that so large a book as the Bible could have had a comprehensively illustrated archetype. But there were cycles for each book—even for the Prophets—though none of these have survived. The effort of combining these different cycles, many of them in different styles, must have been considerable and it had its inevitable effect on the final result. But a book like the *Great Bible of Corbie* (*c.* 880) shows that a wonderfully rich effect could still be obtained in spite of varying styles.

These manuscripts, especially the *Vivian Bible*, show the disintegration of the cyclic system and the breaking up of the traditional interconnections between pictures which derived from the frieze. Miniatures are now becoming separate compositions and the artists begin (some 700 years after the introduction of the codex) to have a feeling for the page.

Some time during this century appeared the style of drawing which is associated with Rheims and its famous *Utrecht Psalter*. It consists of outline drawing, sketchy and vigorous, and while it is totally unlike the usual Carolingian style, both styles are sometimes found together in the same manuscript. It is seen occasionally in classical manuscripts but its abrupt appearance now and sudden widespread popularity present one of the great mysteries of medieval art. With its unadorned impressionistic line, its fluttering draperies and its figures all in violent motion it must have produced on the contemporary eye an overpowering contrast to the static, highly coloured illumination of the time, the more so as it was applied to the same traditional subject matter.

Of the *Utrecht Psalter*, which is the masterpiece in this manner, Hanns Swarzenski says that its drawings rival those of Leonardo, Rembrandt and Van Gogh and thus have their place among the few genuinely original productions in the history of art. The fact that it was itself almost certainly a copy[3] of a previous manuscript does not alter this fact. The 180 drawings (there is one for every Psalm) are not themselves coloured, but coloured outlines and washes are often used in copies of this book. Frames are never put round the drawings and where they are implied they are often broken through as it were by the feverish activity of the figures. Later there is a tendency to elongate and stylize but at its best the work is wonderfully vigorous and expressive. This style, which embraced not only drawing but all the decorative arts as well, had enormous influence throughout the whole of Northwest Europe and it helped to form the Romanesque and Gothic styles. When the *Utrecht Psalter* came to England at the end of the tenth century it was copied three times in 200 years, and each copy was a new work of art. But before that its influence was seen in the *Bury St. Edmunds Psalter* (now in the Vatican Library), which dates from early in the eleventh century. Here most of the drawings are marginal and the style is suited to this sort of thumbnail sketch.

So far we have concentrated on book illustration in France and England because there the most far-reaching developments were taking place. But all this time beautiful manuscripts were being produced in Italy, Spain and Southern Germany. These, however, were still in the Late Antique tradition and what was happening in the north seems to have had curiously little effect on them. Of early Italian illumination little remains to enable us to judge its quality accurately. But we do know that Byzantine influence was very strong and with it is also found the Hiberno-Saxon type of decoration. This is not so strange when we remember that there were Irish foundations like Bobbio in Northern Italy; and some authorities believe that this style originated in Italy and migrated to Ireland and Northumbria. Books like the *Bobbio Psalter*, now at Munich, however, have an almost undiluted Byzantine flavour.

By the tenth century we find manuscripts in all countries with whole pages occupied by pairs of miniatures, placed one above the other. Sometimes, as in the St. Gall *Book of Maccabees*, two pages of pictures face each other and the illustration is thus separated even more completely from the text. This segregation, which we noticed very early on in the sixth-century *Rossano Gospel Book,* had the technical advantage that the scribe and the illustrator could work separately and this no doubt was often done, their sections being collated later. Short inscriptions were then added to the drawings to identify them and so the explanatory caption or legend grew up.

During the second half of the ninth century Alfred was reigning in Wessex and his capital was Winchester. The northern part of England had repeatedly been devastated by Danish invaders and, although Alfred was himself a scholar and encouraged book production by importing instructors from France, the art of illumination had suffered a setback and took some time to recover. It was given the vital impetus by the monastic reforms which were started on the Continent by Odo of Cluny and in England by St. Dunstan. In Winchester, St. Aethelwold (who probably brought the *Utrecht Psalter* to England) was associated with St. Dunstan in his reforms, and the *Benedictional of St. Aethelwold* (*c.* 970) is one of the great books of this school. It has 28 full-page miniatures, mostly scenes from the life of Christ and each framed with an elaborate border. The figure drawing in these shows a distinct advance on any previous English manuscript, but it owes little to the *Utrecht Psalter* except for a lightening of the rather heavy Carolingian style on which it is based.

Canute in the eleventh century did a great deal to encourage literature and art and for the latter purpose is said to have introduced large numbers of Roman manuscripts, presumably in the Byzantine style which was then so much favoured in Italy. But although due weight must be given to the Byzantine element in the Romanesque work of the following century, its influence in Britain as compared with the Italian and Ottonian Schools was curiously ephemeral, and by the thirteenth century that influence was quite thrown off. The *Pontifical of St. Dunstan* in Paris is a good example of early eleventh-century work, but it has no gold. Instead it has the drawings in coloured outline that were so characteristic of English illumination. Sometimes in manuscripts of this period we find the outlines filled in with colours, sometimes the outline is in brown ink shaded with colour. But it is essentially linear and it is in this type of drawing that English artists excelled. Another unfinished manuscript of this century in the Cottonian Collection gives us a valuable insight into the way the illuminators worked in stages on their books. This one contains some outline drawings tinted with colour; but most are painted with body colour in various stages and we can see the the colours of dresses were often applied without any previous outline. Afterwards the figures were drawn in outline and last of all the features were added.

The Norman Conquest, which had such a serious effect on our native literature, caused no break in the continuity of illumination. National boundaries as we know them meant so much less in those days and the only result was to bring the French and English styles closer together and to foster the Anglo-Norman school on both sides of the Channel. There were signs of the *rapprochement* before 1066 and it seems likely that the Conquest only hastened a natural process. Nevertheless it was the collapse of the Carolingian Empire that marked the end of a truly international manner and the beginning of national styles. English illumination, too, was so far ahead of French at this period that it gave more than it received in the exchange. Just before the Conquest the Harley version of the *Utrecht Psalter* had been made in coloured outline. Far from being a slavish copy it is a completely new work of art which in its rejection of all naturalistic illusion foreshadowed the Romanesque style. By the time the next copy was made in the middle of the twelfth century Romanesque had arrived and the drawings have become solid and stylized, 'the triumph,' as Clark calls it, 'of symbol over sensation.'

After the Carolingian period until almost the end of the tenth century there was a period of anarchy and disorder in France when few books were produced. Then, however, the revival of monasticism which had already had such a great effect in England spread from Cluny. *Beatus* manuscripts copied from a famous Spanish prototype are among the most important of this period; and Joan Evans has shown how great an effect they had on sculpture. She goes so far as to say, 'To the illuminated manuscripts nine-tenths of the sculptural innovations of the second half of the eleventh century can be directly traced.' It was in decorative initials rather than illustration proper that this period excelled and by the middle of the twelfth century even these had become monochrome in manuscripts, by the Cistercian Order of 1134.

Italian illumination, which had produced under Carolingian influences several fine books during the tenth century like the *Ambrosian Psalter,* was in eclipse during the eleventh century. Germany and Northern Italy were politically connected at this time so that it is not surprising to find echoes of Ottonian illumination in the manuscripts of Lombardy and Tuscany. In the Romanesque period the best work came from the great Benedictine monastery at Montecassino. Books like *The Life of St. Benedict* have, as one would expect, a strong Byzantine flavour. From Montecassino also came many fine examples of *Exultet* rolls on which was inscribed a liturgy illustrated with pictures. These latter were the opposite way up to the text so that they could be seen by the congregation while the priest read from the roll.

For the true inheritors of the Carolingian tradition we must look to Germany which now was also the centre of the Holy Roman Empire. Here in 962 Otto I became Emperor and was succeded by Otto II and Otto III who gave their name to the Ottonian revival of the arts. It was a period of political aggrandizement for the Empire too and by the twelfth century it was the dominant power in Europe. The Emperors ruled from Bamberg which became a cultural centre, attracting many Greek artists. And to Bamberg from Constantinople, where Byzantine art was now at its peak, came Otto II's wife, Theophano.

But Bamberg did not become one of the great centres of Ottonian book illumination until comparatively late. From the Benedictine Abbey of Reichenau came the best German manuscripts of the tenth and eleventh centuries and its influence spread as far as Trèves and Hildesheim,[4] where there were also famous schools. The Heidelberg *Sacramentary* was one of the most influential Reichenau books and its decorative work was copied *ad nauseam* during the following century. The *Egbert*

Pericope, which is a more interesting work because of its miniatures deriving from Roman models, is much less typical of the Ottonian taste for heavy, isolated figures. This was a decorative period with its strapwork initials, its bird and serpent patterns, its vine stems and foliage, all of them showing an astonishing persistence. Monumentality is achieved by strict symmetry in the use of ornament and by reducing background to a minimum. It is, as Jantzen says, an art of the significant gesture rather than of naturalistic representation; and this can be seen in the reproduction from the Bamberg *Apocalypse,* another Reichenau book.

By now the *Pericope* had appeared, the collection of Gospel texts arranged not in their original sequence but according to their place in the liturgy. This made the insertion of author portraits impracticable and it forced artists to look for new illustrations. Rather than invent they usually had recourse to the old cycles.

From Ratisbon early in the eleventh century came the *Uta Gospels* in which, as Herbert says, the Gothic miniature of 200 years later is clearly foreshadowed and in which the symbolism is heightened by mysticism. This was perhaps the beginning of the Romanesque revival which resulted from the impact of Byzantine on Ottonian art. It did not appear in England until the twelfth century; but the results are curiously similar in both countries—largeness, severity and dignity together with a subtle beauty of design which often eludes at the first glance. There is another connexion, too, in the traces of the Northumbrian style of decoration which are found in German work of this period; only now the patterns of interlaced foliage have taken on a distinctly Teutonic flavour. In Germany particularly there is a love of symbolism which is seen at its best in the famous *Hortus Deliciarum.* This was a sort of philosophical and religious compendium which the Abbess of Hohenburg wrote and illuminated for her nuns and which is a forerunner of later Emblem Books. But more typical of the Carolingian tradition are the big Bibles like the *Arnstein Bible* in the British Museum with its huge initials and bright rather florid colours. Although it was produced under Cluny restrictions it is nevertheless profusely decorated in a style that reflects contemporary architecture.

By now illuminated books were also being produced in the Netherlands. Later on Flemish illumination was to lead the world but at this time it followed in the wake of France, and it is often difficult to distinguish between German and Dutch or French and Flemish work. Enormous Bibles were also produced and the *Stavelot Bible,* which actually preceded the German ones we have just mentioned, shows the influence of the Rheims school as well as of Byzantium. By the beginning of the thirteenth century Flemish artists had begun to demonstrate their superiority to those of Holland and Germany, although they were still behind French and English illuminators; and long before the end of the century they were producing books like the minute *Maestricht Book of Hours* in the British Museum that could hardly be surpassed anywhere.

The Romanesque style which came to fruition in Germany, France and England during the twelfth century is generally supposed to have been the offspring of the Ottonian schools of the tenth century and the Rheims style, unpromising though such a marriage might seem to be. Byzantine influences were strong in the German books and this made for solemnity and rigidity in illumination, for upright poses rather than diagonals which have been common hitherto. But fortunately the Rheims manner was powerful too, especially in England, and while it lightened the Ottonian style its own extravagances were in turn curbed. The synthesis which resulted has a powerful beauty and impressiveness of its own, not so immediately attractive as the Gothic which followed, but not so prone either to descend to mere prettiness. Its severity, or what seems severity to us, had no spiritual counterpart, for this was an age of devotional fervour which produced hymns like *Jesu dulcis memoria*. 'It seems to be,' says Morey, 'the maturity of centuries of growth, and the universality of the Romanesque manner in its larger aspect shows how completely it met the needs of European thought and feeling in the centuries of the Crusades.'

Byzantium and the West shared one characteristic in the tenth century which helps to account for the monumentality to be found in Eastern and Western books and which flowered 200 years later in the Romanesque style. This potent thing was the increasing influence of the Church, helped forward in the West by the reform of the monasteries. 'The need for expressing and propagating transcendental truth,' says Kitzinger, 'turns the scales against the classical tradition in art which came so much into prominence during the Carolingian period.' With the rejection of classical models came a new Biblical iconography in the typological system which interpreted the scheme of Redemption by means of parallels from the Old and New Testaments. This applied not only to Biblical illustration but to other works which we should think of as secular. All of them, even the Bestiaries, were made to contribute to this central doctrine of the Church.

There is no abrupt break in style between the eleventh and twelfth centuries in any of the arts except perhaps in architecture. From now on large scale painting and sculpture came into their own and the influence of their monumentality is seen in the organization of the book. Even the text page now has a fixed plan and its initials become 'historiated' rather than decorated. In the historiated initial text is intimately combined with illustration and the fusion of text, illustration and decoration is complete.

The *Albani Psalter* from St. Albans is one of the very first manuscripts in which we find the real Romanesque manner, but the *Winchester Bible* (c. 1160) is the great English monument of the period; and it is indeed monumental in every sense of the word. Perhaps, as Oakeshott says, it attempts too much and makes illustrations of what should have been wall-paintings. Like so many of the great books of the Middle Ages it contains the work of several hands and as it was many years in the making it shows at least two widely differing styles; there is the dynamic style reminiscent of the *Utrecht Psalter* with hot colours and everything in violent motion; and there is the Byzantine style, classical and static in cooler colours, using drapery to outline the body.

In the *Winchester Bible* there are initials that stretch the whole length of the page, nearly twenty inches. These contain actual illustrations and they are called historiated initials to distinguish them from initials which are merely decorated. Sometimes the illustration is fitted into the initial without affecting its structure, sometimes it is planned (or distorted) into the shape of the letter itself. This type of initial appeared first in about the eighth century and it continued side by side with the more popular decorated initial right down to Victorian times, ·when it was relegated to children's books.

The twelfth century was a period of developing technique. Decoration which, as far as we know, had always been carried out by the illustrator or miniaturist now began to demand its own practitioners. But in spite of their accomplishment the work does not seem to have been done by such skilled artists as the miniatures. Towards the end of the century an even greater innovation was brought about by the discovery that gold could be put on vellum by means of gold leaf with far more brilliant effect than fluid gold could ever produce. The leaf was laid on top of a smooth hard pad or mordant which not only set it in relief but also allowed it to be burnished.

As the century wore on the Rheims element seems to lose ground in England, though it was to reappear later in the work of Matthew Paris. There is little of it in the *Lambeth Bible*, which was roughly contemporary with the *Winchester Bible*; and when at the very end of the century the *Utrecht Psalter* is copied at Canterbury for the third time it is quite transformed. And it is preceded by a series of Bible pictures grouped together in a style that was to become popular in the following century. But things were different on the other side of the Channel where the Gothic style was already on the way. As if conserving her energies for her most glorious period of illumination France produced fewer great books in this century than England or Germany. No doubt Cistercian discouragement of illumination in the twelfth century had something to do with it too, but inasmuch as this concentrated attention on the calligraphic decoration of initials it may have been beneficial rather than otherwise. However, in the middle of the twelfth century the Cistercians forbade even the decoration of initials, and illumination gradually passed into secular hands. Literature too became more secular and a few manuscripts survive with lightly scribbled instructions to the illuminator on the illustration of unfamiliar subjects for which tradition afforded him no guidance. An early thirteenth-century *Treatise on Surgery* by Roger of Parma shows a curious combination of the sacred and the profane. In it are several pages of small pictures, nine to the page, with backgrounds of alternating colours. The top row of each page shows scenes from the life of Christ while the lower two rows show surgical cases, delineated with an extraordinary degree of accuracy.

There has often been a remarkable coincidence between the architecture of buildings and the architecture of books; this is especially noticeable in the Middle Ages when all the arts were more closely interconnected than they are now and when architecture and illumination were both practised by ecclesiastics. Just as the solid heavy Romanesque buildings gave way to the lighter airier Gothic so the same thing happened in illumination. The whole scale suddenly decreases and books become smaller and more delicate. The first Gothic churches that were built in the Ile de France during the second half of the century were not, it is true, any smaller than Romanesque churches which came before them, but they were totally different. By the last decade the Gothic style in architecture had been perfected and pointed arches were already appearing in manuscript decoration. Text and initials, which were distinct in Romanesque design, both assume a certain spikiness which has a unifying effect. Nor was it long before the fashion affected clothes for we find in these same miniatures the tall headgear of the women and the long pointed shoes of the men together with a general elongation of the human figure and an insistence on parallel verticals that is the artist's own contribution to the pattern. It is still a pattern rather than a picture, flat and two-dimensional like the stained glass of the time which it often closely resembles.

The leadership which France now begins to assume in the art of illumination and which was unquestionably hers by the end of the thirteenth century is one of the most striking things in the history of art. From France too came the idea of romantic love which appeared at the same time as the Gothic and which was to have a greater effect on literature, and so indirectly on its illustration. The magnificent *L'Histoire du Graal* in the Bibliothèque Nationale is one of the first romances to be illustrated. Other secular books, such as herbals and bestiaries, become commoner and a change takes place too in the layout of manuscripts. Hitherto the miniature had usually been fairly independent of the text and we often find a group of them all together at the beginning of a book. But now the miniature is often combined with an initial, serving the purpose of decoration as well as of illustration. Sometimes it is combined with the border and grows with it to occupy a whole page; only now the border lends it a decorative effect whereas before it was wholly illustrative. The simple full-page illustration became less common except in luxury manuscripts and the text itself generally occupies less space on the page.

The great French books of this period are those made for the private devotions of noble patrons; the *St. Louis Psalter*, the *Ingeburge Psalter* and the *Psalter of Blanche of Castile*. Now Bibles begin to appear with miniatures on a minute scale, precursors of the exquisite *Books of Hours*. And we find books specially designed for the unlearned and illiterate, books like the *Biblia Pauperum*, the *Golden Legend* and the *Speculum Humanae Salvationis* (in which each scene from the New Testament was paralleled by an anecdote from the Old Testament or from ancient secular history), which relied a great deal on their pictures. In these is seen a popular iconography which was to last on into the block book and the printed book. The *Bibles Moralisées* were far more splendid books with their whole text illustrated and their pictures enclosed in medallions.

At the beginning of the thirteenth century English illumination bore a very close resemblance to French. National boundaries had not yet segregated the art of one country from that of another and with monasteries still the chief centres of book production[5] and Latin still the universal language of learning there was continual interchange which helped to produce not so much uniformity as solidarity. To this may be traced those strange simultaneous changes of style which appear all at once in different places. Gothic appeared in England very soon after France and as in France it produced some fine service books like the *Windmill* and *Tenison Psalters* which are yet quite distinct from French manuscripts. In the latter there are borders containing some very accurately painted birds and short lines in the text are filled out with bands of ornament so that the whole surface of the page is decorated—a custom that was imitated in some early printed books. Many illuminated Bibles and psalters were produced during this century; very small ones similar to the French with tiny lettering and often with shortened text; and big ones with historiated initials which sometimes occupied a whole page. Backgrounds are formed of solid gold and there are architectural backgrounds too which copy the prevalent Gothic style. The thirteenth-century artist seems to have felt no more incongruity in a Gothic setting for a Biblical scene than the seventeenth-century engraver when he gave it a classical one.

Psalters were often prefaced with a series of Bible pictures in monumental style. Margaret Rickert has pointed out their connexion not only with contemporary stained glass but also with the wall-paintings of the time; and she says that this latter relationship is not found in French illumination. She concludes that both forms of art were probably based on cycles which were available for copying.

As the century proceeds we find more freedom of drawing and those delightfully informal marginal sketches or 'drolleries' which were never seen in the previous century make their appearance again and incidentally tell us a great deal about the costumes and everyday life of the time. With them we find a new feature which was later to become a characteristic of English work, the introduction of animal grotesques. Some of them, perhaps in imitation of the Bestiaries, are quite naturalistic; but their purpose is always decorative. St. Albans Abbey was famous for combining outline drawing with a monumental style, owing more to Byzantine than to Gothic art. This is to be seen in the work of Matthew Paris, who trained a school of illuminators at St. Albans and who is one of the earliest English illuminators to sign his work. His best known manuscript is the *Historia Anglorum*.

The middle of the fourteenth century is one of the turning points in the history of illumination. Hitherto the manuscript had in some respects anticipated the printed book which was so soon to oust it, and the persistence of the cycle system points the similarity by emphasizing the continuity of manuscript illumination. The survival of that system up to this time is in fact quite astonishing and illustrations in bestiaries for instance were still being copied (at many removes) from the Latin *Physiologus* which was itself a translation from the Greek. Many of the books we have dealt with, like the *Utrecht Psalter*, were illustrated by men of genius and were truly original, even when they used the old iconography. But the great majority were more or less faithful copies of other books. Now however the time of the virtuoso had arrived and he disdained to copy other men's work. The *Books of Hours* painted for the Duc de Berry were not copies nor were they copied afterwards. This work was book-painting rather than illumination and in it the pictures are of far greater importance than the text.

But with all that gain in technique there was a loss in feeling. Along with these superb books went a wholly inferior sort which can only be called mass-produced. Cheap *Books of Hours*, for instance, were turned out in large quantities to a set pattern in fifteenth-century France for the new bourgeois reading public. The production of books was gradually being secularized and even devotional books (which still comprised the greater part) were made less for the glory of God than for that of the patron or even the artist—who was fast losing his anonymity. Often he was known as a panel-painter as well, and for him illumination was only one way of making a living. That he saw little essential difference between the two arts is evidenced by the habit of painting frames for miniatures to make them look like panels. The natural consequence of all this was a general lowering of standards because speed became more essential when a man's livelihood depended on the amount of work he could turn out.[6] Here the monk had the advantage of knowing that his bread was assured besides the greater satisfaction of more selfless aims.

With illumination falling into secular hands it is not surprising to find Guilds growing up. These appeared towards the end of the thirteenth century and eventually it became as obligatory for an illuminator to join his local guild as it is for a printer today to join his trade union. Weale has given us some fascinating details about the Guild of St. John and St. Luke in Bruges—how those who wished to join had to submit a specimen of their work and how they were liable to a fine if they used inferior materials; limits were even set on the number of apprentices which could be taken.

Jean Pucelle was one of the first of the virtuosi illuminators in France, and in his work we find a wholly new conception of space—new, that is, to France though we find something similar in contemporary Italian painting. His *Hours of Jeanne d'Evreux* contains miniatures which begin to have depth and incidentally pose many problems for the illustrator with his flat page. In his best book, the *Belleville Breviary* of about 1340, there is a new naturalism, too, in the attitude of the Virgin to her Baby. At this time many beautiful manuscripts of the Apocalypse were being produced both in France and England. But towards the end of the century English illumination declined, and French and Flemish were left paramount. This was the time when the great masterpieces of the Paris school were produced, the *Books of Hours* for the Duc d'Anjou and the Duc de Berry, the *Rohan Book of Hours*, the *Bedford Book of Hours* and the rest. However disastrous the reign of Charles VI might be politically, it turned out to be a glorious period for the arts in France. The unpopular Duc de Berry took advantage of his relationship to the King to build up his wonderful library with public money. The names of some of the artists who worked for him are known to us—Pol de Limbourg who illuminated the *Très Riches Heures*, Jacquemart de Hesdin and André Beauneveu—and we know, too, that most of them were Flemish, and a few Italian. In the calendar section of the *Très Riches Heures*, which dates from about 1415, we find exquisite landscapes painted for their own sake and foreshadowing the work of the great Dutch masters in their truth to nature, yet still in the scale of the miniature. Symbolism is beginning to decay. A new unity of light and tone makes its appearance.

Sir Kenneth Clark has pointed out that this 'sense of saturating light grew out of a school of manuscript illumination and first appears in miniatures. For in such small images a unity of tone is far more easily achieved and the whole scene can be given the concentrated brilliance of a reflection in a crystal.' What he calls the first modern landscapes appeared in the *Turin Hours* which was probably painted by Hubert van Eyck in about 1416. A section of this manuscript was destroyed by fire in 1904, but enough survives to indicate the astonishing leap forward not only in the painting of light but also in the importance of landscape in the miniature.

This startling change in technique and in subject-matter reflects a new attitude to life itself which is found also in the poetry of the time. The decay of medieval symbolism indicates a growing secularism, a turning away from things eternal and unchangeable to things temporal and fleeting. Men were becoming conscious of the beauty of change. They were, as Joan Evans says, 'peculiarly sensitive to things that were lovely because they were not lasting: to flowers that fade and to moments that cannot endure. . . . It is this poetic naturalism expressed first in poetry, then in the manuscript illuminations to poems and then in the manifold decorations of castles that sets the note for the imagery of ornament in the later Middle Ages.'

The *Bedford Book of Hours* (c. 1430) for all its magnificence and its four thousand vignettes looks slightly old-fashioned in comparison with the *Turin Hours*. But it is a wonderful book with its work by three different schools, Parisian, English and Franco-Flemish. National styles begin to be distinct in the fourteenth century and by the fifteenth it is comparatively easy to assign illumination to its appropriate school. But it cannot be assumed that the illuminators themselves were natives because they seldom stayed long in one place.

Besides these devotional books many secular works appeared during the fourteenth and fifteenth centuries, and histories were especially popular. There were the *Grandes Chroniques de France* and of course Froissart, who was equally fashionable in England. In these books we find warriors and others represented not in contemporary dress but in that of fifty years earlier than the date of the illustrations; Middleton has suggested that this is because the artist wished to suggest antiquity and went back as far as his memory would carry him. Then there were the Arthurian romances, the books on natural science like Glanville's *Treatise on the Properties of Things*, the books on hunting, and the illustrated *Fabliaux* or short stories in verse. All these, whatever period they purport to describe, are invaluable to the historian because of their pictures of contemporary life and customs. This in fact is the beginning of genre painting.

Two interesting innovations now claim our attention, the first the use of grisaille, the second the striking development of the background and border. Grisaille is first seen during the fourteenth century in France and it lasts nearly to the end of the fifteenth century. By the time it appears the old system of pen outlines filled with flat colours was almost obsolete, and grisaille marks another step forward in the search for depth. It consists of painting in a blue-grey tone with highlights in white or gold, and in the hands of a master it is strikingly effective. In Italy it became chiaroscuro and the principle was applied later to printed woodcuts under the same name. Pächt suggests that it was an expedient to distinguish illumination from the richer effects of the panel picture and to place it in a category of its own, midway between painting and the graphic arts. That may be so, but it is of course found in manuscripts long before the introduction of printing.

During the early fourteenth century backgrounds were purely decorative. The typical background is a sort of chess-board of alternating gold and coloured squares. Towards the end of the century we find gold patterns on coloured grounds, but with the growth of landscape painting and the discovery of the horizon a naturalistic background very gradually replaces this decoration, especially in Franco-Flemish work. So the miniature becomes just a smaller version of the panel paintings which the same artist was probably producing: a development that was not necessarily for the good of the book.

The rectangular border developed in the thirteenth century as a pendant of the initial and even when it grew to surround the whole page it still retained its connexion with the initial. From the bud of the pendant grew the 'ivy-leaf' border which was typical of fourteenth- and fifteenth-century French work. Usually it covered a very wide margin and sometimes there were leaves of burnished gold in the pattern which added greatly to its splendour. But it always formed an integral part of the text and it hardly developed at all. It was left to the Flemish illuminators to make their borders three-dimensional using the same perspective for border and miniature. And as naturalism thus increases, so symbolism declines.

In 1419 Philip the Good of Burgundy became ruler of great and wealthy lands which later included what is now Holland and Belgium. Here the Flemish school of panel painting in oils which is associated with the van Eycks had already grown up, itself an offspring of book illumination. Under its influence the third dimension, seldom found in miniatures of the previous two or three centuries, and never in borders, became common in books, and not altogether with the happiest results. The problem (which is as much the problem of the illustrator today) is to reconcile the flatness of the text with the depth of the picture; and Pächt has shown how one solution was found by the anonymous painter whose best work was done between 1475 and 1485 and whom he calls the Master of Mary of Burgundy. The name comes from the two wonderful *Books of Hours* which this unknown man painted for the wife of the Archduke Maximilian, one now in Vienna and the other in Berlin. In them and in his *Oxford Book of Hours* is brought to perfection the technique of the 'scatter border.' This is an adaptation of the naturalistic still-life border which had already been used in the *Très Riches Heures du Duc de Berry*, and it consists of flowers, butterflies, jewels and so on, surrounding the miniature and, by means of shadows, giving its own feeling of depth quite independently of the miniature which it frames. The reader has the illusion that the border is nearer to him than the text and that the miniature is further away; and always 'the plane of the page is the central organizing factor.' In a famous miniature from the *Book of Hours* painted for Charles the Bold are the jewel case, the cushion and the open prayer book, all belonging to Mary of Burgundy. Framed by architecture is the crucifixion scene which has become almost the background and which is far less vivid and less real than the foreground. We have here the interpenetration of heaven and earth that is typical of fifteenth-century Dutch painting. The picture becomes an extension of the spectator's own world, the flat surface an open window.

These manuscripts also mark, as Bergström has pointed out, the beginning of still-life painting. Religious symbols have been separated from the miniature in the interests of naturalism and relegated to the border where they assume a disproportion-ate importance. To give them an independent existence in a separate painting was only a small step.

The book-painter in the Netherlands at this time was in fact a bold experimentalist and the easel-painters were content to follow in his path. This development had far-reaching consequences not only in the Ghent-Bruges school of illumination[7] which this Master founded but also in the art of Bourdichon in France and Glockendon in Germany. It seems to have had an immediate effect on the illuminators of the famous *Grimani Breviary*, one of whom was for a long time supposed to have been Gerard David.[8] That book was painted at about this time and it contains borders of startling naturalism, besides many fine miniatures. And a hundred years later Georg Hoefnagel (who came from Flanders but did his best work in Bavaria) carried this decorative system to its conclusion in such works as the *Prayer Book of Albert V of Bavaria* (1574) and the *Missale Romanum* (1590). The idea of a framework has been abandoned completely, and the flowers and insects are the *raison d'être* of the miniatures. We feel that these were his chief interest; and he was in fact one of the founders of the Dutch school of still-life painting.

One great French illuminator who seems to have been unaffected by the Flemish fashion was Jean Fouquet. He was working in Tours during the second half of the fifteenth century; and in his hands the art of Tours becomes quite different from that of Paris which at this period is often indistinguishable from Flemish work. He uses mostly the ivy-leaf border but our attention is concentrated on his wonderful miniatures with their backgrounds of Loire landscape. Already the influence of the Italian classical Renaissance is seen in his architecture, which is emancipating itself from the Gothic, as well as in his handling of perspective. In his mastery of crowd scenes he is far beyond any of his contemporaries and his use of colour is always unerring. His chief books are the *Hours of Etienne Chevalier* and Josephus's *Jewish Antiquities*. In the former we find again the conception of the miniature as something seen through a window. A strip of lettering at the foot which appears to be at right angles to the ground above acts as part of the frame. Jean Bourdichon also worked at Tours but a little later than Fouquet. His great work is the *Grandes Heures* of Anne of Brittany, which has more than a flavour of Flanders in its flower painting and in its very early 'scatter-borders' with their deep shadows. These incidentally surround the text only; the miniatures or 'histories' have plain frames. But beautiful and accomplished as this book is we are already reminded that illumination is a dying art and that Bourdichon was a court painter first and an illustrator second. Under Francis I the Tours school moved to Paris where the Italian architect Rosso was enjoying great favour and the Italian taste for emblems had already taken hold. The *Hours of Anne of Austria* (c. 1530) was one of the last great French manuscripts and it shows a significant degree of over-ornamentation. By the turn of the century printing had established itself as the chief method of producing books and the illuminated manuscripts must have begun to seem an anachronism. Elsewhere in France quality had declined badly, and in some late French manuscripts we find transfers being used for the borders—a form of competition with the printer.

During the thirteenth century when English, French and Flemish illumination was at such a high level, German work, unaffected by the Gothic style, continued with the old formulae. Consequently its quality inevitably declined. But in the fourteenth century an important Germanic school sprang up in Prague, which was now the capital of the Holy Roman Empire. Here under the patronage of the Emperor Charles IV was developed that distinctive style of decoration called Bohemian. There is Gothic architecture for instance in Princess Cunigunda's *Passionale* (*c.* 1312) but it is not French Gothic. For Charles was written the celebrated *Golden Bull* which contained all the constitutions of the Empire, and was copied many times in varying degrees of splendour. For his son the *Wenzel Bible* was illuminated and though it is unfinished it is still a magnificent work. In the fifteenth century there was a steady deterioration such as indeed occurred throughout the whole of Germany. This was accelerated by the introduction of printing which seemed to be the signal for illumination of ever increasing gaudiness, e.g. the *Kuttenberg Gradual* at Vienna. And now the virtuosity enters which we shall find especially in France and Flanders during this period, when illumination partakes more of the nature of painting than of illustration. Already there have been many instances where the name of the illuminator is known but now he loses all anonymity and leaves us in no doubt about his identity. The books painted for Albert of Brandenburg early in the sixteenth century by Nicolas Glockendon and the *Prayer Book of William of Bavaria* by Albert Glockendon differ in nothing but dimensions, as Bradley says, from the works of the greatest contemporary painters. But as Bradley also points out, painters and illuminators seldom trespassed on each other's preserves because of the strict rules of the guilds.

In England printing seemed to kill illumination much more quickly. During the thirteenth century the Gothic style came from France and there was a general reduction of scale both for pictures and for text, together with a more delicate and freer style of drawing. But early in the fourteenth century the work of the East Anglian School begins to show some independence, with its flair for the illustration of exciting narrative and profusion of decoration which is sometimes carried too far. From it came some of the finest of all English manuscripts, and Margaret Rickert says that these manuscripts represent 'in all respects the most characteristically English phase of medieval painting.' East Anglia was at this time the centre of the wool trade and very prosperous, and as many books were now being produced for the laity as for the Church. *Queen Mary's Psalter* (*c.* 1330) is a magnificent example of this school, its first sixty-six pages a series of miniatures of Bible scenes with captions but without any other text. These are outline drawings coloured with transparent washes, looking back to the *Utrecht Psalter* and quite different from the more conventional pictures which come later in the book. In the lower margins of these later miniatures however is a series of small tinted drawings of sports, hunting scenes and animals—a form of decoration that was carried much farther, almost too far in the famous *Luttrell Psalter*. Now the flowers in the borders begin to be of recognizable species, reminding us more of Flemish than of French work. We find too in borders that the conventional leaf pattern is developing into a pattern of feathery scrolls.

From about 1348 when England was ravaged by the Black Death until the end of the century there is a dearth of good books. French illumination was now at its peak but we lacked the princely patronage that fostered it there. At the end of this period however there was a revival, exemplified by such books as the great *Carmelite Missal* and the *Sherborne Missal* painted by John Siferwas and now in Alnwick Castle Library. A new influence can be discerned which seems to have come from Bohemia in exchange as it were for the benefits of the East Anglian style which had recently spread as far east as this. Bohemian illumination was now flourishing under Charles IV. Charles's daughter, Anne, married Richard II of England and among other things she introduced to the court the fashion of pointed toes which we find reflected in miniatures of the period. The representation of foliage too seems to be copied from Bohemian borders. But gradually French and Flemish styles prevailed and later work, apart from an occasional masterpiece like the *Hours of Elizabeth the Queen*, tends to be a reflection of foreign virtuosity, growing ever more florid. The new book-buying public seems often to have been content with flashy and inferior work and the more accomplished artists must have forsaken illumination for other branches of the arts. The death-blow given by the Wars of the Roses was indeed a *coup-de-grâce*.

In Italy the thirteenth century, though it was the century of Cimabue and Giotto, was not productive of many fine books.[9] Most of the early scribes there seem to have been French, just as, later on, the early printers there were German. Illustrated choir-books, some of them with initials more than twelve inches high, are among the most beautiful manuscripts of this period and production of these continued by hand until long after the introduction of printing. Fra Angelico is known to have illuminated some at Fiesole in the fifteenth century. Law books from Bologna were famous all over Italy and beyond for their decoration and, curiously enough, their drolleries. Oderisi da Gubbio (whom Dante praised) worked on some of them.

Bologna led the other Italian cities in the art of illumination throughout the Gothic period. Miniature painting still held its own with large scale painting but in the fourteenth century Florence began to vie with Bologna and at the same time the miniature began to take second place. The broader style of the Florentines seems to show that they were panel painters first and miniaturists after. In Siena on the other hand artists like Tegliacci made no distinction between the two arts. Tegliacci may have been responsible for a wonderful Dante now in Perugia, one among many copies of the *Inferno* which was now being illuminated by masters of all schools.

The Gothic style as it was known in France did not greatly affect Italy as a whole. Byzantine tendencies still persisted, especially in Venetian manuscripts and are to be seen in certain antiphonals in St. Mark's Library. And Venetian manuscripts also show a definite Byzantine feeling throughout the period. In Lombardy however French influences were stronger, and the Gothic style lingers there. In the work of Giovannino de' Grassi we find spiky pinnacles similar to those in French manuscripts of the time. 'Giotto and his followers changed the course of art in many things,' says Morey, 'but they did nothing so extraordinary as their transformation of the form and formulae of the French decadent Gothic style.' Towards the close of the fourteenth century Italian artists were working in France on books for the Duke of Berry and so, although her own great period of illumination was not to come until just before the arrival of printing, Italy made her contribution to France's glory.

On the other hand the fifteenth century, particularly the period between 1455 and 1484, was an age of great achievement, in illumination as in the other arts. It was ironical that illumination flowered so much later in Italy than elsewhere and that it was at its height just when printing arrived. It was bound to succumb but it held out for a surprising length of time. The effects of the Renaissance, which we associate with the revival of classicism in fifteenth-century Italy, were as potent on the printed book as on the manuscript. After the sack of Constantinople of course many Byzantine manuscripts reached Italy but they appear to have been valued more for their literary contents than for their illumination. Perhaps one reason for their comparative lack of influence was the close relationship between illumination and painting in Italy at this time. Just as in the north, painting grew out of illumination and then made itself independent. But in Italy, where the *quattrocento* was one of the most glorious periods of painting that the world has ever seen, the arts remained more closely allied and wherever there was a school of painting we find also a school of miniaturists, the influence of whose art is often to be seen in the altar-pieces of the time.

But the first generation of great Renaissance painters were more interested in monumental art and it was not until later that their influence began to be felt. There is indeed a monumental quality about the huge Graduals that were produced between 1463 and 1471 for Florence cathedral. At the other end of the scale were the little *Books of Hours* with exquisitely detailed borders by Francesco d'Antonio, notably the one executed in 1485 for Lorenzo the Magnificent which is known as the *Uffiziolo*, and Bishop Donato's *Lectionary* of 1436 in the Morgan Library with its host of little miniatures about two inches square. Gherardo and Monte de Giovanni are celebrated for their landscape backgrounds in the manner of Fouquet, giving the page a depth more suitable perhaps to the mosaics on which they worked with Ghirlandaio and Botticelli. They also illuminated, for Matthias Corvinus, King of Hungary, Didymus's *De Spiritu Sancto*, which has a text written by Sigismundus de Sigismundis, the most famous scribe of his day. Attavante, whose workshop produced the famous *Urbino Bible* (1476-78) for Federico di Montefelto, was highly esteemed in his own time but to us his pages seem too ornate even in that decorative age and his compositions too crowded. For Matthias Corvinus he too produced, among other manuscripts, a fine breviary in 1487, but it is certain that much of the work that came from his shop was not his. His followers in the early sixteenth century tried to outdo him and this marks the decline of Florentine work.

Italian manuscripts have always been famous for their calligraphy and there is a calligraphic quality about much of their ornament, especially of their initials. By now the roman hand was replacing the Gothic, anticipating the introduction of roman type by Jenson, the printer. Italian illuminators were more sensitive than most to the physical matching of pictures and text and the new style of writing had its effect on miniatures as well as on initials. The humanist book, which we are apt to associate with roman type and with printing, thus had its origins much earlier. There was an enormous demand for books, especially in Florence. Vespasiano da Bisticci, a famous Florentine publisher, employed numerous copyists and illuminators to produce the Greek and Latin classics for wealthy nobles, as well as liturgical works for the monasteries. We can trace the beginning of an antiquarian style in the humanistic book with its opening page framed in the Romanesque manner, a fashion that was even perpetuated in the earliest printed books. This subdued decoration was probably felt to detract less than true illustration from the literary value of the book which, for the humanist, was always paramount. It gives us too a curious side-light on what the Renaissance artist thought classical illustration was like.

If the Renaissance style may be said to have started in Florence it was in Ferrara that it produced some of its most original manifestations. The Este Court was from 1450-71 a scene of unparalleled brilliance and from here, between 1455 and 1461, came one of the great masterpieces of the Renaissance, the *Borso d'Este Bible*. Crivelli, Franco de' Russi and the two or three others who provided the miniatures were all under the spell of Piero della Francesca who himself was painting at the Court. The little pictures embedded in the borders have in fact the same characteristics as the big easel pictures of the time.

De' Russi combined with Guglielmo Giraldi to produce a wonderful *Divina Commedia* in about 1480. One of the finest of all the many Dante manuscripts, its 110 large miniatures stand out even in such a rich period by their originality of conception. There is also a fine four-volume Bible illuminated by Giraldi a few years before the Dante. The *Ercole d'Este Breviary* (1502), on which three artists worked, is the most notable late Ferrarese book, and here we find an imitation of the Flemish border which is a feature of Italian illumination in decline. Most Italian books of the time, irrespective of origin, have borders on the first few pages in which are embedded miniatures in medallion frames with a coat of arms at the bottom. But Ferrarese borders are even more elaborate, except when they imitate the twelfth century in antiquarian style with interlaced bands of white or gold which are thrown into relief by filling the interstices with alternating colours.

Bologna, long displaced from her former primacy, was now producing manuscripts that imitated those of Ferrara; but in the beautiful *Book of Offices of Giovanni II Bentivoglio* (1497) and the *Ghislieri Book of Hours* (which contains a miniature by Perugino) Bologna is seen to be reasserting her own individuality. In Padua at the end of the fifteenth century we can identify in Benedetto Bordone a great miniaturist who also produced wood-engravings. Many artists of this time must have worked for both manuscripts and printed books but it is difficult to identify them, for they never signed their engravings as they did their miniatures. In Verona Francesco and Girolamo dai Libri, working like Bordone under the influence of Mantegna, seemed to carry the art of illumination to a point beyond which it could progress no further.

In Lombardy the Gothic style lingered on long after everywhere else. The influence of Leonardo has beeen discerned in certain manuscripts from Milan such as the *Book of Hours* in the Fitzwilliam, But a far more important figure for the book is Belbello da Pavia, one of the greatest of all Renaissance miniaturists. His work in the second part of the *Visconti Book of Offices*, for certain Venetian choir-books and for a fine *Plutarch* in the British Museum shows a love of brilliant colour, of minute detail and of exquisite landscape backgrounds. Salmi comments on the 'calligraphic bravura of his rapid, agitated and vigorous line.' His borders are often over-elaborated and when, as in the *Plutarch*, he dispenses with them altogether the miniatures benefit considerably. At the end of the century the famous *Sforza Book of Hours* came from Milan and to this book, rich as it is, Charles V later added some beautiful Flemish miniatures. The *Libro dell' Iesus*, also executed for the Sforzas right at the end of the century, has full-page miniatures without any ornamentation save for gold frames which emphasize their detachment from the book.

By the sixteenth century, with printing now well established, manuscript illumination was being practised only to please wealthy patrons by artists like the admired Giulio Clovio whose miniatures, inspired by Michelangelo and stippled with minute points of colour, have been likened to reduced versions of large-scale paintings. Nevertheless his *Book of Hours* of 1546 for Cardinal Alessandro Farnese is a *tour de force*. In it we can see reflections of the mannerist style which was fashionable in Italy at that time.

Illumination at this period was generally confined to religious books but at the same time there was a curious revival of copying the classics and giving them new illustrations; Vasari for instance performed this service for the well-worn *Dioscorides*. At the opposite extreme from this antiquarianism are the occasional miniatures that seem to imitate the printed illustration. Could anything indicate more clearly the decline of illumination?

Spain has been left thus late, not because her work is any less interesting than that of other countries but because it was subject to alien influences and requires separate treatment. From the eighth to the eleventh century Spain was almost the only repository of the classical tradition which was lost elsewhere in the West. Moslem rule affected chiefly the south and as in Islamic countries it was tolerant towards Christianity and it encouraged learning. Cordova in fact became in the tenth century a centre of learning and a place of pilgrimage for scholars from all parts of the civilized world.

Mozarabic art is the name given to the Christian art which flourished under the Moslems; Mudejar art that of the Moslems who stayed after the Christian conquest and kept their own culture. The former was more productive of illumination but it had a great deal in common with the latter, particularly the richly decorative Oriental element. There are of course many early Spanish manuscripts which show strong Carolingian influences, particularly those of the tenth-century Catalan school. Two famous Bibles of this category may be mentioned, that of St. Peter of Ronda and the *Farfa Bible*—both of great beauty. But Spain's most original examples of illumination are Mozarabic and the most remarkable Mozarabic manuscript is the famous *Commentary of St. Beatus* on the Apocalypse. It was written in the eighth century and frequently copied during the next 400 years. Even in the eleventh century copy made at Saint-Sever in the south of France and illuminated by Etienne Garcia the Mozarabic character of the pictures is unchanged, the violent colours, the dreamlike atmosphere of the apocalyptic vision.

After the defeat of the Moslems the Oriental element in Spanish illumination gradually decreased, and it became less and less distinctive. It succumbed to the

Gothic fashion in the thirteenth century, and there are one or two delightful books by Alfonso X illustrated in this style—the *Lapidary* and the *Book of Chess* for instance. Alfonso was a great patron of letters and with his encouragement the *Cronica General* was written and illustrated. From then until the introduction of printing Spanish illuminators contented themselves with imitations of Italian or Flemish work, the difference being that colouring is generally subdued in deference to the Inquisition. So we find, in the fifteenth century, miniatures with black backgrounds and draperies. But these restrictions were eased in the sixteenth century and under Philip II some of the finest Spanish manuscripts appeared. The introduction of printing was a very slow affair in Spain and Portugal, and illumination therefore persisted longer than in most other countries and perhaps influenced printing design more. The magnificent and enormous choir-books ordered by Philip for San Lorenzo of the Escorial between 1572 and 1589 were partly produced by Italians (Scorza of Genoa, a famous miniaturist of the time, was one of them) and display an Italian richness. The flowering of Spanish painting in the next generation must have owed much to these miniaturists—in whose work however one can hardly expect to see as yet the emergence of a national style.

Calligraphy was always highly esteemed in Spain, even more in Portugal, and many fifteenth-century manuscripts depend entirely on their writing for their beauty. Portugal was politically connected with Burgundy and Flemish strains are apparent in Portuguese manuscripts. Her greatest manuscript was perhaps the Bible of the Hieronymites which was mostly written by Italians. In Portugal, as in Spain, good manuscripts continued to appear long after printing arrived. The British Museum has a *Missale Romanum* dating from about 1557, its title-page reminiscent of contemporary engraved titles with its formula of Roman soldiers supporting a tablet.

When in 1519 Cortes arrived in Mexico he found a highly developed form of picture writing which survived long after the Spanish conquest. Many of the wonderful books which were written by this method were preserved by the Spaniards (though unfortunately many more were destroyed), so it seems proper to give some account of them here although they have nothing in common with European illumination at all.

The books themselves were folded rolls of deerskin or of tree-bark paper, and the pictures were painted in the most brillant colours imaginable. The subject-matter was generally magic or history, going back in time to the era before the Toltec Empire. The magic books have been described by C. A. Burland but few of them survive, the best being the *Codex Borgia* and the *Codex Laud* at Oxford. Of the history books the best are the Aztec *Codex Boturini*, the Mixtec *Vienna Codex*, the *Codex Zouche Nuttall*.

These books are unique because they demonstrate the evolution of writing and its origin in picture. In those which have no writing, like the *Vienna Codex*, the illustration *is* the text, so to say. And there is a barbaric splendour in the color and pattern as well as a more subtle skill in their disposition on the page. 'There is,' says Burland, 'an insistent rhythm in the pattern that is almost like music. . . . This is all exciting to the eye and at the same time regularized by its dependence on a very strictly observed code of proportion.'

Even in Spain and Portugal the illumination and indeed the production of manuscripts had virtually ended by the seventeenth century. Manuscripts like those which Jarry produced for Louis XIV are few and far between. It is a commonplace to say that manuscripts were killed by printing but this does not seem quite to account for the decay of illumination which relied on colour inaccessible to printers until the nineteenth century. That curious but often very effective hybrid, the printed book with painted decoration, was only a transitional apparition. The answer seems to be an economic one. Where, as in Spain, the Church continued her patronage, illumination flourished to a comparatively late date. But elsewhere lay patronage was not enough to arrest its decay.

In Russia, where printing developed relatively late the production of manuscripts continued well into the sixteenth century and beyond. Although Byzantine and Balkan influences were strong, important native and some oriental elements appear. The style of the icon is often seen in the frontispieces depicting the Evangelists that embellish the Gospel manuscripts. A highly characteristic feature is the oblong headpiece made up of interlacing ornaments or flower and plant motifs, all carefully and accurately drawn. Initials, though often decorated in the earlier manuscripts, were never historiated.

In the fifteenth and sixteenth centuries we find a curious subjectivism in the miniatures which appear in the manuscript books. They comment on the text rather than illustrate it, and as in Western marginal drawings of an earlier date, they often reflect the everyday life of the world around. In other manuscripts, for instance the much copied Cosmography of Cosmas Indicopleustes, an ancient Byzantine traveller in India, we find strange invented grotesque animals, similar to those in Western bestiaries.

NOTES

[1] But many of the best Carolingian and Ottonian books were also made for princely patrons and contain portraits of them.
[2] Françoise Henry however believes that the separation of the scribe from the illuminator had already begun and doubts whether Eadfrith was really responsible for the illumination.
[3] E. M. Thompson pointed out that the text is written in archaic rustic capitals presumably to preserve the same relative positions of text and drawings as in the prototype.
[4] Hildesheim was famous for its metal-work too, which is much more to our taste than its illumination. This was a period of integration of the arts in Germany. Contemporary murals and stained glass were often based on manuscript illumination, and books like the St. Bernard Gospel Book show a hard unyielding quality in their illustrations as if they were from the hand of a metal-worker.
[5] Scriptoria appeared in the monasteries during this century.
[6] This did not apply to those who worked for princely patrons on a salaried basis.

7 This school is famous also for some of the very earliest examples of pure landscapes in its miniatures, i.e. landscapes which are not just a setting for heaven or for divine activities. These are painted with a beautiful and characteristic atmospheric quality and with a peculiar softness of colour.

8 David, a master painter, is known to have belonged also to a guild of miniaturists. But this was probably exceptional and already a distinction seems to have grown up between painters and miniaturists.

9 It may be worth mentioning that an early thirteenth-century book of Astronomical Treatises in the British Museum is one of the oldest Western books written on paper. But after the introduction of printing, paper was used much for manuscripts.

Hellmut Lehmann-Haupt

The Heritage of
the Manuscript

Histories of book printing usually begin somewhat abruptly with the invention of typography. There is some reference to manuscripts as the models of early printers. But there is never a very clear account of what these manuscripts looked like and in what way they really did influence early printed books. Actually, there is no better way to approach the beginnings of mechanical bookmaking than by looking quite carefully at the manuscripts written and illustrated toward the end of the Middle Ages. Early book printing will then appear to us in a new light. It will be seen not so much as a tentative step in a new art, but as the rendering of existing forms and conventions in a new medium; it will appear more as a process of evolution.

As a matter of fact, the transition from the late mediaeval manuscript to the early printed book is not the one and only great revolution in the history of bookmaking. It is possible to mention at least three other major changes which I do not hesitate to call equally important and revolutionary in their time.

Books in the ancient world, as we all know, existed in the form of rolls usually made of papyrus leaves, and sometimes of animal skins, pasted or stitched together. The early rolls were of tremendous length. We have reason to believe that the whole of Homer's Iliad was sometimes written on one continuous scroll. It is easy to imagine how tiresome the reading of such a book must have been, and it is fairly clear that this

SOURCE: Reprinted from Lawrence C. Wroth, Editor, A *History of the Printed Book, The Dolphin*, No. 3 (New York: The Limited Editions Club, 1938), Chapter I, "The Heritage of the Manuscript," by Hellmut Lehmann-Haupt, pp. 3-23, by permission of the publisher. Copyright © 1938, 1966 by The Limited Editions Club, Westport, Connecticut.

Illustrations mentioned in "The Heritage of The Manuscript" by Hellmut Lehmann-Haupt are located in *The Dolphin* between pp. 81-115. Reprinted by permission of the Limited Editions Club.

1a. Latin Bible manuscript of the fifteenth century.(Reduced.)

was not an exception but that in those early days practically all existing books were of such mammoth dimensions. Books of course were very rare then, and people relied much more on their memories than they do today. In fact, those huge book rolls can be looked upon more as records than as actual reading texts. As time went on, literary works increased until there were too many different texts for people to remember by heart. Scholars and literary men took to reading instead of discussing and debating, and the large size of book rolls began to be looked upon as impractical and old-fashioned. As a result, the first important change took place in the history of bookmaking: the copying of the entire literature of the classical era from the large, old, continuous scrolls into new, convenient, short ones. It was in Alexandria, in the great libraries of the Ptolemies, during the third century before Christ, that this change took place. A complete copy of Homer's Odyssey would now consist of twenty-four rolls, each containing one book of Homer. As a matter of fact, the division of the works of classical literature into such "books" goes back to those Alexandrian days, and can be looked upon as a striking example of the deep effect which a purely physical change has had upon literary composition. The introduction of short, handy rolls not only made it necessary to rewrite and edit the whole of the ancient literature up to the Alexandrian period; it also fundamentally affected all future writing.

The second great revolution in the form of the book was the change from the small book roll of the late classical world to the codex of the early Christian civilization. No longer were the individual sheets combined into a continuous roll; each sheet was now folded in itself to form a quire of at least two leaves (that is, four pages); then the quires were sewn to each other and protected at the back and the sides with a binding. Some papyrus was used this way, but from the very beginning the parchment or vellum leaf was the standard material of the early mediaeval book, and it remained so until the arrival of paper toward the end of the Middle Ages. It is interesting to observe how, in the change from the small roll to the codex, the one great advantage of the old giant roll—namely, continuity of text—was once again recaptured, but how at the same time the disadvantage of both the older large rolls and the more recent smaller ones was eliminated. With a roll it had been impossible to open a book at more than one place at a time, or to refer back to an earlier page without losing the place one was actually reading. This disadvantage was felt most acutely in the Christian Church service and in law practice. Accordingly, the Bible, with some early liturgical works, and law books were among the earliest texts to appear as codices.

By the year A.D. 400 the codex was in full command of the field, and since then the form of the book, roughly speaking, has not changed up to the present day. The next change, that from the handwritten to the printed book, is of a different nature from the two preceding ones. Yet, as an evolutionary step in bookmaking history, it bears some resemblance to its predecessors.

The last change to be mentioned is a fairly recent one; so recent, in fact, that it is still going on today. I am referring to the industrialization of book production; that is to say, the replacement of hand-driven equipment and tools by power-driven machinery, the introduction of photography into the graphic arts, and mass-

1b. Thirty-six-line printed Bible. (Reduced.)

production methods in general. The beginnings of this most recent transition are fairly well defined, and lie within twenty years before and after the year 1800.

The interesting thing about these various changes, different as they may appear to us, is a certain resemblance in principle. The acutal features that are subjected to change are different, of course, each time, and the results are different each time. Yet there seems to be a hidden law somewhere which determines the course of events on each occasion, and which invariably forces the elements in certain directions.

One of the most remarkable aspects seems to be the effect, as it were, of the law of inertia: these changes never seem to be complete, never entirely logical—there is always a certain clinging and holding on to older features that have lost all significance through the altered conditions; yet they are still kept, either without any modification at all, or with very small concessions.

Another thing that happens each time is that the old, obsolete method seems to get a second wind after the first hard blow has been struck. It comes to life again, and for a while it almost looks as though the old would be victorious and drive out the new.

In the following pages, only one of the major changes in book-production methods will be described in greater detail. It is the one which has the greatest interest for us because it gave to our civilization the form of book production that our fathers inherited. The most recent change that I have spoken of, the one still going on today, is too close to our eyes. We cannot as yet detect its full significance or foresee its final results. But if there is a law of development in all these changes, and if we can define this law in one instance, we may learn something that can be applied to future conditions as well. So a study of the transition from the handwritten book to the printed book may help us in some ways to understand the seemingly contradictory trends of forces that are at work today. This, however, is not the main purpose of the following pages, which are primarily concerned with an intelligent understanding of the background of early printing.

The most obvious connection between manuscripts and printed books exists in the interdependence of certain early woodcuts and illustrations in fifteenth-century manuscripts; but the most important link is the connection between handwritings of late mediaeval calligraphers and certain printing types used in the early years of the press. There are also several other interesting parallels. An attempt will be made not only to describe the connections within one medium, but also to give an account of the entire process of transition.

It would be useless, and even tedious, to describe and to illustrate all individual cases of parallels which we know today, nor would even this produce a complete picture. For instance, we know more about the development in Germany than in France, and illustrations have been studied more carefully than for instance, initial letters. Therefore, it will be better to describe some typical exaiaples, each of them showing how the manuscripts of a given locality were used by the early printers of the same region in solving a specific problem of bookmaking. In this way we shall gradually be able to gather a view of the entire evolution, and in the end it will be possible to discuss the principle of this development.

In order to show how each individual feature of manuscript production was treated

2a. Latin Breviary, written at Piacenza in 1480. (Reduced.)

by the early printers, we shall take as a basis of our description the typical production method of a late mediaeval manuscript. There was of course no one and only method of procedure by which to go, but leaving aside variations of minor importance and the possible changes in the order of execution, the following points may be accepted as the typical steps.

First, the *writing* of the actual text in black ink.

Then, the *rubrication*. This was the writing in red, and sometimes in blue and other additional colors, of initial letters of medium and small size at the beginning of paragraphs and sometimes at the beginning of sentences; the crossing through in color of the capital letters in the text; the writing in of paragraph marks in red or blue; also the writing in of penstroke ornaments in red and blue in a fine, calligraphic style, around some of the initials and up and down the borders.

Next, the illuminated *decoration*. This was the painting-in with brush in miniature technique of the larger initials at the beginning of the book and at beginnings of important sections; also the execution of border decorations, either free or in connection with initial letters, on the opening page and at other textually important places. Gold and sometimes silver were employed, together with a full range of illuminator's colors.

Next, the *illustrations* proper. These were not merely decorations or initials, but actual pictorial scenes to illustrate the text. They were done either in the illuminator's technique with gold (or silver) and opaque miniature colors, applied on top of each other, and with white as a separate color; or pen-and-ink drawings in outline, filled in with transparent water colors in a sketchy, open manner, and the white of the paper left shining through as a separate "color." Illumination and illustrations were not necessarily made later than the borders and initials; they were often made at the same time, and by the same person, and sometimes perhaps even earlier.

Next, the *binding*. This was not necessarily the last step to be carried out. Like the cutting and folding of pages to the size desired, and like the ruling of the pages in preparation for writing, the binding could have been done before the writing and decorating. But in a typical fifteenth-century manuscript shop, where it is likely that more than one scribe and illuminator were working simultaneously on the same copy, the binding would naturally come last.

THE WRITING

To the modern mind, the variety of printing types found in the fifteenth century is well-nigh incomprehensible. Nevertheless, this variety is merely the reflection of an even greater wealth of handwriting forms in use at the time when printing was invented. In handwriting, there are not only national differences, but also different styles for different purposes, used simultaneously. When and how these various forms developed can be answered only from a knowledge of handwriting history in the Middle Ages. This history of writing is really not difficult to understand if we can interpret it in universal terms, and apply our present-day experience to the older conditions.

iuftus cocidet feruices peccatoz. Deide legitur euangeliz cum rubea alba in qua viagefimak tono. pinatis ut tantus a cir cunstantib poffit audiri a quatro viacono. Qſam fero factuz effet. uenit qdam homo di ues abarimathia noie iofeph. q et ipe vifcipulus erat iefu. Ihic acceffit av pillatuz et petiit cozp? iefu. Tunc pillat? iuffit redvi cor pus. Et accepto cozpoze iofeph inuoluit illud in fyndone munda. et pofuit illud in monumento fuo nouo. quod exciderat in petra. Et aduoluit faxum magnum ad boftiuz monuméti et abiit. Erat autem ibi maria magdalene. et altera maria fedentes ptra fepul chzum. Et tam viaconus non falutat cum legit. Et qzuis vicat fequentia fan cti euangelii fecundus matheuz. Nullus refponder. Gloria tibi vie. hoc finito. bic incipiut capelam uefpum et vicit. Bñz Bridicrus vns qui uiuit et. Deide inci pit. hyn. Ihymnu vicamus vño. Sine gloria tibi vie. Ihoc finito fubiungie. Bñz. Bridicrus vns qui uiuit et. K archidiaconile. Anime impiozz fremebat aduerfum me et grauari eft fuper eos cor meus pzo eo quod ftatuerut pretium mei triginta argenteos quod apretiatus fuz ab eis. Diuiferunt fibi ueftimenta mea et fuper ueftem meam miferunt forte. tri ginta. Ihoc finito fubiungit pzesbiter Bñz. Bridicrus vns q uiuit. N. Diuiferunt fibi ueftimenta mea et fuper ue ftem meam miferunt fortem. pſ Deꝰ vcus meus refpice in me. finito hoc pfal. mo fine gloria et fine lectioe poftea fequit. Bridicrus vns qui uiuit fegt. Oratio. Largire fenfibus nris fume

reparator omps veus. ut per té pozalem filii tui moztem per opa fancta uitaz ppetuam effe creda mus. Per eudes. Tunc fubiungie pñ. Bridicrus vns qui uiuit. Hec refponfozia cantente. viaconi. Eras qua fi agnus innocens ductus fum av imolan dum et nefciebam pfcilius fecerunt inimici mei aduerfus me vicentes uenite mittam? lignum in panem eius et peramus eus ve terra uiuentium. Exurge vne preueni cos et fubuerte illos qui cogitauerut aduer fum me vicentes. uenite. Iherufales luge et exue te ueftibus iocuditatis iduere cinere cum olio. qa in te eft occifus fal uator ifrael. Luctus unigenith fac tibi planctu amarus. quia in te eft. N uj. Uelum templi fciffum eft 7 omnis terra tremuit latro ve cruce clamabat vicens memeto mei vne vum ueneris in regnum tuum. al Siferere mei veus miferere mei quomaz in te pfidit anima mea. mem to mei vne. Finito ultimo refponfono. Archieps vicit follenes fuper ambonem a parte vertera chou. pesbiteri uero ui ciffim vicunt orationes. archiepo femper iacente ante altare. Tuc viacon? vicit. Flectamus genua. Tunc profternant omnes fe in terras. et vebent vicere un? quilqs in corde fuo fecrete. Flecto genua mea av patrem vni mei iefu xpi. ex quo omnis paternitas in celis 7 in terra noiat. Et poftqs orauerint vicat. Leuate uos. Similiter av ceteras orationes faciendus eft. Flectamus genua. ORemus. vilectiffimi nobis in pzimis pzo ecclefia facta vei. ut eam veus 7 vominus no fter. pacificare. multiplicare. 7 cuftodire vignetur. toto ozbe ter raruz fubinens ei pancipatus et

2b. *Missale Ambrosianum*, printed at Milan by Zarotus in 1474 or 1475. (Reduced.)

3a. Latin Bible manuscript, probably French, late thirteenth or fourteenth century. (Approximately actual size.)

auennt. 7 fecū Romā adduxit. ut
eū Aglegie būns petv̄ i epm ofe-
onet. Sufcepto itaq; Dermacoraf
pōūcat9 officio. cū Aglegēfem ec
dam optie gubnaffet. tandē ab i-
fidelibo capit. 7 ibidē marririo co-
ronat.Eoce quemō brūs. M. ī me
oio ecclie apuit os. ad fufcipienda
cona ōi.q bo merito fieret utilis to
ti collegio ecclie catholice ad femi-
nandum fidē xpi.

Apernit os eius.

Ad mundanoz oerelichonem.
Ad alrifimoz ocemplarionē.
Ad teoz conuerfarionē.
Ad cruciandoz ppreffionem.
Ad uenetoz gubnationem.
Ad fupplicandoz ipetrationem.
     Rimo brūs. M. apuit os. i. ī
     rellcm ad Mundanoz oereli
chionē. Scēdū q̄ ini guia pctā
q̄ regnabāt ī mūdo.erat pctm ifi-
delitad. Joh.io9 ca9. Arguet mun-
oū oe pctō. qa nō credit ī me. Vñ
Aug9 exponēs illud Joh. Si ñ ue-
nifem 7 loque9 eis nō fuifez pec-
catū ñ bērēt.ioicit fic. Magnā qō-
oā pctm fub generali noie uff itel
ligi. B.n. ē pctm infidelitatis quo
tenētur cūcta pctā. ß ille. OÉ eni;
pctm formalr ofiftit in auerfione a
oeo. Vñ tāto aliqō pctm ē graui9
q̄o p ipm hō magl fepat a oeo. Sz
p ifidelitatē bō maxie a oeo elōga
tur. qa nec uerā oei cognitionē h;
p falfam sūt cognitionē ipo9 ñ ap-
propinqūtur ei. ß magl ab ipo elon
gat. nec pōt eē q̄ oeū cogfoat q̄ fal
fam oe eo optionē h;. qa id qō ipfe
opinat nō ē oeus. Vñ manifeftu;

ē q̄ pctm ifidelitatis ē mai9 oībuf
peccatis q̄ otingunt in puerfitate
moz. Qō pz in feptē generib; pec
catoz . p ifidelitas ē gui9 pctm
q̄ fuperbia.Nā celfitudo quā fupb9
iordiate appetit fcōm fua tōem . ñ
h; maxima repugnantiā ad bonū
orutis.qa etiā ex bono orutis con-
furgit. Vñ Aug9 oicit.q̄ fuperbia
etiā bois opib9 ifidiat ut pereant.
Et p̄s oic. Jn uia hac q̄ ābulabam
abfcondert fupbi laq̄u mihi. 7 io
mot9 fupbie occulte furrepēs. ñ h;
maxima guitatē. Sed pctm ifide
litatis gui9 reddit cū ex otēptu oi
uine maieftad poedat. z9 ifidelitas ē gui9 pctm q̄ iuidia. Nō.n.
iuidia ē maximū pctōz. qa ouz qs
uani nois potentiā appetit.ne quif
hāc adipifci ualeat. tabefcit. Sz infidelitas ē quedā iuidentia frae
gre.fcōz quā aliqs oolet o ipfo au-
gmēto gre oei. 7 ñ folū oe bono p
ximi. 7 fic ē pctm in fpm fcm.qa p
hāc inuidentiā q̄dāmodo hō inui-
oet fpūi fcō q̄ in fuis opib; glorifi-
cat . f9 ifidelitas ē gui9 pctm q̄
auaricia.Nā oē pctm ex b ipo q̄ ē
malū ofiftit in quadā corruptioe
feu puatioe alic9 boni.Et fic ex pte
boni qō p pctm otēpnit ul̄ conum
pit. q̄to maius ē.rāto pctm gmiuf
ē.7 fcōm b pctm ifidelitatis qō ē
otra oeū ē guiffimū. 7 fub b ē pec-
catū qō ē otra pfonā bois.fub q̄ ē
pctm qō ē otra res exteriōes. que
fūt ad ufū bois oeputate.qō undet
ad auariciā prine. q9 infidelitas
ē grauius pctm q̄ ebrietas. Nam
ex b oī aliqd eē malū . q̄ puat bo-
nū.uñ q̄to maius ē bonū qō puat
per malum.tanto malū graui9 eft.

3b. Leonardus de Utino, *Sermones de Sanctis*. Venice, Renner,
1473. (Approximately actual size.)

There are today three different ways of using "writing," or rather, of using the letters of the alphabet for purposes of visual communication.

First: *printing;* for books, magazines, newspapers, job printing.

Second: *lettering;* this is a formal, artistic writing, similar in appearance to printing, and in use for special occasions.

Third: our everyday *handwriting,* such as used for correspondence, diaries, notes, accounting, etc.

(The typewriter is not important in this connection. It is a new thing without precedent and does not help us to understand early conditions.)

Now the interesting thing is that this triple use of "writing" can be found at practically all times and in many civilizations. It is one of the fundamental conditions of writing. The classic example is the writing of the ancient Egyptians. They had the "hieroglyphs," which were very formal, conventionalized signs used for dynastic and religious purposes. Then they had the so-called "hieratic writing" developed from the hieroglyphs, and resembling them somewhat, but written with greater speed and ease, and for not quite so holy or official purposes. It is more a regular book hand, for law, medicine, and other scientific texts. And then they had a third kind of writing, also developed from the hieroglyphs by rapid and much repeated use: the so-called "demotic," or popular writing, used for private notes, correspondence, accounts, etc.

All three forms of handwriting were for a long time used simultaneously, though the hieroglyphs are of course the oldest, and the demotics the youngest, in age.

This leads us to the second fundamental law of writing development. Within the most formal group of writing, certain letter forms are continuously becoming obsolete, and are continuously being replaced from the less formal groups. Private cursive writing of today is, so to speak, the official, formal hand of tomorrow. The change is of course very gradual, but it is clearly visible; and as individual forms become obsolete and are therefore replaced, the general character of the formal writing changes as well.

One other factor has to be considered as a continuous influence in the development of writing: that is, the tool with which, and the material upon which, it is done. In the ancient world, in Egypt, Greece, and Rome, the formal writing was primarily used on stone inscriptions, and the more informal, cursive hands were practiced on more perishable material.

Thus, when the formal stonecutter's capitals of classical Rome were used for the writing of vellum manuscripts in the early mediaeval centuries, they gradually assumed a more rounded appearance, that is, the "square capitals" changed to uncial capitals. Next, certain cursive forms that had previously been developed and used in private handwriting in ancient Rome crept in and mixed with the uncials to form the so-called semi-uncial script. Finally, these cursive forms outnumbered, and at last drove out completely, the capital forms. This process was completed around the year 800. Today we call these new forms the *Carolingian minuscules.* They are really nothing else than small roman letters developed in the classical roman cursive writing, and now admitted as book characters into the respectable society of official letters. The square capitals and uncials did not die out entirely; they were now used as

4a. From a fifteenth-century German manuscript, written at
Augsburg in *lettre bâtarde*. (Slightly reduced.)

"display" letters for headings, captions, special sections in the liturgy, and so on. After their establishment, these Carolingian minuscules were never abandoned again; and especially in Italy they were practiced all through the Middle Ages, till at last they became the models, as we shall discuss later on, for the roman printing types of the fifteenth century.

The change from the roman square capital alphabet to the Carolingian minuscule is the most important phase of letter development in the Western world; it established the letters of the roman alphabet in their essential "anatomical" structure. The further developments are merely changes of physiognomy, so to speak—expressions of various artistic styles in terms of the roman alphabet. The most important among these physiognomical changes is the development of the gothic minuscule toward the beginning of the thirteenth century, and on to the fifteenth century. Compared with the variety of gothic letters, the differences in the shape of the roman minuscules appear very small indeed!

Gothic writing forms at the beginning of the fifteenth century represent a separate universe within themselves. A great number of different terms, that sometimes contradict themselves, are used by the various authorities to describe these varieties. It will not do to be very literal in the use of these names, and it is more satisfactory to use a flexible terminology. On the whole, it will be found most convenient to use our friends, the three fundamental categories of writing: formal, semiformal, and cursive. The first kind has appropriately been called *lettre de forme* by the French paleographers; it is also called *pointed missal* type or *textura*. There is a round variety of it, used most frequently in Italy, which is called *round missal* or *rotunda*. Both forms are used primarily for the Bible and for liturgical texts.

Next, the semiformal writing has the official French name of *lettre de somme*. This can best be described as a regular book hand. It is in the main a smaller variety of the missal type, often very similar to it in design, only a little rounder in proportion. Sometimes it is not at all easy to distinguish the two categories. There are several transitional forms and no absolutely final test can be given by which to tell the two apart in cases of great similarity. But it is very convenient to think of the normal, conveniently sized book letter in a category by itself. It is used for regular scientific texts, such as law and medicine, and also in some theological other than liturgical texts.

The third category is a very interesting one, and quite definitely to be distinguished from the two former groups. It is the so-called *lettre bâtarde*, a convenient French term which it is possible to use regularly. This is a cursive book hand which resembles the respective private handwriting of the time and place where we find it used. But it is not identical with a private writing hand. It is younger than the first two categories and is used for the most recent form of literature found in the fifteenth century, the literature in the vernacular languages of France, England, and Germany. Thus, a form of writing closely related to the way in which the people themselves would write was used for texts that were closely related to the people's everyday language. We must not forget how universal the use of Latin was in the Middle Ages and what an innovation this growth of vernacular literature really was.

It is very interesting to observe that the earliest type faces cut in the fifteenth century were of the formal, pointed missal kind, and that the last type faces of the fifteenth century based on handwriting were cursive script letters. It is more or less correct to say that the formal liturgical hands were first translated into type, that the regular book letters came next, and that the *lettre bâtarde* was the last.

It has been established beyond doubt that Gutenberg's famous missal type, the one used for his forty-two-line Bible, is closely based on the missal hand found in liturgical manuscripts of the diocese of Mainz. Actually, all the early typographic experiments of Gutenberg were made with this missal type. These early steps in the development of Gutenberg's invention are visible to us in terms of progressive cuttings, always of the same missal letter, which was not only used for liturgical texts, but also for the Latin school grammars and calendars that preceded the forty-two-line Bible.

Figure 1b is a reproduction, considerably reduced, from the mysterious thirty-six-line Bible, which was undoubtedly composed with Gutenberg types, but which was perhaps printed in Bamberg and not in Mainz, as one would naturally assume. The manuscript page, also reproduced in considerable reduction (Figure 1a), offers a very interesting parallel indeed. It is a fifteenth-century Bible manuscript in the John Rylands Library at Manchester. Mr. Henry Guppy, who kindly gave permission to reproduce the two pages, which he was good enough to provide for this article, was the first to point out the remarkable resemblance of the manuscript to the thirty-six-line Bible. As a matter of fact, the actual hand in which the manuscript is written is not very similar. The capital letters are much more ornamental than the Gutenberg capitals, and their general appearance is not typically German. The manuscript, according to an entry found in the book, once belonged to a monastery in Metz. This, perhaps, is an indication of some French influence. Much closer manuscript models for Gutenberg types could be shown from liturgical manuscripts written in the Rhineland. But apart from this, the similarity is striking. The same passage from the Bible, II Kings 4.1, has been deliberately chosen to show the same arrangement of the text in two columns, the same type of initial letter in the same place, and above all, the same number of thirty-six lines in the manuscript and the printed page. This similarity is not an accident found on two picked pages, but holds true throughout. One feels inclined to assume that the printer of the thirty-six-line Bible had before him, to put it carefully, a manuscript Bible of the same kind as the one preserved today in the John Rylands Library. There cannot be much doubt that the "layout" of the thirty-six-line Bible was not original with the printer, but that he reproduced in the printing press an established kind of Bible manuscript.[1]

It is interesting to note here that the unknown, undated, earliest printer of Holland also used the missal hand for his types. In their experimental character they are comparable with the early Gutenberg types; but they differ from them in the same way in which a Dutch Bible text written in pointed missal differs from a German one.

For an example of a *manuscript rotunda* and its rendering in print we turn to Italy, where this form of letter was most popular in the fifteenth century. Figures 2a and 2b show pages from two Latin service books, one a Breviary written at Piacenza in 1480,

wiſſen dz alle cardinäl der zwelffpotē ſtat hältē ſüllē
als ſÿ xpus erwelt hat in d welt do ſÿ ſeinē namē vnd
ſein gerechtikeyt ſei ſrid vn dē gelaubē veſtnē vn pauē
ſüllen/wēn aber die cardinäl mit mügē an alē ſtettē dz
vſorgē vn tůn noch d pabſt/ſo ſind zů hilff die biſchoff
erdacht vn geordnet/Auch dē ſrid vn die gerechtikeyt
zů pauen vn zů beſchirmē nit ſeiner wirdigen prieſter
ſchafft als wir leſen in dem ewangelio.luce.Ein hauß
vater dz iſt xpus d hat ſein ſchetz enpfolhē ſeinē hauß-
geſind/einē enpfalhe er fünff ſchetz/dem andern zwen
dē drittē einē.Dz ſind d pabſt vn cardinäl fünff ſchetz
dēn biſchoffē zwē/der prieſterſchafft einē. Jn diſen ſch =
etzen leit alle gerechtikeit götlicher ordnūg vn troſtlich
lebē d menſcheit. got hat nichtz vgeſſen er hat vns den
weg gezeygt der ewigen ſelikeyt/vil wöllē in aber mit
geen/An wem aber dz erwindet od wer es hindert dz
würt mā wol merckē wēn mā ÿegklichē ſtat rüren ſol
Jch main wol an d ſimoney ſey d pabſt ſchuldiger dān
die cardinäl.Sie nemen vill eicht iren teil an den ſtuckē
ſānt Peters patrimonÿ lieber dann auf den kirchē/ap=
teyen oder biſtumen/doch erkennen ſÿ wol das es wid
got iſt.Sie ſölten es auch dem pabſt mit nichtē nit ver
hengen/wann nach rechtem ſtat ſo ſol der pabſt in der
heiligē kirchen nichtz vendrē on rat d Cardinäl/darüb
ſÿ auch ſind in ſchuldē wān ſÿ vhengē dz im rechten mit
mag beſteen/vn das wol wiſſen.Seid es dē pabſt vn
cardinälē leicht iſt d gerechtikeit aufzů geen/ſo volget
ÿederman nach mit allem vnrechtē/ vnd iſt kain mittel

4b. Koenigshofen Chronicle. Augsburg, Baemler, 1476.
(Reduced.)

and the other a *Missale Ambrosianum* printed at Milan in 1474 or 1475. The general appearance of both pages is strikingly similar and even the expert will take a few moments to make out which is the manuscript and which the printed page. The general arrangement of the text on the page, the use of a smaller book hand along with the round missal type, and the handwritten rubrication on both pages have of course much to do with this resemblance. But the general ductus of the script as well is closely related, and along with minor variations of letter forms there are such striking similarities as the small *a* and the small *g*. The appearance of the printed page is naturally more regular, or more mechanical looking, and there is a sharp angularity which the manuscript does not show. We have observed the same in the previous example, and we begin to recognize it as an unavoidable, constant factor in the transformation of handwriting into print. So we can really say that Antonius Zarotus, the printer of the *Missale Ambrosianum*, was completely successful in "reproducing" in type what was the usual hand employed for North Italian service books in his time.

The Italian *rotunda*, especially in the smaller sizes and approaching in appearance and function the *lettre de somme*, became one of the most popular letters of the entire early printing period. After it had once been cut as a type, it was copied over and over again by the printers of many countries. Copies were made not only of the first printing types of this kind, but also of copies of them.

Another type face that has played a rôle similar in importance and influence is the regular book type of Fust and Schoeffer, which will be mentioned later on with the *fere humanistica* group of letters. This process of making type not from a manuscript model, but from a type already in existence, is one of the most powerful influences away from the manuscript and toward an early standardization of printing. In the present discussion we must limit ourselves to the creation of the original forms only.

As a matter of fact, the early book hands of the *lettre de somme* category are a little difficult to analyze in this way. Already in the manuscript era they were highly formalized and standardized, and the variations even in two countries are but small.

To illustrate this point a manuscript page and a printed page are shown in Figure 3 which originated in different countries and at widely separated periods. The manuscript page (Figure 3a) is from a Bible, probably French, written in small *lettre de somme* characters at the end of the thirteenth, or in the fourteenth, century. The printed page (Figure 3b) is from a book of sermons set in *lettre de somme* type by Franz Renner, in Venice, in 1473. In spite of the great difference of time and place of origin the similarity of general page appearance is remarkable. It would be possible to take many other examples from different localities and periods, and the effect would be the same. Closer inspection will of course reveal many individual differences of letter form, but they do not seem to influence the general appearance greatly.

Much greater varieties are seen in the third group of gothic letters. It has already been pointed out that the *lettre bâtarde* is the closest approach of a book hand to the everyday writing of the people. This is the reason why fifteenth-century manuscripts written in this hand show the most striking reflection of national character. This impression is also due to the use of the vernacular, as against the universal Latin of service books and of the scientific literature of the time. Further, these popular

5a. From a manuscript of *Le Livre des Propriétez des Choses*, written at Bruges in 1482. (Reduced.)

mes predecesseurs autant grant comme latre
pe corage qui viue :pourroit desirer. ⟨Premie-
rement iap les maisons de mes peres qui sont
tresamples et tresaorneez telement quelles ne
sont pas moindres des ediffices royaulx .⟨
Jay en la douce prouince tusculaine vn tresbel
village .Jay aussi en campane tresbeaux la:
bourages de champs et de vignes dont seulement la famille dune maison pourroit estre
nourrie .ou presques vn tresgrant ost en pour
roit estre repeu . Tous les vtensiles de mon
maisnage quelz quilz soient sont fais et forgi-
ez dor dargent et dyuoire comme a paine tout
le pueple rommain le scet bien par auoir hate
en mon hostel . ⟨Drayement la dignite de
tant de belles choses si riches et si reluisans come dit est :mest vne tresnoble et tresclere decoration de noblesse q en ceste cite sauue la paix
de tous :que on ne pourroit trouuer plusgrant
ne plusnoble .

Par ainsi conques se taise Sapus flami-
mius et en ce debat de noblesse delaisse a de-
mander Lucresse .lui qui nest pas seulement

5b. From Colard Mansion's undated Bruges edition of Surse de
Pistoye's *La Controversie de Noblesse*. (Reduced.)

[metrical life of St. Edmund — early fifteenth-century manuscript facsimile]

6a.   From a metrical life of St. Edmund by John Lydgate; early fifteenth-century manuscript. (Reduced.)

[Occleve's De Regimine Principum — early fifteenth-century manuscript facsimile]

6b.   From Occleve's *De Regimine Principum*; early fifteenth-century manuscript. (Reduced.)

[Caxton printed text facsimile]

contre. Thus wente hercules by the ryuage of the see m
to the liste and furthermest partye of Europe And say
&c. so ferre that he entrid m to the Ryuer of guadiana
where as the traunt gerion dwelde and aboute m the cpte
of megida/ The same tyme that hercules entrid m to the
ryuere. Gerion wente vp in to the toppe of an hygh
tour where he myght see all aboute the contre for to see

7a.   Lefèvre's *Recuyell of the hystoryes of Troy*, translated and printed by Caxton at Bruges. (Reduced.)

[Caxton printed text facsimile]

egall/andr so shal godr leue him & his succession   And
sayd that may none escape to be atte grete day of Jugemt
andr his helpe shalbe there by iij thinges/ Discracion chas/
tete/andr goode Werkes/Alle thinges may be lefte/Siue
goode dedis/Alle thinges may be chaungedr/Saue nature
Alle thynges may be redressh dr and reformed/Saue euil
dedis/Alle thinges may be escheued/Saue deth/andr the

7b.   *Dictes and Sayings of the Philosophers*. Westminster, Caxton, 1477. (Slightly reduced.)

"chapbooks," as we may call them, are very frequently illustrated with free pen-and-ink illustrations filled in with water colors, which also help to give them a spontaneous, fresh appearance. Therefore it is only natural that the early printed editions in these *bâtarde* types show a great deal of life and variety. Compared with the somewhat dreary monotony of the mediaeval Latin texts of a scholastic and dogmatic nature, these first documents of living contemporary literature are pleasant and enjoyable to the modern mind, and their physical appearance also is a pleasant relief from the very formal script of church service books and theological and scientific texts. A study of *lettre bâtarde* manuscripts from various European countries makes it clear that this hand was most significant in Paris and the north of France, Belgium, and Holland. The *lettre bâtarde* written in this region is quite uniform, the variations being of minor importance. England too has its *lettre bâtarde*, which resembles the Western Continental group, but shows some distinct peculiarities of its own. The *lettre bâtarde* in Germany is not as clearly defined as in the countries just mentioned. There is no one dominating type, and the absence of a uniform standard for this hand allows for innumerable variations in the different German districts, which make it difficult at times to decide whether one is still dealing with a real book hand or merely with a private hand employed for the copying of a text.

Figure 4a shows a Swabian *lettre bâtarde* which is definitely a book hand, written by Conrad Mueller von Oettingen, a professional scribe, who was probably the head of a secular manuscript workshop in Augsburg between 1450 and 1480. Figure 4b shows a page from a book printed in 1476 by Baemler, one of the printers who definitely used type faces cut to reproduce the local manuscript hand. As a matter of fact, the resemblance of manuscript and print is not as obvious as in the examples of more formal script already shown. One great difference is that the manuscript shows a definite slant to the right, while the printed page has a perpendicular appearance. Also, the letters in the manuscript are all connected with each other in much the way in which we connect letters when we write today. Both differences are easily explained: Had the Augsburg punchcutter attempted to retain both ligatures and the slanting character of the script he would have encountered difficulties far beyond his ability; furthermore, the composition of such slanting letters would have presented insurmountable obstacles. Not until some twenty years later, when Aldus Manutius had his first Greek type and soon afterward his first italic type cut, were these problems successfully overcome. A closer inspection of the two Augsburg examples will satisfy the critical reader as to their connection. It is sufficient to point to the letters s, f, ff, and tt, which are not only similar in shape, but also manage to reproduce some of the slope of the manuscript.

Of the Franco-Flemish *lettre bâtarde*, there is reproduced a fine example from Bruges. All in all, it is perhaps correct to say that the Netherlandish variety is apt to be a little heavier and also larger than the French examples. Figure 5a is reproduced from a finely illuminated manuscript copy of *Le Livre des Propriétez des Choses* in the British Museum, which was written, as the book itself tells us, in 1482 by Jehan du Ries in Bruges. It is very fortunate that we can show a *lettre bâtarde* manuscript actually written in Bruges, for it was in that city that the famous Colard Mansion used

8a. An example of Italian *fere humanistica* writing, from a manuscript of Gregorius's *Moralia*. (Reduced.)

8b. *Fere humanistica* printing type as used by Sweynheym and Pannartz in their St. Augustine. (Reduced.)

a very interesting heavy *bâtarde* printing type, Figure 5b, that is obviously based on the local handwriting. The similarity is very obvious and it is not necessary to point out individual resemblances. As in the case of the Augsburg *bâtarde*, previously shown, the printed page does not appear quite as slanting as the manuscript. Another characteristic difference is the greater delicacy of the manuscript letters. They are of approximately the same size as the type, but they show much greater contrast of hairlines and body strokes. Modern printers who have worked with extremely delicate script type will appreciate the early Flemish type-cutter's reluctance in reproducing the finer portions of his manuscript models.

Colard Mansion has always interested the English-speaking world as an associate of William Caxton, the first English printer, during his Continental apprenticeship. It was at Bruges and in collaboration with Mansion that Caxton started to print English books for the English market. Discussing possible manuscript models of the types employed by Caxton both in The Netherlands and in England raises some very interesting points.

It is quite clear that Caxton began printing with a *bâtarde* type that he got from Colard Mansion; Figure 7a shows Caxton's first type, which he used in Bruges, and which is identical with Mansion's third type face. When Caxton went to England, he used other type faces. It has been said of them that they bear general resemblances to the Flemish *bâtarde* letters, but also show some peculiarities of their own. What these peculiarities are, has as yet not been stated very clearly. It is therefore very interesting to compare Caxton's type faces with English manuscripts of the fifteenth century. Figures 6a and 6b show two early fifteenth-century English manuscripts in the characteristic English *lettre bâtarde*. A glance at the Flemish *bâtarde* in Figure 5a will prove that the English hand has a definite character of its own. Individual letter forms are quite similar, but the general appearance is different; the body strokes are not so heavy, the general appearance is not so regular and shows more flourishes, and the writing is more upright (Figure 6b). It is very interesting to see that all this can be said with equal justification of Caxton's second *lettre bâtarde* type (Figure 7b), which he used after his return to England. The resemblance of this type to the Occleve specimen (Figure 6b) especially is conclusive. We may assume then that, like the printers of the Continent, Caxton also took the national handwriting of his country as a model for some of his printing types.

The inspiration which the early printers received from late mediaeval gothic script of the cursive variety was undoubtedly refreshing and valuable. However, this influence turned out to be an impermanent one. There is only one really notable exception. The German "Schwabacher" type face, which developed from German *bâtarde* script toward the end of the fifteenth century, has lasted through the sixteenth and the following centuries to the present day.

Robert Granjon's *lettre de civilité* which was used in Lyons from the middle of the sixteenth century, and which spread to Holland and England, is another example of a gothic script type based on handwriting forms. However, it was not based on a script employed for book writing, but on a secretary hand.

Before going on to look at the manuscript foundation of roman printing types, there

9. Italian humanist manuscript of *Vegetius, De Re Militari.*
(Reduced.)

is to be considered one transitional group of handwritings and of printing types derived from them which is of considerable importance in the fifteenth century. In the English-speaking world the term *fere humanistica* has been coined to describe the minuscule hands that contain elements of both the gothic and the roman style. This hand was very popular in Italy, where there has always been some reluctance in accepting purely gothic forms, whether in architecture, painting, or writing. The Loggia dei Lanzi, well known to anyone who has ever visited Florence, is an extraordinary architectural document of romanized gothic or of gothic roman. In Germany, where the term *Gotico-Antiqua* is used to describe this *fere humanistica* hand, there is very little use of it in manuscript writing; but the first distinguished regular book hand in German printing, the one used by Fust and Schoeffer (Figure 30), is a *fere humanistica*. It proved to be a most successful design, and the subsequent imitations and adaptations by other fifteenth-century printers can be regarded almost as a symbol of the spreading of typography from Mainz.

In Italian printing history we find that the earliest printers used a *fere humanistica* before they used a purely roman type face. In Figure 8b is shown a section from a St. Augustinus, printed by Sweynheym and Pannartz. For comparison, a typical Italian *fere humanistica*, written in the fifteenth century, is shown in Figure 8a. It is interesting to see on this manuscript page the purely roman capital letters M and N beside capital letters in other styles. In the small letters, too, the conflict between smooth curves and narrow, angular forms is marked.

Compared with this mixed hand, the pure humanist minuscule, an exquisite example of which is reproduced in Figure 9, is a direct descendant of the Carolingian minuscule; this in turn was the adaptation, as a formal book hand, of the classical roman cursive writing. With very few interruptions, the Carolingian minuscule was used all through the Middle Ages in Italy. It is true that in the late thirteenth and in the fourteenth centuries the *fere humanistica* more or less took the place of the pure roman minuscule, and it is true that in the early fifteenth century the Italian humanists who were engaged in classical research adopted the roman hand as their favorite book hand; but to speak of a "revival" of the Carolingian minuscule is an exaggeration. The only real revival that did take place was the renewed interest in the roman square-capital letters, such as were seen on the ancient ruins. They were studied with a new love and interest. As a result, these capital letters were introduced once again into book writing, and they were now established as the definite, permanent companions of the humanist minuscules.

It is not quite easy to say in what Italian city and by what scribes the actual manuscripts were written which served as models for the early printers. Figure 9 and Figure 11a show how great the differences between the individual examples of humanist minuscule handwriting can be. Our quest is further complicated by the fact that the first actual appearance of a purely roman printing type was not in Italy at all, but in Germany. Adolph Rusch of Strassburg is the first printer to use a roman type face, an example of which is shown in Figure 11b. It is fairly certain that it was his own type, because the letters A ad R, which are his initals, show some curious variations from the normal shape.

10. The Epistles of St. Jerome, printed at Rome by Sixtus
Riessinger. Reproduction from the British Museum copy, with
hand-painted border and initial. (Reduced.)

In Italy, too, the first attempts at roman type design were made by German printers—in the city of Rome. Sweynheym and Pannartz (Figure 12) and Ulrich Han (Figure 11c) made independent experiments in the cutting of roman type faces. Compared with the Venetian designs, their type faces are not very successful. But in the obvious imitation of whatever manuscript models they may have used, these early type faces cut in Rome are fascinating documents of experimentation. Figure 10 shows another interesting example of this phase.

By comparison, the Venetian attempts aim from the very beginning at a definite printing type, rather than at a mechanical rendering of manuscript models. The brothers John and Wendelin of Spires used a type face which has the finality of a definite accomplishment, and which, shown in Figure 13a, was the basis of Jenson's famous type (Figure 13b). And from there on the course of roman type design was a straight line of steady development and gradual refinement. The roman type of Erhard Ratdolt (Figure 14) and of Aldus Manutius (Figure 35) are both direct descendants of Jenson's roman.

If one were to gather from this that Aldus Manutius, who started his career as a printer late in the century, did not use any more handwriting models for his type, one would be quite mistaken. His Greek type is a very close rendering of Greek handwriting, and also in the italic type—his distinguished contribution to typography—handwriting forms were closely imitated. It is true that Aldus is a somewhat belated example of a printer who used current manuscript hands for his type designs. It is generally accepted today that this method was abandoned by about 1475. There is another significant difference between his use of manuscript forms and those of printers earlier in the century: Aldus did not go back to writing hands that had been established and used as book letters for a long time; instead, he took script forms which had been adopted as book hands only recently, and which were thus made into printing types after a very short trial period as manuscript letters.

There had been some experiments with Greek printing type previous to Aldus in which the more formal, upright varieties of Greek book hands were used for models. When Aldus decided to print regular editions of Greek classics, he turned to the cursive hand, as written by the Greek scholars who had fled from the Near East to Venice when the Turks conquered Constantinople in 1453. There are manuscripts preserved today written in this hand, and Figure 15a shows the opening lines of Homer's Iliad in a British Museum manuscript. Figure 15b, a section from Aldus's famous Aristotle of 1495-1497, shows how successfully Aldus managed to reproduce the refined, civilized handwriting of the scholarly calligraphers who wrote manuscripts like the Homer in the British Museum. The two initials also are interesting to compare.

For the beginnings of the sloping humanist hand which served as a model for Aldus's italic type we have to look at the Italian chancery hand as written in Rome in the course of the fifteenth century. From that source it was adopted as a book hand in the second half of the fifteenth century. Not many manuscripts written in this hand are known today. In Figure 16a is reproduced an exquisite copy of Catullus, which is now in the Scottish National Library at Edinburgh. It is probable that this manuscript

pulfi uox in aere profertur. Ex his cum foluta frequetia
eft. Qua deinde die pro lege promulganda iterum conuenif
fent Pompeiuf in agrum profectuf eft. Cum uero legem
intellexiffet promulgatam noctu in urbem reduic inuidia
ex incredibili multitudine que fibi fieret uitanf. Vt aut
illuxit dief in medium profectuf facra egit. In contionem
deinde perductuf operam dedit ut alia legi adderentur.
apparatu propemodum duplia. Quingente etenim na

11a. From a humanist manuscript of Plutarch's Lives of Great
Men, written in the middle of the fifteenth century. (Reduced.)

Rurſus & alios principes legimus ſapiencie ſtudiũ di
lexiſſe. Nero eni quáæ crudelis eſſet: elegit tamé Se
necam ſapientem in doctorem:qui de clemencia librũ:
eius occaſione ſcripſit:nunquid troyanus habuit Plu-
tarcum : cui9 occaſióe factus eſt liber de inſtructione
trayani:ut patet ex epiſtola quam ſibi ſcripſit : in qua
trayanus plus laudabat ſapienciã plutarci æ ſuá fortu
nam uel potenciam. Ceterũ de Iulio ceſare legimus æ
ſtudioſſimus extitit : curſúæ ſolis inveſtigás dies per
horas & momenta diuiſit:biſextum inuenit:& mul-
tos alios libros ſcripſit:ut patet í libro de vita ceſaris

ABCDEFGHILMNOPQuQRSTVXYZ
aáàbBcctddeëéfffgğhbiiílPmnoóópppp̃p̄pqqq̃
φφφ̃φ̃rŕsſſſſtßttuũvxyʒɔ&9ꝣ,:

11b. First Roman printing type, as used by Adolph Rusch in
Strassburg. (Reduced.)

VM igitur uehemetius inuehereretur in cau
ſam principum conſul philippus druſiæ
tribunatus ,p ſenatus actoritate ſuſceptis
infringi iam debilitanæ uideretur : memi
ni dici mihi ludorũ romanorum diebus
L .craſſum quaſi collegendi ſui cauſa ſe in
tuſculanum contuliſſe : ueniſſe codé ſocæ-
eius :g hiiſſe . Q. mutius dicebatur : et . M. antonius homo
et conſiboqum in re.p .ſocius :& ſumma cum craſſo familia-
ritate comunctus . Exierant cũ ipſo craſſo adoleſcétes & druſi
maxime familiares & in qbus magnam cũ ſpem maiores na
tu dignitatis ſue collocarant:C. cocta qui.tr.petebatur :&.P.
ſulpicius qui deinceps cum magiſtratum petituus putabatur

11c. Cicero, De Oratore. Rome, Ulrich Han, 1468. (Reduced.)

was written at Venice in 1495. For comparison, the same text from the Aldus edition of Catullus, Tibullus and Propertius, printed at Venice in 1515, is shown in Figure 16b. It is interesting to compare not only the handwriting with the type, but also the arrangement of the text on the page, the headings of the poems, and the use of the roman capital letters at the beginning of lines. The Edinburgh manuscript is undoubtedly a good example of the kind of manuscript that was used in the Aldus composing room for his edition of the ancient Roman poet.

In comparing manuscript forms with early printing types, we have had the opportunity to observe more than once how not only the letter forms, but also the way in which they were arranged on the page, were taken directly from the manuscript. A particularly obvious example of manuscript layout slavishly followed by the early typographer is the usual arrangement in early printed books of a text along with a commentary. The text, in regular book-size letters, is set in one or two columns in the middle of the page, and the commentary in smaller letters is arranged around the text like a border. Already in the manuscript this was a particularly difficult arrangement. Since the amount of commentary varied for each section of the text, each new page had to be planned separately. For the printer to follow this arrangement must have meant no end of trouble in adjusting and rearranging. Nevertheless, it simply was "the thing to do," and the early printers do not seem to have known any alternative way of avoiding this trouble.

RUBRICATION AND DECORATION

After the actual writing of the text the next thing that would be done in a late mediaeval scriptorium was the rubrication. The pages of manuscripts reproduced in this chapter show ample examples of the kind of thing that the rubricator would have to do, and how he did it. Figure 1a shows what today we would call a "running head," done in red; the opening lines of the text in red; and the large calligraphic initial letter. Figure 2a shows calligraphic initial letters of smaller size and with some border decoration. In Figure 4a the crossing through of capital letters at the beginnings of lines and the marking in of paragraph marks can be seen.

In the early years of the printing press the simple way in which the printer would solve the problem of rubrication was to have it worked in by hand. Figure 3b is an interesting example of a page printed in black with spaces left open for the rubricator. Pages where the rubrication has been carried through can be seen in Figures 1b, 2b, and 5b. (Initial with border scrolls, paragraph marks, red underlining of headlines and crossing through of capital letters.) Leaving aside the Colard Mansion specimen, which bears no date, all these examples were printed before the year 1480, and it is possible to say that by that time printers had found a way to reproduce rubrication mechanically. We remember that the use of manuscript models for type designing had really come to an end by that same time!

The first experiments in reproducing rubrication mechanically are very early. Gutenberg actually used some red printing in his forty-two-line Bible. Fust and Schoeffer, too, made notable experiments in their famous Psalter of 1457 and 1459.

12. The Epistles of St. Jerome, printed at Rome by Sweynheym
and Pannartz, 1468. Reproduction from the British Museum copy,
with hand-painted border and initial. (Reduced.)

ficiis boinu & copellar iniuriis:facile patior ea me de re publica fentire ac di′
cere:quę maxime cu mibi multu etia reipublicę rationibus putem coducere
Apertius auté hęc ago ac fępius:ꝗ & Q · frater meus Legatus eſt Cęſaris &
ꝑullu meu minimu dictum non modo factu pro Cęſare interceſſit quod illę
no ita illuſtri gratia exceperit:ut ego eum mibi deuinctu putaré.Itaꝗ eius oi
et gratia quę fumma eſt: & opibus quas intelligis eſſe maximas fic fruor ut
meis: nec mibi aliter potuiſſe uideor hominu perditoꝗ de me cofilia fragere
nifi cum pręfidiis bis quę femp babui.Nunc etia potétiu beniuolétia coiux′
iſſem.His ego confiliis fi te pręfenté habuiſſem:ut opio fert eſſem uſus eiſdé

13a. A passage from De Spire's edition of Cicero's Epistles,
Venice, 1469. (Reduced.)

de republica fétire ac dicere.quæ maxime cu mihi multu
etiam reipublicæ rationibus putem conducere.Apertius
autem hæc ago ac fępius:ꝗ &.Q.frater meus Legatus eſt
Cæſaris:et multum meu minimum dictu no modo factu
ꝑ Cæſare íterceſſit:quod ille no ita illuſtri gratia exceperit
ut ego eum mihi deuinctum putarem. Itaꝗ eius omni et
gratia(quæ fuma eſt)et opibus quas ítelligis eſſe maximas
fic fruor ut meis:nec mihi aliter potuiſſe uideor hominu
perditorum de me confilia frangere:nifi cu pręfidiis his
quæ femp habui.Hunc etiam potentium beniuolentiam
coiunxiſſem.His ego cofiliis fi te præfentem habuiſſem:
ut opinio mea fert:eſſem uſus eiſdé.Noui enim téperátia

13b. The same passage in Jenson's edition, Venice, 1471.
(Reduced.)

They succeeded in reproducing mechanically in red and blue printing initial letters with a very complicated calligraphic scroll running up and down the page! But they must have realized that these experiments were impractical and did not lead to an acceptable, everyday working method. It is usually said that Erhard Ratdolt, in Venice, carried on some twenty years later where they had stopped. This is not quite correct, because what he "reproduced" mechanically was not rubrication but illuminated decoration. We shall hear more about this presently. First, another word must be said about the further development of rubrication in terms of typography. As time went on, the merely decorative features were neglected and only those points were transferred to the press that had real textual significance. Thus, we find a good deal of red and black printing in liturgical books all through the fifteenth century. In other books, the headlines that would have been red in the manuscript were printed in black in a larger type of different design from the text. Paragraph marks would be printed as black spots a little heavier than the general weight of the type face. Perhaps we can also say that some of the rather flourished capital letters that were developed for certain gothic type faces toward the end of the century were meant to stand out from the run of the text in much the same way in which a manuscript capital letter with a red stroke through it would have stood out!

The story of initial letters and their transformation from manuscript forms into printing units is a very interesting one and much more could be said about it than is possible in a survey such as the present one. Like all other products of the rubricator, initial letters were at first simply added by hand to the printed page, as can be seen on Figures 1b, 5b, and 8b. As a guide to the scribe the printer would often print a small, lower-case letter in the actual space where the initial was to be put in.

Mechanical reproduction of initials is a very old practice; in fact, it developed quite independently from the invention of printing and is found much earlier. Manuscripts are known into which the initials are pressed with some kind of engraved stamp. There also seems to have been some use of stencils to simplify the rubricator's tedious task.

Of the attempts of Fust and Schoeffer to print calligraphic initials in red and blue we have already spoken. Subsequent attempts by other printers were less ambitious, and they led to a possible routine method: the printing of woodcut initials in simple black outline which were at first intended for subsequent hand coloring, but were very soon developed into self-sufficient black and white units. The famous lily-of-the-valley initials, first used by Günther Zainer of Augsburg, are good examples of this development, which we can trace step by step in our figures. Figure 1a, the Manchester Bible manuscript, has a calligraphic initial P which clearly belongs to the lily-of-the-valley type of decoration. Figure 17a, from the British Museum copy of the *Zamorensis Speculum*, shows an incunable printed by Günther Zainer in 1471 with the same kind of initial drawn in by hand; and Figure 17b shows the same letter as it finally appears in Zainer's woodcut alphabet.

The illuminator's initial letter is to be distinguished from the rubricator's calligraphic initial. It was not drawn with the pen in red and blue ink, but painted with fine brushes in the full range of illuminating colors and with gold and sometimes silver.

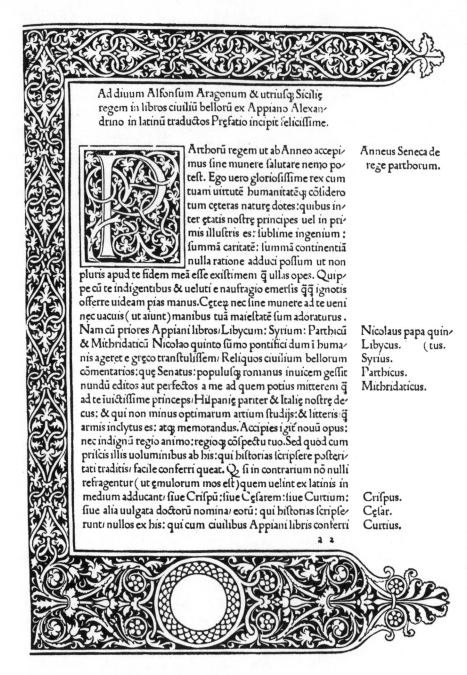

Ad diuum Alfonfum Aragonum & utriufq; Sicilię
regem in libros ciuiliū bellorū ex Appiano Alexan⸗
drino in latinū traductos Prefatio incipit feliciſſime.

Arthorū regem ut ab Anneo accepi⸗
mus fine munere falutare nemo po⸗
teft. Ego uero glorioſiſſime rex cum
tuam uirtutē humanitatēq̃ cōlidero
tum cęteras naturę dotes: quibus in⸗
ter ętatis noſtrę principes uel in pri⸗
mis illuſtris es: fublime ingenium :
fummā caritatē: fummā continentiā
nulla ratione adduci poſſum ut non
pluris apud te fidem meā eſſe exiſtimem q̃ ullas opes. Quip⸗
pe cū te indigentibus & ueluti e naufragio emerſis q̃q̃ ignotis
offerre uideam pias manus. Cęteq̃ nec fine munere ad te ueni
nec uacuis (ut aiunt) manibus tuā maieſtatē fum adoraturus .
Nam cū priores Appiani libros/Libycum: Syrium: Parthicū
& Mithridaticū Nicolao quinto fūmo pontifici dum i huma⸗
nis ageret e gręco tranſtuliſſem/ Reliquos ciuilium bellorum
cōmentarios: que Senatus: populuſq̃ romanus inuicem geſſit
nundū editos aut perfectos a me ad quem potius mitterem q̃
ad te iuictiſſime princeps/Hifpanię pariter & Italię noſtrę de⸗
cus: & qui non minus optimarum artium ſtudijs:& litteris q̃
armis inclytus es: atq̃ memorandus. Accipies igit nouū opus:
nec indignū regio animo: regioq̃ cōfpectu tuo. Sed quod cum
prifcis illis uoluminibus ab his: qui biftorias fcripfere pofteri⸗
tati traditis/ facile conferri queat. Q̃ fi in contrarium nō nulli
refragentur (ut ęmulorum mos eft) quem uelint ex latinis in
medium adducant/ fiue Crifpū :fiue Cęfarem: fiue Curtium:
fiue alia uulgata doctorū nomina/ eotū: qui biftorias fcripfe⸗
runt/ nullos ex his: qui cum ciuilibus Appiani libris conferri

Anneus Seneca de
rege parthorum.

Nicolaus papa quin⸗
Libycus.   (tus.
Syrius.
Parthicus.
Mithridaticus.

Crifpus.
Cęfar.
Curtius.

a 2

14. *Appiani Romanorum Liber,* printed by Ratdolt in Venice,
1477, with woodcut initial and border in red. (Reduced)

Therefore its mechanical reproduction presented considerable difficulties. More designing skill was necessary to translate this symphony of color into simple black and white lines, and the printer who used such outline initials must have relied on subsequent hand coloring even more than in the case of the calligraphic initials. Figure 15 shows a rather late example of an illuminated initial letter and a black and white rendering of a similar letter. When looking at the woodcut initial alone it does appear somewhat incomplete in its outline, and a glance at its illuminated forerunner makes it clear just what it is that is missing.

It so happens that all other examples of illuminated letters on our plates appear in connection with illuminated borders.

In decorated manuscripts at large many separate initial letters can be found, but at least on the opening page of the manuscripts they are usually found in some connection with borders of the same style and technique, so that we are justified in treating initials and borders at the same time. A splendid example of a richly decorated opening page, Figure 20, is a fifteenth-century copy in French of Boethius's Consolation of Philosophy, from the Morgan Library in New York. The finely painted initial letter, about which more will be said later on, is connected with an elegant border in gold and pen work of typical French character, on the left. On the right is a more realistic floral border of wild berries and leaves combined with coats of arms and heraldic animals. There is yet another initial letter with the same design as the left border, on a gold background. The colors are brilliant, and the general effect is extremely rich and gorgeous. An equally brilliant, but more restrained, opening page is shown in Figure 9, an Italian fifteenth-century manuscript in the British Museum, where the initial letter, with an author's portrait in it, is an integral part of the border decoration.

As in the case of rubrication, the first step of the early printer in getting his books illuminated in the same way as his manuscript models was to have the printed pages finished off by hand. Figure 12, the opening page of the 1468 Rome edition of the Epistles of St. Jerome, shows a charming border with initial letter and coat of arms woven into a decorative pattern which differs in no way from the decoration of Italian fifteenth-century manuscripts.

In decoration also, the middle of the 1470's seems to mark an important turning point. In Figure 18 can be seen a woodcut initial and woodcut border on the opening page of a Strassburg book of 1483. Both are very clearly derived from manuscript decoration of the fifteenth century. The animals and the amusing wild men and women playing in the floral border are of the so-called *drôlerie type*, which is much more frequent in French and Flemish than in German manuscripts; but, as this example shows, there is now and then some influence from neighboring France in books made on the shores of the Rhine.

The Strassburg example is by no means one of the earliest attempts to reproduce illuminated borders by a woodcut. Already in the 1470's Venetian woodcut borders had reproduced successfully a very popular type of Italian border decoration. This style of ornament has an old and distinguished ancestry. It goes back in the last analysis to Celtic Models, brought to the Continent by Irish monks from the eighth

15a. Opening page of a fifteenth-century Greek manuscript of
Homer's Iliad. (Reduced)

ΑΡΙΣΤΟΤΕΛΟΥΣ ΓΕΡΙ ΖΩΩΝΙΣΤΟΡΙΑΣ

ΤΟ Δ.

15b. Aristotle, Works. Venice, Aldus, 1497. (Reduced.)

century on; these motives became an integral part of Continental book decoration in the ninth and tenth centuries. Figure 9 shows its use in a fine humanist manuscript; Figure 10 is an early printed book of Rome with hand-drawn border and inital in the same style; and Figure 14 shows Ratdolt's Venetian woodcut border and initial derived from the manuscript models.

There is a good reason why the opening page in mediaeval manuscripts and in many early printed books was decorated with such special care: the absence of a title page. Title pages, as is generally known, are essentially a feature of the printed book, and their development in the fifteenth century makes an interesting study in itself. But here, too, careful investigation would show that title pages were not entirely unknown during the manuscript era and at least the rudiments of later developments could be discovered.

It is very interesting to observe that the decorated opening pages by no means disappeared with the arrival of title pages. Their persistent occurrence, in spite of a much diminished *raison d'être*, is one of the most remarkable proofs of the power of tradition and custom. By the beginning of the sixteenth century, the full border around all four sides of the page, with the initial letter as part of it, had shrunk to a mere headband with a separate initial, which, however, was still drawn in a style of ornament closely related to the pattern found in the border. Figure 15b is an example of this "abbreviated formula." It is found in many Italian books of the sixteenth century; in Paris the Estiennes, as well as other printers, made good use of it; and Plantin carried it over into The Netherlands. By 1600 it was a universal practice, and it has lasted to the present day. In our times both D. B. Updike and Bruce Rogers have made much use of it in their books.

An interesting side line is the influence of the "opening page formula" on early newspaper typography. In looking over the plates of Stanley Morison's monumental volume on English newspapers,[2] it is most fascinating to observe how title-page layout and opening-page layout struggled for supremacy on the first page of the early newspaper. The opening page came out on top, and it is actually true that the little emblem in the masthead of the daily edition of the London *Times* is the last survivor of the splendidly illuminated opening page of a mediaeval manuscript.

ILLUSTRATION

We know perhaps more about the interdependence of illustrations in late manuscripts and early printed books than about any other individual feature. Nevertheless, a clear view of the development is obstructed by an astonishing number of transitional manufacturing stages between a regular illustrated manuscript and a regular illustrated printed book. This can best be seen by a simple enumeration of the transitional steps actually observed in fifteenth-century illustrated books. There is:

1. The manuscript illustrated with illuminated miniatures.
2. The manuscript with pen-and-ink drawings, colored in water colors.
3. The manuscript with pasted-in woodcuts or copper engravings.

4. The manuscript with printed-in wood blocks or metal cuts.
5. The block book.
6. The printed book (movable types) with hand-drawn or pasted-in illustrations.
7. The printed book with outline woodcuts to be colored by hand.
8. The printed book with self-sufficient black and white woodcuts.
9. The printed book illustrated with copper engravings.

This list has been arranged in what would appear to be a logical development of subsequent stages. However, there are some peculiarities of chronology which upset this order and which must be dealt with before we can pursue our main line of observation. It will be advisable, so as not to complicate matters further, to disregard some of the less important experiments that are interesting enough in themselves, but have not much symptomatic value. The numbers 3 and 6 on our above list can therefore be neglected.

It will be useful for us to think of the dates at which the various stages described in our list actually begin. Illuminated manuscripts, our starting point, are the oldest of all; they go back practically to the beginning of the codex in early mediaeval times. It might be said right away that they by no means stopped abruptly with the beginnings of printed illustration, but were carried on well into the sixteenth century and even further.

Manuscripts with pen-and-ink illustrations are old too, but although there are examples to be found through the Middle Ages, the fifteenth-century ones belong to a group of manuscripts that rose to importance in the course of the fourteenth century.

Most of the manuscripts with printed-in wood blocks or metal cuts are to be considered as predecessors of the regular block books. They deal with the same subjects, are arranged in the same way, and bear general resemblances to the block books. Schreiber, the great authority on early woodcuts, calls the woodcut volumes of this category *Xylo-Chirographa*. The volumes with metal cuts, called *Metallo-Chirographa*, are much rarer.[3] These block books with handwritten text appear in the neighborhood of the year 1450, and they do not seem to last much later than 1460. About that date the regular block books appear on the scene, those in Latin marking the beginning, and German and Dutch texts appearing as late as about 1470.

These dates are surprisingly late if one considers that as early as 1461, Albert Pfister in Bamberg printed the first book in movable type with woodcut illustrations; and that other printers followed soon afterwards. This fact is the main reason why until quite recently block books were dated much earlier in the century. This view was based on the logical assumption that block books represent a natural step of evolution between the manuscript and the movable-type printed book. However, more accurate research in early book illustration, such as comparisons of graphic design with the general development of artistic style, and careful consideration of chronological entries in the block books, have established their later date. As a result, we have to revise our opinion of the block books as an intermediate step between illustrated manuscripts and printed books. Rather, we have to think of block books as a separate, independent movement that has its own momentum and fulfils itself in its own time.

Ad claras Asiae uolemus vrbes :

Iam mens praetrepidans auet vagari :

Iam laeti studio pedes vigescunt :

O dulces comitvm ualete caetvs

Longe quos simui a demo profectos

Dwersae & variae uiae reportant :

Om et Socration duae sinistrae

Pisonis scabies famesqz Memmi

Vos veranniolo meo & Fabullo

Verpus praeposuit priapus ille :

Vos convivia lauta sumptuose

De die facitis mei sodales

Quaerunt in trivio vocationes :

Ad Iuventum :

Elluos oculos tuos Iuuenti

Si qvis me sinat vsque basiare :

CATVL.

Vidit? quis uenerem auspicaciorem ?
        Ad seipsum de aduentu ueris.
    Iam uer egelidos refert tepores,
I am caeli furor aequinoctialis
I uandis zephyri silescit auris ,
L inquantur phrygij Catulle campi ,
N iceaeq; ager uber aestuosae ,
A d claras Asiae uolemus urbes ,
I am mens praetrepidans auet uagari ,
I m laeti studio pedes uigescunt ,
O dulces comitum ualete coetus ,
L onge quos simul a domo profectos ,
D iuersos uariae uiae reportant .
        Ad Porcium, & Socrationem.
    Porci, & Socra:ion,duae sinistrae
P isonis scabies, fame: q; Memmi ,
V os Veraniolo meo, & Fabullo
V erpus praeposuit priapus ille ,
V os conuiuia lautae sumptuose
D e die facitis,mei sodales
Quaerunt in triuio uorationes.
        Ad Iuuencium.
    Mellitos oculos tuos Iuuenci,
S iquis me sinat usque basiare ,
V sque ad millia basiem trecenta ,
N ec unquam saturum inde cor futurum est ,
N on si densior aridis aristis
S it nostrae seges osculationis .
        Ad Marcum T. C.
    Disertissime Romuli nepotum,

16a. Catullus manuscript, probably written at Venice in 1495. (Reduced.)

16b. The same passage in the printed edution Catullus, Tibullus and Propertius. Venice, Aldus, 1515. (Reduced.)

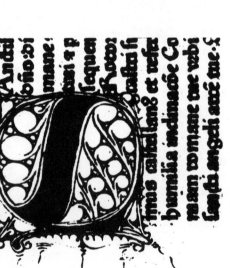

17b. Woodcut initials of the same design used by Günther Zainer. (Reduced.)

17a. From Rodericus Zamorensis's *Speculum*, printed at Augsburg by Günther Zainer in 1471. Initial drawn in by hand.

How else are we to understand why block books continued until the 1470's, when regular illustrated books were at the height of their popularity?

For these illustrated books we can assume, then, a direct evolution from illustrated manuscripts; and the historical facts bear out this assumption. Before going on to observe these relations, a word should be said about the relation between manuscripts and block books. There is hardly a block book the illustrations of which do not have a parallel in slightly earlier or in contemporary manuscripts. The purpose of both these block books and manuscripts is the same: popular religious and moral instruction by means of many pictures and few words. At the same time there is a certain chapbook element in these products, catering to the same instinct that sends people to the movie theatres today. Children must have loved these brightly colored pages!

Naturally, there are many close connections between the manuscripts and block books. Mr. Henry Guppy, in *The Beginnings of Printed Book Illustration*, describes and reproduces a manuscript Apocalypse that is closely related to the block book *Apocalypse*. For the *Speculum Humanae Salvationis*, too, such parallels are known. As a matter of fact, manuscript illustration has had an influence on woodcutting in a stage even more primitive than block books or "block books with handwritten texts." A manuscript has been discovered which contains the models for several well-known single-leaf woodcuts.[4] Leaving aside textile printing and playing cards, these single-leaf cuts, or broadsides, represent the earliest form of European wood engraving. So we know now that from the very beginning pictorial reproduction methods were based on existing hand-drawn manuscript models.

Mr. Guppy has also pointed out that the woodcuts in the Bamberg *Biblia Pauperum*, another early illustrated book, represent the same subjects, and are arranged page for page in the same combinations as in the block book *Biblia Pauperum*. It is not necessary to assume that the Bamberg printer had a copy of the block book in front of him when he had his cuts made and his pages set up. As in all similar cases there is the possibility of a parental manuscript from which both the block book and the Bamberg printed book could have been derived. And even if the block book is really the model, it would not allow us to conclude therefrom that fifteenth-century illustrated books in general are derived from the block books. We know too many cases where this is not true, and where we can point to direct manuscript models.

Our knowledge of these connections, it must be admitted, is at present rather unequal, as far as the various European countries are concerned. We know much more about the development in Germany than in any other country, and it is therefore advisable to start there. One of the most interesting cases is the relationship of the famous woodcuts in Quentell's Cologne Bible of 1479 to the illustrations of a German Bible manuscript in the Staatsbibliothek in Berlin, shown in Figure 19. The manuscript was written about 1460 in Cologne dialect in or near that city. As is usually the case in these connections, the relationship is once removed; that is to say, the wood blocks and the drawings do not depend on each other directly, but go back to the same original manuscript. This accounts for all those differences that are not due

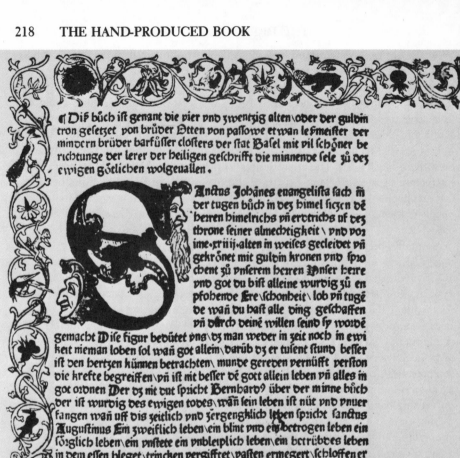

18. Otto von Passau's *Buch der Vierundzwanzig Alten*. Strassburg, Martin Schott, 1483. (Reduced.)

to the process of translating delicate, lively, pen-and-ink designs into terms of the wood block. To those who have known, and perhaps loved, the Cologne woodcuts, a glance at the lovely, spontaneous drawings must come almost as a shock. There can be no doubt that the drawings are far superior to the woodcuts, which in spite of their primitive charm appear only as rather clumsy reproductions.

Another famous German woodcut book for which the manuscript model is known is Dr. Hartlieb's German version of the Romance of Alexander, printed at Augsburg by Johann Baemler in 1473. All its woodcuts appear to be copies of a manuscript that was written and illustrated by a certain Voelkhardus Landsberger of Kaufbeuren, who lived and worked in Augsburg between 1455 and 1465. This manuscript was in the Library at Maihingen in southern Germany, and is now in the Morgan Library in New York. There, again, the manuscript illustrations are much freer and more spontaneous than the woodcuts. These woodcuts are charming when looked at alone, but when compared with their manuscript predecessors, their crudity and roughness become rather obvious.

We know a good many manuscript models for Augsburg woodcut illustrations. During an extensive study of the illustrated manuscripts of southwestern Germany I had the good fortune to discover manuscript predecessors for about ten different Augsburg woodcut books. These manuscripts all date from between 1450 and 1470. The earlier ones turned out to have the greater artistic value. In no case did the woodcuts appear superior to, or in any creative way independent of their models. Merely the redesigning of these illustrations in simplified lines and the skilful cutting of these lines in wood can be counted to the credit of that first generation of woodcutters who worked for the Augsburg printers.

A very interesting thing about these manuscript models is the fact that none of them is what we would call an illuminated manuscript. They are, all of them, popular paper manuscripts, written generally in a cursive hand, illustrated with pen-and-ink drawings and painted with light, transparent water colors. The texts for which these illustrations were made are popular religious or moral tracts, usually in the vernacular, and popular versions in local dialects of the romances that had been the delight of the nobility a hundred years earlier. These manuscripts were not written and illustrated in monasteries, as the illuminated manuscripts of that time and of earlier days, but they were written in an almost mass-production manner in secular workshops in the towns. We know of one workshop in Augsburg, that of Conrad Mueller von Oettingen, where such manuscripts were turned out as late as 1470-1480, that is to say, actually at the same time as the illustrated printed books.

In other towns also, such workshops have existed. Earlier in the century a thriving business in popular, illustrated romance manuscripts was carried on in the town of Hagenau, in Alsatia, by one Diebold Lauber. Similar workshops seem to have existed in Strassburg and Stuttgart, and it would not be surprising if traces could be discovered in many other towns. We know of several other cases of the dependence of illustrated woodcut books on such popular manuscripts, which have as yet not been attributed to a definite workshop. But we know enough to be able to say that the fifteenth-century woodcut illustration in Germany is based not on traditional illuminated manuscripts, but on a new type of manuscript production that worked in a new manner and obviously for a new public!

Is this also the case in the other European countries? Not much research has been done along these lines and there is no definite answer today to that question.[5] One thing is certain: The kind of popular manuscript just described in Germany does exist in the other countries. We know Dutch, French, Spanish examples, and also, which is more surprising, Italian and English. Then, too, there are in these countries, with the definite exception of Italy, woodcut illustrations that look very much as though they were derived from such manuscripts. But our assumptions are not always borne out literally. For instance, the 1489 edition of the works of Alain Chartier, printed in Paris by Pierre le Caron, has an interesting opening woodcut of the author inspired by "Entendement" and "Merencolie" (meaning the light and the dark powers of the human mind), shown in Figure 21. Professor Panofsky has suspected for a long time that this woodcut is derived from a manuscript illustration, and he had the satisfaction at last of finding in reality what he had imagined. Figure 20, which is being reproduced with the kind permission of the Morgan Library, is the opening page of a manuscript of Boethius's Consolation of Philosopy, in French. We have already had occasion to admire the rich border decoration and the fine workmanship of the initial letters. Once again we regard this figure with renewed interest, because the larger of the two initials turns out to be the unmistakable model for our woodcut. It is not the identical scene, but a similar "author's portrait" with the author reclining on his bed and an allegorical figure beside him. Obviously, we have here a type of illustration customary at the beginning of certain writings. This initial is not a pen-and-ink drawing, but a regular piece of illumination.

There are other indications that in France the formal illuminated manuscript rather than the popular manuscript has influenced printed book illustration. Illuminated books of hours were much more popular in France than in Germany; in fact we can call them a typical French product. The Parisian workshops really worked for a world market. It is told how, soon after 1480, Parisian printers began to produce such books of hours by the printing press, and how certain printers and publishers specialized in their manufacture. It is certain that their border decorations, initials, and illustrations, printed from metal cuts, were closely based on the contemporary manuscripts. They were frankly competitive products; printed books of hours on vellum are preserved that are illuminated so much in the manuscript manner, covering up in the illustrations all traces of printed lines, and using gold and silver, that it takes some time to decide whether or not they are printed books. Because the manuscript production was so well organized and its market so firmly established, the printers had to fight much harder for recognition of their books of hours than for any other of their books, and the battle lasted much longer than in any other branch. In the early sixteenth century manuscript books of hours were still doing very well.

In England, as in the case of Caxton's type faces, one has so far been satisfied to explain everything as direct or indirect Continental importation. Only one exception is known for English fifteenth-century woodcut illustrations. The cuts in Caxton's second (first illustrated) edition of The Canterbury Tales show some dependence

19a. Illustration of the Dance of David in a Low German
manuscript of the Bible, written in or near Cologne about 1460.
(Reduced.)

19b. The same scene in the Cologne Bible, printed by Heinrich
Quentell in 1479. (Reduced.)

20. Opening page of a fifteenth-century French manuscript of
Boethius. (Reduced.)

O ꝝ diⱦiefmᵉ aꝯ de moꝯ
doufant eⱦil
Apꝛes mait dueil ꝗ mait
mortel peril
Et les dãgiers quap iuſꝯ
ques cꝩ paſſeꝫ
Dont iap ſouffert graces a dieu aſſeꝫ
Na pas grantmentes cꝛoniques liſoie
Et es haulꝫ faiꝫ des anciens Biſoie
Qui au pꝛemier noble france fondeꝛẽt
Leuſꝝ eꝯ Bertu tellement abõdeꝛẽt

Que du pape fuꝛẽt Bꝛaie poſſeſſeuꝛe
Et lont laiſſie a leuꝛe bõs ſucceſſeuꝛe
ꝗ tãt leuꝛe mie's ꝗ le's doctꝛines cꝛuꝛẽt
que le' ropaume ꝗ le' poũoit acteurent
Et ſi firent honnouꝛet et aꝛmet
Cꝛaindꝛe ꝗ doubter deça et dela meꝛ
Juſtes eꝯ fais ſecouꝛãs leuꝛe amis
duꝛe auⱦ mauuais ꝗ fieꝫ auⱦ ẽnemiſ
Aꝛdans dõneuꝛꝗhaulⱦ entꝛepieneuꝛ
Amans Bertus des Bices ꝛepieneuꝛ
Regnans paꝛ diꝛoit euꝛeuⱦ ꝗ glorieuⱦ
a.ii.

21. Opening page of Alain Chartier's Works, printed in Paris by
Pierre le Caron in 1489. (Reduced.)

upon the illustrations of the manuscript in Cambridge and the Ellesmere manuscript, now in the Henry E. Huntington Library. Perhaps this is the only example in England that we shall ever know of, but it must be said that the English popular illustrated manuscripts of the fifteenth century have not been much investigated; in fact, the whole question of English fifteenth-century manuscript production, illustrations or no illustrations, has not been dealt with very extensively.

In Italy, we have a situation that differs fundamentally from that of the northern countries.

Italian woodcut illustration, apart from a few individual forerunners, did not get under way until the last decade of the century. It began at a time when in other countries manuscript models had already been absorbed, and printers were finding their way more independently. But even in earlier Italian examples there does not seem to have been much imitating of manuscript illustration. In the following passages I would like to quote from a study of fifteenth-century illustration by Mr. William M. Ivins, Jr. (*Some Artistic Aspects of Fifteenth Century Printing*, published in the Papers of the Bibliographical Society of America). About the Verona Aesopus of 1479, a noted early Italian woodcut book, Mr. Ivins says:

> It was the first, and until quite recent times the last, book to be illustrated with woodcuts conceived not as imitations of pen drawings but in immediate terms of knife-work upon the block.

Of the later Florentine woodcuts he says:

> Their pictures are not only the loveliest to be found in any early books, but they are more closely allied to and based upon the contemporary design of a great school than any of the woodcuts produced before the outstanding masters of painting themselves took to designing book illustrations.

For Venetian woodcuts, too, the relations with the monumental art of the time are important. Ivins knows of only one book, a small edition of Meditations of the Passion of 1489, which shows some relation to miniature painting. The cuts in this book are by two different hands, one of whom with some reason has been identified with the Paduan miniaturist Benedetto Bordone. However, this artist's work is in itself under the immediate influence of Mantegna and the Bellinis.

This independence of Italian book designing from manuscript models is really not surprising, if we consider that it was first in Italy that the makers of books, as Mr. Ivins has put it, realized and adapted themselves to the physical conditions which in the event have produced the modern book.

BOOKBINDING

Of all the steps in the manufacture of a book the only one that is left to examine is the binding. It is very fitting that this factor should be considered at the end, for it will be

Beati qui lauant stolas suas in sanguine a=
gni:ut sit potestas eorum in ligno vite:et per
portas intrent ciuitatem. Foris autem canes
et venefici et impudici et homicide et ydolis
seruientes; et omnis qui amat et facit men=
dacium. Ego ihesus misi angelum meum te=
stificari vobis hec in ecclesijs. Ego su radix
et genus dauid: stella splendida et matuti=
na. Et spiritus et sponsa dicunt veni. Et qui
audit:dicat veni. Et qui sitit veniat:et q̃ vult
accipiat aquã vite gratis. Contestor enim
omni audienti verba prophetie libri huius. Si
quis apposuerit ad hec · apponet deus super
illu plagas scriptas in libro isto : et si quis
diminuerit de verbis libri prophetie huius · au=
feret deus parté eius de libro vite et de ciui=
tate sancta : et de hijs que scripta sunt in li=
bro isto. Dicit qui testimonium phibet istorum.
Etiam :Venio cito amen:Veni dne ihesu.
Gra dni nri ihesu cristi cu omnibus vobis ame.
Explicit liber apocalips beati iohãnis apli.

Presens hoc opusculu Artificiosa admiuetione
imprimendi seu caracterizandi · absq; calami
exaracõn · in ciuitate Moguntini sic effigiatu·
et ad eusebiã dei industrie per Johe3 fust ciue
et Petru schoifher de gernsheym clericu di=
oces eiusdem est consumatu3. Anno dni. M.
cccc.lxij. Jn vigilia assumpcõis virg̃ marie·

30. Latin Bible. Mainz, Fust and Schoeffer, 1462. Reproduced
from the Morgan Library copy on vellum. (Reduced.)

seen that the relationship of manuscript bindings to the bindings of printed books is a very eloquent indication of the true course of events. The current, popular theory in bookbinding handbooks is that the invention of printing changed the character of bookbinding fundamentally. Actually, this is not at all true.

The typical binding on an early printed book is a brown calf binding with blind-stamped decoration. There are of course other types of binding, but this one is found so predominantly that its history can be considered as a satisfactory clue to the entire situation.

This type of binding, then, has quite a distinguished parentage. There was a clearly recognizable vogue of such bindings as early as the twelfth century. Mr. E. P. Goldschmidt, who has investigated the entire field of early bookbinding with masterly skill, is inclined to see in these bindings an early indication of semicommercial manuscript production. This early blind stamping is perhaps a set type of binding decoration for certain ecclesiastical manuscripts, which would be written and bound in monasteries to be sold to customers, who would again be chiefly monastic and episcopal libraries.

In the thirteenth and fourteenth centuries there are hardly any examples at all of this kind of binding. But at the beginning of the fifteenth century there is a revival of the craft, and by the time book printing started, these blind-stamped calf bindings were popular all over Germany and Austria, France, The Netherlands, and England. It is absolutely correct to say that there is no difference in either technique or decoration between the typical manuscript binding of the fifteenth century and the typical binding of the incunables!

The first change in the technique of blind-stamped bindings did not begin until the 1480's. To save some of the labor involved in the building up of borders with single close-set rectangular stamps, rolls with the design engraved on them were introduced at that time. But their use did not become general until about 1510. The next step toward mechanization, as books became more frequent, cheaper, and also smaller in size, was the engraving of the decoration on to a single large metal stamp, from which an entire panel could be printed with one impression. This innovation, too, does not come into regular use until after 1500. A more important, fundamental change in bookbinding was the introduction of pasteboard to take the place of the heavy wooden boards that had so far been used as the basis for the covers. This change, too, did not take place until the sixteenth century.

It is clear, then, that the kind of bookbinding found on early printed books started independently of, and earlier than, the invention of printing. Also, it can be said that it was not affected by it until the early sixteenth century, when the entire aspect of bookmaking reached a new stage.

A RÉSUMÉ

We have now come to the end of our study, and it will be interesting briefly to sum up what the detailed observation of manuscripts in relation to printed books has taught us

POLIPHILO QVIVI NARRA,CHE GLI PARVE AN-
CORA DI DORMIRE,ET ALTRONDE IN SOMNO
RITROVARSE IN VNA CONVALLE,LAQVALE NEL
FINE ERA SERATA DE VNA MIRABILE CLAVSVRA
CVM VNA PORTENTOSA PYRAMIDE,DE ADMI-
RATIONE DIGNA, ET VNO EXCELSO OBELISCO DE
SOPRA.LAQVALE CVM DILIGENTIA ET PIACERE
SVBTILMENTE LA CONSIDEROE.

A SPAVENTEVOLE SILVA,ET CONSTI-
pato Nemore euaſo,&gli primi altri lochi per el dolce
ſomno che ſe hauea per le ſeſſe & proſternate mébre diſ-
fuſo relicti,me ritrouai di riouo in uno piu delectabile
ſito aſſai piu che el præcedente.Elquale non era de mon
ti horridi,&crepidinoſe rupe intorniato, ne falcato di
ſtrumoſi iugi. Ma compoſitamente de grate montagniole di non tro-
po altecia. Siluoſe di giouani quercioli, di roburi, fraxini & Carpi-
ni , & di frondoſi Eſculi, & Ilice , & di teneri Coryli,&di Alni,& di Ti-
lie,& di Opio, & de infructuoſi Oleaſtri, diſpoſiti ſecondo laſpecto de
gli arboriferi Colli. Et giu al piano erano grate ſiluule di altri ſiluatici

35. From the *Hypnerotomachia Poliphili*, Venice, Aldus, 1499.
Reproduced from facsimile copy of Columbia University Library.
(Reduced.)

about the general evolution of book printing in the fifteenth century.

It was only toward the end of the century that a clear conception of bookmaking in genuine printing terms had evolved. It took another fifty years for this conception to be accepted generally in the various countries of Europe. Looking back at the beginnings of printing, this means that about a hundred years of experimentation had to pass before something like a universal standard of book production was evolved.

The fifteenth century as a whole really appears in a new light. To put this quite simply, one can say that a new era in book production did not start with the beginnings of typography, but earlier in the century; that there were several subsequent movements to supply the new demand for popular, inexpensive books; that these movements conflicted somewhat with each other and that there was a battle of the powers involved, in which the printing with movable types came out on top. It is immensely interesting to observe how the demand of new classes of readers, the rise of universities, the awakening of vernacular literature, together with the revived interest in classical literature and the intimations of reformation in the Church, really preceded the invention of printing. It is quite clearly visible how the makers of books early in the century prepared themselves to meet the new demands even without the printing press, of which they had no knowledge. It is possible to "predict" how book production would have developed if printing had not arrived at that crucial moment.

In this regard the secular manuscript workshop in the cities has great importance, together with such ecclesiastical organizations as the Brothers of Common Life, who made it their chief aim to produce inexpensive books for popular consumption. This movement got under way in the first quarter of the century; it reached its best period between 1450 and 1470, and fell off rapidly after 1480. However, the members of these writing shops did not give up without struggle. We have knowledge of complaints of their guilds against members of the printers' guilds in several cities. Another way by which they hoped to keep their hold on the market was to imitate in their manuscripts certain characteristics of the printed book. This is especially visible in the illustrations of some popular manuscripts, and there are also observable some pathetic attempts to outdo the woodcuts by tricks that only the pen could do!

The traditional ecclesiastical art of illumination did not feel the competition of printing and wood engraving so keenly. It lasted undisturbed all through the century and well into the next one, when at last the illuminators had to surrender.

The first step toward mechanization was the block book, with its predecessor, the block book with handwritten text. The latter, as has been said before, had started by 1450, the regular block books beginning around 1460 and going on, like the popular manuscripts, until the end of the 1470's. First, they had to gain ground from the manuscripts, then they had to struggle against the regular printed books. One amusing phase of this struggle is that some makers of block books, like some manuscript scribes, imitated the printed books. There are some block books known which actually are copied from regular printed books.

Printing with movable type, then, is the final step in the mechanization of bookmaking. It has been carefully shown in this article how the earlier printers depended in every detail on the model of the manuscript. Perhaps it has not been made clear enough that this was not a deliberate choice, but absolute necessity. There is still the idea alive with some writers that the fifteenth-century printers, like the makers of certain finely printed books today, looked around in earlier centuries for "interesting" models. That is not the case. What they did, simply and purely, was to take the manuscripts of their own immediate neighborhood.

It took the early printers about twenty-five years to translate the mediaeval manuscript methods into printing terms; and they needed another twenty-five years to forget them and gain the freedom necessary to answer the call of a new era of human civilization.

NOTES

[1] As in other such instances there is, of course, the possibility that the manuscript was copied from the printed book. Close study of such relationships is needed before questions of this kind can be definitely determined.

[2] Stanley Morison, *The English Newspaper*, 1622-1932, Cambridge University Press, 1932.

[3] *See* Warren Chappell's article, "Illustrations Made with a Tool," in *The Dolphin*, No. II, 1935, for a reproduction of a metal cut.

[4] Fritz Saxl. "Aller Tugenden und Laster Abbildung." In the Julius v. Schlosser *Festschrift*.

[5] Since these lines were written, Professor Adolph Goldschmidt devoted an entire course of lectures at the Morgan Library to these popular manuscripts.

THE HAND-PRODUCED BOOK
Additional Readings

THE ANCIENT WORLD

Chiera, Edward. *They Wrote on Clay: The Babylonian Tablets Speak Today.* Edited by George C. Cameron. Chicago: University of Chicago Press, 1956.

Diringer, David. *The Hand-Produced Book.* New York: Philosophical Library, 1953.

Hussein, Mohamed A. *Origins of the Book: Egypt's Contribution to the Development of the Book from Papyrus to Codex.* Greenwich: New York Graphic Society, 1972.

Kenyon, Sir Frederic G. *Books and Their Readers in Ancient Greece and Rome.* 2d ed. Oxford: Clarendon Press, 1951.

Pinner, H. L. *The World of Books in Classical Antiquity.* 2d ed. Leiden: A. W. Sijthoff, 1958.

Thompson, Edward. *A Handbook of Greek and Latin Paleography.* 3d ed. London: Kegan Paul, Trench, Trübner, and Company, Ltd., 1906. Reprint. Chicago: Argonaut, 1966.

_____. *An Introduction to Greek and Latin Paleography.* Oxford: The Clarendon Press, 1912. Reprint. New York: Burt Franklin, 1964.

Turner, E. G., *Greek Manuscripts of the Ancient World.* Princeton: Princeton University Press, 1971.

_____. *Greek Papyri: An Introduction,* Princeton: Princeton University Press, 1968.

Weitzmann, Kurt. *Ancient Book Illumination.* Cambridge: Harvard University Press, 1959.

THE MEDIEVAL WORLD

Alexander, J. J. G. *Italian Renaissance Illumination.* New York: George Braziller, 1977.

Ancona, P. d' and Aeschlimann, E. *The Art of Illumination: An Anthology of Manuscripts from the Sixth to the Sixteenth Century.* New York: Phaidon, 1969.

Dain, A. *Les Manuscrits.* Paris: Societé d'Éditions-les Belles Lettres, 1964.

Dupont, Jacques and Gnudi, C. *Gothic Painting*. Translated by Stuart Gilbert. Geneva: Skira, 1954.

Formaggio, Dino, and Basso, Carlo. *A Book of Miniature*. Translated by Peggy Craig. New York: Tudor, 1962.

Mitchell, Sabrina. *Medieval Manuscript Painting*. New York: Viking, 1964.

Mutherich, Florentine. *Carolingian Painting*. New York: George Braziller, 1976.

Nordenfalk, Carl. "Book Illumination," in *Early Medieval Painting from the Fourth to the Eleventh Century*. New York: Skira, 1957.

_____. *Celtic and Anglo-Saxon Painting: Book Illumination in the British Isles 600-800*. New York: George Braziller, 1977.

Pirani, Emma. *Gothic Illuminated Manuscripts*. London: Hamlyn, 1970.

Porcher, Jean. *Medieval French Miniatures*. New York: Abrams, 1959.

Putnam, George H. *Books and Their Makers During the Middle Ages*. 2 vols. New York: G. P. Putnam's Sons, 1896. Reprint (2 vols). New York: Hillary House Publishers, 1962.

Reynolds, L. D. , and Wilson, N. G. *Scribes and Scholars: A Guide to the Transmission of Greek and Latin Literature*. 2d ed. Oxford: Clarendon, 1974.

Robb, David M. *The Art of the Illuminated Manuscript*. South Brunswick and New York: A. S. Barnes and Company. 1973.

Salmi, M. *Italian Miniatures*. New York: Skira, 1956.

Sinks, Percy. *The Reign of the Manuscript*. Boston: Richard G. Badger, 1927.

Swarzenski, H. *Early Medieval Illumination*. New York: Oxford University Press, 1952.

Thompson, Daniel B. *The Materials and Techniques of Medieval Painting*. London: Allen and Unwin, 1956. Reprint. New York: Dover, n.d.

Weitzmann, Kurt. *Late Antique and Early Christian Book Illumination*. New York: George Braziller, 1977.

_____. *Studies in Classical and Byzantine Illumination*. Edited by Herbert L. Kessler. Chicago: University of Chicago Press, 1971.

_____, et al. *The Place of Book Illumination in Byzantine Art*. Princeton: The Art Museum, Princeton University. Distributed by the Princeton University Press, 1975.

Williams, John. *Early Spanish Manuscript Illumination*. New York: George Braziller, 1977.

IV.

THE PRINTED BOOK

Part IV. THE PRINTED BOOK

Introduction

Between Gutenberg's invention of printing with movable type and today stand 500 years of the printed book. Although each era brought new developments, the printing of books remained a hand-craft operation until the mechanization of book production during the Industrial Revolution. Thus from 1450 A.D. to 1800 A.D. book production was essentially the same and although it was a faster process than the hand-produced book of earlier times, it still produced rather limited quantities of books for a small reading public. It was not until after the Industrial Revolution that mass production of books became a reality, or as stated in "Caxton to Computers" by J. M. Kerby: "Few technical developments have been more significant for the human race than the invention of printing by movable type [in Europe] in the fifteenth century and the introduction of the electronic computer in the twentieth."

Otto W. Fuhrmann surveys the invention of printing with movable type, discussing its beginnings in the Far East and early developments in Western Europe. Fuhrmann reveals that Gutenberg's invention came to full fruition during the decade preceding his death in 1490 and concludes: "When the great inventor, whom we may all admire as a mechanical genius, closed his eyes, the craft he had developed was well on its way to become the most potent factor in the intellectual advancement of Europe."

Although Gutenberg was responsible for this technological development it was for the scholar-printers of the Renaissance to realize the power of the printed word. John Edwin Sandys examines the contributions of Aldus Pius Manutius, of Venice, with his printing of the ancient Greek and Roman authors in his *editiones princeps* ("first printed editions"), bringing back into the mainstream of Western culture the literature and language of the ancient world. Deno John Geanakoplos studies the contribution of the Greek scholars who came to Venice and other parts of Western Europe after the fall of Constantinople in 1453 A.D., bringing with them their manuscripts and their knowledge of Greek culture. Frederick B. Artz believes that the humanists "restored the whole surviving heritage of Greek and Latin literature, edited all of it,

235

and later, brought out printed editions of the whole." John Rothwell Slater's talk before the Fortnightly Club of Rochester, New York appeared as *Printing and the Renaissance*, in which he states: "Printing did not make the Renaissance, the Renaissance made printing." He examines the works and influences of Aldus, Estienne, Froben, Koberger, and Caxton, revealing how "each stands for a different aspect of the art of printing," forming a "sort of composite picture of the Renaissance."

The "Introductory Remarks" in the British Museum Catalogue of the "Exhibition of Fine Printing in the King's Library of the British Museum" entitled *Printing and the Mind of Man* succinctly presents a survey of printing in the next five centuries. John Clyde Oswald looks primarily at printing in England from the typefounder William Caslon to the revival of printing with William Morris. Holbrook Jackson examines the aesthetics of printing where "self-effacement is the etiquette of a good printer." J. M. Kerby bravely goes from Caxton to computers in his address to a printer's meeting in the City of Leeds. Kerby feels that "clearly we are on the threshold of immense technical advances and the printer must move with the times. . . ." He also believes that printing will survive all the changes of the electric and electronic age because "it is more convenient and attractive, for many purposes, than any of the new techniques of communication." Robert Escarpit asks the question "what is a book?" and states that "like anything that lives, the book is not to be defined." He traces the mutations of the book and gives a brief history from the earliest printed books to the best sellers, mass communication, and paperbacks of today. The concluding essay contains the remarks of Marshall McLuhan in *Do Books Matter?* in which he states that the book "serves a myriad of roles, ornamental, and recreative, and utilitarian." He examines the effects of the new technology on the printed book which he believes is actually "in the process of rehearsing and re-enacting all the roles it has ever played."

The final unit traces the growth of books and printing in America. Douglas C. McMurtrie examines the work of the American printers from Bradford to the pioneer printers of the West stating that "In the Americas the press accompanied the cross and the sword, the ax and the plow, into the world's most magnificent pioneering adventure." Joseph Blumenthal, in the exhibition catalog to the Pierpoint Morgan Library's show "The Art of the Printed Book, 1455-1955," examines the book in the United States from Benjamin Franklin to Bruce Rogers concluding that: "Whatever its name, whatever its form, something will always exist to uphold the civilized word. 'In the beginning was the word.' So it will be at the end."

Otto W. Fuhrmann

The Invention of
Printing

THE CHINESE INVENTION OF PAPER

"Back of the invention of printing lies the use of paper, which is the most certain and the most complete of China's inventions" — thus Thomas Francis Carter opens his scholarly book on *The Invention of Printing in China and Its Spread Westward.* The date A.D. 105 is somewhat arbitrarily chosen since such an invention must necessarily have been, like printing itself, a gradual process; but as it is documented, it serves as a milestone. In that year Ts'ai Lun, privy counsellor and later inspector of public works, reported to the emperor Ho Ti the invention of a process of papermaking which may have been his own or merely sponsored by him, according to an account by Fan Yeh about A.D. 470 in the official history of the Han Dynasty (206 B.C.-A.D. 220).

This first paper was made from "tree bark, hemp, rags, and fish nets." While silk was then in use as material for writing and painting, it was unsuitable then, as it is now, for papermaking. The "silky" appearance of some Chinese and Japanese papers is not due to silk fibers, as is popularly believed. It is true that the commonly used Chinese ideogram for paper has the radical for "silk" as indication of the material, in preference to the other form with the "cloth" radical, but that is simply due to the scribe who dealt with a new material and, in naming it, grouped it with the silk fabric known to him.

SOURCE: Reprinted from Lawrence C. Wroth, Editor, *A History of the Printed Book, The Dolphin,* No. 3 (New York: The Limited Editions Club, 1938), Chapter II, "The Invention of Printing," by Otto W. Fuhrmann, pp. 25-57, by permission of the publisher. Copyright © 1938, 1966 by The Limited Editions Club, Westport, Connecticut.

Illustrations mentioned in "The Invention of Printing" by Otto W. Fuhrmann are located in *The Dolphin* between pp. 101-108. Reprinted by permission of The Limited Editions Club.

Up to recent years it was generally believed that mulberry bark and cotton constituted the chief ingredients of old Chinese paper, and that pure rag paper was a
European invention of the fourteenth or fifteenth century; ever since Marco Polo's
travels, Oriental paper has been known as "cotton paper."· The Arabs of Samarkand
have been credited with the first use of linen rags. In 1911 some paper brought back
by Sir M. Aurel Stein's second expedition to Tun-huang in Turkestan (nine undated
letters among documents dated A.D. 21-137 were found in a watchtower on a spur of
the Great Wall) was microscopically examined by Dr. Wiesner of Vienna and proved
to have been made purely of rags. This precious find carries the age of existing paper
back even further than Dr. Sven Hedin's recent specimens of Loulan (about A.D.
200), into the very period of Ts'ai Lun. The correctness of the early account is thereby
established.

FIRST IMPRESSIONS

Although paper quickly became the universal writing material of the Orient the time
of its use for some mechanical form of duplicating an inscription is in doubt. Seal
charms, sold to the pilgrims by the Taoist priests and later by the Buddhist priests,
were probably the first mechanically produced "prints," both the rubbing and
stamping methods being employed. But neither this activity nor the more elaborate copies of the canonical texts and the Confucian classics, obtained by rubbing from inscriptions incised in stone slabs, nor the rubbings from texts cut in relief on wooden
tablets (block printing) can properly be called "printing" as we today understand it. All
of this is a necessary forerunner to our form of printing, definitely circumscribed in its
possibilities, and suited to Oriental conditions but not capable of expressing the needs
of the Western world with its vastly different construction of languages.

A seal "impression" on paper can be made readily by stamping a flat surface, into
which designs or ideograms have been engraved, after the surface of the seal has been
dabbed with writing ink; that method produces a reversed or negative image (the
design white on black background). If the lines or characters are to appear as they are
painted or written originally, the pattern must be engraved in relief (with the
background cut away) and reversed right to left; the ink dabbed on the relief will then
be transferred to paper in the form of lines, and the characters will read as they were
written. The stamping of blocks produced by either method is limited to small sizes,
for it is not possible to exert enough pressure on areas larger than a few square inches
without a mechanical contrivance such as a press—which the Orientals never used.
The early existence of text inscriptions engraved on stone[1] slabs was due to a desire to
keep the official texts free from copyists' errors. There was only one practical way in
which the engraved inscription could be transferred to paper. A sheet of paper,
dampened and thereby made pliable (much more pliable than any of our modern
Western papers), was placed on the slab and dabbed until the paper had sunk into the
incised characters; the surface then was covered with writing ink, with brushes and
pads, which left the characters white. When the sheet was peeled off, one had a

"negative"; i.e., white characters on black background. It might seem simpler to dab the surface of the stone first, lay the damp paper on it, and rub it on the back; but the result would be a *reversed* (right side left) image, and therefore not suitable, unless viewed as a transparency.

The practice of cutting in stone the texts of the classics continued through the important dynasties, each thereby preserving the best textual criticism of the day. The stones of the T'ang Dynasty, which served later as models for the wood-block prints of the classics, were erected between A.D. 836 and 841. At about the same time smaller stones were used in Buddhist monastaries for the making of book scrolls, simultaneous with the first appearance of block-printed books.

BLOCK PRINTING IN THE FAR EAST

Block printing is a method of duplication whereby the characters are cut and reversed in relief, in wood, and an "impression" is taken by laying the paper on the ink-stained relief and rubbing the back. Its beginnings are shrouded in mystery. The emperor Wên Ti is reported in A.D. 593 to have caused "the cutting in wood of old pictures and the holy scriptures handed down to him." And a later historian says that during following centuries of the T'ang Dynasty "minor literary works and elementary textbooks were block-printed and sold in the markets." *For the Chinese the invention of this method is the invention of printing.* European printing differs fundamentally, as we shall see.

For the successful transfer of a design by pressure from a relief block to paper or fabric, the ink is important. Ordinary writing fluid is not satisfactory because the liquid has no viscosity and, therefore, tends to escape the pressure area, with the result that it collects along the edges, giving an "outline effect." At least by the year 200 B.C., if not earlier, the kind of ink known in the English-speaking world as "India," but more correctly described by the Germans and French as "Chinese," was used; its pigment is lampblack obtained from burning various kinds of oil, and the vehicle is made up of water-soluble gums. In the dry state it is quite permanent. Its chief quality is the indestructibility of the pigment and its resistance to water once it has dried, even in a thin layer. For printing from wood blocks this Chinese ink is ideal, because the wood absorbs excess moisture; for a metal surface, however, it is unsuitable because it collects in globules, and under pressure it is squeezed toward the edges.

An "impression" from a wood block is taken by laying the paper on the ink-dabbed block and rubbing its back with a blunt-edged stick of bamboo or bone, or a dry brush. This method of pressure application elimates the necessity for an absolutely plane-parallel surface and for uniform thickness of all blocks, and allows gentle or stronger pressure as the subject may require; furthermore, even warped, old blocks will not crack, as would be the case if a press were used. The method is by no means crude and produces excellent results, as the well-known Japanese color prints show; however, it renders the paper unfit for printing on the reverse side, the fibers being roughened by the procedure; hence the development of a style of bookmaking wherein the leaves are folded back to back, the folds being at what we would call the fore edge and the open ends being stitched together sideways, forming a square back. A contributing factor is the thinness and consequent translucency of the paper; according to the amount of water-resisting "sizing" in the paper the ink spreads more or less through the paper and makes the rather bold text characters visible on the reverse side.

What recommends the wood-block method for Oriental text printing is (1) the solidity of the page which guarantees unchangeability once it is made; if an error occurs in the making, or damage is done to the block in handling, corrections and repairs can be made by mortising and inserting plugs, and recutting; (2) the availibility of the block for subsequent editions, with the correct text unimpaired, save for physical damage (which can be remedied); (3) light weight—which makes handling easy; (4) long life—because the amount of wear from the rubbing is slight, and blocks yield several thousand prints; (5) the Chinese (and Japanese) characters being ideograms, not letters of a phonetic alphabet, form compact groups, and do not need careful alignment and uniformity; (6) ready availability of the material (wood) and ease of converting it into a printing block; and (7) speed of production without complicated mechanical devices (one man with a helper can take several thousands of impressions per day, varying with the size of sheet and other factors.) According to DeVinne "the usual performance of the Chinese printer is two thousand sheets per day, which is about one fourth more than the daily task of an American hand-pressman."[2] The only drawback is the cumbersome storage problem; however, reasonable protection against the elements offers no more difficulty than a well-kept lumberyard encounters.

In the light of all this, it occasions no great surprise to hear that the *first recorded block-print* edition was one of a million prints. To be sure, they were not books but merely "charms," small strips of paper, eighteen inches long and two inches wide, to be placed in tiny wooden pagodas which were distributed to temples as protection against demons of sickness, by order of the Japanese empress Shotoku, an ardent disciple of Buddha. Some of these charms are preserved in the temple Horyuji in Yamato; specimens are in the British Museum and the Deutsches Buchmuseum in Leipzig; moreover, we have the account in the official Japanese history, *Shoku Nihongi*, volume thirty, according to which these charms were produced between the years 764 and 770 of our era.

How soon this first recorded "job printing," as Carter calls it, was followed by the printing of a longer text (in essence a "book"), we do not know. The year of 868, however, is memorable as the year in which one of the *oldest preserved block-printed "books"* (in scroll form) was produced in China: the fanous Diamond Sutra. On May 11 of that year, the statement printed at the end says, "Wang Chieh" finished it "for free general distribution, in order to perpetuate, in deep reverence, the memory of his parents." This "book" consists of six sheets, each two and one-half feet long by nearly one foot wide, pasted together to form a roll sixteen feet long; it is now in the British Museum together with other treasures discovered by Sir M. Aurel Stein in a walled-up chamber of a Buddhist monastary in Tun-huang, in 1907.

The Diamond Sutra is significant for a feature that caused much trouble to the later

European printers when they attempted it; viz., the combination of text and illustration. It will be readily understood that in Chinese wood-block printing there is no conflict between the two, both being pictures, both being done with the same tools, and on the same block of the same material. How different from European wood blocks in combination with single, cast, metal letters!

To the Prime Minister Fêng Tao, who held his position under various emperors, belongs the credit of having caused the printing of the Confucian classics (932-953). Significant as this undertaking was, it cannot really be compared with the publication of the forty-two-line Bible in the Western world. For Fêng Tao's aim was the establishment of the correct text of the classics and their commentaries and *not* to make literature more available to the masses, whereas the European invention of printing brought about a wider distribution of *all* forms of literature. Private printing of the classics was forbidden for more than a century afterwards. *Fêng Tao is not the inventor of printing in China*, as he is sometimes referred to; he had, so far as records go, no hand in the technical work, although his name is forever connected with a venture that ushered in the so-called Renaissance of China under the Sung and Mongol dynasties (960-1368). In this era, when the magnetic needle was applied to navigation, gunpowder to warfare, and porcelain became an article of export, block printing, too, reached a high state of perfection; the National Academy embarked on the printing of the dynastic histories, a task of seventy years, and of the classics; one of the most monumental works history records was published (about 972) during the reign of the first Sung emperor: the *Tripitaka*, the whole Buddhist canon (sacred scriptures), consisting of 1,521 works, in over 5,000 volumes making 130,000 pages and requiring the stupendous number of 130,000 wood blocks. Twenty reprint editions were published by succeeding Sung and Mongol dynasties. A revised edition was cut in wood and printed in Korea, 995-1009; a reprint copy in 6,467 volumes made in 1457 has been preserved in Tokyo. This official activity found its reflex in the growth of private printing and publishing.

In 1157 the Diamond Sutra—a favorite with the Buddhists—was printed in Japan. In the four centuries between then and the printing of the prayer charms (A.D. 770) very little is recorded of printing in that country. Of other religious groups under the Chinese domain no printing by or for the Nestorians and Roman Catholics, whom Marco Polo found flourishing, is recorded, and only one large almanac edition of 3,123,185 copies for the Mohammedans (in 1328) is mentioned by historians. No blockprinted issue of the Koran is known. It must be remembered, however, that the Confucian historians were biased, and ignored, for instance, the vast Buddhist literature, including the *Tripitaka*.

Throughout the Sung dynasty books exerted an influence upon intellectual life in China comparable to the reawakening of Europe in the century following Gutenberg.

Block-printed paper money was made in China at least as early as the middle of the tenth century. Paper money was the first form of Chinese printing met with by European travelers and described in European writings before Gutenberg, chiefly by Marco Polo. Playing cards, originally a modified form of dice and widely used in the Orient, were destined to become the first paper-printed product of Europe.

THE SPREAD OF PAPER WESTWARD

While it has been said that the absence of arabic block-printed books is due to early religious scruples against mechanical duplication, I believe it is chiefly due to the unsuitability of the method to express clearly the sharp-pointed, curved, and connected phonetic characters of the arabic script, especially when written with diacritical marks. The Chinese ideograms were developed from pictograms; the tool was a brush; the character was an entity, complicated yet clearly showing the basic form and the modifying additional signs. The over-all dimensions, while roughly corresponding to a rectangle, did not have to be uniform, nor did the characters have to stand exactly in line. By contrast, the word picture in a phonetic script is long drawn out, with a straight horizontal (rarely a vertical) line as a base; the Semitic people used finer brushes and pens which made possible delicate swellings and sharp curves, and an abundance of hairlines, as well as numerous diacritical marks. While it is not impossible, technically speaking, to cut, for instance, a fine Persian manuscript in a wood block (if we use crosscut boxwood and the experience of *our* times), a glance at the script should be sufficient to satisfy anyone that the woodcutting method of the Chinese would not recommend itself to the Mohammedan scribe as a logical, easy, and practical one. Moreover, there was lacking in the Islamic world the vast background of revered philosophic wisdom and literary writing, manifested in thousands of volumes. One single book, the Koran, filled the need for moral and spiritual guidance of the followers of Mohammed, and that book was always copied by handwriting.

It is, therefore, not surprising that, while papermaking became an industry throughout the domain of Islam, with large domestic comsumption and a sizable export to Christendom, no authentic block prints from that quarter are known. Some extant Kufic manuscripts, in a heavy, squarish, and angular hand, found in Egypt, may have been cut in wood and block printed, or may have been produced by the widely practiced stencil method; the sharp rectangular grouping of characters found in Kufic gravestone inscriptions is undoubtedly due to its formal character and to the use of chisels as tools; stone and chisel yield readily straight lines and right angles, while curves and gradual swellings, on the other hand, are the logical result of the use of brushes and pens on a smooth surface.

It was due to the Saracens that the manufacture of paper finally penetrated into Europe: first into Spain, then into Sicily and lower Italy. The Spanish city of Xativa is mentioned in 1150 as a place where "paper is manufactured, such as cannot be found anywhere in the civilized world, and is sent to the East and to the West." The first recorded paper mill in Christian lands was believed, until very recently, to be the one at Hérault, on the French side of the Pyrenees, 1189. There was, however, an earlier one, in the same section of the country, founded in 1157 by Jean Montgolfier among whose descendants we find the first balloonist, Pierre Montgolfier (who made a successful ascent at Vidalon, December 14, 1782). Jean Montgolfier took part in the Second Crusade, 1147, was taken prisoner by the Saracens, and was sent to work in a paper mill at Damascus. Having managed to escape, he returned to his home in

1157, where he employed the knowledge gained and set up a paper mill; his descendants acquired the Vidalon mill during the sixteenth century and have been manufacturing paper there ever since; the present firm of Canson & Montgolfier proudly points to its little-known record. In Italy the first recorded paper mill was at Montefano, 1276; it was soon followed by the famous Fabriano mill in Umbria, which is still in existence. The crossing of the Alps into Germany occurred much later; the first authentic date is that of Ulman Stromer's mill at Nuremberg, 1390. During the fourteenth century, the paper needed for writing purposes in Germany was mostly imported from Italy via the trade routes from Venice and Milan; it was only in the latter part of the century, when block printing was practiced in centers like Augsburg and Nuremberg, that the demand for paper became sufficient to justify domestic manufacture.

EARLY MOVABLE CHARACTERS

The opinion is often expressed that the essence of the European invention of printing is the separate, movable, cast-metal letter. If that were so, the Mongolian Orientals would be the inventors of our printing for the Chinese had *movable* characters three hundred years before Gutenberg's time, and the Koreans even had *cast metal* characters fully thirty years before Gutenberg's first attempts.

To understand the essential difference between the Eastern and the Western systems, it should be said that the idea of assembling texts from separate, movable characters into a (temporarily) solid block for printing purposes originated in the Orient. Various methods of obtaining the single characters were employed: (1) individual moulding in china clay and subsequent baking; (2) cutting a relief wood block into small pieces, one for each character, for direct printing; and (3) using such wooden characters as patterns for *sand* moulds from which metal shapes were cast in tin or bronze.

That is as far as the Chinese and Koreans went. The European method is characterized by Gutenberg's invention of the *metal* casting mould of exact dimensions (adjustable) which produces plane-parallel metal shapes of two uniform dimensions (height-to-paper and depth, or body size) and one flexible one (width, or set-width), with the position of the face on the shank of the type under control, for the purpose of alignment and close spacing. This ingeniously constructed casting instrument is the heart of Gutenberg's invention, its essential features still being in use today.

The metal casting mould, the application of the press, and the use of oil varnish ink by Gutenberg together constitute the basis of European printing.

As stated above, the Chinese block printing at its full development must not be thought of as crude; the workmanship of many existing specimens is excellent. Block cutting, moreover, gave the scribe freedom for expression of his individual artistic taste. In the face of this is it rather surprising that an inventive mind should have attempted to mechanize the Chinese characters into individual bodies, to be composed. An unlearned "man of the common people," by name Pi Shêng and by calling a blacksmith, was not deterred by the enormous number and variety of characters. He must have been a most uncommon person; for while it is possible to express simple thoughts with a few hundred Chinese characters, for the highest forms of literature upward of eight thousand characters are needed. Pi Shêng mastered all the ideograms necessary to produce literary works. He created baked porcelain characters and set them upon an iron plate, into a layer of wax and resin; when they were all in position, the plate was warmed to make the sticky mass pliable, and an even printing surface was obtained (regardless of uneven thickness of the clay pieces) by pressing another iron plate against the face of the porcelain characters. When cooled, the wax and resin would harden and hold the clay pieces firmly in position. An ingenious method indeed, giving freedom of assembling and correcting characters (movability) and yet resulting in a most desirable fixed block for printing (what we today obtain by stereotyping and electrotyping). Once the equipment of characters was provided, printed sheets could be produced "marvelously quickly." Common characters were produced in multiples and rarer ones were made easily as occasion required. Mere heating liberated the clay characters for further use. Of course, the classified array in storage for instant use was quite a problem, but that was also solved by Pi Shêng.

Printing from porcelain characters went on from 1041 until 1049 when Pi Shêng died; then his method fell into disuse because there was nobody among the craftsmen with the requisite scholarly knowledge to carry on, and no scholar would descend to the level of a handworker. The clay characters became souvenirs, and none have survived. We have, however, the exact account from a comtemporary writer, Shên Kua, who was probably an eyewitness.

The story is hidden in the reminiscences of a learned statesman and does not seem to have been known in Europe until 1847, when a summary was published in the transactions of the Paris Academy of Sciences. De Vinne (in his *Invention of Printing*, 1876) quotes from a condensed translation by Sir John Francis Drake, onetime British minister to China. Accurate and annotated translations of the account have been published recently by Hülle (1923) and Carter (1925).

Whether the facts of this Chinese invention penetrated into the Western world, as did wood-block printing, and thereby influenced the European invention of typography, is a moot question. Its short practice by a single individual at that early age makes such an influence seem unlikely. In China, however, the essential principle of *movable* characters was not forgotten, for in 1344 the writer Wang Chêng reviewed the previous development of block printing and described in detail the *movable wooden* characters of his day. He mentions briefly *tin* characters that were strung on an iron wire, to hold them in line, and says further "but none of these take ink readily, and they rapidly deteriorate in printing." Then he praises the characters obtained by sawing apart an engraved wood block, as being more exact and convenient, and writes concerning their use that for printing they were held in a wooden frame, small wedges of bamboo serving to hold them rigidly. There we have the principle of the "chase" and locking devices of the European printers, a perfectly logical (and simple) construction when one deals with small blocks having a thickness of about one inch.

The account mentions that somewhat more than thirty thousand characters were needed. It has been corroborated by the recent discovery of several hundred wooden printing characters in one of the caves of Tun-huang by Professor Paul Pelliot; they are in Uigur (Mongolian) language, 2.2 cm height-to-paper, 1.3 cm wide, length (varying according to word) from 1 cm to 2.6 cm and are well preserved. The Metropolitan Museum of Art in New York possesses several of them; Professor Carter (in his book mentioned) shows an actual-size photographic view as well as an impression of their faces. In all respects, save the face which represents a word in each case, they exemplify the method described by Wang Chêng. Books printed from separate wooden characters cannot readily be distinguished from block prints. It is likely, however, that they were more frequent than those made with Pi Shêng's porcelain characters, or those of tin. An absolute proof of the use of separate wooden characters is furnished by a case known since 1775: in a book of the Sung Dynasty a character is lying on its side.

The reader might be tempted to see, in these characters of hardwood, models for early European inventors struggling with the problem of reproducing alphabetic writing by mechanical means. A mere glance at the size of these blocks, however, and comparison with a formal manuscript page of a European early fifteenth-century scribe will convince anyone that the movable wood-block method did not commend itself readily for the reproduction of connected pen writing in books, or of the large formal gothic lettering, closely spaced.

KOREAN BRONZE CHARACTERS

One other important element of typography was developed in the East prior to its invention in Europe; viz., the *casting* of *movable metal* characters. There is a natural temptation to look for a possible connection between the East and the West, but up to this day no proof of such a connection has been offered.

Wang Chêng's reference to *tin* characters establishes Chinese priority in that field. Of greater importance, however, because of their practical use, were the *bronze* characters developed in Korea, a country which enjoyed a period of remarkable activity after it had been brought into the domain of the great emperor Jinghis Khan.

For the year 1392 the annals record: "A department of books was established which had as its responsibility the casting of type and the printing of books." It was not until 1403, however, that actual printing began, and it is this date that Korean writers hail as a milestone; prefaces of books contain references to and descriptions of the new invention—the recognition of which stands in marked contrast with the gradual adoption of block printing—and praise of the king whose munificence made the enterprise possible. Several hundred thousand characters (the number is only thus vaguely given) of *bronze* were cast. The king, T'ai Tsung, declared "The costs [for the printing of books] shall not be taken from the people in taxes. I and my family, and those ministers who so wish, will privately bear the expenses." Truly a noble sentiment and a noble deed! As a matter of fact, the venture needed continued government support; when that ceased, in 1544, block printing was once more resorted to. Private enterprise could not bear the heavy investment needed. As late as 1770 a new font of 32,000 wooden models and 300,000 cast bronze characters was made, but it fell into disuse in the nineteenth century.

Some Korean bronze characters are preserved at the American Museum of Natural History in New York. They are about 1 cm square, ½ cm height-to-paper, and grooved on the under side, evidently so that they could be lain on a rod for alignment; their sides are not squared, making locking against each other impossible. Most likely wax or pitch was filled in when all the rods were filled, and thus a solid page form was obtained. For distribution the iron base plate was heated—the way Pi Shêng had done earlier. In a description the Korean writer Song Hyon gives about 1500, it is said that the wax-filled plate was not firm enough and that the characters, therefore, were "fitted into a bamboo frame" (corresponding to the locking-up of European type in a chase). The characters preserved in New York are quite rough in finish, the result of sand-casting from wooden models; the jets were filed off, as were sharp corners and burrs.

Professor Carter, fortunately, submitted impressions of the New York characters to the curators of the Seoul Museum in 1924 and established that they were *not* of the fifteenth-century fonts, as had been believed before, but belonged to the last font of 1770. As, however, neither their physical shape nor the process of manufacture is likely to have differed materially from the earlier product, we have in them at least a tangible basis for speculation as to manner of making and use—which is more than we can say about Gutenberg's type. (Figure 22.)

Many of the important books printed with cast bronze type are still in existence, especially in Japan. The method itself was practiced in Japan from 1596 to 1629 for Chinese as well as Japanese literary works; it does not seem to have found favor, however—probably due to the likelihood of compositor's errors—for the technique reverted to the old and practical wood block.

As for printing from bronze characters in China proper, a reference hitherto believed the earliest mentions the year 1522, during the Ming Dynasty. That the whole system originated in China and that its appearance in Korea was an importation, has been considered likely by research workers. An oral information from Professor Paul Pelliot of Paris indicates that proof of Chinese origin has been discovered by him, and we may soon hear more about his researches on this fascinating phase of early printing.

The last recorded fonts of Chinese bronze printing characters were melted up for coins in 1736. That was practically the end of Oriental "type"—for, as Carter says, "By the nineteenth century the use of type had almost ceased in all three countries, and was reintroduced from the West as an entirely new art."

It would be interesting to investigate the kind of ink that was used on these metal characters, for it is known that watery solutions do not lie and print evenly on metal surfaces, the problem which forced Gutenberg to turn to linseed oil has been solved by our ink manufacturers only in the last few years; we can now print water color (on a glycerine base) satisfactorily from metal plates on our presses, but the small shapes of our type still offer difficulties. It must be remembered that Korean and Chinese

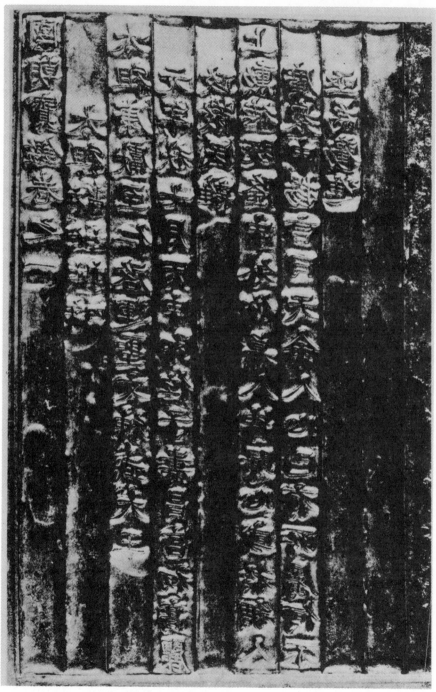

22. *Korean bronze characters. From Bogeng,* Geschichte der Buchdruckerkunst. *(Reduced)*

characters offer considerable surface to the ink brush or pad, and also to the stiff brush or rounded bamboo stick with which the paper is rubbed in the "printing."

It is not likely that the typographic method will supersede block printing in the Orient, in spite of the application of even the linotype machine to Chinese commercial work. The full beauty of Chinese calligraphic work is best rendered not in mechanized type, but in individual cutting or, as done most recently, by lithographic or photomechanical means.

As to the question whether the knowledge of the Far Eastern invention of cast-metal printing characters reached Europe and thus stimulated speculative minds, all that can be said is: we do not know. The process of sandcasting of small objects from wooden patterns, a basic feature, had been familiar to European goldsmiths long before the fifteenth century. We do not hear of experiments in European printing in which *metal* played a role, until the 1430's, in connection with Gutenberg; there is also evidence of other efforts.

The specific invention that made printing, as we know it, possible, was undoubtedly European: John Gutenberg's casting instrument. Through it was added to the features known in the Orient—mobility and metal casting—the decisive one, namely controlled, exact dimensions, with the possibility of quantity production as a result.

In order to make clear the difference between Far Eastern printing, whether from blocks or movable characters, and European typographic printing, I offer the following definition of the latter: the art of reproducing phonetic writing by means of assembling separate, cast-metal characters, of exact, plane-parallel dimensions, into a rigid form which can be printed and then distributed again into its separate units, making them available for new composition.

Before we can discuss typography, however, we must trace the appearance of the older Oriental block-printing method in Europe, in the wake of paper.

EARLY EUROPEAN BLOCK PRINTS

For centuries after paper had first become known in Europe it served as writing material only. Even if a Chinese block-printed book occasionally reached the Western world, it is unlikely that its mechanical production was recognized. When and where the first block prints were made in Europe and what their nature was, is impossible to determine definitely. Textile prints probably were first because the technique of stamping wooden patterns was known in Egypt as early as the sixth century of our time as a specimen of Panopolis, Egypt, in the Forrer Collection (Deutsches Buchmuseum) in Leipzig shows. Such "prints" were ornamental and pictorial; the oldest existing block-printed European textiles date from the twelfth century and point, by style features, to the lower Rhineland with Cologne as a center, as the region of origin, whence the art spread into southern Germany as well as into Flanders.

An actual relief block for printing on fabric was found in France in 1898, in demolishing the Cistercian Convent at La Ferté-sur-Grosne (Department of Saône-et-Loire). The block depicts part of the Crucifixion scene and bears an inscription of several words in uncial characters. Its large size, about nine by twenty-four inches, indicates its use for printing a fabric which was to be viewed from a distance. The costumes and arms of the soldiers pictured are of a style that enables us to date the work as belonging to the latter part of the fourteenth century.

Cloth printing was one of the decorative arts practiced in monasteries. Cennini, the Florentine painter, refers to it as a form of painting in his treatise on the arts (1437).

Just when pictures were first stamped on paper or parchment is unknown; authorities, such as W. L. Schreiber, see in the playing cards the medium that furnished the incentive for European block printing on paper. We know that Chinese playing cards were originally a form of dice; the Oriental gambling devices reached Europe via the trade routes, and the Crusaders brought knowledge of games and implements back with them. The Church was powerless to stop the spread of gambling; the more frequent were the injunctions, the greater the demand. Hand-painted, stenciled, stamped, finally block-printed—playing cards had an important share in the development of European block-making.

Illuminators of fine manuscript books not only employed stencils for the initials to be filled in, in blank spaces left by the scribes, but they also made use of stamps. Such wooden or metal relief stamps were colored and impressed individually by hand. We know of a manuscript of the thirteenth century, written in the Vauclerc monastery and now in the Bibliothèque Muncipale at Laon (France), in which the ridges of ink at the edge of the initials and the embossing on the back furnish proof of the method of "impressing."

Literacy was much less prevalent in the Europe of the thirteenth and fourteenth century than in China a thousand years before. Handwritten manuscripts filled the needs of the small number of educated persons. For the masses of people, impoverished through wars and pestilence, crowded into the narrow confines of cities, and frequently active to earn a precarious living—in a world with the mere rudiments of transportation facilities—manuscript books were out of reach; nor did the common man, lacking learning, require more than a visual stimulus by way of a picture. The Saints of the Church, and more often the horrors of Hell—so vividly painted by zealous servants of the Lord—became objects of contemplation in the form of crude block prints; such prints, however, are not much older than the latter part of the fourteenth century.

The Buxheim St. Christopher block print bearing the earliest authentic printed date (1423) at the end of a two-line verse, represents an advanced state of block cutting which allows the inference that at least a generation or two of development preceded it. It should be noted, since practically all reproductions of it in books show only the black lines, that the print was colored by hand, and therefore, presents a much more finished appearance than the bare outline drawing suggests. A still earlier date (1418) on a print "Marriage of St. Catherine" is much disputed.

EUROPEAN BLOCK BOOKS

It is not known just when the single-leaf block prints, combining pictures and brief texts, developed into books, the so-called "block books." This development was the logical result of an increased demand for *popular* literature; there is no evidence that the block books and fragments still in existence antedate the first appearance of typographic printing. The popular belief that they represent the forerunner of type-printed books is erroneous.

To my knowledge McMurtrie's *Golden Book* was the first historical account written in America that stated clearly: "Block books must be considered, not the forerunners of typography, but in a way competitors—the two arts developing almost simultaneously though along independent lines."

The purpose of block books was *not* the dissemination or preservation of literature, but the pictorial dramatization to semiliterate people of legends and miracle stories, of moralizing tendency, with explanatory captions and brief texts; their technique was the Chinese method, suitable for this kind of work in which the text played only a minor role. The wood-block method could be applied to the production of ephemeral pieces in small and even larger editions, and was especially practical when a constant demand necessitated reprints; it did not require large capital, nor more than a small workshop, and consequently fitted perfectly into the then existing state of production governed by the individual craftsman. This explains why we have early references to *formschneider* (1423), "letter snyder," *briefdrucker* (1428), etc., long before typographic printing.

The undated single-leaf block prints extant *might* antedate typography; the existing copies of block books, however, mostly bear printed dates or contain other evidence of proceeding from the decades beginning with 1470 and 1480; for instance *Biblia Pauperum* 1470, *Defensorium inviolatae virginitatis Mariae* 1470, first edition of *Speculum Humanae Salvationis* 1471, *Entkrist* 1472, *Ars Moriendi* 1473, *Ars Memorandi* (not before 1470), *Mirabilia Romae* (184 pages, decorated with the arms of Pope Sixtus IV, therefore datable between 1471 and 1484), the calendar of Regiomontanus (not before 1475), that of Johannes de Gamundia (1468), etc.

Block books are completely a German and Dutch product; they occur in a region where paper had been available for some time, along the trade routes from Venice to the Lower Rhine, and where the cutting of wood blocks (Chinese fashion) had had an early start. W. L. Schreiber, the greatest authority on woodcuts, is of the opinion that at first the pictures alone were cut and the text was handwritten, that from about 1460 on the (Latin) text also was cut, and that by 1470 the *formschneider* had become publishers and favored popular (German and Dutch) texts.

Of all block books the *Speculum Humanae Salvationis* deserves special mention because a technical peculiarity has given rise to the myth, cherished by bibliographers for centuries, that its printer was the first Dutch printer and typographer, meaning Laurens Coster of Haarlem. In three of the four editions the text is printed typographically; in the other edition a third of the pages are completely cut in wood; the remaining portion of the book is type-printed. From the signs of wear of the wood-block illustrations, Ottley has proven (in his book *An Inquiry into the Origin and Early History of Engraving,* 1816) that the mixed edition was the third one.

De Vinne states that the xylographic pages correspond perfectly with those of the first type-printed edition, in length of line and the use of abbreviations and contractions; the woodcutter even went so far as to reproduce the small blemishes of defective letters. The work, therefore, seems to have been done from exact tracings; it illustrates the mechanical skill of the cutter but at the same time his illiteracy, or unfamiliarity with type, for he treated the letter shapes as mere designs.

From such simple observations it appears unlikely that a Dutch block printer could have been the inventor of typographic printing. Some unexplained disturbance during the printing of that edition must have led to the substitution of wood blocks as a makeshift. Such scholars as Bradshaw and Wyss assign the printing of the *Speculum* to 1471-1474.

From the existing German and Dutch block books the deduction can be made that the block cutting of texts did not antedate 1460; hence it is eliminated as a direct forerunner of typography. The only completely extant xylographic Donatus (Latin school grammar) is of a late date for its maker identifies himself as Conrad Dinckmut whom we know as a bookbinder from 1476 to 1481 and a printer from 1482 to 1499 in Ulm (Swabia).

If the block books had been a mere forerunner of the type-printed books, they would have given way immediately to the new and improved technique; that they persisted until the last quarter of the fifteenth century, parallel to printed books, is an indication that they represented merely the last phase of development of an independent craft.

Two factors account for their elimination: (1) a growing demand for serious literature (the emphasis being on the text), (2) the development of perspective in design and the introduction of shading into woodcuts, simulating plasticity in monotone (black) heretofore obtained only by hand-coloring. A contributing factor to (2) was the great effort and expense involved in coloring illustrations in printed books, the number of leaves as well as of copies in an edition running into the hundreds. By the year 1500, the end of the incunabula period, printing of illustrations in books in black, together with type, had become universal; and where refined taste desired greater detail and delicacy that even the Dürer school could provide in woodcut illustrations, copper engraving, a method that developed at the same time as typography, though independently, took its place.

METAL TECHNIQUE IN EARLY FORMS OF EUROPEAN PRINTING

When we observe the advanced state of the metal work of the goldsmiths and the armorers of the fourteenth and fifteenth centuries and further find that the engraving technique practiced by them was the basis of the first pictorial intaglio printing in the 1440's, the thought of a possible connection between the field of metal work and early relief printing suggests itself. Bibliographers of printing heretofore have almost completely centered their attention on the wood-block technique; yet there is undeniable evidence that many of the important steps leading to typography belong to the sphere of metal craftsmen.

A metal worker, accustomed to engraving in relief and intaglio and to fusing and casting, would seem to be the logical person to engage in an activity requiring precision, such as the making of types. These small shapes, as mentioned before, had to be of accurate dimensions, so that an assembly of them would produce a squared-up group of horizontal lines, with a plane surface—the group combining mobility with rigidity.

The standards of beauty evolved by the manuscript makers being high, a mechanical method of letter construction, therefore, had to meet their standards of alignment, close spacing, flexibility in the length of lines through contractions and abbreviations, and sharpness of details such as hairlines and serifs.

The problem of the making of the first types is much more complicated than most people realize. The modern technician has, in my opinion, a much better grasp of the technical foundations of early printing than the scholar steeped in the voluminous wood-block literature, and it is, therefore, due to the recent efforts of men like Wallau, Hupp, Bauer, Enschedé, and Mori, that we now have plausible explanations of the way the invention of typography may have taken place.

As a matter of fact, we have actual examples of early *metal relief* prints in the so-called "metal cuts," with the special group of "dot prints." They form a well-defined category among the printed products of the fifteenth century.

That metal appears in European printing first in the form of picture-printing plates, is readily understood when one considers how readily the line-drawing technique can be expressed with them. If engraved into depth (the easiest form of engraving), an intaglio plate is created; if in relief (which requires more effort), the resulting plate can be printed like a wood block. In either case it is necessary, however, to use an ink having viscosity or "tack"; thus we see that a change of material immediately affects another factor, the ink, and brings about the substitution of oil-varnish ink for a water-soluble fluid.

We find the intaglio engraving and printing technique well developed in Germany between 1440 and 1450, the oldest dated copper engravings of a Passion series showing the year 1446. Its beginnings may, therefore, be dated several decades earlier.

With the same tools used in intaglio work, but with considerably more labor, an engraver can produce relief metal plates, the printing of which is more nearly like that of wood blocks. Such plates have actually been used, as evidenced by the "metal-cut" prints.[3]

The relief prints classed as metal cuts show unmistakable earmarks of the graver rather than the cutting knife; they also have punch-like indentations producing white dots in a black area; when the dots predominate the prints are known as "dot or shot prints" (French, *criblé*; German, *schrotdrucke*). Whether the plates were of lead, bronze, brass, or copper, we do not know; any metal that was ductile as well as sufficiently hard was serviceable. Contrary to the general belief that the dots were created by punches (which leaves unexplained how the engraver eliminated the ring-shaped buckles of the displaced metal) I find that the dots were *engraved individually*, dug out, or "flicked out," as the technician would call the process. From the oldest specimens down to the *criblé* backgrounds in initials, borders, and printers' marks of early sixteenth-century French printers, the magnifying glass shows them to have sharp and irregular angles, produced by an *engraving tool*.

The art of metal-cut or engraved relief plates flourished especially in the centers along the Rhine and in northeastern Germany: a large number of the existing prints have been found pasted into incunables in the libraries of Königsberg, Danzig, Pelplin, Leipzig, and Halle, while woodcut prints are almost completely absent in that region of middle northern and northeastern Germany. It is very significant that the oldest and best metal-cut prints extant, now in the Bibliothèque Nationale in Paris (among them St. Bernard, dated 1454) were found in Mainz and its environs in 1804 by Maugérard, and that others were discovered inserted in copies of the forty-two-line Bible. The famous engraver E. S. whose work numbers, according to Lehrs, about four hundred pieces, is supposed to have begun around 1450 in Mainz—this is important as showing a possible influence of metal technique upon early typography.

The prints extant show such an advanced technique that the assumption of a generation, at least, of development from crude beginnings seems entirely justified.

In this connection it is interesting that the woodcuts of the block book *Ars Moriendi* were copied from a series of copper engravings made by the master E. S. about the middle of the fifteenth century. The "Master of the Erasmus," whose work ends about 1460, imitated the series by E. S., and he was himself imitated by a third engraver. In each case only the pictures were engraved, and of the latter two editions a complete copy each, with handwritten text, is preserved; so the inference is permissible that the first series, and also the series of seven leaves of the 1446 Passion, were intended for a *block book with written text*, as the pictures without text were unintelligible. To the wood-block picture books with handwritten text we must now add those where the pictures were cut in metal relief blocks, as products of a period in which inventors wrestled with the problem of mechanical book production.

There is another field through which the metal technique might have exerted some influence upon early attempts at typography; viz., bookbinding. Not only were the brass locking devices of books engraved with ornaments and short inscriptions before 1400, but as early as 1430 are found bindings with words the *letters of which are stamped in with single punches;* these were, however, unlike the well-known typefounders' punches; they had the lines engraved into a flat base, the way seals are made, so that the stamped letters would stand in relief on a depressed background, and, of course, blind (i.e., without color or gold). Leather bindings since the twelfth century also show the use of punches in round, square, or diamond shapes, with or without engraved ornaments. Letter punches, by the way, are mentioned among the tools of goldsmiths and leather workers as *totum alphabetum;* both of these crafts had much contact with later mediaeval binding, and their tools and methods became those of the later bookbinders.

The use of such letter stamps is authenticated for the period in which Gutenberg made his experiments, in southern and western Germany. One must, however, remember that these punches were engraved in intaglio, the opposite of the later typefounders' punches.

In addition to these evidences of the use of metal in bookbinding and picture printing during the early fifteenth century, we have a somewhat obscure reference to mechanically made books in the diary of the Abbot Jean le Robert of Cambrai in Flanders, who mentions that he had bought in 1445 (i.e., 1446 new style) a *Doctrinale* from a scribe (*escripvand* Marquet) and that it was *jette en molle*. This expression, generally translated as "cast from a mould," has also been interpreted as "cast into a mould"; i.e., "bound into covers." Just what the process might have been is, in the absense of a tangible specimen, wholly a matter of conjecture. Schreiber has (in *Gutenberg Jahrbuch*, 1927) given a plausible explanation of the obscure term; he thinks it refers to the book having been printed from metal relief plates which were cast from a mould of slate; characters engraved in the slate would appear reversed in the relief cast and facing properly on the print taken therefrom. The basis of this theory is the discovery of a direct reference to slates engraved with the *abece*, though of somewhat later date.

All the foregoing evidence points to the conclusion that typography, essentially a metal technique, was developed with the tools and processes known to metal workers. The difference in material and technique between wood block and type is so great that no bridge leads from the one to the other. The invention of types becomes less miraculous—though it remains ingenious—if the role metal has played in early printing, and in fields adjacent to it, is understood, and if we assume that the inventor was a metal craftsman. Such a man would have melting oven and casting box, gravers and files in his equipment; would know metallurgy and mechanics; understand plane-parallelity and rectangularity—all of which are factors essential in typographic printing; against this rich background the wood-block technique could only offer planer and cutting knife as tools, neither of them essential for the production of printing type.

It has been said that "every inventor stands on the shoulders of his predecessors." We might elaborate the thought and say that inventions grow out of the use of known tools, materials, and processes, that they are rooted in their background. Such an inner connection is lacking between the wood block and the typographic metal technique; and because of this gap the explanations of the invention of printing types have been unconvincing in the past when the basis was sought in the wood block. Substituting now for it the metal craftsman's background and equipment, we shall be able to understand more readily the puzzling aspects of the origin and the march of the invention.

THE BASIS OF OUR ACCOUNT OF THE INVENTION OF PRINTING

So far we have observed the historical and technical foundations of printing in the Orient and in Europe. We must now focus our attention on the evolution in the West, for it is there that we find, in the German cities of Strassburg and Mainz and connected with the person of John Gutenberg, actual historical evidence that enables us to gather, at least in its most important outlines, how and when typography started in Europe.

Direct documentary and other evidence about its early stages is meager. We depend largely on two incomplete sources: (1) the so-called "Strassburg Documents," records of a lawsuit of 1439, and (2) the "Helmasperger Notarial Instrument" of 1455, one remaining document of another court action—both of which center around John Gutenberg. Some additional information is contained in scattered records, covering the years from 1430 to 1444, but relating only to the person, not the work, of Gutenberg while he lived in Strassburg. For the second period, that of Mainz, we have a few documentary references to financial matters; most important, however, are the specimens of printed work of that period, from small fragments to the stately volumes of the forty-two-line Bible, extending over a span of about ten years.

While none of these printed pieces bears his name, they must be ascribed to Gutenberg, for their origin in Mainz seems well founded and no other person than he was then and there engaged in printing. Close study of these specimens, especially in the last few decades, has yielded important technological data that enable us to reconstruct the development of the technique. While there is still room for interpretation and speculation on minor points, we are now able, due to modern research methods, to see more clearly in matters that have been controversial for centuries.

The old question "who was the inventor of printing?" is likely to arouse our emotions; by rephrasing it into "what has been invented, where and by whom?" we are now led into technological considerations that yield, as a matter of logic and not of sentiment, the answer as to time, place, and person.

The Strassburg Documents engage our interest because in this lawsuit against Gutenberg about a partnership disagreement occur the first known references to "printing," a "press" and tools, implements and "material pertaining to printing." These (unfortunately incomplete) records, long the center of controversy, were found in the archives by Wencker and Schoepflin and later edited and published by the latter (in 1760) in his book Vindiciae Typographicae together with a Latin translation. Schoepflin's interpretations have been severely criticized by later writers; his motives have been suspected; he and Wencker have even been accused of having forged the papers. Recent finds by the former librarian of Strassburg, Karl Schorbach, however (they were published in the Gutenberg Festschrift, 1925, and the Gutenberg Jahrbuch, 1926), have increased confidence in the veracity of the men involved and reestablished belief in the genuineness of the records.

It will always be a matter of keen regret that the original documents are no longer in existence. One section was destroyed by the revolutionary mob in 1793, when a bonfire was fed with part of the archives of Strassburg. The bulk of the records perished with the library during the siege of 1870. Fortunately we have another transcript of them, made by DeLaborde and published, with a French translation and facsimiles of some passages, in 1840 under the title Débuts de l'Imprimerie à Strasbourg. The facsimiles are lithographed from careful tracings and are invaluable. An English text by Hessels (in his Gutenberg–was he the Inventor of Printing?, 1882) follows the mistranslations of DeLaborde, so that for the purpose of research, reference must be made to the original text in the difficult Alsatian dialect. The best available rendering of the text, in roman type, is found in the Festschrift . . . der Stadt Mainz, 1900, where Schorbach has collected and critically edited all the documents about Gutenberg. This volume constitutes the main source of our present knowledge of the documentary material about the invention.

THE STRASSBURG LAWSUIT OF 1439

The main part of the Strassburg Documents consists of the record of the testimony of numerous witnesses and of the judgment of the court, in a suit brought against John Gutenberg in 1439 and decided in favor of the defendant. We gain the best understanding of this partnership disagreement from the judgment, for it sets forth (1) the complaint by the brothers Dritzehn, (2) the defense of Gutenberg, and (3) the decision.

As to the complaint: Georg Dritzehn, sheriff of Strassburg, speaking also for his brother Claus, demanded to be admitted, as heirs of their deceased brother Andreas, to a partnership which John Gutenberg had formed with several men, and to which Andreas had contributed a large part of his property; as an alternative, repayment of all the money invested was asked. Neither request having been granted by Gutenberg, Dritzehn marshaled twenty-five witnesses before the court, the testimony of thirteen of whom is preserved.

Gutenberg's defense sets forth that the demand was unjust, since the precise terms of the partnership were contained in a written agreement. In explanation, he relates how Andreas Dritzehn, some years ago, had come to him wishing to learn "certain crafts," that he had taught him to "polish stones," and that Andreas had profited therefrom. Sometime after that Gutenberg had joined with Hans Riffe in an enterprise for making mirrors which were to be sold at the forthcoming pilgrimage and fair at Aix-la-Chapelle, then expected to be held in 1439. Andreas Dritzehn, learning of this, had asked to be admitted, for a consideration, and so had the priest Antonius Heilmann for his brother Andreas.

Gutenberg consented and determined the shares of his new partners; each were to pay eighty guilders as fee for the training. When it became known during 1438 that the pilgrimage was not to be held until 1440, the new partners wished to learn "all the other arts and crafts" that Gutenberg practiced. Gutenberg, after some hesitation, consented. Under the new agreement the two Andreases (Dritzehn and Heilmann) were to pay together 250 guilders, of which 100 guilders were to fall due immediately. Heilmann paid his part of fifty guilders while Dritzehn remained in arrears with ten guilders. The balance of 150 guilders was to be paid to Gutenberg in three installments. Andreas Dritzehn became ill and died in December, 1438, still owing eighty-five guilders (ten guilders from the first payment and seventy-five from the balance.)

The agreement was for a partnership from 1438 to 1443 and provided that, in case a partner should die, "all his tools and finished work and the art [i.e., the knowledge]" should belong to the remaining partners, with the sole obligation that they should pay to the heirs 100 gilders after the end of the five-year period.

This stipulation, with other terms, was put on paper at the time, the intention being to have a signed and sealed contract made; while Andreas Dritzehn held the concept (for consideration and signature) he died. The "paper" (*zedel*) was found among the belongings of the deceased, who furthermore had admitted on his deathbed that he had received the instruction (which entitled Gutenberg to the stipulated compensation). Gutenberg, therefore, demanded that the plaintiffs deduct the eighty-five guilders due him from the one hundred guilders wanted, offering also to pay the fifteen guilders immediately, although the agreement gave him the right to defer payment until 1443.

The testimony of only three of Gutenberg's fourteen witnesses has been preserved.

The judgment, dated December 12, 1439, was in favor of Gutenberg. After he and his partners had affirmed upon oath that the terms of the concept of the contract actually were in force, the plaintiff's claim was denied, and Gutenberg was merely instructed to pay fifteen guilders in settlement to the brothers Dritzehn.

That is the substance of the lengthy legal records. All of this would be quite uninteresting, were it not for a few incidental references to *printing* that occur in the testimony, and the deductions we may draw from them. We hear of material "pertaining to printing" procured as early as 1436, also of contractual relations extending to 1443, and thereby gain glimpses of a fairly long period. An analysis of the trial records, therefore, is important on our quest for the beginnings of printing.

The first contract related to the making of mirrors which were to be sold at the forthcoming fair. "Mirror" is *spiegel* in German, *spighel* in Dutch, and *speculum* in Latin. From the fact that these words appear in the title of editions of an undated block book (best known under the Latin title *Speculum Humanae Salvationis*) the theory has been derived that the object of the activity briefly referred to as "printing" was the production of books, in connection with the fair. However, a study of the text reveals a remark by a witness that disposes of the assumed connection of Gutenberg with the group of early block books; Hans Niger relates that he had asked Andreas Dritzehn the nature of his occupation, and that Dritzehn had answered that "he was a mirror-maker" (*spiegel-macher*).

The second contract, to run from 1438 to 1443, covered the exploitation of other schemes; Gutenberg was to teach his partners *new* crafts that were to be kept *secret*—hence the clause about money indemnification in case of death.

Now what was the secret art that Gutenberg and his partners had been practicing from the summer of 1438 to the time of the trial, and that he had previously hidden even from his companions? The answer is definitely "printing." But what it consisted of, and how near it came to the technique later known by that name, we do not know. We can only surmise, from indications in the testimony, that it was still in an experimental stage. The documents themselves are incomplete; of the depositions of thirty-nine witnesses only sixteen have been preserved. Chiefly, neither the defendant nor his witnesses were willing to disclose the secrets; the opposing witnesses lacked the comprehension of the details they related; and finally, the judges were concerned only with the legal aspect of the agreement and, therefore, needed no definition of the enterprise.

Matters of technical interest occur in only six of the depositions; they are mentioned vaguely and are open to interpretation. Gutenberg himself refers to the new enterprise in a general way as *afentur und kunst* ("novel and artful activity"); Andreas Dritzehn calls it "the work" (*das werck*). Part of it was a "press," made by Conrad Saspach and placed in Andreas Dritzehn's house. In the lower part of the press were lying "four pieces" which would fall apart when two hand screws (*würbelin*) were opened, so that nobody could see what the apparatus was. Mention is further made of "tools and finished work," forms (*formen*—possibly but not necessarily what printers now call forms; casting moulds also are called *formen* in German), and *Gezügk* which can be translated as "tools" but might also mean "metal" or "alloy" (in the German typefounders' language the type metal is called *zeug*). The partnership also purchased lead and "other material belonging to it." It is also disclosed that on Gutenberg's order some "forms" kept by the two partners were called in and "melted up" shortly before Christmas. Finally, there is a most important but very brief statement of the goldsmith, Hans Dünne, that about three years before (i.e., 1436) he had made a profit of about one hundred guilders on material "pertaining to printing" (*das zu dem trucken geböret*) sold to Gutenberg. (Figure 23a.)

Based on these few technical references many attempts have been made to determine Gutenberg's secret undertaking. The Strassburg historian Schoepflin, who first published the documents, asserted that it was book printing with movable letters; and living at a time when national, regional, and municipal jealousy sought to establish the honor rather that the facts of the invention he declared Strassburg the birthplace of typography. Thereupon a voluminous controversial literature developed, covering almost a century and a half, three theories being advanced: (1) that typographic letterpress printing was done; (2) that blocks, wood or metal, served for printing; and (3) that the terms related to the earlier business, i.e., mirror making.

The last point is now untenable; modern writers agree on printing of some sort, or at least the experimental steps leading to the technique that was later successfully practiced at Mainz. For the assumption of printing pictures of saints, or of textile printing (block printing), there is no evidence whatever in the testimony. That leaves the possibility of printing from types.

According to the goldsmith Dünne, "printing" was done by Gutenberg as early as 1436; i.e., before the partnership concerned in the lawsuit was formed. Dünne had sold Gutenberg "material pertaining to printing" and has profited to the extent of one hundred guilders (a considerable sum). The term "printing," however, is vague, as it covered also the old method of block printing on paper and textiles. That it later became the technical term for typographic book printing (so used in the colophon of the Psalter of 1457) does not help to clarify its meaning at this earlier time. However, other incidental references point more directly to typographic printing.

The "forms" mentioned were melted up before Gutenberg's eyes; evidently they were useless, yet the destruction of some of them "pained him." That they were of metal, is established; but whether they were letters for printing, or for bookbinders' stamping, or some intermediate stage of matrices, is impossible to determine.

The "press" was to be kept secret. Immediately after Dritzehn's death (Christmas 1438) Gutenberg sent his servant to the abode of his deceased partner with the order

23a. Portion of the testimony in the Strassburg lawsuit of 1439. From tracings by DeLaborde, in Débuts de l'Imprimerie à Strasbourg, 1840. (Reduced)

Transcription: Item Hanns Dunne der goltsmyt hat geseit das er vor dryen joren oder dobii Gutemberg bij den hundert guldin abe verdienet habe alleine das zu dem trucken gehöret

Translation: Item, Hans Dünne, the goldsmith, has said that three years or so ago he had profited from Gutenberg by about one hundred guilders, alone on (material) pertaining to printing.

that nobody should be allowed to see the press. This was a necessary precaution as Dritzehn's house was to be visited by a throng of mourners. Now presses—consisting of two heavy upright beams, with cross connection at top and bottom, and a wooden screw spindle that moved a flat platen downward—were then in common use among papermakers and bookbinders. The press to be hidden, therefore, had features that were new, presumably those that made a mere press into a printing press. I suggest that these features may very well have been (1) a sliding arrangement of the bed, the bed being table-high and in the open for the ease and convenience of the necessary operations before it was shoved under the platen, for taking the impression; (2) some form of hinged frame for holding the paper, which developed into the frame and frisket, the use of which in the earliest Mainz press products is evidenced by pin marks.

The extensive buying of lead may pertain to the mirror business—it could have been used in the glass as well as in the frames—but lacking definite information we are free to see in it the basic metal for types, since other evidence points to typography.

The "tools and implements" might appertain to printing; the word *gezüge* occurs later in Dr. Conrad Humery's document of February 26, 1468 (disposing of Gutenberg's second workshop, after his death) in connection with "forms" (*formen und gezüge*, also *formen, buchstaben, instrument, gezauwe und anders zu dem truckwerck gehörende*; i.e., forms, types, casting instrument, *gezauwe* = *gezüge*, and other things pertaining to printing).

Unlike the later Mainz document of 1455, which speaks of the "work of books," the Strassburg account refers to the activity of the partners merely as "the work" (*das werck*); there was no legal necessity to go into details of a secret process, hence we hear nothing of paper, parchment, and ink. We have, however, indirect evidence in a later document of 1446 about a suit between Georg and Claus Dritzehn on the division of the inheritance of their brother Andreas (Gutenberg's partner). Among the items left by Andreas are mentioned a supply of "large and small books" (*grossen und cleinen buchern*), *snytzel gezug*; i.e., "engraving tools," and "the press," And for the characterization of the brothers who had brought suit against Gutenberg in 1439, it is interesting to note that they accuse each other of having secreted part of the estate, Claus having taken the books, Georg the press and the engraving tools—among other things, such as money, a ring, and precious stones. To assume that the books mentioned were printed by the partners, is unwarranted; they may have been manuscript books, books to be bound, perhaps stamped on the binding, or to be decorated with semiprecious stones (which Andreas Dritzehn had learned to cut and polish).

A further corroborative bit of evidence is the fact (which we learn from a document of 1441) that Gutenberg's other partner, Andreas Heilmann, together with his brother Nicolaus, owned a paper mill not far from the convent of St. Arbogast, where Gutenberg lived.

In the testimony we also hear, repeatedly, of "four pieces" with "two screws"—a much-discussed item of greatest importance. Up to now all attempts but one to explain the "four pieces" convincingly have been in vain. De Vinne, the only technician among the earlier writers, says in his *Invention of Printing* (1876): "It is obvious that these four pieces were not a part of the press. *Properly put together they constituted one tool.*" Another witness [Saspach] repeats the story, describing this tool as *it*.[4] Gustav Mori, an eminent modern technician, suggested in 1921 that the four pieces were the essential parts of a sand-casting mould. I go even further in assuming that the tool ("it") was a compact instrument of steel for casting types; i.e., a casting mould—the heart of the invention!

The witness Saspach relates that "the thing had disappeared" when he came to take it apart by opening the two screws. We now have a possible explanation of its disappearance in the above-mentioned document of 1441; perhaps it was stolen by the two avaricious brothers of the deceased Andreas Dritzehn, the same men who, in 1439, tried unsuccessfully to learn the secret of the invention by bringing suit against Gutenberg.

To sum up: the *internal* evidence of all Strassburg documents reveals Gutenberg as a metal craft worker and points to the possibility, even probability, of the invention of the basic elements of typographic printing by him, during his residence in Strassburg. *External* evidence in the shape of printed work is, unfortunately, not available, and there is scant probability—although it is not impossible—that a piece of experimental printing of that period will come to light at this late date.

The archives are silent on the partnership's business after the lawsuit; that it was very profitable may be doubted, for in 1442 Gutenberg obtained a loan. His name appears in the tax registers for the last time on March 12, 1444; soon afterwards he seems to have left Strassburg, and it is presumed, with good reason, that he returned to his native city of Mainz.

EXPERIMENTS IN "PRINTING" IN AVIGNON

At that time there appeared in the southern French town of Avignon a Bohemian goldsmith, Procopius Waldfoghel by name, whose activities during two years point to some form of printing—according to records in the archives of the Department of Vaucluse, found and published by the Abbé Requin in 1890. The documents being sales contracts and receipts, executed by Waldfoghel, the exact nature of the process that the goldsmith taught others and that is referred to as "a mechanical art of writing" (*artificia causa artificialiter scribendi*) cannot be determined, yet the mention of alphabetic letter forms of steel and iron, tin, copper, and brass, and of tools, points in the direction of printing. On July 4, 1444, the Magister Manuel Vitalis, so one record says, received from Waldfoghel "two alphabets of steel, two iron forms, a steel vise, and forty-eight forms of tin" for "mechanical writing" which the two men were to practice; two years later Vitalis ended the partnership and returned "the instruments. . . of iron, steel, copper, brass, lead, tin, and wood" (*instrumenta. . . tam de ferro, de callibe, de cupro, de lethono, de plumbo, de stagno, et de fuste*), and had to affirm, moreover, that what he had been taught was "a special, valuable art, practical and useful to everyone who practiced it diligently" (. . . *esse veram et verissimam,*

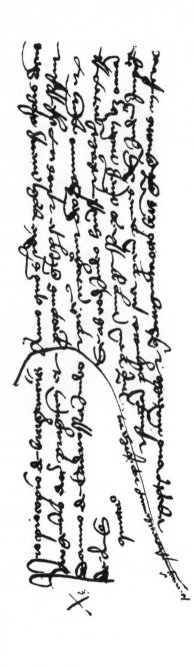

23b. Portion of the Avignon records: release given by Waldfoghel to Davin de Caderousse, 1446. From Requin: Origines de l'Imprimerie en France—Avignon 1444. (Reduced)

Transliteration: Quittacio pro Procopio de Braganciis, argentario diocesis Praguensis, et Davino de Cadearossia, judeo, de Avinione

Anno quo supra et die XXVI mensis aprilis, dictus Procopius quantum per se et suos, confessus fuit et publice recognovit dicto Davino presenti, etc., se ab eodem judeo habuisse et realiter recepisse, juxta per eum nuper promissa X mensis marcii, videlicet omnia et singula pignora sua per eum penes dictum judeum impignorata, excepto uno mantello et quadraginta octo litteris gravatis in ferro

Translation: Release by Procop de Bragancia, silversmith, of the diocese of Prague, to Davin de Caderousse, jew, of Avignon.

On April 26 of the year above (i.e. 1446) said Procop has, for himself and his heirs, etc., declared and publicly acknowledged in the presence of said Davin, etc., that he has actually received from said jew, according to promises made on March 10, all the tools and implements loaned to said jew, with the exception of a coat and 48 letters engraved in iron

Last line of facsimile is indicated by roman type.

esseque facilem, possibilem et utilem laborare volenti et diligenti eam). The craft was also taught to certain individuals who paid a fee and had to agree not to instruct others without permission, nor to practice it within a certain distance from Avignon.

Under date of March 10, 1446, Waldfoghel contracted to furnish Davin de Caderousse with twenty-seven Hebrew letters engraved in iron, for the practice of the art he had been teaching him "for these last two years," also apparatus of wood, tin, and iron (*viginti septem litteras ebreaycas formatas, visas in ferro bene. . . ingeniis de fuste, de stagno et de ferro*); Davin also had to promise to keep the art a secret and not to teach it to anyone within thirty miles of Avignon.

The last document preserved is a receipt of Waldfoghel's for pledges returned by Davin, dated April 26, 1446. Davin retained "forty-eight letters engraved in iron" (*quadraginta octo litteris gravatis in ferro*) which are referred to as "two Latin alphabets," and acknowledged that he had received instruction in their use (*realiter recepisse. . . omnia artificia, ingenia et instrumenta ad scribendum artificialiter in litera latina*). (Figure 23b.)

That the activity thus vaguely indicated was *printing* is an assumption, unsupported by further evidence, of the Abbé Requin; it seems more plausible to consider it a form of *stamping* with metal characters, in the making of which *steel punches* played a role. The variety of metals seems to indicate the use of matrices and of cast characters. Evidently the process was far from perfect; hence the declaration of the Magister Vitalis, that it was practical if one applied oneself to it diligently, seems to have been inspired by Waldfoghel's desire to protect himself against later claims.

Waldfoghel's name does not occur in any further records of Avignon, or elsewhere. No specimen of work done by him or his pupils is known. It is also an open question whether he was trying to market his own invention, or a process learned from someone else. Of the man himself we know that he had come from Prague and that he had acquired, by purchase, citizenship in Lucerne (Switzerland) in 1439. Extensive traveling was then, and later, common among European craftsmen; it is, therefore, entirely possible that he may have worked for a while in Strassburg with one of the goldsmiths who had dealings with Gutenberg, and that in this way he had learned something of the new process of printing. He does not seem to have been in the possession of all the knowledge.

A most recent attempt by Audin (in his *Histoire de l'Imprimerie*, 1929) to interpret the notary's *quadraginta octo* (i.e., 48) in the record of April 26, 1446, as *quadringentis octo*, meaning 408 letters, and thereby, to prove that Waldfoghel possessed several alphabets with contractions, abbreviations, and ligatures, lacks corroborative evidence and is, furthermore, philologically unsound.

Whatever Waldfoghel produced was outdone at the very time by Gutenberg, whose oldest extant *printed* specimen is believed to have originated in Mainz about 1445.

What is significant in the Avignon affair is the definite reference, at this early time, to engraved steel letter punches, tools, and implements of various metals that may readily be interpreted as casting mould, matrices, and types. I believe I have established the probability that all these things, plus some others necessary for printing, had been in the hands of Gutenberg in Strassburg *before* Waldfoghel's appearance in Avignon. That the latter's activity began so soon after Gutenberg's last mention in the records of the Rhenish city is most easily explained by the assumption that Waldfoghel's employment either with the goldsmith Dünne or Gutenberg himself, ceased with the removal of the latter's workshop from the city. For the theory that Gutenberg may have gone to Avignon under an assumed name, there is no proof whatever; moreover, there are weighty reasons to believe him established in Mainz, and *actually printing*, before the year 1446.

BASIC REQUIREMENTS FOR TYPOGRAPHIC PRINTING

Before we enter the discussion of the period in which the Strassburg experiments came to fruition in Mainz, of which actual printed specimens give us evidence, it might be well to summarize what really was needed for a successful production of books in the typographic manner, which of the important implements and materials were available, and which had to be invented.

Paper was being manufactured at the time in various places in southern Germany. It was still expensive, but was available in reasonably large quantities—although it has been found that the printing of about 200[5] copies of the forty-two-line Bible, each needing 320 sheets of about 16½ by 23½ inches, required the output of several mills. As for thickness, strength, finish, and color, high standards could be met. Parchment, also, was readily available, although not with the uniformity of color and texture that paper offered. A scribe could easily select his skins, but when thousands were needed for a number of copies of a printed volume, one could not be so particular.

The printing of books being the aim, the problem was one of constructing *characters* that would give the print the appearance of the formal gothic manuscript hand, not for any reason of wilful deception but in order to meet the established style of the period.

The standards of letter formation, close spacing, use of ligatures and abbreviations, horizontal line-up, even space between the lines, rectangular appearance of the block of text on the page, sharpness of hairlines, yet fullness of strokes—all that formal detail evolved and practiced by good scribes had to be followed rigorously. The best manuscript work of the time served as model; there was no other standard, nor had the conception arisen that a mechanical process might find its own forms of expression.

These letter shapes had to have a body of exact dimensions so that the characters could be assembled at will into a rigid group from which an impression could be taken; they had to be constructed so that they could be taken apart and used again; their bodies had to be plane-parallel on all sides and rectangular, so that they would fit closely with each other; and each character had to be straight on the body and be of uniform alignment in relation to its neighbors in the line. Moreover, the hundreds of type characters in a page, when composed, had to be of uniform height—analogous to the surface of an engraved wood block.

The metal used for such characters had to be sufficiently hard to stand up under repeated use and to retain its height-to-paper under pressure, but soft enough to be free from pores, and to allow a sharp casting of pointed corners and hairlines. Futhermore, it had to be noncorroding; there was water in the damp paper and in the water-soluble India or sepia ink; dried ink had to be removed from the letters by washing. And for an ink on an oily base, if that was tried, there was no volatile chemical such as benzine available; sharp lye, highly corrosive on most metals, was the only practical solvent (it is still in use today). And last, but not least, the metal shapes, if they were cast, had to retain their predetermined exact dimensions when the molten metal solidified; that required an alloy the composition of which was a matter of experimentation.

Assuming the letters were ready, there still remained the problem of *inking* and *presswork*.

Metal letters, as pointed out before, offer no "grip" to watery ink—a much tackier vehicle for the pigment was needed, and this was found in the linseed oil varnish, then in use by the early Dutch painters. This viscous ink could not be applied with the customary brush; it had to be dabbed on with a leather-covered stuffed ball or pad.

European rag papers, lacking the pliability of the Oriental product (which is due to difference in fibers), do not take the tacky ink unless a *strong pressure* is exerted. (What was true in the fifteenth century is equally true today whenever handmade paper is used.) Rubbing on the back was not sufficient; force in rubbing would have caused waves and wrinkles in the sheet and tended to smear letters, distort hairlines, etc. Therefore, a device for exerting strong pressure at once over the whole page area had to be developed. The answer was the press.

The prototype of the early printing press was not, as is popularly believed, the wine or fruit press, but a much more practical form then already in use by all papermakers: a "standing press" or "baler" (unchanged today, except for metal construction). What was needed in additional features to make such a press a printing press, I have described above (in the discussion of the Strassburg Documents). The "frame" and the "frisket" are especially important because only they make possible clean printing in register; i.e., in position back to back. The sheet was held by pins, the marks of which would serve as guides for printing the reverse side. A clean impression was obtained by having the frame so adjusted that the sheet did not touch the form until the platen pressed it down uniformly and at once. These devices are so practical that they are still in use on modern hand presses!

Since the manuscript books were written on both sides of paper or parchment, with no waste of material, it is logical that a mechanical method would follow this style rather that that of block printing in which the rubbing on the back roughened the paper and made it unsuitable for impression and writing on that side. Printing by means of a platen was the only possible answer to the problem.

The person unfamiliar with printing technique hardly realizes how important each one of the fundamentals just mentioned is. Let one of them remain unsettled—and good or tolerable printing cannot be done! The fact that fairly good printing (as measured by our standards) *was done in Mainz* from about 1445 on—ten years before the forty-two-line Bible was finished—is proof that the man who did it had solved all important problems. Can anyone deny that the many questions involved required years and years of experimentation—to say nothing of the crux of the whole matter, viz., the mechanical construction of type of which more will be said below?

It seems to be well established that the printing press is Gutenberg's invention; that he was the first to use linseed oil varnish ink, the vehicle then being scarcely known in the field of painting; that he constructed the adjustable type mould for casting letters from metal matrices—a device unchanged in principle today. Moreover, the only alloy which combines strength with ductility, hardness with smooth casting quality, which is non-porous, noncorrosive and—most important—which does not shrink in the casting process and thus keeps its perfect plane-parallel shape, that alloy was evolved by Gutenberg. Today, we are still using it, not having found a better one! Need we wonder now why Hans Dünne, the goldsmith, earned such a large sum in 1436 in supplying Gutenberg with *material pertaining to printing*, presumably metal?

The proof that the aforesaid requirements for successful printing had been met is found in the earliest extant specimens of the Mainz press. No other printer than Gutenberg existed in Mainz in the 1440's. Nobody before him had used the implements and methods described.

We, therefore, can answer the questions *"what* has been invented, *where,* and *by whom?"* with a fair degree of certainty: The essentials of typographic printing technique were in possession of Gutenberg when he began work in Mainz, presumably in 1445.

THE "HELMASPERGER DOCUMENT"

Documentary evidence about the early stages of printing in Mainz is almost wholly centered in a parchment dated November 6, 1455, the famous "Helmasperger Notarial Instrument," the one remaining piece of the records of a lawsuit against Gutenberg. It contains a summary of the complaint of one John Fust in a loan and forecolsure matter and Gutenberg's defense, the plaintiff's oath about the loan, and the judgment of the court on the legal question involved. The document is now extant, and its genuineness is unquestioned.

We learn from it that Gutenberg had obtained, some years previously, a loan of 800 guilders, in order to "further his work," and later another one of the same amount, for "the work of books," a partnership venture; that Gutenberg could not pay when the loan was called, and that Fust asked for a judgment in the sum of 2,020 guilders (capital and interest). We hear about the contractual relations between the two men, and we find guarded references to their secret enterprise; viz., the printing of books (*das werck der bucher*).

Again, as in the Strassburg lawsuit, the record does not clarify the undertaking of the partners, being concerned only with the legal aspect of the matter. However, the inferences that can be drawn enable us, in conjunction with the examples of actual printing, to reconstruct events covering about five years previous to the date of the document.

As to other direct evidence about Gutenberg, the archives contain little: he appears in money deals in 1448 and 1457, and as a pensioner of the archbishop in 1465; and his death previous to February 26, 1468; is inferred from a document of that date in which a Dr. Humery disposes of his printing equipment.

The scarcity of records need not surprise anyone who is familiar with the sufferings of that region on the Rhine during the Thirty Years War (1618-1648) and subsequent catastrophes in the wake of warfare and revolution. Beginning with the sack of Mainz in 1462 by the troops of the victorious Elector Adolf of Nassau, and ending with riots during the French Revolution in 1793, the city has had more than the usual share of misfortune. Considering all this, it is almost miraculous that any documentary and printed evidence has been preserved at all.

In view of the importance of the main documentary source of information, a brief analysis of its contents will be in order.

The business connection between Gutenberg and Fust was twofold: the first loan was meant for Gutenberg's own work, the second one for an enterprise of both of them.

For the first 800 guilders Gutenberg was to complete his equipment, the ownership and use of which were expressly reserved by him. However, it was pledged as security to Fust; payment of the debt should free him of all obligations. All of this had been agreed upon in writing.

The conditions attached to the second loan are not known; no written agreement is mentioned, and some verbal understanding seems to have existed. It is reasonable to suppose that Fust, before advancing another considerable sum, must have become convinced that the work was developed far enough to yield a profit soon. But now he wanted a share in the business, and with it, he became the controlling interest. According to Gutenberg's defense, Fust also had agreed to pay 300 guilders annually for board and keep, wages, rent, paper, parchment, and ink—and had given verbal assurance that no interest would be charged.

Presumably, early in 1455 Fust called in the loans. The work not having produced finished books, Gutenberg could not pay and lost his pledge (what that was, will be explained below). Fust demanded a total of 2,020 guilders; viz., 800 plus 6 per cent interest (= 244), 800 plus 140 for interest and 36 for compound interest. How great this sum was cannot be judged from the gold value alone (it has been computed as about 16,000 German gold marks); a better conception may be gained from its buying power. From other sources we know that at that time ten guilders bought a suburban house with garden, 100 guilders a substantial city house; a prize ox was worth eight guilders, and horses sold for from four to fifteen guilders.

The decision of the court, as contained in this document, was: (1) Gutenberg was to render an accounting of the sum used for the second, the partnership, venture; (2) if it was found that he had received altogether more than 800 guilders, this money—unless used for the partnership—should be repaid to Fust; (3) if Fust would swear that he had had to pay interest for money raised and advanced to Gutenberg, he would be entitled to interest payment according to the first written agreement.

Fust affirmed by oath that such was the case.

The document stops with that record. What followed must be surmised: judgment was entered against Gutenberg, his pledge was forfeited, other assets were taken to satisfy the claimant—all in accordance with the strict letter of the law. It would be of great interest to us to know what equipment Gutenberg saved, but that remains a matter of speculation.

THE FINISHED PRODUCTS OF THE INVENTION

Within a year of this court action there appeared printed copies of a folio Bible in two volumes, with forty-two double-column lines on the page, without date or name of printer (one extant copy, now in Paris, bears the rubricator's colophon with the dates of August 24 and 15, 1456)—and on August 14, 1457, there was completed, according to the printed colophon, the magnificent Psalter, the *magnum opus* of early printing, elaborately embellished with decorative initials *printed* in red and blue, with the text printed in black and red throughout, in large types of stately beauty.

These are the books that have given rise to the myth that printing came into being all at once, in marvelous perfection. To contemporaries their appearance must have seemed miraculous; the brief explanation in the colophon of the Psalter that the book was not produced by the pen but by printing, did not enlighten them. The art was being kept secret, and an air of mystery hung about it. Added to that feeling of awe was the reverence for Holy Writ; it seemed eminently fitting that the Book of Books, and such service books as psalters and missals, should have been the first products of an invention inspired by the Almighty. This uncritical view, a beautiful sentiment, has persisted into our times and has moved poets and painters and writers to innumerable efforts.

Both of these books, famous for their rarity, fully deserve praise for their beauty; they excite our admiration and our wonder. For how are we to explain the remarkably perfect technique? We may say with reason that they could not have been the *first* fruits of a new invention, that they must represent the end of a long development. The stages of this development are pictured to us, fortunately, in a number of remnants of earlier printing, and it is from a study of these pieces (some of them having come to light only in recent years) that we now can reconstruct the progress of the invention during those years for which documentary evidence is lacking; viz., chiefly 1445 to 1455. This study has been carried on very intensely during the last thirty years and has yielded much valuable information. Not only have such details as various crude stages of the type and of its composition been observed, together with other points of technological importance, but it has been possible to date certain pieces and bring all existing fragments of printing into a chronological order; moreover, we can make deductions upon the technical process of making the type; and finally, in looking over the whole field, we now begin to understand the aim of Gutenberg and the logic of the development, as it is pictured in the fragments and in its crowning achievements.

The known older prints consist in the main of (1) a fragment of a German poem known as the "World Judgment"; (2) two leaves of a Latin school grammar (by Aelius Donatus) with twenty-seven lines on the page, printed on parchment (Figure 24); and

24. *Gutenberg's first type: Twenty-seven-line Paris Donatus. From* Bogeng, Geschichte der Buchdruckerkunst. *(Reduced)*

me amaſtis: et credidiſtis quia
ego a deo exiui· Exiui a pre ⁊ ueni in mudu: iteru relinquo mudu: et uado ad prem· Dicunt ei
diſcipuli eius· Ecce nuc palam
loqris: et puerbiu nullu dicis·
Nuc ſcim⁹ ǫa ſcis omnia: et nō
opus eſt tibi ut ǫs te interroget·
In hoc credim⁹: ǫa a deo exiſti·
Reſpōdit eis iheſus· Modo cre-
ditis: Ecce uenit hora: et ia ueſt
ut diſpgamini onuſquiſǫ in-
propria: ⁊ me ſolu reliquatis·
Et nō ſum ſolus: ǫa pater me-
cu eſt· Hec locutus ſum uobis:
ut in me pacē habeatis· In mu-
do pſſurā habebitis: ſed cōfidi-
te: ego uici mudu·

    et locutus eſt iheſus: et ſu-
    leuatis oculis ī celu dixit·
Pater uenit hora: clarifica fili-
um tuu· ut fili⁹ tu⁹ clarificet te·
Sicut dediſti ei poteſtate omnis
carnis: ut omne qd dediſti ei det
eis uitā eternā· Hec eſt aut uita
eterna: ut cognoſcat te ſolu deu
ueru: et que miſiſti ihm criſtu·

opera tua: et dirigentur cogitacōnes tue·
Uniuerſa ppter ſemetipm operatus e
dns: impiu ǫ ad diem malu· Abho-
minatio dni ē omnis arrogas· etiā
ſi man⁹ ad manu fuerit nō ē innocs·
Inicium uie bone facere iuſticiā: acce-
pta eſt apud deu magis ǫ immolare
hoſtias· Miſericordia et ueritate redi-
mit iniquitas: et in amore domini
declinat a malo· Cū placuerint dno
uie hominis: inimicos quoǫ eius
couertet ad pacem· Meli⁹ eſt paru cu
iuſticia: ǫ multi fruct⁹ cu iniquitate·
Cor hominis diſponit uiā ſuā: ſed
dni eſt dirigere greſſus eius· Diuina-
no in labijs regis: in iudicio nō erra-
bit os eius· Podus et ſtatera iudicia
dni ſut: et opera eius omnes lapides
ſeculi· Abhominabiles regi qui agut
impie: quoniā iuſticia firmat ſoliu·
Uoluntas regu labia iuſta: qui recta
loquit dirigetur· Indignatio regis
nucij mortis: et uir ſapiens placabit
eu· In hilaritate uult⁹ regis uita: et
clementia eius quaſi imber ſerotinus·
Poſſide ſapientiā quia auro melior
eſt: et acquire prudentiā ǫa prolior
eſt argento· Semita iuſtoru declinat
mala: cuſtos anime ſue ſeruat uitam
ſuā· Cōtricionē precedit ſupbia: et ante
ruinā exaltabit ſpiritus· Melius eſt
humiliari cu mitibz: ǫ diuidere ſpolia
cu ſupbis· Erudicus in uerbo reperiet
bona: et qui ſperat in dno beatus eſt·

25. *Type of the Thirty-six-line Bible. From*
Bogeng, Geschichte der Buchdruckerkunst.
(Reduced.)

26. *Type of the Forty-two-line Bible. From*
Bogeng, Geschichte der Buchdruckerkunst.
(Reduced.)

(3) part of a parchment broadside of an undated calendar. The moon phases of the latter have been found to fit the year 1448; we may, therefore, assume that it was printed at the end of 1447. The Donatus shows the same type in a less perfect state, and still more primitive is the type of the "World Judgment," which may have been printed as early as 1445. Thus we have established, at least circumstantially, the connection with the Strassburg experiments which ended, as we know, in 1444. That Mainz was the scene of this printing activity is a well-founded assumption, although Gutenberg's presence in his native city is documented only for the year 1448 when he obtained a loan.

The type in which the fragments mentioned are printed is quite large and seems strangely formal and unsuited to such ephemeral products; it has been proven to represent the more primitive stages of a type we find much later in the (undated) folio Bible with thirty-six lines on the page—which was finished between 1457 and 1460—and also in books printed by Albert Pfister in Bamberg after 1460. (Figure 25.)

The type of the forty-two-line Bible (Figure 26), while of similar design and construction, is smaller and more elaborate. That the Bible with the more perfected type should have preceded the one with the older, cruder type is a riddle that has been solved only in our time. It is, however, not the only puzzle confronting us. When we consider the character of the contents of the fragments and find it to be popular literature, we must wonder why such a large, formal type was used—a type which was so radically different from the common manuscript hand of the early fifteenth century and which seemed so much more appropriate for stately folio volumes of religious character. And that leads to the question: Was the aim of the inventor merely the mechanical production of ordinary "job printing," as represented by the earliest specimens? We may well be in doubt when we see that such an elaborate, extensive and costly book as the forty-two-line Bible followed so soon afterward, and with such evident mastery of the problems involved. And then we find the elaborate Psalter completed within less than two years more—a time that has been estimated to cover the *composition and presswork* alone and forces us to the conclusion that the equipment for it—an extremely complicated equipment!—must have been prepared during the association of Gutenberg and Fust.

At the bottom of all these puzzling questions lies the process by which type was made; if we can reconstruct it, by observation of all printed specimens, by experiment, and by the use of circumstantial data—then we can see the chronological order of the printed work and the logical progress of the invention from the Strassburg experiments to the Psalter of 1457.

The mass of data gathered by European scholars and technicians, mainly during the last three decades, and published in numerous monographs, allows certain conclusions which are briefly set down here:

(1) The activity that resulted in the printing of the great Bibles, of the Psalter, and of missals immediately following, was started by Gutenberg in Strassburg and developed or perfected by him in Mainz.

(2) The aim of Gutenberg was the mechanical production of the elaborate service books of the Church, especially of psalters and missals. This required large type of

formal design, in several sizes, as well as printing of the text in black and red throughout, with additional two-color printing of decorative initials. The books, in order to meet the highest requirements, had to be printed on vellum.

(3) The purpose determined the style of the first type. The medium size of text type, serviceable for a future missal, was probably the starting point. It occurred in the earliest fragments because it was the only type then made.

(4) The early prints served as trials toward the larger aim.

(5) The fragments show the gradual development of a complicated, specifically Gutenbergian system of type construction, that culminated in a font containing 292 characters (forty-two-line Bible). This system disappears as soon as books lose their formal manuscript character (with the introduction of small book type in the Durandus of 1459 and the *Catholicon* of 1460).

(6) When the sum of 150 guilders was lent to Gutenberg in 1448, the work done so far had established the practicality of procedure as to typemaking, composition, and presswork. The purpose of the capital may well have been the production of a short missal, requiring printing of text in red and black throughout, such as the *Missale speciale* (which up to now has remained a much disputed item), as a further step toward the ultimate goal.

(7) According to the "Helmasperger Document," Gutenberg obtained his first loan from Fust in 1450 for his own work. The security pledged for such a large sum must have consisted of something more tangible then pamphlets and broadsides, or even a trial missal; presumably it consisted of the basic secret, the casting instrument, and the steel punches and moulds of the equipment needed for the planned Psalter, including the technically complicated initials.

(8) Trial pages of a folio Bible with thirty-six lines on the page were printed about that time, the font of the first type having been improved to meet the exacting requirements of calligraphy. A Bible edition with plain text lay within the capacity of staff and equipment, and promised a quick sale while the preparations for the Psalter were going on. Three hundred guilders annually were to be provided by Fust for rent, wages, paper, parchment, and ink, indicating a *large* enterprise.

A second capital of 800 guilders was obtained, Fust now becoming a partner with controlling interest. It was found that the Bible as planned would run into too many pages to make its production economical. (We see here the influence of a coolly calculating business mind.) A smaller size of type was decided upon, and a whole new equipment for it was made, with refinements which resulted in a larger number of characters. The new type accommodated forty lines in the same space as before, and a few sections were printed, with chapter heads *printed in red* in a separate operation. Additional saving of paper, parchment, and press labor seemed desirable, and an additional line on the page was made possible by cropping the ascending letters at the top. Since this mutilated them, new and shorter letters were made; at the same time the body of all letters was slightly reduced so that forty-two lines found room on the page. The printing of red chapter heads was discontinued. The saving of paper, parchment, and press labor was so considerable that the edition could be increased; thereupon the sections already printed were reset and reprinted with forty-two lines.

27. *Colophon of the Psalter of 1457. From the Vienna copy. In the original the initial letter P is blue; ornament, text, and emblem are red. (Reduced)*

ꝓns ſpalmoꝝ roꝺeꝫ · ꝟenuſtate capitaliū ꝺecoꝛ⸗ ata⸗ Rubricatiōibuſꝗ ſufficieter ꝺiſtinctus ·

Aꝺinuetiōe artificioſa impmēꝺi ac caractrizandi · abſꝗ calami ꝟlla exaratōe ſic effigiatus · & aꝺ euſe⸗ biam ꝺei induſtrie eſt ſūmatuſ · Per Iohēm fuſt ciuē magūtinū · Et Petrū Schoffer ꝺe Gernſzheim · Anno ꝺni Ꟁ· illeſio· ccc· lvij· In vigilia Aſſūpcōis ·

There we have briefly the explanation of the puzzling features of the famous Bible. It should be added here that the thirty-six-line Bible has been proved to be a later edition in the larger type.

(9) Before the printing of the forty-two-line Bible was finished, disagreements arose between the partners. We know nothing about the cause. (About Fust we know that he was without definite occupation; his brother Jacob was a goldsmith, also burgomaster; a Clas Fust, perhaps a relative, is also listed in the records as a goldsmith.) As a result of the foreclosure suit brought by Fust, Gutenberg lost his pledge (specified above under 7). Fust was probably able to realize a handsome profit from the sale of the Bible. Financially strong, he could now turn to the production of the Psalter, being in possession of the elaborate equipment and a well-trained staff headed by Gutenberg's able young assistant, Peter Schoeffer, a master craftsman proficient in both composition and presswork.

(10) In less than two years the stupendous undertaking was finished. The pride of Fust and Schoeffer is reflected in the colophon which reads (in translation) as follows:

> The present book of the Psalms, decorated with beautiful capital letters and profusely marked out with rubrics, has been thus fashioned by the added ingenious invention of printing and shaping of letters without any exertion of the pen, and to the Glory of God has been diligently brought to completion by Johann Fust, a citizen of Mainz, and Peter Schoeffer of Gernszheim, in the year of the Lord 1457, on the eve of the Feast of the Assumption [i.e., August 14]. (Figure 27.)

Their elation over the successful completion of this outstanding book is further shown by the printing of their mark under the colophon. Of the few extant copies, however, only the one in Vienna contains it, which explains the many wrong statements as to the earliest appearance of this frequently used mark. The Psalter shows the Gutenbergian type system in full development, not only as to ligatures, contractions, accented letters, but in three separate sizes according to the importance of the parts of the text concerned. It shows also the mastery of the technique of printing in two colors.

With the Psalter, not with the Bible, the invention of printing was completed.

What followed was the application of the new technique to an ever-widening circle of books, with a corresponding simplification and standardization of the technical production features. We see, beginning with the Letters of Indulgence, printed in 1454 (the first printed date), the development of a small, more rounded type suitable for small texts and books, and of the first real book face in the Durandus of 1459 and the Catholicon of 1460. The appearance of book type signifies independence from the contents of the book, a greater freedom, in the style of type design, from the manuscript pattern, and a resulting growth of features based on the technical background, on steel punch and graver—with only slight reminiscences of the original pen strokes.

Gutenberg's activity after the separation from Fust does not seem to have been extensive. He evidently had been left only his oldest font of type, for in the years following the break there appeared an almanac, a twenty-eight page booklet (the bull of Pope Calixtus III against the Turks), and two calendar broadsides—all in German and in this oldest type, in the stage known as that of the thirty-six-line Bible. Of each, only a single specimen has been preserved. Presumably before 1460, when the Bible type passed into the hands of Pfister in Bamberg, the thirty-six-line Bible was printed—we do not know by whom, nor where. Gutenberg's connection with it is probable; whether the place of printing was Mainz, Bamberg, or Frankfort, is still a matter of dispute. Recent researches by Mori in the Frankfort archives indicate the possibility of hitherto unknown relations of Gutenberg with that city.

With greater certainty we can ascribe the *Catholicon* of 1460 to him, although the colophon does not mention his name. A number of small pamphlets follow; then comes the sack of Mainz in 1462, and his printing activity seems to have come to an end. The victorious Elector Adolf of Nassau appointed the aged inventor to a small honorary office in his retinue, in 1465. Indirectly we hear, through a document of

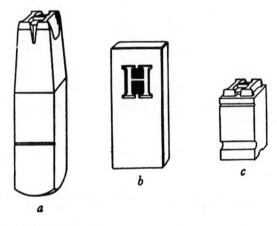

(a) Steel punch; (b) matrix (bar of copper); (c) type cast from matrix in the casting instrument.

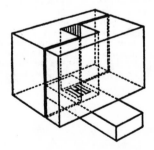

Schematic diagram showing the principle of the casting instrument. Above the matrix are two L-shaped steel blocks built on rectangular lines and leaving a rectangular opening between them, which is variable in one dimension and always centered over the eye of the matrix.

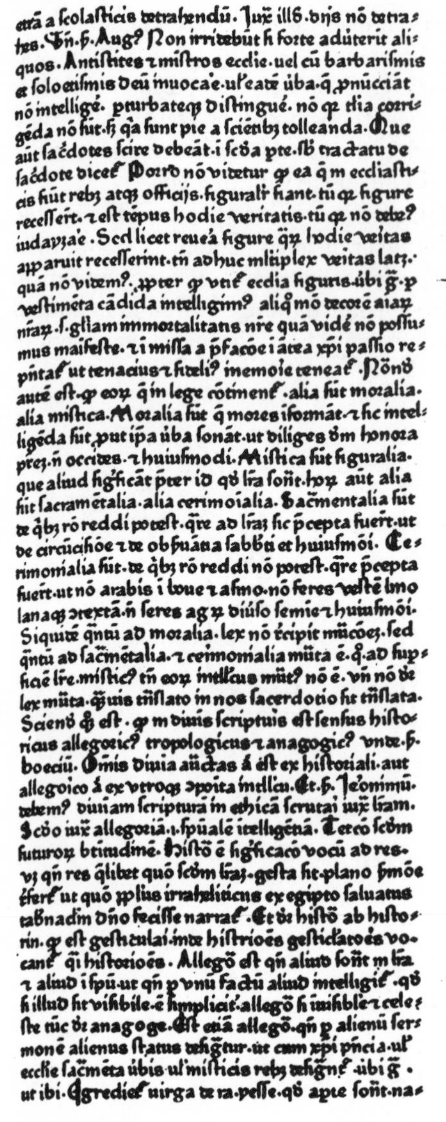

etrā a scolasticis detrahendū. Iuxª illδ. dn̄s nō detra-
hes. Ṽn̄. s. Aug⁹ Non irridebūt h forte adūterit ali-
quos. Antistites τ ministros ecclie. uel cū barbarismis
et soloecismis deū inuocare. ul' eatē uba. q̄ pnūciāt
nō intelligē. perturbateq̄ distinguē. nō q̄ ita corri-
gēda nō sūt. h q̄a sunt pie a scientibz tolleranda. Que
aūt sacerdotes scire debeāt. i. scōa pte. sb tractatu de
sacerdote dicet'. Porro nō videtur q̄ ea q̄ m ecclasti-
cis sūt rebz atq̄ officijs. figuralr' fiant. tū q̄ figure
recesserīt. τ est tēpus hodie veritatis. tū q̄ nō debe⁹
iudayzare. Sed licet reuera figure q̄r hodie veitas
apparuit recesserint. tn̄ adhuc mltiplex veitas latz.
quā nō videm⁹. ppter q̄ vnit' ecclia figuris. ubi g̃. p
vestimēta cādida intelligim⁹ aliq̄ mō decorē aiarz
nr̄arz. s. gliam immortalitatis nr̄e quā vidē nō possu-
mus maifeste. τ i missa a pfacōe i ātea xp̄i passio re-
pn̄tat' ut tenacius τ fideli⁹ inemoie teneat'. Nōnd
autē est. q̄ eorz q̄ in lege cōtinent'. alia sūt moralia.
alia mistica. Moralia sūt q̄ mores ifōrmāt. τ hec intel-
ligēda sūt, put ipa ūba sonāt. ut diliges dn̄m honora
patrē. n̄ occides. τ huiusmodi. Mistica sūt figuralia.
que aliud signicāt pter id q̄d lr̄a sonāt. horz aūt alia
sūt sacramētalia. alia cerimoialia. Sacmentalia sūt
de q̄bz rō reddi potest. q̄re ad lr̄az sic pcepta fuerīt. ut
de circūcisiōe τ de obsuāta sabbti et huiusmōi. Cerimonialia sūt. de q̄bz rō reddi nō potest. q̄re pcepta
fuerīt. ut nō arabis i boue τ asino. nō feres vestē lino
lanaq̄ cōtextā. n̄ seres ag'r diuiso semie τ huiusmōi.
Siquidē q̄ntū ad moralia. lex nō recipit mūcōez. sed
q̄ntū ad sacmētalia. τ cerimonialia mūta ē. q̄. ad sup-
ficiē lr̄e. mistic⁹ tn̄ eorz intellect⁹ mūt⁹ nō ē. vn̄ nō de
lex mūta. q̄uis trāslato in nos sacerdotio sit trāslata.
Sciend̄ q̄ est. q̄ in diuinis scripturis est sensus histo-
ricus allegoric⁹ tropologicus τ anagogic⁹ vnde. B.
boeciū. Omis diuia aūctas ā ēst ex historiali. aut
allegorico ā ex vtroq̄ cōposita intellcu. Et. B. Ieronimū.
debem⁹ diuinam scripturā in ethicā scrutari iux̄ lr̄am.
Scdo iux̄ allegoriā. i. spūalē itellīgētiā. Tercio scdm
futurorz btitudinē. Histō ē signicacō vocū ad res-
pz q̄n res q̄libet quō scdm lr̄az. gesta sit. plano smōe
refert' ut quō pplus israheliticus ex egipto saluatus
tabnacl'm dn̄o fecisse narrat'. Et dr̄ histō ab histo-
rin. q̄ est gesticulai. inde histrioēs gesticulatoēs vo-
cant' q̄i histozioēs. Allegō est q̄n aliud sonāt in lr̄a
τ aliud i spū. ut q̄n p vnū factū aliud intelligit'. q̄d
si illud sit visibile. ē simpliciter allegō. h inuisibile τ cele-
ste tūc dr̄ anagoge. Est etiā allegō. q̄n p alienū ser-
monē alienus status designatur. ut cum xp̄i p̄ncia. ul'
ecclie sacmēta ūbis ul' misticis rebz designat'. ubi g̃.
ut ibi. Egredie' uirga de ra. yesse. q̄d apte sonāt. na-

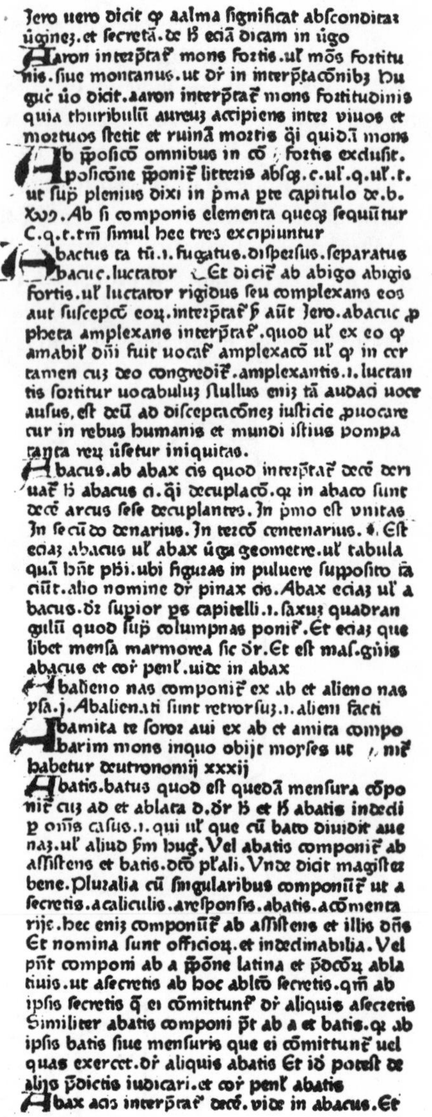

Iero uero dicit q̄ aalma significat absconditaz
uirginez. et secretā. de h̄ etiā dicam in uirgo
Aaron interptat' mons fortis. ul' mōs fortitu
nis. siue montanus. ut dr̄ in interptacōnibz hu
guc' uo dicit. aaron interptat' mons fortitudinis
quia thuribulū aureuz accipiens inter uiuos et
mortuos stetit et ruinā mortis q̄i quidā mons
Ab cōposicō omnibus in cō ; fortis exclusit.
Aposicōne ponit' litteris absq̄. c. ul'. q. ul'. t.
ut sup plenius dixi in pma pte capitulo de. b.
Xvij. Ab si componis elementa queq̄ sequūtur
C. q. t. tn̄ simul hec tres excipiuntur
Abactus ta tū. i. fugatus. dispersus. separatus
Abacuc. luctator Et dicit' ab abigo abigis
fortis. ul' luctator rigidus seu complexans eos
aut suscepcō eoz. interptat' s aūt Iero. abacuc p
pheta amplexans interptat'. quod ul' ex eo q̄
amabil' dn̄i fuit uocat' amplexacō ul' q̄ in cer
tamen cuz deo congredit'. amplexantis. i. luctan
tis sortitur uocabuluz Nullus eniz tā audaci uoce
ausus. est deū ad disceptacōnez iusticie puocare
cur in rebus humanis et mundi istius pompa
tanta rez ūsetur iniquitas.
Abacus. ab abax cis quod interptat' decē deri
uat' h abacus ci. q̄i decuplacō. q̄ in abaco sunt
decē arcus sese decuplantes. In pmo est vnitas
In secūdo denarius. In tercō centenarius. ¶ Est
eciaz abacus ul' abax ūga geometre. ul' tabula
quā hn̄t phi. ubi figuras in puluere supposito fa
ciūt. alio nomine dr̄ pinax cis. Abax eciaz ul' a
bacus. dr̄ supior ps capitelli. i. saxuz quadran
gulū quod sup columpnas ponit'. Et eciaz que
libet mensa marmorea sic dr̄. Et est mas. gn̄is
abacus et cor' penl'. uide in abax
Abalieno nas componit' ex ab et alieno nas
ysa. j. Abalienati sunt retrorsuz. i. alieni facti
Abamita te soror aui ex ab et amita compo
Abarim mons inquo obijt moyses ut nu'
habetur deutronomij xxxij
Abatis. batus quod est quedā mensura cōpo
nit' cuz ad et ablata d. dr̄ h et h abatis indecli
p om̄s casus. i. qui ul' que cū bato diuidit aue
naz. ul' aliud sm hug. Vel abatis componit' ab
assistens et batis. dcō pl'ali. Vnde dicit magister
bene. Pluralia cū singularibus componūt' ut a
secretis. a calicuis. a responsis. abatis. a cōmenta
rijs. hec eniz componūt' ab assistens et illis dn̄s
Et nomina sunt officioz. et indeclinabilia. Vel
pn̄t componi ab a pōne latina et pdcōz abla
tiuis. ut asecretis ab hoc ablcō secretis. q̄m ab
ipsis secretis q̄ ei cōmittunt' dr̄ aliquis asecretis
Similiter abatis componi pt ab a et batis. q̄ ab
ipsis batis siue mensuris que ei cōmittunt' uel
quas exercet. dr̄ aliquis abatis Et id potest de
alijs pdictis iudicari. et cor' penl' abatis
Abax acis interptat' decē. uide in abacus. Et

28a. *Type of Durandus,* Rationale. *Fust and Schoeffer, 1459. From* Veröffentlichungen der Gutenberg-Gesellschaft, V-VII. *(Reduced)*

28b. *Type of the* Catholicon, *1460. From* Veröffentlichungen der Gutenberg-Gesellschaft, *IV. (Reduced)*

Dr. Humery who seems to have provided money for Gutenberg's workshop (for he owned the equipment), that he had departed this life before the date of the record, February 26, 1468.

GUTENBERG'S TYPES

As to the manner of making the early types, opinions still differ. Since Wallau has convincingly demonstrated that the two-color Psalter initials were made of metal, not of wood (in *Festschrift. . . Mainz*, 1900) the view that steel punch and matrix determined the procedure, if not from the very beginning, then at least at an early stage, has gained ground. For a long time Peter Schoeffer has been credited with the introduction of the steel punch; considering his age and his background as a calligrapher, it is highly improbable that he should have first used a fundamental tool with which Gutenberg as a metal worker must have been familiar for decades before (Schoeffer was still in Paris in 1449). Schoeffer did, however, first use copper for matrices, and the result shows clearly in the superior type of the Durandus; Gutenberg's *Catholicon* type was evidently cast from leaden matrices of the sort that had previously been satisfactory for the larger types. (Figures 28a and 28b.)

The Dutch typefounder, Charles Enschedé, has expressed the opinion that a process used by founders until quite recently, and known as *abklatsch*, was employed by Gutenberg. Its principle is the pressing of a model (which may be wood or metal) into a quantity of molten lead that has been poured upon a stone slab, at the moment of solidification; thus a matrix is formed which may be justified to fit into a casting instrument. Such a matrix, while not permanent like one punched into copper, is known to yield a number of good casts. The method is primitive and has limitations.

Another modern technician, Gustav Mori, likewise basing his opinion on a known typefounders' process, assumes models of brass or bronze, either sand-cast from wooden patterns or engraved in relief by hand, which were driven into blocks of type metal, thus forming the matrices; he even suggests that the earliest types were made entirely by the sand-casting method from wooden models, and experiments carried out by him have proven the practicability of his assumed progress—in the twentieth century! Whether the experiments of the fifteenth century, in the absence of precision tools, would have led to the same results, is, however, an open question.

It cannot be denied that both Enschedé and Mori have demonstrated methods that *might* have been employed at the very beginning. All other theories may safely be disregarded, except the assumption of the early use of the steel punch, which is made by such technicians as Otto Hupp and Friedrich Bauer and concurred in by the present writer.

Shaping the type face in steel (right-side-left) at the end of a conically shaped bar, and sinking this "punch" into a softer metal, is not a difficult feat. More difficult was the casting from such a "matrix" of letters that met the strict requirements repeatedly mentioned before. We know that the casting instrument was the solution.

Our only tangible evidence, the early fragments, does not yield directly an answer

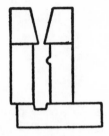

Cross section through casting instrument. Above the matrix the steel blocks determining the "body" size, with the jaws for the "jet." The hollow space is filled with molten type metal.

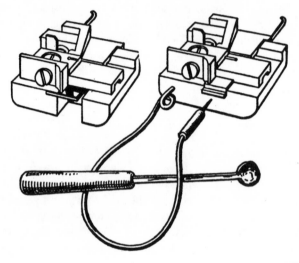

Typical form of the casting instrument (opened), with casting spoon.[6]

to the question as to how the types were made. It is fallacious, however, to judge from the crude appearance of the earliest cuttings that the process of making the type was crude!

In the formal Rhenish manuscript books of his time Gutenberg found a system of writing which relied for its effect mainly upon close and rhythmical spacing. To obtain the same balanced rhythm with metal characters was found impossible unless and until a system of special characters was invented. Gutenberg spared no time and effort to create such characters.

In the formal gothic letters there is no mingling of curved and straight lines, as in the roman; all curves are "broken" and transformed into emphatic vertical lines with sharply spurred corners. The parallel vertical strokes are nearly evenly spaced

Variants of letters i and s in Gutenberg's first type (Enlarged—from *Veröffentlichungen der Gutenberg-Gesellschraft*, III).

The Gutenbergian type system illustrated (from Hupp, *Zum Streit um das Missale speciale Constantiense*).

throughout the line and give it the appearance of a "grating," heightened by the fact that the spurs of adjacent letters actually touch each other.

The earliest fragments show clearly how difficult it was to achieve rhythmical spacing with single, assembled types.

The type of the forty-two-line Bible shows the Gutenbergian system fully developed as to characters and sorts. From the minute investigations of Schwenke, we learn that the font contained 240 lower-case letters, including abbreviations, contractions, and ligatures, and 52 caps, altogether 292. For comparison: the modern German Fraktur type, rich in ligatures, averages forty punches for the lower-case alphabet.

The font consisted of: (1) regular upper- and lower-case alphabet; (2) so-called succeeding letters (*Anschluss-Buchstaben*); i.e., regular letters with the spurs filed off on the left; (3) letters with pointed heads and no spurs on the left (specially made that way); (4) secondary letter forms (two and even three different designs of the same type); (5) ligatures (tied or combined letters in one piece); (6) overhanging, or "kerned" letters; (7) accented letters (i.e., with abbreviation marks); (8) independent special marks (prefixes, suffixes, punctuation).

Of these, only the regular and kerned letters and the ligatures and punctuation marks have survived until today; accented letters were used throughout the incunabula period and disappeared gradually, early in the sixteenth century. Numbers 2, 3, and 4 constitute the typical Gutenbergian system.

THE UNKNOWN EARLY DUTCH PRINTER

No account of the invention of printing can overlook the work of an unknown Hollander. Although we cannot be sure about the identity of the individual and must leave open the question whether the hero of a local tradition of Haarlem, Laurens Janszoon Coster, can be connected with the *two* Laurens Janszoons mentioned in incomplete Haarlem records, yet of the existence of an early printer in Holland we have proof in the form of numerous fragments of books of small extent, such as the Donatus, the *Doctrinale*, the *Speculum*, and others. All these fragments are printed on parchment with types of distinctly Dutch design, both the types and the printing revealing a primitive technique, that *may* antedate Gutenberg's work. (Figure 29.)

Neither date nor place and individual can be assigned to these specimens. The only supporting evidence is a vague reference in the Cologne Chronicle of 1499 which speaks, under the head "Of the Invention of Printing," of the Dutch Donatuses as forerunners (*eyrste vurbyldung*) to the improved method of Gutenberg, who is given full credit for having invented and perfected printing in the form in which it was being practiced at the time the Chronicle was written.

A somewhat legendary account by Hadrianus Junius, a learned physician, in his *Batavia* (a history of Holland), published in 1588, is based on the local tradition then current in Haarlem that Laurens Janszoon Coster invented printing in that city, and that his servant Gensfleisch absconded with the whole equipment one Christmas

Xpũs mraͤ figͤns moreͤ ſuͤ figuns poͤrneͤ

Criſtus ladͤ voor ſijn cruers
Jn den voergaeͤde capitel hebͤ wi gewerͤ
hoe criſtus ſyn cruys droech veruolghendͤ
laeſ ons hoe he hi ladͤ vociteͤ ghenͤ die
hem crueceͤ Die riddeͤ leydͤ dat cruys op
ter aertͤ en criſtum ontcleedͤ ſo reckeͤ ſi
hem daer op wͤ Die eerſte hant nagͤldͤ ſi
uͤ enͤ nagel dier an En die ander hantͤ
nagheldͤ ſi daer na wͤ treckende mit linen
toten anderͤ gaeͤ En wen ſi dien an geſͤ
ghe ladͤ toghͤ ſi die voeten wͤ nuͤ linen
en uͤ enͤ nagel ſloghͤ ſi leidͤ die voeͤ an
Deſe wuͤreckinghe ſcit die heͤ inͤ ſalm
ende werͤ daer van Si hebben werboͤr
mijn hantͤ en voetͤ en hebͤ al mijn gebeͤ
te gheteͤ En we zͤs deſe wͤeerhaͤ ghele
den ladͤ leuͤes hy hem ſijn alte goedͤtie
enſte minne waͤ hy ſinͤ hemelſchͤ vadͤ
voeͤ hem ladͤ En gaf ons een exempel
onſe vianderͤ te minnͤ wanneeͤ wi onſe viͤ
dͤ minnͤ en voer lͤ bidͤ ſo lewiſͤ wi ons
te weſen ſonen gods ende broederen criſt
Criſtus heeft ons gheleerͤ onſe vianten te
minnͤ op dat wi moghͤ weſͤ ſonͤ ſijns vͤ
ders die inͤ hemel is Ten is nieͤ groͤ
te minnͤ die ons wel doen en onſe viendͤ
Matheus xxv lucas xxiii iohes xiɟ

29. From Speculum humanae salvationis, *by the unknown early Dutch printer. First Dutch edition. The line at top belongs to the woodblock illustration. From Zedler,* Von Coster zu Gutenberg. *(Reduced)*

night. Why the "inventor," even if his tools were stolen, did not fashion new ones, having the knowledge, is not explained! The fanciful tale is critically dealt with by the historian Pater B. Kruitwagen in the *Gutenberg Festschrift,* 1925.

Little evidence can be gleaned from the Haarlem archives, for the data about the two Laurens Janszoons are partly contradictory as to time.

The printed fragments, however, are real evidence; new bits have been found in recent years in bindings of old books and records, and more are likely to be discovered. What is known now, has been recorded, illustrated, and investigated minutely by Professor Gottfried Zedler in his book *Von Coster zu Gutenberg* (1921). He comes to the conclusion that in the Dutch method, more primitive and older, the type was cast in *two* operations; i.e., the heads first, and the shanks joined with them subsequently. This assumed procedure complicates an admittedly difficult technical problem still more, and opinions on it differ widely. Zedler admits that Gutenberg invented the casting instrument which produced types in *one* operation—the only practical method.

We may regard the following as certain: The technique of *one* man appears in all extant Dutch specimens. The books of which they were a part were small in size and extent, and unpretentious; judging from the contents—school texts and popular literature—they were meant for mass consumption by a clientele interested in low price.

The Dutch books comprise a limited field that is covered, after the middle of the fifteenth century, by the wood-block printers. Gutenberg's printing, starting with a higher aim, was applicable to all forms of literature; by its technical superiority it developed and lived, while the Dutch method, due to basic technical limitations, enjoyed only a brief existence.

The work to which John Gutenberg had devoted his life had come to full fruition during the decade preceding his death. When the great inventor, whom we may well admire as a mechanical genius, closed his eyes, the craft he had developed was well on its way to becoming the most potent factor in the intellectual advancement of Europe.

NOTES

[1] Annals of Han Dynasty: A.D. 174, Ts'ai Yung, Supervisor of the Imperial Archives, had the texts of six canonical books, from his own handwriting, engraved on large stone tablets and had them placed in front of the state academy "so that scholars and students of all ages could come any day to interrogate these tablets and to make exact copies or correct their copybooks."

[2] Did Mr. DeVinne mean sheets printed on one side or both sides; the wooden press or the iron hand press; inking by balls or by rollers? The comparison is valueless unless these factors are accounted for. Editor.

[3] For a description of tools and processes used in intaglio work, as well as a reproduction of a metal cut, see Warren Chappell's article "Illustrations Made with a Tool," in *The Dolphin,* No. II, 1935.

4 Italics mine. Saspach said: "do was das ding binweg"; i.e., "the thing had disappeared."
5 Schwenke's estimate; Zedler's is now 86, but formerly was as high as 270; Hupp's is still larger.
6 This illustration and those on the preceding page are from *Das Moderne Buch* (*Graphische Künste der Gegenwart* III), Stuttgart, 1910.

The nontechnical reader will find the illustrations of this article, "The Making of Printing Types" (*The Dolphin*, No. I, 1933, pp. 24-57), very helpful.

John Edwin Sandys

The Printing of
the Classics in Italy

While we gratefully recall the preservation of Latin manuscripts in the mediaeval monastaries of the West, as well as the recovery of lost Classics by the humanists of the fourteenth and fifteenth centuries, and the transference to Italy of the treasures of Greek literature from the libraries of the East, we are bound to remember that all this would have proved of little permanent avail, but for the invention of the art of printing.

The old order culminates in the name of Vespasiano da Bisticci (1421-1498), the last of mediaeval scribes and the first of modern booksellers. The date of his birth falls exactly a hundred years after the death of Dante (1321) and before the death of Leo X (1521), and he is himself one of the most interesting representatives of Medicean Florence. An intimate friend of the many-sided Manetti, he was conscious of not having such a mastery of the best Latin as would warrant his using that language in answering the Latin letters of his friend, yet he possessed a thorough knowledge of the commercial value of Latin, Greek and Hebrew MSS. Besides executing orders for Hungary, Portugal, Germany, and England, he was the trusted agent of the three greatest collectors in the fifteenth century, Cosimo de' Medici, Nicolas V, and Frederic of Urbino. When Cosimo, the founder of three libraries, the private library of the Medici, that of San Marco, and that of the Badia between Florence and Fiesole, proposed to found a fourth library for the monks of San Lorenzo, he applied to Vespasiano, who promptly engaged 45 copyists, and, in less than two years, produced 200 MSS for the purpose. [1] The library was divided into classes according to

---

SOURCE: Reprinted from John Edwin Sandys, A *History of Classical Scholarship*, Third edition (Cambridge: Cambridge University Press, 1921), 3 volumes. (Reprint-New York: Hafner Publishing Company, 1967), Volume II, Chapter VIII, "The Printing of the Classics in Italy," pp. 95-105, by permission of Cambridge University Press. Copyright 1921 by Cambridge University Press.

a scheme drawn up by Tommaso Parentucelli, afterwards famous as Nicolas V, the founder of the collection of MSS in the Vatican Library. In the formation of that library, Vespasiano was one of the Pope's principal assistants, and the bookseller of Florence dwells in glowing terms on the services rendered by Nicolas V to the cause of learning.[2] Similarly, Vespasiano spent fourteen years in forming for the duke of Urbino a fine library including all the Greek and Latin authors as yet discovered, all the volumes being bound in crimson and silver, and all in perfect condition, all 'written with the pen,' for the duke would have been ashamed (says Vespasiano) to possess a single printed book.[3] Such is the phrase found in one of those delightful biographies of the hundred and three men of mark, the patriots, patrons of learning and scholars of the fifteenth century, biographies founded on personal knowledge and inspired by a love of virtue, which have made the name of Vespasiano dear to all who are interested in the literature of the time of transition from the age of the mediaeval copyist to that of the modern printer. He rests in Santa Croce among the great men of Florence, after proving himself faithful to the old traditions of learning down to the very end of his life.[4] Twenty-eight years before the death of Vespasiano, we find Filelfo genuinely interested in the new art of printing, and resolving on the purchase of 'some of those *codices* they are now making without any trouble, and without a pen, but with certain so-called types, and which seem to be the work of a skilled and exact scribe,' and finally inquiring as to the cost of a printed copy of Pliny and Livy and Aulus Gellius.[5]

Printing had been introduced into Italy by two Germans, Sweynheym and Pannartz, who had worked under Fust at Mainz. They set up their press first at the German monastary of Subiaco in the Sabine mountains (1465) and next at the palace of the Massimi in Rome itself (1467). At Subiaco they produced the *editio princeps* of the *De Oratore* of Cicero. At Rome they reprinted that work, and added the earliest edition of the *Brutus* and *Orator* (1469); moreover, they produced the *editiones principes* of Cicero's *Letters* and *Speeches*, Caesar, Livy, Gellius, Apuleius, Virgil, Lucan, and Silius (1469-71), the prefaces being generally written by Giovanni Andrea de'Bussi, bishop of the Corsican see of Aleria, who also saw through the press their Ovid of 1471. Cardinal Campano edited Quintilian and Suetonius for Philip de Lignamine, and Cicero's *Philippics* for Ulrich Hahn (1470). Pomponius Laetus edited for Georg Lauer the first edition of Varro *De Lingua Latina* (1471), and the second of Nonius Marcellus (1476). In Venice, the first edition of the elder Pliny was produced by John of Spires in 1469.[6] At Florence, Bernardo Cennini, the first Italian who cast his own type, printed the commentary of Servius on the whole of Virgil (1471-72). By the year 1500 about 5,000 books had been produced in Italy, of which about 300 belong to Florence and Bologna, more than 600 to Milan, more than 900 to Rome, and 2,835 to Venice, while presses were set up for a short time in fifty places of less importance.

Before the year 1495 only a dozen Greek books had been printed in Italy, viz., the Greek grammars of Lascaris[7] and Chrysoloras;[8] two Psalters,[9] Aesop[10] and Theocritus,[11] the 'Battle of the Frogs and Mice',[12] and Homer,[13] with Isocrates,[14] and the Greek Anthology.[15] This last was in capital letters, and was succeeded in Florence by similar editions of Euripides, Callimachus, Apollonius Rhodius, and Lucian. The latter were, however, preceded by the earliest of the Greek texts printed in Venice by Aldus Manutius.

Aldus Manutius (1449-1515) is the Latin form of Aldo Manuzio, whose original name was Teobaldo Manucci. Born in the neighbourhood of Velletri, he was early imbued with classical learning by two natives of Verona, having studied Latin in Rome under Gaspare, and Greek as well as Latin under Guarino at Ferrara.[16] His younger fellow-student, the brilliant Giovanni Pico of Mirandola, recommended Aldus as tutor to his nephews Alberto and Lionello Pio at Carpi, and it was at Carpi that Aldus matured his plans for starting a Greek press with the aid of Alberto Pio. The press was ultimately founded in Venice, the model for the Greek type was supplied by the Cretan Marcus Musurus and most of the compositors were natives of Crete. The Greek books published by Aldus between 1494 and 1504 included Musaeus, Theocritus, and Hesiod, Aristotle, nine plays of Aristophanes, Sophocles, Herodotus and Thucydides, Xenophon's *Hellenica*, with eighteen plays of Euripides, and, lastly, Demosthenes. After an interval caused by the troubles of war, we have first the Greek rhetoricians, including the first edition of Aristotle's *Rhetoric* and *Poetic*, and next, the *Moralia* of Plutarch. Another interval, due to the same cause, was followed by the publication of Pindar, with the minor Attic Orators, and Plato, and Athenaeus.[17]

With a view to promoting the study of Greek and the systematic publication of the Greek Classics, Aldus formed in 1500 the 'New Academy' of Hellenists. Greek was the language of its rules; Greek was spoken at its meetings; and Greek names were adopted by its Italian members. Thus Scipione Fortiguerra of Pistoia, the earliest editor of the text of Demosthenes, and Secretary of the Academy, translated his name into Carteromachus.

One of the aims of the Academy was to produce in each month an edition of at least 1,000 copies of some 'good author.'[18] Among the ordinary members were Janus Lascaris and his pupil Marcus Musurus, besides other scholars from Crete. Among the honorary foreign members were Linacre, whose Latin rendering of the *Sphere* of Proclus was published by Aldus in 1499, and Erasmus, who visited Venice in 1508, when he was engaged in seeing through the press a new edition of the *Adagia*.[19]

As a printer of Latin Classics Aldus had been preceded in Venice by John of Spires (1469), Nicolas Jenson, and Cristopher Valdarfer (1470). In 1501 Aldus began that series of pocket editions of Latin, Greek, and Italian Classics in small 8vo, which did more than anything else towards popularising the Classics in Italy. The slanting type then first adopted for printing the Latin and Italian Classics, and since known as the 'Aldine' or 'Italic' type, was founded on the handwriting of Petrarch by Francesco de Bologna[20] and it was first used in 1501 in the Aldine editions of Virgil, Horace, Juvenal and Persius, as well as in the *Cose Volgare* of Petrarch.[21] The later Latin texts include Valerius Maximus (1502), Pliny's *Letters* (1508),[22] and Quintilian (1514).

In 1499 Aldus had married the daughter of Andrea Torresano d'Asola, who had, twenty years previously, bought up the printing business of Nicolas Jenson. In course of time Aldus and his father-in-law, Andrea, went into partnership, and the above edition of Pliny's *Letters*, printed *in aedibus Aldi et Andreae soceri*, supplies us with the first public record of the fact. Aldus was far more than a printer and bookseller; he rejoiced in rescuing the writings of the ancients from the hands of selfish bibliomaniacs, many of his texts were edited by himself, and he was honoured as a scholar by the foremost scholars of the age. One of the most generous of men, his generosity was appreciated by Erasmus, and by his own countrymen. The editor of the *Prefaces to the Editiones Principes* justly describes 'the dedications of Aldus as worth all the rest; there is a high and a noble feeling, a self-respect, and simplicity of language about him which is delightful; he certainly had aspiring hopes of doing the world good.'[23] He is probably the only publisher who, in the preface of a work published by himself, ever used such language as the following: –*nihil unquam memini me legere deterius, lectuque minus dignum.* Such are the terms in which he refers to the Life of Apollonius by Philostratus; but he hastens to add that, as an antidote to the poison, he publishes in the same volume the refutation by Eusebius, translated by the friend to whom he dedicates the work. In the twenty-one years between 1494 and 1515, Aldus produced no less than twenty-seven *editiones principes* of Greek authors and of Greek works of reference.[24] By the date of his death in 1515, all the principal Greek Classics had been printed.[25] Before 1525, the study of Greek had begun to decline in Italy, but meanwhile an interest in that language had happily been transmitted to the lands beyond the Alps.

Paolo Manuzio (1512-1574), the youngest son of Aldo, was educated by his grandfather Andrea, who carried on the business till his death in 1529, when Andrea was succeeded by his sons, with whom Paolo was in partnership from 1533 to 1540. From that date forward, Paolo published on his own account a series of Ciceronian works, beginning with the complete edition of 1540-46, and including commentaries on the *Letters to Atticus* (1547), and *to Brutus* and *Quintus* (1557), and on the *Pro Sextio* (1556). One of the daintiest products of his press is the text of Cicero's *De Oratore, Brutus* and *Orator*, printed in Italic type, with his own corrections, in 1559. He published his Italian Letters in 1556-60, and his Latin *Epistolae et Praefationes* in 1558. He had a branch house in Rome, on the Capitol, and it was mainly in Rome that he lived from 1561 till his death in 1574, producing *scholia* on the Letters *Ad Familiares* (1571) and on the *Pro Archia* (1572). At Venice and Rome he published several works on Roman Antiquities, while his comments on Cicero's *Speeches* were posthumously printed in 1578-79, and his celebrated *commentarius* on the Letters *Ad Familiares* in 1592.[26] Tiraboschi, who refers to the eulogies paid him by Muretus and others, happily describes him as having been worthy of a far longer life, and still more worthy of immortal remembrance.[27]

Paolo bequeathed his business to his son Aldo Manuzio the younger (1547-1597), who held a professorship in Venice before succeeding Sigonius in Bologna and Muretus in Rome. At the age of eleven, he had produced a treatise on the 'Elegancies of the Tuscan and Latin languages,' and, at fourteen, a work on Orthography founded on the study of inscriptions (1561). The second edition of the latter (1566) contains the earliest copy of an ancient Roman calendar of B.C. 8-A.D. 3 discovered by his father in the Palace of the Maffei and now known as the *Fasti Maffeiani*,[28] His other publications include a volume of antiquarian miscellanies entitled *De Quaesitis per*

Epistolam (1576). He is somewhat severely denounced by Scalinger as 'a wretched and slow wit, the mimic of his father.'[29] After little more than a century of beneficent labour in the cause of classical literature the great house of printers came to an end when the younger Aldus died in Rome without issue in 1597.[30] The vast library which had descended to him from his father and his grandfather was dispersed, but the productions of the Aldine press are still treasured by scholars in every part of the civilised world.

The present chapter may fitly close with a chronological conspectus of the *editiones principes* of the Greek and Latin Classics. The list is mainly confined to the principal classical authors, with the addition of the two earliest texts of the Greek Testament (1516-17) and of the Latin Fathers (1465), but to the exclusion of translations, grammars, and minor bibliographical curiosities. Not infrequently an *editio princeps* comes into the world without any note of time or place, and without the name of any editor or printer, and the determination of these points is often a matter of considerable difficulty. Possibly the unique *Batrachomyomachia* in the Rylands Library, Manchester (ascribed by Proctor to Ferrandus of Brescia, c. 1474), and the rare copies of Virgil (Mentelin, Strassburg, c. 1469), Juvenal (Ulrich Hahn, Rome, c. 1470), and Martial (Rome, c. 1471), are earlier than those entered in the list; and it is uncertain whether the *editio princeps* of Curtius (c. 1471) is that of G. Laver, Rome, or Vindelin de Spira, Venice. In the list, approximate dates are (as here) distinguished by the usual abbreviation for *circiter*; and conjectural names of printers, or of places of publication, are enclosed within parentheses. For all these details the best bibliographical works have been consulted.[31] The name of the 'editor' has been added, wherever it can be inferred either from the colophon or title-page, or from the preface or letter of dedication. It will be seen how large a part of the editorial work was done, in the case of Latin authors, by Giovanni Andrea de' Bussi, bishop of Aleria, and, in the case of Greek, by Janus Lascaris, and Aldus Manutius (with or without the aid of Musurus). Besides frequently indicating the names of the editors, the Aldine prefaces are full of varied interest. Thus Aldus laments that his work as a printer is interrupted by wars abroad[32] and by strikes at home,[33] and by difficulties in procuring trustworthy MSS.[34] But he exults in the fact that Greek is being studied, not in Italy alone, but also in France and Hungary and Britain and Spain.[35] A Greek scholar at Milan begins the *editio princeps* of the great lexicon of Suïdas with an adroit advertisement in the form of a lively dialogue between the bookseller and the student, who finally produces three gold pieces and buys the book.

Date	Author	Editor	Printer	Place
1465	Cicero, *De Officiis, Paradoxa*		Fust and Schoeffer	Maintz
c. 1466	Cicero, *De Officiis*		Ulrich Zell	Cologne
1465	Cicero, *De Oratore*		Sweynheym and Pannartz	Subiaco
	Lactantius; 1467 Aug.*Civ. Dei*		..	..
1467	Cicero, *ad Familiares*		..	Rome
1469	Cicero,*De Or.,Brutus,Orator*		..	..
	Apuleius	Jo. Andreas de Buxis	..	..
	Gellius	..	..	..
	Caesar		..	..
	Lucan	..	..	
	Pliny, *Hist. Nat.*		J. de Spira	Venice
c. 1469	*Virgil	..	Sweynheym and Pannartz	Rome
	Livy	..		
1470	Cicero, *ad Atticum*	..		
	Sallust		Vindelin de Spira	Venice
	*Juvenal and Persius		..	..
	Priscian		..	..
	Cicero, *Rhetorica*		N. Jenson	..
	Justin		..	..
	Quintilian, *Inst. Or.*	Campanus	(Phil. de Lignamine)	Rome
	Suetonius	..	..	..
c. 1470	Cicero, *Philippicae*	..	Ulrich Hahn	..
	Terence		(Mentel)	(Strassburg)
	Valerius Maximus		..	..
	Boëthius, *De Phil. Cons.*		Hans Glim	Savigliano
	Tacitus, *Ann.* 11—16, *Hist.,* *Germ., Dial.*		J. de Spira	Venice
1471	Ovid	Franc. Puteolanus	Azzoguidi	Bologna
	Silius Italicus	Jo. Andreas de Buxis	Sweynheym and Pannartz	Rome
	Cicero, *Orationes*	..	..	..
	Pliny, *Epp.*. libri viii	Ludovicus Carbo	(Chr. Valdarfer)	(Venice)
	Pomponius Mela	Zarotus	Zarotus	Milan
	Nonius			(Italy)
	Florus		Gering,Crantz, Friburger	Paris
	Varro, *L.L.*; c.1471 *Curtius	Pomponius Laetus	Georg Lauer	Rome
	Eutropius		..	..
	Aem. Probus, *i.e.* Nepos		N. Jenson	Venice
c. 1471	Horace		..	(Venice)
	*Martial	G. Merula	Vindelin de Spira	Venice
1472	Plautus	..	..	..
	Tib., Prop., Cat , Stat. *Silv.*		..	..
	Macrobius		N. Jenson	..
	Ausonius and Calpurnius	Bart. Girardinus	Bart. Girardinus	..
	Scriptores de Re Rustica	Merula and Colucia	N. Jenson	..
	Manilius	Regiomontanus	Regiomontanus	Nuremberg
c. 1473	Lucretius		Ferrandus	Brescia
1474	Valerius Flaccus		Rugerius and Bertochus	Bologna
	Amm. Marcellinus, libri 13	Sabinus	Sachsel and Golsch	Rome
c. 1474-84	Seneca, *Tragoediae*		Andreas Gallicus	Ferrara
1475	Quintilian, *Decl.* 3	Dom. Calderinus	Schurener	Rome
1475-83	Statius	..	Octavianus Scotus	Venice
1475	Hist. Aug. Scriptores	Bonus Accursius	Philippus de Lavagna	Milan
	Seneca, *Moralia et Epp.*		Moravus	Naples
1477	Dictys Cretensis	Masellus Beneventanus	(Philippus de Lavagna)	Milan
1478	Celsus	Bart. Fontius.	Nicolaus Alemannus	Florence
1481	Quintilian, *Decl.* 19	Jac. Grasolarius	Lucas Venetus	Venice
1482	Claudian	Barn. Celsanus	Jac. Dusensis	Vicenza
c. 1482	Pliny, *Pan.*, Tacitus, *Agr.*	Puteolanus, Lauterius	(Zarotus)	(Milan)
1486	Probus	Franc. Michael	Boninus	Brescia
c. 1486	Vitruvius	Joan. Sulpitius	G. Herolt	Rome
	Frontinus, *De aquaeductibus*	..	..	..
1487	Vegetius, Aelian, Frontinus		Eucharius Silber	..
1494	Quintilian, *Decl.* 138	Thad. Ugoletus	Ang. Ugoletus	Parma
1498	Apicius	Ant. Motta	Guil. Signerre	Milan
1498-9	Cicero, 4 vols. folio	Alex. Minutianus	.. Gulielmi fratres	
1502	Prosper, Sedulius	Aldus Manutius	Aldus Manutius	Venice
c. 1508-13	Symmachus	Bart. Cyniscus	Bern. de Vitalibus	..
1515	Tacitus, *Annal.* 1—5 etc.	Beroaldus II	Steph. Guilleroti	Rome
1520	Velleius Paterculus	Beatus Rhenanus	Jo. Froben	Basel
1533	Amm. Marcellinus, libri 18	M: Accursius	Silvanus Otmar	Augsburg
1596	Phaedrus	Pierre Pithou	J. Odot	Troyes

Editiones Princeps of Latin
Authors

Date	Author	Editor	Printer	Place
c. 1478	Aesop	Lat. trans. Rinutius	(Bonus Accursius)	(Milan)
1486	*Batrachomyomachia		Leonicus Cretensis	Venice
1488	Homer	Dem. Chalcondyles	Bart. di Libri for	Florence
			Bern. Nerli	
1493	Isocrates	..	(Uderic Scinzenzeller)	..
c. 1493	Theocritus, 1—18, and Hesiod, *Opera et Dies*		(Bonus Accursius)	Milan
1494	*Anthologia Graeca*	J. Lascaris	Laur. de Alopa	Florence
c. 1495	Euripides, *Med. Hipp. Alc. Andr.*	..	..	..
	Callimachus, 1—6	..	..	..
c. 1494-5	Musaeus	Lat. trans. Musurus	Aldus Manutius	Venice
1495-8	Aristotle, 5 vols. folio and Theophrastus,*Hist.Plant.*	Aldus Manutius	..	..
1496 N.S.	Theocritus, 1—30, Bion, Moschus,Hesiod,Theognis	..	..	..
1496	Scriptores Grammatici	Guarino, Politian etc.	..	..
	Apollonius Rhodius	J. Lascaris	Laur. de Alopa	Florence
	Lucian	..	..	..
1497	Zenobius	Bened. Ricciardini	Phil. de Junta	Florence
1498	'Phalaris'	Bart. Capo d' Istria	Printers from Carpi	Venice
	Aristophanes, 9 plays	Aldus et Musurus	Aldus Manutius	..
1499	*Epp. Graecae*	..	..	..
	Astronomici veteres	Aldus Manutius	..	..
	Dioscorides and Nicander	..	..	..
	' Etymologicum Magnum'	Musurus	Zach. Callierges	..
	Simplicius in Ar. *Categ.*		Z. Callierges	Milan
	Suïdas	Dem. Chalcondyles	Printers from Carpi	Venice
1500	Ammonius *in v voces*		Z. Callierges	..
	Orpheus		Phil. Junta	Florence
1502	Stephanus Byz.	Aldus Manutius	Aldus Manutius	Venice
	Pollux	..	..	..
	Thucydides	..	..	..
	Sophocles	..	..	..
	Herodotus	..	..	..
1503	Euripides, 18 plays	..	..	..
	Ammonius in Ar. *Interp.*	..	..	..
	Ulpian and Harpocration	..	..	..
	Xenophon, *Hellenica*	..	..	..
1504	Philostratus, *vita Apoll.*	..	..	..
	Philoponus in Ar.	..	..	..
	Demosthenes	Aldus et Carteromachus	..	..
1508-9	*Rhetores Graeci* (incl. Ar. *Rhet. Poet.*)	Aldus Manutius	..	..
1509	Plutarch, *Moralia*	Aldus et Demetrius Ducas	Aldus et Andreas Asul.	..
1512	Dionysius Periegetes	Bondenus, & printer	J. Maciochus	Ferrara
1513	Pindar, Lycophron etc.	Aldus Manutius	Aldus et Andreas Asul.	Venice
	Orationes Rhet. Gr.	..	..	..
	Plato	Aldus et Musurus	..	..
1514	Alex. Aphrod. in Ar. *Top.*	Aldus Manutius	..	..
	Athenaeus	Aldus et Musurus	..	..
	Hesychius	..	..	..
1515	Oppian, *Halieutica*	Bern. Junta	Phil. Junta	Florence
1516 N.S.	Aristoph. *Thesm. Lys.*	..	..	..
1516	*Testamentum Novum*	Erasmus	Jo. Froben	Basel
	Xenophon	Euphrosynus Boninus	Phil. Junta	Florence
	⌐Pausanias	Musurus	Aldus et Andreas Asul.	Venice
	Strabo	Ben. Tyrhenus	..	..

Editiones Princeps of Greek Authors

Date	Author	Editor	Printer	Place
1517	Libanius	Coelius Calcagninus	Jo. Maciochus	Ferrara
	Didymus, *Homerica*	J. Lascaris	Ang. Collottius	Rome
	Aristides	Euphrosynus Boninus	Phil. Junta	Florence
	Plutarch, *Vitae*	Phil. Junta		..
1514-7	Complutensian Polyglott	Cardinal Ximenes	Arnold Gul. de Brocario	Alcalá
1518	Biblia Sacra Graeca	Andreas Asulanus	Aldus et Andreas socer	Venice
	Aeschylus, 6 plays	Fr. Asulanus	..	..
	Porphyrius, *Homerica*	J. Lascaris	'Monte Caballo'	Rome
1525	Galen, in 5 parts	Asulani fratres	Aldus et Andreas Asul.	Venice
	Xenophon, *Opera*		Aldi in aedibus	..
1526	Hippocrates	Fr. Asulanus	Aldus et Andreas Asul.	..
1528	Epictetus and Simplicius		J. Anton. et fr. de Sabio	..
1530	Polybius	Vinc. Obsopoeus	Jo. Secerius	Hagenau
1532	Aristophanes, 11 plays	Simon Grynaeus	Cratander	Basel
1533	Diogenes Laërtius	Hieron. Froben et	Hieron. Froben et	..
		Nic. Episcopius	Nic. Episcopius	
	Euclides	Simon Grynaeus	Jo. Hervagius	..
	Ptolemaeus	Erasmus	Hieron. Froben et	..
			Nic. Episcopius	
1535	Arrian	Jo. Bapt. Egnatius	J. F. Trincavelli	Venice
	Stobaeus	Victor Trincavelli	..	..
1539	Diodorus, 16—20	Vinc. Opsopoeus	Jo. Oporinus	Basel
1544	Josephus	Arnoldus Arlenius	Hieron. Froben	..
	Archimedes	Thomas Gechauff	Jo. Hervagius	..
1545	Aelian, *Var. Hist.*, etc.	Camillus Peruscus		Rome
1546	Dionysius Halic.	Rob. Stephanus	Rob. Stephanus	Paris
1548	Dion Cassius, 36—58		..	..
1542-50	Eustathius. 4 vols.	Majoranus & Devarius	Ant. Bladus	Rome
1551	Dion Chrys.	F. Turrisanus	F. Turrisanus	Venice
	Appian		Car. Stephanus	Paris
1552	Aelian, *Tactica*	Robortelli	Spinelli	Venice
	Aeschylus, 7 plays	..		
1553	Menander, *Frag.*		F. Morel I	Paris
1554	'Longinus'	Robortelli	Jo. Oporinus	Basel
	Anacreon	Putschius, & printer	H. Stephanus	Paris
	Aretaeus	Jac. Goupyl	Andr. Turnebus	
1555	Apollodorus, *Bibl.*	Ben. Aegius	Ant. Bladus	Rome
1556	Claudius Aelian, *Opera*	C. Gesner, Robortelli,	Gesneri fratres	Zürich
		Gillius		
1557	Aeschylus, *c. Ag.* 323—1050	Victorius	H. Stephanus	Paris
	Maximus Tyrius	H. Stephanus	..	
1558	Marcus Aurelius	Xylander et C. Gesner	And. Gesner	Zürich
1559	Diodorus, 1—20	H. Stephanus	H. Stephanus	Geneva
1565	Bion, Moschus	Adolf Mekerch	Goltzius	Bruges
1566	Poëtae Gr. Principes	H. Stephanus	H. Stephanus	Paris
	Aristaenetus	J. Sambucus	Plantin	Antwerp
1568	Antonius Liberalis,	Xylander	Thomas Guarinus	Basel
	Phlegon, Apollonius			
1569	Nonnus, *Dionysiaca*	Falkenburg	Plantin	Antwerp
1572	Plutarch, *Opera*	H. Stephanus	H. Stephanus	Paris
1575	Stobaeus	Guil. Canter	Plantin	Antwerp
1580	Plotinus	Lat. trans. Ficinus	Petrus Perna	Basel
1583	Hierocles	Jo. Curterius	Nic. Nivellius	Paris
1587	'Empedocles,' *Sphaera*	Florent Chrestien	F. Morel II	..
1589	Polyaenus	Casaubon	J. Toinaesius	Leyden
1594	Andronicus Rhodius	Hoeschelius	M. Manger	Augsburg
1598	Iamblichus	Jo. Arcerius Theo-	Aegid. Radaeus	Franeker
		doretus		
1601	Photius, *Bibliotheca*	Hoeschelius	Jo. Praetorius	Augsburg
1621	Diophantus	Cl. G. Bachetus	Seb. Cramoisy	Paris

Editiones Princeps of
Greek Authors
(continued)

292   THE PRINTED BOOK

NOTES

1 *Vita di Cosimo*, § 12, p.255.
2 *Vita di Nicola* V, § 25 f, p. 38 f.
3 *Federigo, duca d'Urbino*, pp 27-31, esp. p. 99 "tutti iscritti a penna, e non v'è ignuno a stampa, che se ne sarebbe vergognato".
4 The *Vite* first published by Mai, in *Spicilegium Romanum*, 1839 f, and afterwards by Bartoli (Florence, 1839). Cp. in general, Voigt, i 399 f³; Symonds, ii 306 f.
5 Letter dated 25 July, 1470, in Rosmini's *Vita di Filelfo*, ii, 201; Symonds, ii 306.
6 See list of Latin *Editiones Principes*.
7 Milan, 1476; Vicenza, 1488.
8 Venice, 1484; Vicenza, 1490.
9 Milan, 1481-6.
10 Milan, c. 1493.
11 Florence, 1488.
12 Florence, 1494.
13 Milan, c. 1479.
14 Venice, 1486.
15 Milan, 1493.
16 Pref. to Theocritus, 1495, p. 194 of Botfield's *Prefaces*.
17 See list of Greek *Editiones Principes*.
18 Pref. to Euripides, 1503, p. 226 Botfield.
19 Didot's Alde Manuce, 147-152, 435-470; and Symonds, ii 385-8.
20 Of the Griffi family (not Francia); cp. Fumagalli, *Lexicon typographicum Italiae*, Florence, 1905, s.v. Bologna, p. 42. Aldus himself calls this style of type, *cancelleresco* (ib. 471).
21 Didot, 155-169. Of the rare texts above mentioned, I happen to possess Munro's copy of the Juvenal and Persius, bound with the Catullus, Propertius and Tibullus of the following year.
22 The first complete ed. with *all* the correspondence with Trajan (and the *Panegyricus*)
23 Botfield, p. vi.
24 Nine of these 27 'editions' included two or more works, 69 in all besides the 27, making a total of 96.
25 On Aldus Manutius, see Didot's *Alde Manuce*, 1875; Renouard, *Annales de l'imprimerie des Aldes* (1803-12; ed. 2, 1834); and Omont, *Catalogue. . . en phototypie*, 1892. Cp. A. Schück, *A. M. u. seine Zeitgenossen* (1862); and Symonds, ii 368-391. Portrait, published in Rome, probably by Antoine Lafrery, now in Library of San Marco, Venice, copied by Phil. Galleus, *Effigies*, ii (1577) 32, and in frontispiece to Didot's *Alde Manuce*, Portraits of all the three Aldi in Cicero, ed. 1583.
26 Ed. Richter, 1779f; 'optimi etiamnunc interpretis' (Orelli's *Cicero*, ed. 1845, III p. XXXV f).
27 vii 208 f; Cp. *Epp.* 1581, ed. Krause, 1720; *Epp. Sel.* (Teubner, 1892), *Lettere Volgari*, 1560, Renouard, *Lettere di P. M.* (Paris, 1834). Portrait in his *Liber de Comitiis*, (1585), and in Phil. Galleus, ii 33, and Boissard's *Icones*, VIII *mmm* 2.
28 Cp. *C. I. L.* i pp. 303-7; J. Wordsworth, *Fragments. . . of Early Latin*, 266 f. 539.
29 *Scaligerana*, 149. 'P. Manucius quidquid scripsit bonum fuit, magno labore scribebat epistolas. Aldus filius miserum ingenium, lentum; quae dedit valde sunt vulgaria; utrumque novi; Patrem imitabatur, solas epistolas bonas habet; sed trivit Ciceronem diu. Insignis est Manucii commentarius in Epistolas ad Atticum et Familiares. Manucius non poterat

tria verba Latine dicere, et bene scribebat. . . .'

30 Portrait in *Eleganze* (1580), an in Cicero, ed. 1583.

31 Dibdin's *Introduction*, ed. 4 (London, 1827); Panzer, *Annales Typographici*, ad ann. 1536, 11 vols. (Nürnberg, 1793-1803); Hain, *Repertorium Bibliographicum*, ad ann. 1500, 2 vols. in 2 parts each (Stuttgart, 1826-38; now in course of reprinting), with *Indices* and *Register* (Leipzig, 1891), Copinger's *Supplement*, 3 vols. (London, 1898), and Reichling's *Appendices* (Munich, 1905-); R. Proctor, *Index to the Early Printed Books in the British Museum* to 1500, 2 vols. (London, 1898), Germany, in 1501-20 (1903), and *The Printing of Greek in the xvth cent.* (*Bibliographica*, Dec. 1900); Renouard, *Annales des Imprimeries des Aldes*, 3 vols. ed. 3 (Paris, 1834); Didot, *Alde Manuce* (Paris, 1875); Botfield, *Praefationes et Epp.* (London, 1861); R. C. Christie, *Chronology of the Early Aldines* (1894), in *Selected Essays* (London, 1902), 223-246; and H. Guppy, *The John Rylands Library* (Manchester, 1906), 49-78.

32 Plato, 1513.

33 Aristotle, i 2, and iv 1495-8.

34 Prudentius, 1502 N.S.

35 Aristotle, i 2 (*init.*); Steph. Byz.

Deno John Geanakoplos

"Conclusion"
The Contribution of
the Greek Scholars

There are special reasons and the most cogent of motives which impel the Venetians to undertake and constantly to strive to bring to a happy conclusion the revival of Greek letters. You have been provided most liberally with the means of bringing to fruition this very noble undertaking: you have living among you Greeks as your neighbors, you have under your hegemony not a few of the Greek cities and islands, and you suffer from no lack of as many teachers and books as are needed for this task. . .

> Pietro Bembo, from a speech delivered
> to the Venetian Senate probably in 1531.

How deeply it grieves me to see our (Greek) people suffering everywhere publicly and privately, esteemed lightly, hated, persecuted, abused. . . Learn to bear the jealously flourishing everywhere. . . especially against foreigners, the more so if they are learned men.

> Cardinal Bessarion, letter to
> Michael Apostolis, ca. 1455.[1]

From 1397, when the Byzantine Manuel Chrysoloras delivered his opening lecture at the *studium* of Florence, to 1534 and the death in Rome of the last major Greek scholar-exile, Janus Lascaris,[2] western Europe advanced in its knowledge of Greek from virtual ignorance of the language to the recovery and mastery of almost the entire corpus of Greek literature in the original. In the fourteenth century Greek had

SOURCE: Reprinted from Deno John Geanakoplos, *Byzantium and the Renaissance: Greek Scholars in Venice* (Hamden: Archon Books, 1973), "Conclusion-The Contribution of the Greek Scholars," pp. 279-301, by permission of the Shoe String Press, Inc. Copyright © 1973 by Deno John Geanakoplos.

been known only to a few individuals or in isolated areas, southern Italy in particular; by 1534 it had been communicated to every important cultural area of the West.

But before this process of diffusion could be accomplished, the many Greek works unknown to medieval western Europe (apart, that is, from the culturally separate area of southern Italy)—a large part of the extant ancient literature, including poetry, history, oratory, and some of Plato, not a few of the patristic works, and most of the Byzantine writings and commentaries—had to be introduced from that repository of Hellenic learning, the Greek East. These writings were brought to the attention of the West both by Western scholars who traveled to the East, as did certain of Chrysoloras' pupils and others like Barbaro, Filelfo, and Aurispa,[3] and, more importantly through the mediation of men of letters from the East, who, before or for some years after 1453, emigrated westward in increasing numbers in order to escape the Turkish domination of their homelands. These Greek fugitives brought with them not only whatever manuscripts they were able to carry on their persons but, much more significantly, as is not fully appreciated by many Western-oriented historians of the Renaissance, the intellectual tradition of Byzantium by which their education and general outlook had been to a considerable extent molded. And it was through their work in the West as teachers, scribes, and editors for the press that the diffusion of the Greek language and literature was able to proceed so rapidly in so brief a period.

Opportunistic as perforce they had to be, these Eastern exiles were naturally attracted to the leading Italian humanist centers of the time. First they gravitated to Florence, whose period of leadership in Greek studies extended over the greater part of a century, from Manuel Chrysoloras' appearance in 1396-97 to the collapse of the Medici regime following upon the French invasion of 1494. Other Greeks appeared for a time in Rome during the mid-fifteenth century, under the patronage of Pope Nicholas V and his humanist cardinal, the Byzantine Bessarion. Forced by political conditions at the close of the fifteenth century to leave Florence, many of the learned exiles moved northward to Venice, safely isolated for a time at least from the wars and dislocations of the Italian peninsula. There they remained until the decline of Venetian literary primacy following the Venetian defeat at Cambrai (1509) and the death in 1515 of the famous Venetian printer Aldus Manutius. The promise of another Medici golden age under the patronage of Popes Leo X and Clement VII attracted the exiles finally to Rome, the ascendancy of which was in turn brought to a close by the sack of the papal capital in 1527. This pattern of movement from one center to another is clearly apparent in the careers of most of the Greek scholar-exiles; Marcus Musurus, Arsenios Apostolis, Demetrius Ducas, and Zacharias Calliergis. Of this group Musurus and Arsenios, resided for a time in Florence, mainly during the period of their youth and when Florence was already experiencing a loss of prestige. With the subsequent decline of Florence they, along with Calliergis and Ducas (after his return from Spain), moved on to Rome, now rapidly displacing Venice in humanist endeavors. But the careers of the exiles were most closely associated with the Venetian period of pre-eminence. And it is their activities in Venice and in the areas affected by the influences emanating from that city or its colonies that have constituted the principal focus of this work.

Though the activities of these Greek exiles in the Republic of St. Mark seem almost exactly to coincide with the Venetian period of intellectual supremacy, to say that they alone were responsible for the Venetian advances in Greek scholarship would be to discount other important factors—the contribution of the Latin Hellenists of Venice and, more fundamental, the historical background of the city itself, which seemed to lend itself naturally to the development of an interest in Greek. Actually the Venetian flowering of Greek studies in the early sixteenth century marks the culmination of a tradition of close Venetian involvement with the Greek East that reaches back even earlier than the ninth century. For a long period the relations of the two peoples led to little genuine Venetian appreciation of the classical Greek works as literature. But once Venice had become imbued with the rising humanist ideals emanating from Padua and to a lesser extent Florence, she could take advantage of her traditional orientation to the East and make remarkable progress in the cultivation of Greek letters.

With the fall of Constantinople in 1453, the colonial possessions of Venice in the East, acquired as a result of the fourth crusade of 1204, assumed a greater importance in the cultural sphere. For they became a refuge for fugitives coming from all areas of the old Byzantine world. The island of Crete in particular now became what it was never to be again, a prime European center of intellectual activity, especially for the copying and distribution of manuscripts. Prominent in this occupation were two men the Byzantine refugee Michael Apostolis and his Cretan-born son Arsenios. Both established schools for scribes on the island in which a surprisingly large number of future copyists, editors, and correctors for the Venetian press were trained, including Laonikos the Cretan, Musurus, John Gregoropoulos, Emmanuel Adramyttenos, and John Rhosos. Indeed, in some respects this Cretan milieu offers a direct anticipation of certain aspects of the work of the Aldine circle. But despite the importance of this Cretan activity, which permitted the island to act as a kind of halfway point for the transmission of Greek letters from Byzantium to Italy, little attention has hitherto been directed by historians to this phase of Cretan history.

The conditions obtaining on the overcrowded island soon began to breed frustration among all groups, not least among the scholars, and a desire spread to emigrate elsewhere. From Crete and the other Venetian colonies a stream of refugees, or in some cases voluntary exiles, now flowed into Venice, the principal port of entry to the West. And by the turn of the century the largest concentration of Greeks in western Europe was to be found in that city. It would be a mistake to think that this Greek community of Venice consisted only of intellectuals; actually it embraced a wide stratum of society, from merchants and intellectuals to soldiers (*estradioti*), shipowners, and laborers. This colony grew from its early beginnings to its recognition as a corporate body within the Venetian state, and, ultimately, to its assertion in the sixteenth century of complete independence of the ecclesiastical authorities of Venice. In the cultural sphere the Venetians were able to draw considerable profit from the interaction of their Greek community and colonies with the home city: through increasingly close contact with the Greek language and manner of life the Venetians gradually developed a predisposition for Greek studies. And the wealth of manuscripts brought by the exiles or otherwise procured from the East through their agency—some such codices being then still unknown to the West—contributed to make the city one of the principal custodians of Greek manuscripts in this period of the Renaissance. Moreover, as the wealthy Venetian aristocracy developed its taste for Greek studies, it drew on the Greeks as teachers, and we find schools established in the city not only for the practical purpose of training Venetian colonial officials but to instruct students in the Greek literature and Aristotelian philosophy. Indeed, the Greek chair at the nearby university of Venetian-controlled Padua, during its occupancy by the Cretan scholar Marcus Musurus, became the most famous in all Europe, with students from Italy, France, Germany, the Lowlands, Spain, and Hungary flocking to hear his lectures.

But it was the economic prosperity of Venice in conjunction with the advantages provided by her Greek connections that led to the development of Venice's famous Greek press. Already the leading international entrepôt for the commerce between East and West, Venice by the end of the fifteenth century had become the chief European center for the manuscript and book trade. With easy access to her Eastern colonies, with the papermaking facilities of Padua at her disposal,[4] and with a citizenry not only wealthy but increasingly eager to support humanistic endeavors, Venice was now in a position to vie with her predecessors in the field of Greek publication, Milan and Florence.

The invention of printing in movable type had taken place at almost the moment of Constantinople's fall, thus providing a convenient means of preserving and even multiplying the manuscripts of the ancient Greek masterpieces, many of which were threatened by destruction as a result of the Turkish conquest. Of the many scores of presses established in Venice in the late fifteenth and early sixteenth centuries, the most celebrated is certainly that of Aldus Manutius, and it is in his widely distributed productions that we find the instrument for the broadest transmission of Greek.

There can, of course, be no question of Aldus' extraordinary inspiration in inaugurating and directing the activities of his famous publishing house. He was not only a competent printer[5] but an outstanding editor and humanist scholar as well. But it is not generally realized that in the publication of Greek works in Venice Aldus was anticipated by certain little-known Greek émigrés, the Cretans Laonikos and Alexander, and possibly by Zacharias Calliergis and Nicholas Vlastos (themselves preceded by the Italian Peregrino of Bologna). Moreover, a major portion of the vital and difficult work of typesetting and editing at Aldus' press was done by the Greek exiles. His principal editor was the Cretan Marcus Musurus, while his compositors were likewise in large part Cretans (chief among whom was John Gregoropoulos), because of the difficulty of finding persons competent to read the Greek script from which the printing was done. Of some thirty Greek first editions produced by Aldus,[6] Musurus alone was responsible, presumably, for editing no less than eleven or twelve of the more difficult and important authors. Other Greeks such as Arsenios Apostolis supervised at least one volume, and several were edited by Ducas, whose *Rhetores Graeci*, in the view of the authoritative Renouard, may be considered the most valuable of all Aldine editions.

We certainly cannot overlook the fact that Aldus took a keen interest in all the productions of his press, himself editing or collaborating with others, including Italian scholars, in the editing of a number of Greek authors. Nor should we forget that Aldus offered a means of employment—an outlet as it were—for the talents of the Greek émigrés. Had it not been for the prestige of the Aldine press, even the valuable editions of Musurus would unquestionably have been less widely known. On the other hand, to take nothing from Aldus, it is doubtful whether without the reservoir of talent provided by his Byzantine associates and workmen, with their mastery of the language and technical skill, he could have offered to the public, in the relatively short period of less than two decades, as much as he did of the corpus of classical Greek authors. To quote Aldus' own words: "Musurus' constant aid in the correction of texts is so precious to me that, had Greece produced two more of his merit as councillors of mine, I would not despair of giving before long to people of taste, in very correct editions, the best works of both literatures [Greek and Latin]." By the time of Aldus' death in 1515 his press had given to the world practically all the major Greek authors of classical antiquity. [7]

But the press of Aldus was not a mere publishing house in the narrow sense. With the Greek exiles as a kind of nucleus, Aldus was able to gather around him a group of Western and Greek Hellenists and to establish an Academy (*Neakademia*) where it was prescribed that the Greek language alone could be spoken. There the problems involved in the projected publications of his press were discussed and analyzed, there Hellenists of both East and West in friendly camaraderie could exchange manuscripts and ideas, while not infrequently visitors could benefit from the association, to return later to their homelands enriched by their experience. The contribution of Aldus' Academy is more difficult to assess precisely than is that of his press. But there can be little doubt that this select intellectual circle, composed of eminent Western as well as Greek Hellenists, was during the period of its existence the chief focus for the development of Greek studies not only in Venice but in the entire western world.

Let us look more closely at this period of Venetian primacy in order to distinguish the specific advances made by Venetian scholarship and in particular the nature of the contribution of the Greek exiles. Toward the close of the fifteenth century, Western Europe, despite or perhaps because of the significant advances previously made in Greek studies in Florence and other Renaissance centers, began acutely to feel the lack of Greco-Latin grammars, lexica, and especially readable editions of the Greek classics. It was no accident that the first wholly Greek book to appear in the West was a grammar, the *Erotemata* ("Questions")[8] of Constantine Lascaris, published in Milan in 1476 and followed in 1493 by a grammar of the same title written by the fourteenth century Byzantine Manuel Moschopoulos. But, printed as these were entirely in Greek and without Latin translation, their usefulness was somewhat limited. It was in Venice, with her capabilities for Greek printing and scholarship, that the greatest advances were made in providing the tools for instruction in Greek.

There Aldus, following the appearance in 1484 of the first Venetian Greek book, the grammar of Chrysoloras, produced in rapid succession a series of technical manuals: in 1495 Lascaris' *Erotemata*, with Latin translation, and Gaza's grammar, followed the next year by the collaborative *Thesaurus Cornucopiae et Horti Adonidis*, an important collection in Greek of Greek and Byzantine grammatical treatises, some then unknown. Continuing along these lines, Aldus in 1497 published Urbano Bolzanio's grammar, the first to be written in Latin, and, following this, in the same year, the *Lexicon* of Crastoni (probably edited by Musurus), which when published earlier was the first Greco-Latin dictionary printed in the West. Aldus' enthusiasm for the printing of grammars and lexica, so important in his mind for the diffusion of Greek letters, culminated in the publication of a grammar of his own, which was edited after his death by his friend Musurus. [9] It is a fact worthy of repetition that the grammars most often published in the first half century after the beginnings of Greek printing were not those of the ancients but of Byzantines of the Palaeologan or post-Palaeologan era—of the fourteenth century Moschopoulos and of the Greek émigrés themselves: Chrysoloras, Constantine Lascaris, Chalcondyles, and Gaza. The composition and publication of these grammars on the part of the exiles adds credence to the view that in many ways they were but carrying on in another environment the intellectual tradition of their homeland. [10]

Aldus' interest in the publication of aids for Greek instruction is further indicated by his issuing of a number of texts with corresponding Latin translation, the Musaeus, for instance, edited by Musurus, and Aesop's *Fables*. But it was of course, in his famous series of first editions of the classical authors that Aldus made his chief contribution to scholarship. We have already noted how much he was indebted to his Greek collaborators, especially Musurus, about whose work a word is here in order.

Of the many editions for which Musurus was primarily responsible (it is only in the nineteenth and twentieth centuries that philological methods have permitted more conclusive identification of Musurus' editorial contributions), five are works of poetry (Musaeus, Aristophanes, Sophocles, Euripides, and perhaps Pindar); two are philosophic, the writings of Plato and of Alexander of Aphrodisias on Aristotle; two, the Hesychius and Athenaeus, belong to the category of lexica or literary prose. Still another work comprises the orations of the Byzantine church father Gregory of Nazianzus. There is also an epistolographic collection of ancient and early medieval authors and the edition done later in Rome of Oppian's *Halieutica*. Gifted as he was in the various fields of Greek literature, Musurus' true genius, however, lay in his grasp of the art of Greek poetry. More even than his teacher the eminent Janus Lascaris, he had a keen sensitivity for the style and meters of the ancient poets; and he understood the difficult art of versification with its problems of meter and quantity as did no other person of the age. The editions he produced of the ancient tragedies, comedies, and lyric poets, despite the failings that can be noted by modern philologists with respect to some of his textual changes, are probably the best examples of Renaissance Greek textual criticism, surpassing in insight and technical skill the similar work of any of his contemporaries. A main contribution, in fact, of later Greek Renaissance scholarship (not of the *quattrocento* as a whole but of the late fifteenth and the early sixteenth century) is the editing of Greek poetry, which had hitherto not been attempted, certainly not by Western scholars. And here, of course, Musurus' name is in the foreground.

Despite Musurus' undeniable talent, it must be noted, however, that he too, like all of the exiles, was in many respects but following in the footsteps of his Byzantine predecessors of the Palaeologan era, who had, as early as the later thirteenth century, instituted a revival of classical criticism and of the editing of the old texts. Thus the greatest philologist of the nineteenth and early twentieth centuries, the German classicist U. von Wilamowitz-Moellendorff, could refer justifiably to Musurus as a continuator of Moschopoulos.[11] Nonetheless, despite his debt to his Byzantine forebears, Musurus possessed considerable originality and insight of his own, as may clearly be observed from some of his textual corrections which seem to be based on no known manuscript evidence, the felicitousness of which readings must therefore be attributed to his own remarkable powers of critical divination.

But Musurus' work as editor, as we have noted, was only part of his contribution to Venetian intellectual life. For in his instruction at Padua and later at Venice he attracted pupils from practically every country of the West—ambassadors, men of state, aspiring or established scholars, other refugees. Though it would be difficult to assess the precise influence of his teaching unless one could examine the intellectual development of each of his many students, the vast popularity of his courses and the high regard in which he was held by the Venetian government, the papacy, and many contemporary Hellenists, including the discerning Erasmus, attest to an influence paralleled only by that of Chrysoloras in Florence and Guarino at Ferrara. Neither Chrysoloras nor Guarino, of course, had any connection with the press, and therefore, when one considers Musurus' double editorial and pedagogical career, one is tempted to term him the greatest Hellenist of the entire Renaissance period.

Though none of the other Greek exiles could match Musurus in the number of editions they produced, their work was often of first importance. Ducas' edition of the *Rhetores Graeci*, referred to above, contained many valuable treatises, among them Aristotle's *Rhetoric* and the first edition of Hermogenes, both of which played a major part in the development of Renaissance rhetoric. And Ducas' *editio princeps* of Plutarch's *Moralia* rendered that work easily accessible in the original to those humanists becoming increasingly concerned with the theory and practice of education, so important for the development of the Renaissance intellect.

It has more than once been emphasized here that the Aldine was not the only press to issue Greek books in Venice. Of an even higher quality of printing and sometimes of textual criticism were the productions of the Cretan Zacharias Calliergis. Independently of Aldus and possibly even before him, Calliergis had conceived the plan of founding in Venice a press to publish all the Greek works of antiquity. In view of the often expressed desire of the exiles of the diaspora to preserve the treasures of the Greek legacy not only for the western world but especially for the benefit of future generations of their countrymen[12] (this deep ethnic pride as a basic dynamic in the activities of so many of the Greek exiles is a point that bears repetition), the intention of Calliergis to print Greek works alone seems only natural. Calliergis' press, which was owned and operated exclusively by Greeks, produced as its first work the most important of the medieval Greek dictionaries, the *Etymologicum Magnum* (pages of which resemble the rich leaves of a Byzantine manuscript) and subsequently the *editiones principes* of the commentary of Simplicius on the *Categories* of Aristotle and of Ammonius Hermeiae on the *Five Voices* of Porphyry.[13] Both editions were to prove of significance for the humanistic interpretation of Aristotle which in this period—and in large part under the influence of the Greeks—had begun to develop independently of the medieval scholastic tradition.

Another Cretan, Arsenios Apostolis, early in his career edited one of the very first Aldine works, the *Galeomyomachia*. After his return, however, from his see of Monemvasia, in Greece, his principal contribution to the cultural life of Venice consisted of important editions for the Giuntine and da Sabio presses—various works of Psellus, an edition of Byzantine poetry, Alcinous' precious philosophic summary of and introduction to Plato, and Arsenios' celebrated scholia on Euripides.

Arsenios' father, Michael Apostolis, never resided for any length of time in Venice but spent most of his life on Crete. From that vantage point in the decades following the fall of Constantiniple he scoured the East for manuscripts, which he transcribed and sent on to his patron Bessarion in Rome. Many of these were later to be incorporated into the great collection of manuscripts Bessarion bequeathed to the Venetian government. Codices from this library served as the basis for not a few editions produced by Aldus and other Venetian printers. Michael, as we have mentioned, established some kind of school in Crete, and among his pupils was one of the teachers of Pico della Mirandola and of Aldus himself, Emmanuel Adramyttenus, who, along with Apostolis, seems to have had some as yet undefined connections with the pioneer Cretan printers of Venice. It is to be noted, however, that Michael's method of transcribing manuscripts, however useful for their ultimate preservation, was from the standpoint of modern philology inferior. For his aim, like that of his fellow Cretan scribes, was primarily to provide a complete text of a given author for the amateur patron of the moment, scholarly faithfulness in the process of copying being of only secondary importance. Nor can it be said in general that the Greeks of Venice followed strict standards of philological scholarship in their work of editing for the press. Such canons were not to be formulated until the nineteenth century. Yet it cannot be denied that the editions produced by Musurus and his Greek collegues at Venice were correct within the limits of Renaissance scholarship, and remained, in many cases, for almost three centuries the vulgate versions accepted in Europe. Even today many of the texts they established are still considered very significant factors in the history of the modern transmission of these texts.

But was this role of the Greek exiles in Venice limited only to the technical one of teacher, grammarian, or editor—in other words, to that of purveyor of knowledge? In the case of Musurus the question must be answered in the negative, when we consider the merits of his long poem to Plato prefixed to his edition of that author. Within the difficult metrical and prosodical pattern of the ancients, Musurus expresses true poetic feeling—a moving appeal to the spirit of Plato so to inspire the Pope that he will launch a crusade in behalf of his enslaved Greek compatriots. But Musurus' ability to compose with effect in the larger Greek poetic forms was exceptional among the Greeks. Apart perhaps from some of the well-turned epigrams that all the humanists were in the habit of writing, the exiles seem as a whole rarely to have attemped original composition. This was probably in part because what poetic feeling they possessed they sought to express in the artificial classic language, not in the living demotic Greek. And this attempt to imitate the antique style did not permit the full exercise of imagination. In this respect they were typical of the later phase of Byzantine literature (and not unlike the Western Ciceronians of the Renaissance), which, aside from the Platonic revival at Mistra, was essentially a rhetorical movement, very learned but hampered in the expression of originality by overly strict adherence to the imitation of the antique forms.

And yet one may ask how many of the later Italian humanists reveal genuinely creative literary imagination. Very few, probably, except for the poets Poliziano, Pontano, and Sannazaro.[14] Even the vaunted Erasmus' main talents lay in the direction of critical scholarship—in the editing and translating of classical authors, the amassing of proverbs from recondite sources, and the utilization of these in the editions he prepared for popular consumption—rather than in true artistic or poetic expression.[15] Moreover, one must not forget that the Greek exiles, unlike not a few of their Latin contemporaries, rarely had the leisure to indulge whatever creative impulses they might have possessed. As displaced persons they were preoccupied with eking out a living as best they could. Constantly busy at the press, teaching, or copying manuscripts, they had to carry out whatever demands were made upon their time by their patrons of the moment.[16]

It would appear, however, that in one important respect at least the Greeks did, if almost inadvertently, contribute something more than merely the mechanical to Western humanism. In accordance with the Byzantine rhetorical tradition (the orations of the fourteenth century Thomas Magister are a good example), they emphasized the reading, memorization, and imitation of the style of the original texts,[17] and through this procedure something of the content of these works could not but have been absorbed by their Western students. This would be especially true of the philosophic and educational writings of such authors as Aristotle, Plato, and to a lesser degree Plutarch, a translation of which, however careful, would almost invariably lose some of the nuances of thought or expression of the original. As a result of this method, then, which produced a growing familiarity with the original texts of Greek works containing some of the noblest concepts of classical antiquity, the intellectual horizon of the western world during the *quattrocento* and *cinquecento* could not help being expanded. And this, in fact, to a degree that it had not been since the reception of Aristotle's scientific works from the Arabs several centuries before.[18]

Having examined the contribution of the Greek exiles, in particular with regard to Venice, let us attempt to evaluate the role of that center in transmitting Greek letters to the West. Chronologically the Venetian period of leadership in Greek studies lasted approximately twenty-five years, that of Florence an entire century. Yet within her relatively brief span of time, Venice, in this particular respect, the diffusion of Greek, seems proportionally to have made the greater strides. We have, it is true, not attempted in a rigidly systematic manner to delineate the role of Venice in spreading Greek letters. But on the basis of the variegated experiences of the six representative figures, we may derive a reasonably adequate impression of the Venetian part in this process. For in the careers of these figures may be clearly observed the various methods or channels of diffusion of Greek as well as the distant areas to which a knowledge of the language was carried. In their very movement from Venice to other areas the exiles were themselves responsible for a good deal of dissemination of Greek. Ducas, for example, after being summoned by Cardinal Ximenes to Spain and appointed the first professor of Greek at the newly founded University of Alcalá, spent much of his time supervising the editing of the Greek New Testament of Cardinal Ximenes' celebrated Polyglot Bible. And through his teaching as well as his other publications (it was at his own expense that the first Greek books were printed in Spain), he provided no little impetus to the development of Greek studies in that country. Calliergis, after many years of residence in Venice, introduced the art of Greek printing to Rome, where under the patronage of members of Leo X's court he edited as well as printed some significant first editions, notably the scholia on Pindar and several Byzantine religious works. Arsenios Apostolis too, the exigencies of whose ecclesiastical career made him a frequent commuter between East and West, worked in the later portion of his career in Rome and in Florence, tirelessly copying, printing, or editing texts of both ancient and Byzantine writers. And the great Musurus, whose career was passed almost entirely in Venice, spent the last year of his life at Rome, teaching and editing while moving in the circle of Pope Leo X as one of its chief ornaments.

The influence of the Venetian-based émigrés is also apparent in the activities of their many students, who came from various far-flung areas of Europe. Such persons as Girolamo Aleandro, after a period of tutelage under Musurus at Padua and the closest of associations with the Aldine group (it will be recalled that he lived in Aldus' own house), left Venice to go directly to Paris, where he instituted the first public lectures in Greek. And John Conon, after pursuing the course of study at Padua under Musurus, returned to Germany to become what one scholar has called the "true founder" of Greek studies in that country.[19] We might briefly mention also, among others who studied in Venice, Germain de Brie of France, Janus Vertessy of Hungary, the young Gelenius of Prague (who later settled in Basle, where he produced some Greek editions), and again the cosmopolite Erasmus of Rotterdam, who, soon after leaving Venice, accepted an appointment as professor of Greek at Cambridge University.

In the Venetian sojourn of this most influential of all Western humanists we see what is probably the prime example of a Latin Hellenist who was able not only to assimilate but in his unique manner to exploit the Greek learning of the Aldine circle and to transmit it to the West on a wider and more popular level. Erasmus acquired from the Eastern exiles not only manuscripts—but, hardly less important, advice in the interpretation of difficult Greek passages as well as ideas that would later assist him in the formulation of his program for the reform of Greek pronunciation. In the career of Erasmus, who is generally regarded as the chief link between the northern and southern phases of the Renaissance, we may see the culmination of the process of disseminating Greek learning from Venice to northern Europe.

But there were still other methods of transmitting Greek learning. Venice, as the center of the book trade, attracted many foreign book agents and buyers, eager to purchase not only Aldine and other publications but, no less important for the development of Greek studies in their homelands, Greek manuscripts. Thus it was in Venice that Vittorino da Feltre procured numerous old codices for his library, while Venetian nobles like Barbaro and Lipomanno were able to secure theirs in Venetian-dominated Crete. Giorgio Valla, who taught Greek in Venice in the last years of the fifteenth century, amassed a remarkable collection of manuscripts there,[20] no few of which were used by Aldus in producing his famous Greek editions. Aldus himself had a rich library, which we know was accumulated in considerable part in Venice. Musurus, too, as we have seen, owned a number of valuable manuscripts, and Pietro Bembo formed his library while he was in retirement in Padua. Even after Venetian intellectual primacy had declined, Venice continued to be an important mart for the purchase and exchange of Greek codices. From there in the mid-sixteenth century the wealthy Spanish diplomat Don Diego Hurtado de Mendoza sent the Corfiote Nicholas Sophianos to Greece and Mount Athos, and he returned with no less than 300 Greek manuscripts.[21] Guilelmus Pélicier, then the French ambassador to the Serenissima (1539-1542), bought many valuable manuscripts in that city,[22] and Jean de Pins, another French envoy, also gathered works there. Moreover, Cardinals Domenico and Marino Grimani (pupils of Musurus) in the early sixteenth century left a library in Venice containing hundreds of volumes of Greek and Latin authors.[23] All of these activities helped in one way or another to further the diffusion of Greek learning.

Since during the Renaissance a knowledge of Greek was not so widespread as one might expect—after all, not even all the humanists could read the language—the diffusion of Greek literature depended no less on Latin translations than on editions of the original Greek texts.[24] The Greek exiles, of course, for obvious reasons (including in most cases an insufficient knowledge of Latin) preferred to edit Greek texts for the press. The medieval world, to be sure, had produced a surprisingly large number of translations from the Greek, especially of the Aristotelian philosophic and scientific works. But these were done in a crabbed, overly literal style that did not make for readability and hence for any degree of popularity except within select groups. The humanists, on the other hand, as a result of training from the Greek exiles, had acquired a superior knowledge of Greek syntax and idiom and some awareness of textual variants, together with a greater freedom in word order, style, and terminology. And as a consequence they were now able to produce works that were attractive to a much wider audience.[25] The first substantial humanist translations from the Greek had been made in Florence in the early fifteenth century by Chrysoloras' student Leonardo Bruni and very soon thereafter in Rome by the circle of Bessarion and Pope Nicholas V, where George of Trebizond, Theodore Gaza, and Bessarion himself joined Western humanists in converting Greek texts into Latin.

The Greeks of Venice, however, had little to do with translation into Latin, one of the very few exceptions being Musurus, who did a version of *Musaeus* for Aldus and translated the commentary of the Byzantine John Philoponos on Aristotle's books on generation and corruption. The reason for these exiles' lack of interest in translation (besides an insufficient command of Latin) lay probably in the fact that adequate

Latin versions of most of the Greek works by then already existed: the primary task now was rather to prepare the original texts for the press, an undertaking for which the Greeks were well qualified. So thoroughly was this task accomplished—and by the Greeks centered in Venice particularly—that by the time the last important Greek exiles had disappeared from the scene the body of Greek material that the Latin humanists were able to translate included almost all of Greek poetry, historiography, oratory, much of Greek patristic theology and of non-Aristotelian philosophy, and some writings on mathematics and medicine.[26]

But the chief vehicle for the transmission of Greek in the early sixteenth century was undoubtedly the printed book, especially the Aldine productions. It was Aldus' aim to issue each month from his press an edition of one thousand copies.[27] The great demand for his books throughout Europe is evident from the catalogues he frequently printed (on occasion he even listed the publications of his rivals such as Calliergis), and from the orders for Greek books he received from almost every region of the West, including distant Poland, England, Spain, even Crete. His voluminous correspondence with scholars—with Erasmus, Reuchlin, Bonamico, Vertessy, William Latimer, Celtis, Aleandro, to cite only a few important names—reveals requests for newly printed Greek grammars and lexica and manuals of style and syntax as well as for his eagerly awaited editions of the classic masterpieces.[28] His invention of the small octavo volume, designed to reduce the price of his books and the cost of production (a volume could now be carried in a reader's pocket) helped to increase the circulation of his books far beyond the confines of the Italian peninsula.[29] Though Erasmus was not without some reputation on his arrival in Venice, it was the Aldine publication of his *Adages* that established his reputation on a pan-European scale. Aldus' efforts in behalf of Greek learning did not go unappreciated. The great German humanist John Reuchlin (with whom Aldus enjoyed close relations) could declare that without the work of Aldus in providing Greek texts his own endeavors at teaching Greek in Germany would have been fruitless.[30] But perhaps the most striking testimony to Aldus' efforts is the remark of Beatus Rhenanus, the pupil of Erasmus, who informs us that so successful was Aldus in spreading abroad a knowledge of Greek that he was accused by a fellow-Venetian of a lack of patriotism, as students would no longer find it necessary to come to Italy to learn Greek.[31]

A complete picture of the role of Venice in transmitting Greek letters to the West would of course have to include an equally intensive treatment of the careers of all the other Greeks connected with the period of Venetian primacy[32]—and notably of Janus Lascaris (of whom several biographies are available), who for a time was closely associated with the Aldine press. And it would have to delineate in equivalent detail the role of the Latin Hellenists of Venice, who were at least as numerous as their Greek associates and were able (or thought they were), several of them, to vie with the Greek exiles in their mastery of the Hellenic language. Nevertheless, recognition has been given to the work of the more important of these Western Hellenists of Venice, including, besides Aldus, Scipio Carteromachus, cofounder with Aldus and Gregoropoulos of the Aldine Academy; Urbano Bolzanio, who acquired much of his Greek in the East and was responsible for the first Greek grammar written in Latin;[33]

Varinus Favorinus of Camerino, whose career is more intimately associated with Leonine Rome; and the Venetian nobleman and later Cardinal Pietro Bembo, whose cogently expressed sentiments on the significance of Greek learning and the role of the Greek colonies of Venice therein have been prefixed to this chapter.

Impressive as was the Venetian achievement in the dissemination of Greek, there were in the early sixteenth century certain obstacles which impeded an even more rapid diffusion of the language. In the first place (and in contradiction to the sage advice contained in the 'discourse of Michael Apostolis to the Italians'), Greek was always taught through the instrumentality of Latin. And among the exiles—whose role, as we have seen, was so central for the Venetian period of primacy—very few, except for Musurus, Lascaris, and George of Trebizond, were competent in Latin,[34] a fact which was a certain handicap in their instruction. Moreover, in the later stage of the development of Greek learning in the West, the exiles, Musurus and Lascaris again excepted, were no longer looked upon with the respect, even adulation, that had greeted the earlier arrivals such as Chrysoloras and Bessarion. As the Westerners drew their knowledge of Greek from the émigrés and began in turn to consolidate their own skills, some, like Poliziano, began to believe that their command of the language even surpasses that of their Greek masters. And as more and more émigrés arrived from the East, many from among the lower classes and many pseudo-intellectuals, the Latin feeling of disdain, even mistrust, for the Greeks became more pronounced. But for this attitude, it must be admitted, the exiles were themselves far from blameless. For the most part they would not, or perhaps could not, recognize the exigencies of life in the new world they entered. Bearded, as they often remained, viewing themselves in the traditional Byzantine manner as superior to the Westerners whom they considered it their mission to Hellenize, expressing lip service to Catholicism but at heart retaining their Orthodox loyalties, they aroused a good deal of resentment. This was especially true when, as not infrequently happened, a Greek proved more successful than his Latin opponent in capturing a coveted professorial post. Musurus, to be sure, despite his great learning and success in the West, remained modest in word and act. But his was an exceptional case, and even he was slandered after death. On the other hand, Michael Apostolis, possibly Ducas in Spain, and certainly the devious Arsenios aroused deep feelings of antagonism and professional jealousy and were therefore never able to secure permanent professorial positions. Even so, more important obstacles to the diffusion of Greek than the prejudice and presumptuous ignorance of the Western humanists were certain practical considerations: for all the Hellenists, Latin as well as Greek, there were too few stable university chairs; Greek books, despite the rapid development of the press, remained relatively costly; and it was not always easy to find expert transcribers of Greek texts.[35]

A few years before Janus Lascaris' death in 1534, Greek studies in Italy began noticeably to decline from the pitch of contagious enthusiasm fostered by the propaganda of the Greek exiles[36]—in the last analysis perhaps the émigrés' chief contribution to Renaissance Greek learning—to the narrower, more specialized interests of the native Italian professional scholars. It would be difficult to affirm categorically that it was the gradual disappearance of the Greek exiles that brought about this situation, although, as Burckhardt points out, more than mere coincidence seems to be involved.[37] It should be noted, however, that almost all of the ancient Greek works had now been printed, and that, with the excitement diminished for the production of new ones, a certain satiety with Greek learning had begun to set in. Part of this lessening of interest in Greek may also have stemmed from the developing interest in the Italian vernacular as a literary medium.[38] Important, finally, was the severe blow dealt to Italian humanism by the sack of Rome in 1527, with the consequent ending of the lavish patronage of the papal court—a factor of vital significance in view of the leading role patronage had played in the furtherance of Greek studies in Florence and Venice, as well as in the mid-fifteenth century Rome of Bessarion's circle. After all, like the exiles themselves, the Greek language, for all the admiration of the Westerners, was never really a part of the native Western culture.

The emphasis placed by historians on Venice's economic, political, and artistic life has served to obscure her purely intellectual achievements. Of even greater importance, however, with respect to her role in the development of Greek learning, has been the lack of understanding of the interaction of Venice's intellectual life with that of the Byzantine and post-Byzantine East, in particular the Venetian colony of Crete. It has been the aim to provide a composite picture of East and West by means of a detailed examination of the careers of five little-studied and in many ways representative Greek émigré scholars who (except for the preparatory figure of Michael Apostolis) came to reside in Venice during the years of her intellectual primacy but did not cut the ties with their Greek homeland. In the background of the émigrés was the Greek community of Venice, which was constantly being reinforced by new arrivals from the East and from which, whether the émigrés chose to live in the colony or not, they were able to derive a sense of security which caused them to look upon Venice as almost a second Byzantium. It was chiefly this magnetlike attraction of Venice for the Greek exiles, based on a centuries-old tradition of close relations with Byzantium— not to overlook, of course, the city's economic prosperity and the opportunity for employment afforded by the Aldine press—that enabled Venice not only to appropriate but, with remarkable success, to diffuse Greek letters throughout the Western world.

NOTES

[1] Quoted in Ferrai, *L'Ellenismo di Padova*, 9; also see J. Morelli, "Intorno ad un orazione greca inedita del Cardinale Pietro Bembo alla Signoria di Venezia," *Memorie dell' R. Istituto del regno Lombardo-Veneto*, II (Milan, 1821) 251-62. Also L. Mohler, *Aus Bessarions Gelehrtenkreis* (Paderborn, 1952) 481.

[2] The traditional date of Lascaris' death is 1535 (Knös, *Janus Lascaris*, 214), but Mercati, in *Opere minori*, III (1910) 185, on the basis of Ms. Vat. gr. 2240, fol. 49r, has now placed it as December 7, 1534.

[3] Guarino, Filelfo, Aurispa, and Giovanni Tortelli, the first librarian of the Vatican (who was at Constantinople from 1435 to 1437), actually studied in the East. Fuchs, *Die höheren Schulen*, 68-69, gives a long list, but several of the names he cites are certainly wrong. R. Sabbadini, *Le scoperte*, is a much better authority. South Italian monasteries had a good deal of Greek literature.

4   Brown, *Venetian Printing Press*, 24. Aldus secured the paper for his book manufacture from the small town of Fabriano, in the province of Ancona.

5   Some authorities have criticized from a technical point of view his talent or lack of talent as a craftsman of printing. For instance, his adoption of the new cursive hand for his Greek type has been much criticized in favor of the handsome type used in the Alcalá New Testament.

6   Out of a total of 127 authenticated editions of all kinds (E. Robertson, "Aldus Manutius, the Scholar-Printer," 72; also C. Bühler, "Aldus Manutius," 211).

7   One important omission was Polybius.

8   This was a favorite title for a whole series of Byzantine grammars; works of this name were cast in the form of questions and answers (a kind of grammatical catechism).

9   See Kukenheim, *Contributions à l'histoire de la grammaire*, 7ff.

10 Cf. Krumbacher, *Byzantinischen Litteratur*, 501, who had realized the continuity of the Byzantine tradition in Italy on the part of the Greek exiles. As he writes: "Wer künftig eine Geschichte des Humanismus schreiben will, muss auf Moschopulos, Planudes, ja bis auf Eustathios, Psellos, Arethas, und Photius zurückgehen. Dass sich die Sache geschichtlich so verhält, geht schon aus der einfachen Beobachtung hervor, dass gerade die Werke, durch welche ein Theodoros Gazes, ein Konstantin Laskaris, ein Manuel Chrysoloras das Studium der griechischen Sprache am meisten beförderten aus älteren byzantinischen Vorlagen, aus Arbeiten des Theodosios, Moschopulos u.a. abegleitet sind."

11 See U. von Wilamowitz-Moellendorff, *Einleitung in die attische Tragödie* (= *Euripides Herakles erklärt*, von U. von W.-M., Band I, Berlin, 1889) 194, and cf. 220f. for another extremely complimentary passage on Musurus' talent in textual criticism. These passages also refer to other fourteenth and sixteenth century Greeks.

12 This wish of the Greek exiles to preserve their national legacy for their downtrodden people is frequently overlooked by historians in discussing their activities in the West in connection with the development of Greek learning.

13 Calliergis also printed the *Therapeutics* of Galen.

14 This is not, of course, to say that others in other fields, for example, Ficino in philosophy and Poggio and Bruni in history, did not exhibit a certain imagination.

15 Weiss, "Learning and Education in Western Europe," I, 114, thinks that the works of the Greek poets Homer, Sophocles, and Aeschylus were too difficult for Erasmus: hence his partiality (as he said) for Euripides or Lucian!

16 The Greek exile Marullus wrote some very good Latin poetry in Florence, as did Rhalles. Janus Lascaris wrote some Latin epigrams. Knös, *Janus Lascaris*, 168-69. The verses by Ducas translated above are of course not important.

17 Cf. W. Woodward, *Studies in Education during the Age of the Renaissance* (Cambridge, Eng., 1924) 18, who says that at the schools of Guarino and Vittorino the study of Greek was mainly for its content. Among the Byzantines, the fourteenth century Thomas Magister wrote orations deliberately imitating the form and style of the ancients: see F. Lenz, "On the Authorship of the Leptinean Declamations Attributed to Aristides," *American Jl. of Philology*, LXIII (1942) 154ff., esp. 167.

18 Of course the contribution of the Greek exiles of Venice was only part of the broad movement for the restoration of Greek letters, which began at least as early as the fourteenth century. This point bears repetition.

19 The honor of founding Greek studies in Germany is often awarded to John Reuchlin and Rudolph Agricola.

20 These are the manuscripts that were later purchased by Alberto Pio and are today housed in Modena.

21 Of course the value of all these manuscripts must have been very uneven.

22 On Pélicier see the preface to L. Cohn, *Verzeichniss der von der königlichen Bibliothek zu Berlin erworbenen Meermanhandschriften des Sir Thomas Phillipps* (Berlin, 1892) p. i, which lists the many manuscripts he collected ("quorum codicum maior pars iussu Pelecerii ipsius vel ab hominibus Graecis vel ab Italis doctis, quos per tempus illud quo Venetiis morabatur mercede conductos habebat, Venetiis exarata est").

23 See Mercati, *Pio*, 14ff. Also P. Paschini, *Domenico Grimani* (Rome, 1943) 141.

24 See Bolgar, *Classical Heritage*, 277f., and especially Kristeller, *Classics*, 16. Also Lockwood, "Aristophanes in the 15th Century," *Transactions and Proceedings of the American Philological Association*, XL (1909) p. lvi.

25 See Kristeller, *Classics*, chap. i.

26 Cf. Kristeller, *Classics*, 16. By 1600 virtually all of Greek literature was available in Latin.

27 Preface to Aldine Euripides (1503), in Botfield, *Praefationes*, 226. Also see Putnam, *Books and Their Makers*, I, 423.

28 A rapid perusal of E. Pastorello, *L'epistolario Manuziano* (Florence, 1957), gives an idea of Aldus' vast, far-flung correspondence; for instance, Aleandro from Paris requests a Greek grammar (210); Celtis makes a request (27); Reuchlin (26); Vertessy, (35); and Latimer, from Padua (21).

29 See Putnam, I, 424ff. (who notes that the sales in Paris were interfered with by Lyons piracy editions); Brown, *Venetian Printing Press*, 48, and Robertson, "Aldus Manutius, the Scholar-Printer," 64.

30 See Putnam, I, 430.

31 See Beatus' introduction to the works of Erasmus: "Quidam Venetiis olim Aldo Manutio commentarios Graecos in Euripidem et Sophoclem edere paranti dixit: Cave, cave hoc facias, ne barbari istis adjuti domi maneant et pauciores in Italiam ventitent."

32 As has frequently been stressed, this book focuses primarily on the Greek exiles in or connected with Venice during the period when she attained the primacy in Greek studies. But of course the Venetian role in the transmission of Greek did not cease in 1535 (with the disappearance of the scholars whose biographies have been given here). Venice remained for some years an important center for the manuscript trade, and in fact Greek scholars of lesser importance from Crete, Corfu, and other areas continued to come to Venice until long past the end of the sixteenth century. Some of these, nearly all of whom were copyists, were Anthony Eparchos, Nicholas Sophianos, Angelo Vergikios, Andreas Darmarios, Constantine Palaeokappas, and John and Thodosius Zygomalas. On all these see esp. Legrand, *Bibliographie hellénique*, vols. I and II.

33 According to Rhenanus, Erasmus had a high regard for Bolzanio's Greek knowledge.

34 Gaza and Bessarion had also been good Latinists.

35 Cf. V. Rossi, *Il Quattrocento*, 93.

36 Of course certain exceptions can be cited in the late sixteenth century, such as the excellent Hellenists Pier Vittorio and Francesco Patrizi, and we know that additional translations were made. On the decline of enthusiasm for Greek see Sandys, *Classical Scholarship*, II, 100 and 133 ("Before 1525 the study of Greek had begun to decline in Italy"). Also Burckhardt, *Civilization of the Renaissance* (Oxford and London, 1945) 118. Meanwhile, under the influence of Italy, Greek studies had begun to flourish north of the Alps, especially with Budé, Erasmus, and the Stephani.

37 Burckhardt, *Civilization of the Renaissance* (Oxford and London, 1945) 119.

38 On the development of the vernacular see Kristeller, *Studies*, 492, who affirms that study of the vernacular was influenced by the techniques (on vocabulary, syntax, forms) perfected for the study of Latin. Greek study also, if indirectly, probably played a part here.

Frederick B. Artz

The Significance of
Renaissance Humanism

The task undertaken by the Humanists was an enormous one. It involved first a systematic search for manuscripts, many of which still existed in only a few scattered copies. The collecting, copying, and diffusion of manuscripts was but the beginning of their work. Manuscripts had to be collated to weed out copyist's mistakes, and then they had to be edited, which required a minute study of paleography, orthography, grammar, syntax, and usage, and all this had to be done without the help of printed texts, grammars of any great value, dictionaries and handbooks, all the aids now regarded as indispensable to modern classical studies. In the end, the Humanists restored the whole surviving heritage of Greek and Latin literature, edited all of it, and, later, brought out printed editions of the whole. At the same time, they founded modern philology, archeology, and the writing of history.

The result of their tremendous labors was to bring back into the mainstream of western civilization the whole body of the still extant Greek and Latin literatures. This was a heritage so valuable in itself that human life would be poorer without it, and also a heritage so fraught with power to educate and stimulate that the permanent loss of it would have been the annulment of an inestimable agency in the development of the human faculty. The creative mind of ancient Greece was the greatest originating force which history has known. The ancient Latin mind also was the parent of masterworks which contain a varied wealth of beauty and experience. There was a time when men had allowed the best part of these treasures to be buried, and had almost forgotten their existence. The Humanists found them again, and gave them back to those nations on which the future of civilization chiefly depended.[1]

The Humanists introduced the idea of a lay morality which laid stress on ethical

SOURCE: Reprinted from Frederick B. Artz, *Renaissance Humanism*, 1300-1550 (Kent: The Kent State University Press, 1966), Chapter VI, "The Significance of Renaissance Humanism," pp. 87-91, by permission of the author and publisher. Copyrightx © 1966 by Frederick B. Artz.

conduct as an end in itself. This ideal of lay morality came in alongside the old clerical and monastic views of life. The Humanists increased the sense of the dignity of man and emphasized what man can do for himself, an idea partly derived from the restudy of Greek Fathers of the Church, as Clement of Alexandria and Gregory Nazianzus. One of the clearest statements of this is Pico della Mirandola's *Oration on the dignity of man* of the later fifteenth century:

> Then the Supreme Maker decreed that unto man, on whom he would bestow nought singular, should belong in common whatsoever had been given to his other creatures. Therefore he took man, and having placed him in the center of the world, spake to him thus: 'Neither a fixed abode, nor a form in thine own likeness, nor any gift peculiar to thyself alone, O Adam, in order that what abode, what likeness, what gifts thou shall choose, may be thine to have and possess. The nature allotted to all other creatures, within laws made by ourselves, restrains them. Thou, restrained by no narrow bounds, according to thy own free will, in whose power I have placed thee shall define thy nature for thyself. Thou shalt have power to decline unto the lower or brute creatures. Thou shalt have power to be reborn unto the higher, or divine, according to the sentence of thy intellect.' Thus to man, at his birth, the Father gave seeds of all variety and germs of every form of life. [2]

One is, at once, reminded of many resemblant statements by Greek and Latin writers, but especially of the passage in Sophocles' *Antigone* which begins

> wonders are many but none is so wonderful as man. . . . Man excellent in wit. . . cunning beyond fancy's dream is the fertile skill which brings man, now to evil; now to good.

The same idea reappears in Shakespeare's *Hamlet:*

> What a piece of work is a man. How noble in reason; how infinite in faculty; in moving how express and admirable; in action how like an angel; in apprehension how like a god!

The Humanist Movement, in the next place, was a great stimulus to individualism. The Humanists took themselves very seriously, and they thought all their ideas were worth recording. Thus, treatises even on abstract subjects are intermixed with personal stories, gossip, flattery, and invective which amaze the modern reader. Hence the wide-spread Humanist preference for certain literary forms such as the letter in which the author speaks in the first person, the biography where all details about an individual may be presented, and the diary and autobiography where personal traits can be made to stand forth. The contemporary vogue of the art of portrait painting and portrait sculpture indicates the same tendency.

Humanism had a great influence on education, first on secondary schools, later on advanced education. The Humanists laid emphasis on the study of ancient literature — especially on grammar, rhetoric, poetry, history, and moral philosophy—rather than on logic, natural history, and metaphysics. So the classics gradually became everywhere one of the great staples of the curriculum, only to be pushed aside in the nineteenth and twentieth centuries by science, modern languages, and the social sciences. The first influence of the Humanists on education was on the secondary schools. In spite of all their efforts, Aristotelianism continued to dominate the universities right through the sixteenth century. This Aristotelianism in the universities was not seriously challenged until the growth of new scientific and philosophical ideas in the seventeenth century began steadily to push it aside. With the decline of Aristotelianism in the universities, not only science and a new philosophy came into vogue, but the Humanistic study of the classics of Greece and Rome came to have a larger place in the curricula of most universities. In secondary education, the Humanists rejected the great rigid and closed systems of Scholastic thought, and substituted for them a knowledge derived from concrete and worldly experience. Humanism thus stimulated critical attitudes, and freed minds which refused to be bound by old systems and were prepared to accept new ideas and new experiences. The Humanists helped to lessen the ecclesiastical monopoly of learning, and challenged philosophy to deal with practical subjects, especially with ethics. Though the Humanists were unfavorable to science and philosophy, they indirectly contributed to both by their revival of every scrap of ancient scientific and philosophical writing, and by their worldly and secular attitudes toward life.

All over Europe, the Humanists, with the aid of artists and the writers of vernacular literature, helped to introduce the classical period of European culture, a period that extends from before the time Rabelais said "Thank God we are out of the Gothic night" to Victor Hugo's Romantic pronunciamento, "At last, Parnassus and Olympus are for rent!" In literature, the Humanist theory of imitating the classics was taken over by the vernacular writers. As a result, the vernacular literature of the Renaissance, and again, after Mannerism, of the Baroque period, had a structure and form of much greater clarity and effectiveness than was possessed by most of the vernacular literature of the Middle Ages. Vernacular writers as different as Machiavelli, Montaigne, Shakespeare, Racine, and many others, are not understandable without the background of Humanism. Most Renaissance writers copying from classical literature in vernacular literature believed that the imitator should know his models well enough to reproduce the elements he required without help from notebooks, and even without remembering from whence each gem came. Only such classical materials as came spontaneously to his pen should be used by an author. The aim should be emulation rather than mere imitation. This classical influence began as an inspiration where the vernacular writers borrowed words, figures of speech, subject matter, and general structure from Greek and Latin literature, and ended as an age of literary rules based on classic practice and ancient literary criticism. This becomes clear, at once, if one compares the classical influences in Shakespeare with those in Alexander Pope. There was everywhere in vernacular literature an increased interest in matters of form and style, which parallels the increased interest in both of these fields in the fine arts. At the same time, ancient literary forms were revived—the dialogue, the essay, the familiar letter, comedy, tragedy, the ode, and the literary treatment of history, biography, moral philosophy, and political theory. Unfortunately, in all the influence of classical literature on literatures in the vernacular, the

Latin influence was always stronger than that of Greek literature. The same was true of the fine arts where the influence of Rome was much more marked than that of Greece.

Finally, in Germany, England, and France, Humanism was one of the currents, though not the deepest one, out of which came the Protestant Reformation. The attacks of the Humanists on many aspects of the whole ecclesiastical system of the Roman Church undermined the faith of many of the intellectuals in that church, and prepared them to accept the ideas of reformers like Luther, Zwingli, and Calvin. At the same time, another contribution of the Humanists to the Reformation lay in the Humanist attack on Scholasticism, and their rediscovery of the Bible and the early Fathers of the Church. Unfortunately the Humanist's ideal of an evolutionary reform of the Roman Church was swept aside in the polemics and in the revolutionary fury of the Protestant Reformation and the Catholic Counter-Reformation.

The reason the Humanists, so much esteemed in their own day, were neglected by later generations is that what they found in the classics and strove to disseminate was then new, and later became, thanks to their efforts, an integral part of Western civilization, and as such seemed commonplace. Thus, one of the proofs of the success of the Humanists lies in the fact that they are largely forgotten today.

NOTES

¹ Valuable summaries of the Humanist achievement will be found in P. O. Kristeller, "Humanist learning in the Italian Renaissance," in *The Centennial review*, 1960; in W. K. Ferguson, "The revival of classical antiquity or the first century of Humanism, a reappraisal," in *Report of the annual meeting of the Canadian Historical Association*, 1957; and in several of the essays in A. Renaudet, *Renaissance et l'Humanisme* (Geneva, 1958).
² E. Cassirer and others, eds., *The Renaissance philosophy of man* (Chicago, 1948), pp. 215-254, where the whole *Oration* is given with editorial comment by P. O. Kristeller.

John Rothwell Slater

Printing and
the Renaissance

Printing did not make the Renaissance; the Renaissance made printing. Printing did not begin the publication and dissemination of books. There were libraries of vast extent in ancient Babylon, Egypt, Greece, Rome. There were universities centuries before Gutenberg where the few instructed the many in the learning treasured up in books, and where both scholars and professional scribes multiplied copies of books both old and new. At the outset of any examination of the influence of printing on the Renaissance it is necessary to remind ourselves that the intellectual life of the ancient and the mediaeval world was built upon the written word. There is a naive view in which ancient literature is conceived as existing chiefly in the autograph manuscripts and original documents of a few great centers to which all ambitious students must have resort. A very little inquiry into the multiplication of books before printing shows us how erroneous is this view.

We must pass over entirely the history of publishing and book-selling in ancient times, a subject too vast for adequate summary in a preliminary survey of this sort. With the fall of Rome and the wholesale destruction that accompanied the barbarian invasions a new chapter begins in the history of the dissemination of literature. This chapter opens with the founding of the scriptorium, or monastic copying system, by Cassiodorus and Saint Benedict early in the sixth century. To these two men, Cassiodorus, the ex-chancellor of the Gothic king Theodoric, and Benedict, the founder of the Benedictine order, is due the gratitude of the modern world. It was through their foresight in setting the monks at work copying the scriptures and the secular literature of antiquity that we owe the preservation of most of the books that have survived the ruins of the ancient world. At the monastery of Monte Cassino,

SOURCE: Reprinted from John Rothwell Slater, *Printing and the Renaissance: A Paper Read Before the Fortnightly Club of Rochester, New York* (New York: William Edwin Rudge, 1921), pp. 1-36.

founded by Saint Benedict in the year 529, and at that of Viviers, founded by Cassiodorus in 531, the Benedictine rule required of every monk that a fixed portion of each day be spent in the scriptorium. There the more skilled scribes were entrusted with the copying of precious documents rescued from the chaos of the preceding century, while monks not yet sufficiently expert for this high duty were instructed by their superiors.

The example thus nobly set was imitated throughout all the centuries that followed, not only in the Benedictine monasteries of Italy, France, Germany, England, Scotland, Ireland, Iceland, but in religious houses of all orders. It is to the mediaeval Church, her conservatism in the true sense of the word, her industry, her patience, her disinterested guardianship alike of sacred and of pagan letters, that the world owes most of our knowledge of antiquity. Conceive how great would be our loss if to archaeology alone we could turn for the reconstruction of the civilization, the art, the philosophy, the public and private life of Greece and Rome. If the Church had done no more than this for civilization, it would still have earned some measure of tolerance from its most anti-clerical opponents. It is of course to the Eastern rather than to the Roman Church that we owe the preservation of classical Greek literature, copied during the dark ages in Greek monasteries and introduced into Italy after the fall of Constantinople.

A second stage in the multiplication and publication of manuscript books begins with the founding of the great mediaeval universities of Bologna, Paris, Padua, Oxford, and other centers of higher education. Inasmuch as the study of those days was almost entirely book study, the maintenance of a university library with one or two copies of each book studied was inadequate. There grew up in each university city an organized system of supplying the students with textbooks. The authorized book-dealers of a mediaeval university were called *stationarii*, or stationers, a term apparently derived from the fixed post or station assigned in or near the university buildings to each scribe permitted to supply books to the students and professors. A stationer in England has always meant primarily a book-dealer or publisher, as for example in the term Stationers' Hall, the guild or corporation which until 1842 still exercised in London the functions of a copyright bureau. Incidentally a stationer also dealt in writing materials, whence our ordinary American use of the term. Another name for the university book-dealers was the classical Latin word *librarii*, which usually in mediaeval Latin meant not what we call a librarian but a vender of books, like the French *libraire*. These scribes were not allowed at first to sell their manuscripts, but rented them to the students at rates fixed by university statutes. A folded sheet of eight pages, sixteen columns of sixty-two lines each, was the unit on which the rental charges were based. Such a sheet at the beginning of the thirteenth century rented for about twenty cents a term; and since an ordinary textbook of philosophy or theology or canon law contained many sheets, these charges constituted no inconsiderable part of the cost of instruction. The books must be returned before the student left the university; sales were at first surreptitious and illegal, but became common early in the fourteenth century. Reasonable accuracy among the stationers was secured by a system of fines for errors, half of which went to the university, the other half being divided between the supervisor or head proof-reader and the informant who discovered the error.

The original regulation which forbade the stationers to sell books was intended to prevent students of a profiteering turn of mind from buying books for resale to their fellow-students at a higher price, thus cornering the market and holding up the work of an entire class. In course of time, however, the book-dealers were permitted not only to sell textbooks, at prices still controlled by official action, but also to buy and sell manuscripts of other books, both those produced by local scribes and those imported from other cities and countries.

This broadening of the activities of the university bookstores led naturally to the third and last stage which the publishing business underwent before the invention of printing. This stage was the establishment in Florence, Paris, and other intellectual centers, of bookshops selling manuscripts to the general public rather than to university students. These grew rapidly during the first half of the fifteenth century, receiving a marked impetus from the new interest in Greek studies. Some years before the fall of Constantinople in 1453 Italian book-sellers were accustomed to send their buyers to the centers of Byzantine learning in the near East in quest of manuscripts to be disposed of at fancy prices to the rich collectors and patrons of literature. There is evidence of similar methods in France and Germany during the earlier decades of the Renaissance.

This preliminary sketch of the book-publishing business before printing is intended to correct a rather common misapprehension. Manuscript books were indeed relatively costly, but they were not scarce. Any scholar who had not been through a university not only had access to public libraries of hundreds of volumes, but might also possess, at prices not beyond the reach of a moderate purse, his own five-foot shelf of the classics. The more elegant manuscripts, written by experts and adorned with rich illuminations and sumptuous bindings, were of course not for the humble student; but working copies, multiplied on a large scale by a roomful of scribes writing simultaneously from dictation, might always be had. Chaucer, writing of the poor clerk of Oxford at the end of the fourteenth century, tells us that

> Him was levere have at his beddes heed
> Twenty bokes, clad in blak or reed,
> Of Aristotle and his philosophye,
> Than robes riche, or fithele, or gay sautrye.

We are not sure that he had the whole twenty books; that was his ambition, his academic dream of wealth; but we are assured that he spent on books all the money he could borrow from his friends, and that he showed his gratitude by busily praying for the souls of his creditors.

When we consider the enormous number of manuscript books that must have existed in Europe in the middle ages, we may well wonder why they have become relatively rare in modern times. Several explanations account for this. In the first place, the practice of erasing old manuscripts and using the same vellum again for other works was extremely common. Secondly, vast numbers of manuscripts in the monasteries and other libraries of Europe were wantonly or accidentally destroyed by fire, especially in times of war and religious fanaticism. In the third place, the early binders, down through the sixteenth century and even later used sheets of vellum from old manuscripts for the linings and the covers of printed books. Finally, after the invention of printing, as soon as a given work had been adequately and handsomely printed in a standard edition, all but the finest manuscripts of that book would naturally be looked upon as of little value, and would be subject to loss and decay if not to deliberate destruction. Owing to these and perhaps other causes it is almost entirely the religious manuscripts that have survived, except those preserved in royal libraries and museums from the finer collections of the middle ages.

The invention of printing was not the work of any one man. Not only were printed pages of text with accompanying pictures produced from woodcut blocks in Holland a quarter of a century before Gutenberg began his work at Mainz, but it is pretty well established that movable types were employed by Laurence Koster, of Haarlem, as early as 1430. But Koster, who died about 1440, did not carry his invention beyond the experimental stages, and produced no really fine printing. Moreover, his work had no immediate successor in Holland. Whether it be true, as sometimes alleged, that Gutenberg first learned of the new art from one of Koster's workmen, we have no means of knowing. At any rate, Gutenberg's contemporaries as well as his successors gave to him the credit of the invention. That he was not the first to conceive the idea of multiplying impressions of type-forms by the use of a screw press is evident; but he was the first to develop the invention to a point where it became capable of indefinite extension. He seems to have worked in secret for some years on the problems involved in type-founding and printing before the year 1450, when he set up his shop in Mainz.

The capital for the new business was furnished by a wealthy goldsmith named Johann Fust. Between 1450 and 1455 Gutenberg printed an edition of the Latin Bible, sometimes known as the Mazarin Bible, which is ordinarily regarded as the first printed book. It was a magnificently printed volume, exhibiting at the very foundation of the art a skill in presswork scarcely surpassed by any of Gutenberg's immediate successors. He was a great printer, but not a financially successful one. Fust sued his partner in 1455 for repayment of the loans advanced, and upon Gutenberg's failure to meet these obligations Fust foreclosed the mortgage and took over the printing plant. Although Gutenberg started another publishing house at Mainz, and continued it until his death in 1468, the main development of printing after 1455 was in the original plant as carried on by Fust and his son-in-law, Peter Schoeffer. They printed in 1457 an edition of the Psalms in which for the first time two-color printing was employed, the large initial letters being printed in red and black. This innovation, designed to imitate the rubricated initials of the manuscripts, involved great technical difficulties in the presswork, and was not generally adopted. Most of the early printed books, even down to the end of the fifteenth century, left blanks for the large capitals at the beginnings of the chapters, to be filled in by hand by professional illuminators.

From the establishments of Gutenberg and of Fust and Schoeffer in Mainz knowledge of the new art spread rapidly into many German cities. In 1462 Mainz was captured and sacked by Adolph of Nassau in one of the local wars of the period, and printers from the Mainz shops made their way to other cities throughout the empire. Before 1470 there were printing establishments in almost every German city, and hundreds of works, mostly theological, had been issued from their presses.

In all these early German books, printed of course in Latin, the type used was the black-letter. Gutenberg, in designing his first font, evidently tried to imitate as closely as possible the angular gothic alphabet employed by the scribes in the best manuscripts. Not only were the letters identical in form with the engrossing hand of the monks, but the innumerable abbreviated forms used in the Latin manuscripts were retained. Thus a stroke over a vowel indicated an omitted *m* or *n*, a *p* with a stroke across it indicated the Latin prefix *per*, a circle above the line stood for the termination *us*, an *r* with a cross meant—*rum*, and so forth. These abbreviations, which make printed books of the earliest period rather hard reading today, were retained not only to save space but to give the printed page as nearly as possible the appearance of a fine manuscript. It was not at first the ambition of the printers and type-founders to make their books more legible or less taxing on the eyes than manuscript; their readers were accustomed to manuscript and felt no need of such improvements. The mechanical advance in the art of writing brought about by printing was at first regarded as consisting in the greater rapidity and lower cost at which printed books could be produced.

But the new invention was at first looked upon by some famous scholars and patrons of learning as a detriment rather than a help. The great Trithemius, abbot of Sponheim, wrote as late as 1494 in the following terms:

> A work written on parchment could be preserved for a thousand years, while it is probable that no volume printed on paper will last for more than two centuries. Many important works have not been printed, and the copies of these must be prepared by scribes. The scribe who ceases his work because of the invention of the printing-press can be no true lover of books, in that, regarding only the present, he gives no due thought to the intellectual cultivation of his successors. The printer has no care for the beauty and the artistic form of books, while with the scribe this is a labor of love.

Contrasted with this low estimate of the importance of the new art by some scholars, we note the promptness with which the great churchmen of Italy and of France took measures to import German printers and set up presses of their own. In 1464 the abbot of Subiaco, a monastery near Rome, brought to Italy two German printers, Conrad Schweinheim and Arnold Pannartz, and set them at work printing liturgical books for the use of the monks. Soon afterward, under ecclesiastical patronage, they began to issue, first at Subiaco and then at Rome, a series of Latin classics. During five years this first printing establishment in Italy published the complete works of Cicero, Apuleius, Caesar, Virgil, Livy, Strabo, Lucan, Pliny, Suetonius, Quintilian, Ovid, as well as of such fathers of the Latin Church as Augustine, Jerome and Cyprian, and a complete Latin Bible. This printing establishment came to an end in 1472 for lack of adequate capital, but was soon followed by others both in Rome and especially in Venice.

Early Venetian printing forms one of the most distinguished chapters in the whole history of the subject. The most famous of the first generation was Nicolas Jenson, a Frenchman who had learned the art in Germany. Between 1470 and his death in 1480 he printed many fine books, and in most of them he employed what is now called roman type. He was not absolutely the first to use the roman alphabet, but his roman fonts were designed and cast with such artistic taste, such a fine sense of proportion and symmetry of form, that the Jenson roman became the model of later printers for many years after his death. Roman type, unlike the black-letter, had two distinct origins. The capitals were derived from the letters used by the ancient Roman architects for inscriptions on public buildings. The small letters were adapted from the rounded vertical style of writing used in many Italian texts, altogether different in form from the angular gothic alphabet used in ecclesiastical manuscripts. Jenson's roman letters were clear, sharp and easy to read, and constituted the greatest single addition to the art of printing since its beginning. Germany clung obstinately to the black-letter in its Latin books, as it has adhered down to very recent times to a similar heavy type for the printing of German text; but the rest of Europe within a few years came over to the clearer and more beautiful roman.

There were many early printers at Venice between Jenson and his greater successor Aldus Manutius, who began business in 1494, but we shall pass over them all in order to devote more careful attention to the noble history of the Aldine press. I propose in the remainder of this paper to select five great printers of the Renaissance, and to examine their work both as a whole and as illustrated in typical examples. These five are:

ALDUS MANUTIUS, of Venice.
ROBERT ESTIENNE, of Paris, commonly known by the name of *Stephanus*,
JOHANN FROBEN, of Basel.
ANTON KOBERGER, of Nuremberg.
WILLIAM CAXTON, of London.

Each stands for a different aspect of the art of printing, both in the mechanical features of book-making and also in the selection of works to be published and the editorial methods employed in making them ready for the press. Taken together, the books issued from their presses at the end of the fifteenth and the beginning of the sixteenth century form a sort of composite picture of the Renaissance.

First of all, in our consideration and in order of greatness, stands the name of Aldus Manutius. The books of the Aldine press, all with the well-known sign of the anchor and dolphin, are familiar to most students of the classics. Aldus was born in 1450, the very year of Gutenberg's invention. For the first forty years of his life he was a scholar, devoting himself to the Latin classics and to the mastery of the newly revived Greek language and literature. His intimate association with Pico della Mirandola and other Italian scholars, as well as with many of the learned Greeks who then frequented Italian courts and cities, led him to conceive the great plan upon which his later

career was based. This was nothing less than to issue practically the whole body of classic literature, Greek as well as Latin, in editions distinguished from all that had preceded in two important respects. First, they were to be not reprints of received uncritical texts but new revisions made by competent scholars based upon a comparison of all the best available manuscripts. Secondly, they were to be printed not in ponderous and costly folios but in small octavos of convenient size, small but clear type, and low price. This was not primarily a commercial venture like the cheap texts of the classics issued in the nineteenth century by Teubner and other German publishers, but resembled rather in its broad humanistic spirit such a recent enterprise as the Loeb Classical Library. The purpose in each case was to revive and encourage the reading of the classics not alone by schoolboys but by men of all ages and all professions. But there is this important difference, that Mr. Loeb is a retired millionaire who employs scholars to do all the work and merely foots the bill, while Aldus was a poor man dependent upon such capital as he could borrow from his patrons, and had at the same time to perform for himself a large part of the editorial labors on his books. Mr. Loeb commands the latest and most complete resources of the modern art of printing; Aldus helped to make that art. Mr. Loeb's editors may employ when they choose the style of type known as italic; Aldus invented it. Mr. Loeb's publishers have at their command all the advertising and selling machinery of a great modern business concern, and yet they do not, and probably can not, make the classics pay for themselves, but must meet the deficits out of an endowment. Aldus had to organize his own selling system, his advertising had to be largely by private correspondence with scholars and book-sellers throughout Europe laboriously composed with his own hand; yet it was imperative that the business become as soon as possible self-supporting, or at least that losses in one quarter should be recouped by profits in another.

It was in his edition of Virgil, 1501, that Aldus first employed the new cursive or sloping letter which later came to be known in English printing as italic type. According to tradition he copied it closely from the handwriting of the Italian poet

Petrarch. The type was very compact, covering many more words on a page than the roman of that day, and was used as a body type, not as in our day for isolated words and phrases set apart for emphasis or other distinction from the rest of the text. Aldus also, though not the first to cast Greek type, gave his Greek fonts an elegance which was soon imitated, like the italic, by other printers. By the introduction of small types which were at the same time legible, and by adopting for his classical texts a small format suitable for pocket-size books, Aldus invented the modern small book. No longer was it necessary for a scholar to rest a heavy folio on a table in order to read; he might carry with him on a journey half a dozen of these beautiful little books in no more space than a single volume of the older printers. Furthermore, his prices were low. The pocket editions or small octavos sold for about two lire, or forty cents in the money of that day, the purchasing power of which in modern money is estimated at not above two dollars.

This popularizing of literature and of classical learning did not meet with universal favor amongst his countrymen. We read of one Italian who warned Aldus that if he kept on spreading Italian scholarship beyond the Alps at nominal prices the outer barbarians would no longer come to Italy to study Greek, but would stay at home and read their Aldine editions without adding a penny to the income of Italian cities. Such a fear was not unfounded, for the poorer scholars of Germany and the Netherlands did actually find that they could stay at home and get for a few francs the ripest results of Italian and Greek scholarship. This gave Aldus no concern; if he could render international services to learning, if he could help to set up among the humbler scholars of other lands such a fine rivalry of competitive cooperation as already existed among such leaders as Erasmus and Sir Thomas More, he should be well content to live laborious days and to die poor. Both these he did; but he gathered around him such a company of friends and collaborators as few men have enjoyed; he must have breathed with a rare exhilaration, born of honest and richly productive toil, the very air of Athens in her glory; and he must have realized sometimes amid the dust and heat of the printing shop that it was given to him at much cost of life and grinding toil to stand upon the threshold of the golden age alike of typography and of the revival of learning. In 1514, the year before his death, Aldus wrote to a friend a letter of which I borrow a translation from George Haven Putnam's Books and Their Makers during the Middle Ages. This is the picture Aldus drew of his daily routine:

I am hampered in my work by a thousand interruptions. Nearly every hour comes a letter from some scholar, and if I undertook to reply to them all, I should be obliged to devote day and night to scribbling. Then through the day come calls from all kinds of visitors. Some desire merely to give a word of greeting, others want to know what there is new, while the greater number come to my office because they happen to have nothing else to do. 'Let us look in upon Aldus,' they say to each other. Then they loaf in and sit and chatter to no purpose. Even these people with no business are not so bad as those who have a poem to offer or something in prose (usually very prosy indeed) which they wish to see printed with the name of Aldus. These interruptions are now becoming too serious for me, and I must take steps to lessen them. Many letters I simply leave unanswered, while to others I send very brief replies; and as I do this not from pride or from discourtesy, but simply in order to be able to go on with my task of printing good books, it must not be taken hardly. As a warning to the heedless visitors who use up my office hours to no purpose, I have now put up a big notice on the door of my office to the following effect: Whoever thou art, thou art earnestly requested by Aldus to state thy business briefly and to take thy departure promptly. In this way thou mayest be of service even as was Hercules to the weary Atlas. For this is a place of work for all who enter.

What a picture that letter gives us of the half humorous, half pathetic spirit in which the great publisher endured the daily grind. Twenty years of it wore him out, but his dolphin-and-anchor trade-mark still after four centuries preaches patience and hope to all who undertake great burdens for the enlightenment of mankind.

The Aldine press did not confine its efforts to the ancient classics, but printed editions of Dante and Petrarch and other Italian poets, and produced the first editions of some of the most important works of Erasmus. But all of its publications belonged in general to the movement known as humanism, the field of ancient and contemporary poetry, drama, philosophy, history, and art. Aldus left to others, especially to the great ecclesiastical printers of Venice and of Rome, the printing of the scriptures, the works of the church fathers, and the innumerable volumes of theological controversy with which the age abounded. In France, on the other hand, the great publishing house of the Estiennes, or Stephani, to whom we next direct our attention, divided its efforts between the secular and sacred literature. Inasmuch as the history of the Stephanus establishment is typical of the influence of printing upon the Renaissance, and of the Renaissance upon printing, which is the subject of this paper, we may well examine some aspects of its career.

Printing had been introduced into France in 1469 by the ecclesiastics of the Sorbonne. Like that abbot of Subiaco who set up the first press in Italy five years before, these professors of scholastic philosophy and theology at Paris did not realize that the new art had in it the possibilities of anti-clerical and heretical use. For the first generation the French printers enjoyed a considerable freedom from censorship and burdensome restrictions. They published, like the Venetians, both the Greek and Latin classics and the works of contemporary writers. Both Louis XII and Francis I gave their patronage and encouragement to various eminent scholar-printers who flourished between the establishment of the first publishing-houses in Paris and the beginning of the sixteenth century. I pass over all these to select as the typical French printers of the Renaissance the family founded by Henri Estienne the elder. His first book, a Latin translation of Aristotle's *Ethica*, appeared in 1504. From that date for nearly a hundred years the house of Stephanus and his descendants led the publishing business in France. Both in the artistic advancement of the art of printing and in the intellectual advancement of French thought by their selection of the works to be issued they earned a right to the enduring gratitude of mankind.

Henri Estienne, the founder of the house, who died in 1520, had published during these sixteen years at least one hundred separate works. Although they were mostly Latin, many of them revealed Estienne's knowledge of and devotion to the new Greek studies, and this tendency on his part was at once suspected as heretical by the orthodox doctors of the Sorbonne. The favor of King Francis was not at all times sufficient to protect him from persecution, and an increasing severity of censorship arose, the full force of which began to be evident in the time of his son Robert.

After Henri's death his business was for a time carried on by his widow's second husband, Simon Colines, a scholar and humanist of brilliant attainments. Both while at the head of the house of Stephanus and later when he had withdrawn from that in favor of Robert Estienne his stepson and set up a separate publishing business, Colines added much to the prestige of French printing. He caused Greek fonts to be cast, not inferior to those of the Venetian printers, and began to publish the Greek classics in beautiful editions. It was Colines, rather than either the elder or the younger Estienne, who elevated the artistic side of French printing by engaging the services of such famous typographical experts as Geofroy Tory, and adding to his books illustrations of the highest excellence, as well as decorative initials and borders. Indeed it may be said that after the death of Aldus supremacy in the fine art of book-making gradually passed from Venice to Paris.

The greatest of the Estiennes was Robert, son of Henri Estienne and stepson of Colines, who was in control of the house from 1524 to his death in 1559. The very first book he published was an edition of the Latin Testament. Although following in the main the Vulgate or official Bible of the Roman Church, he introduced certain corrections based on his knowledge of the Greek text. This marked the beginning of a long controversy between Estienne and the orthodox divines of the Sorbonne, which lasted almost throughout his life. In following years he published many editions of the Latin scriptures, each time with additional corrections, and eventually with his own notes and comments, in some cases attacking the received doctrines of the Church. A Hebrew Old Testament, in 1546, was followed in 1550 by the Greek New Testament. The next year he published a new edition of the Testament in which for the first time it was divided into verses, a precedent followed in Bible printing ever since. It was not merely the fact of his printing the scriptures at all that angered the heresy-hunters, but much more Estienne's notes and comments, in which, like Luther in Germany and Tyndale in England, he sided with the views of the Reformers.

What distinguishes Robert Estienne from the ordinary Protestant scholars and publishers of his time is the fact that he was not only a Reformer but a humanist of broad and tolerant culture. In all the illustrious group of that age there is scarcely another like him in this union of religious zeal and of scholarly culture. Luther and Calvin and Tyndale had the one; Erasmus is the most eminent example of the other, with such great publishers as Aldus and Froben his worthy supporters. But Robert Estienne, alongside of his controversial works and Biblical texts, labored at such great enterprises as his monumental edition of Terence, in which he corrected by the soundest methods of textual criticism no less than six thousand errors in the received text, and especially his magnificent lexicons of the Latin and Greek languages, which set the standard for all other lexicographers for generations to come.

The middle of the sixteenth century in France is thus marked by a curious blend of those two distinct movements in human history which we call the Renaissance and the Reformation, and the blend is nowhere more picturesque than in the life of Robert Estienne. At one moment we find him attacking the abuses of the church, at another we find him consulting with Claude Garamond upon the design of a new Greek type, or reading the final proofs of an edition of Horace or Catullus or Juvenal, or discussing with some wealthy and noble book-collector like the famous Grolier the latest styles in elegant bindings and gold-stamped decoration. For beauty and for truth he had an equal passion. All that romance of the imagination which touches with a golden glamour the recovered treasures of pagan antiquity he loved as intensely as if it were not alien and hostile, as the many thought, to that glow of spiritual piety, that zeal of martyrdom, that white, consuming splendor which for the mystical imagination surrounds the holy cross. Humanism at its best is ordinarily thought to be embodied in the many-sided figure of Erasmus, with his sanity, his balance, his power to see both sides, that of Luther and of the Church, his delicate satire, his saving humor, his avoidance of the zealot's extremes. Perhaps a not less striking figure is that of this much less known French printer, striving in the midst of petty cares and unlovely sectarian strife to maintain the stoical serenity of a Marcus Aurelius side by side with the spiritual exaltation of a Saint Paul. There are two types of great men equally worthy of admiration: those of unmixed and life-long devotion to a single aim springing from a single source, such as Aldus Manutius, and those in whom that balance of diverse and almost contradictory elements of character which commonly leads to weakness makes instead for strength and for richness, for duty and delight. Such was Robert Estienne.

The third printer whom I have selected as typical of the Renaissance is Johann Froben, of Basel. His chief distinction is that he was the closest friend and associate of Erasmus, the principal publisher of Erasmus's works, and the representative in the book trade of the Erasmian attitude toward the Reformation. Although he did print the Greek Testament, years before Estienne published his edition in Paris, he accompanied it with no distinctively Protestant comments. Although at one time he issued some of the earlier works of Luther, he desisted when it became evident that Erasmus opposed any open schism in the Church. It was Froben who gave to the world those three famous works of Erasmus, the *Encomium Moriae* or *Praise of Folly*,

FRO BEN

the *Adagia* or Proverbs, and the *Colloquia* or *Conversations*, which did quite as much as the writings of Luther to arouse independent thinking within the Church, and to bring to an end the last vestiges of the middle ages in church and state. And in this relation of Froben to Erasmus there was not the mere commercial attitude of a shrewd publisher toward a successful author whose works became highly lucrative, but the support by one enlightened scholar who happened to be in a profitable business of another who happened to be out of it. The earlier life of Erasmus exhibits a rather depressing illustration of the humiliations to which professional scholars were exposed in trying to get a living from the pensions and benefactions of the idle rich. Literary patronage, as it existed from the days of Horace and Maecenas down to the death-blow which Dr. Johnson gave it in his famous letter to Lord Chesterfield, has never helped the independence or the self-respect of scholars and poets. It was Froben's peculiar good fortune to be able to employ, on a business basis with a regular salary, the greatest scholar of the age as one of his editors and literary advisers, and at the same time enable him to preserve his independence of thought and of action. Aldus and the French publishers had gathered about them professional scholars and experts for the execution of specific tasks at the market price, supplemented often by generous private hospitality. That was good; but far better was Froben's relation with his friend, his intellectual master, and his profitable client Erasmus. In an age when no copyright laws existed for the author's benefit the works of Erasmus were shamelessly pirated in editions, published in Germany and France, from which the author received not a penny. Yet Froben went right on paying to Erasmus not only the fixed annual salary as a member of his consulting staff but also a generous share of the profits upon his books. In a greedy, unscrupulous, and rapacious age this wise and just, not to say generous, policy stands out as prophetic of a better time.

As a printer Froben was distinguished by the singular beauty of his roman type, the perfection of his presswork, and the artistic decoration of his books. In this last respect he was much indebted to the genius of Hans Holbein, whom he discovered as a young wood-engraver seeking work at Basel. With that keen eye for unrecognized genius which marked his career he employed Holbein to design borders and initials for his books. Later, with an equally sagacious and generous spirit, perceiving that the young artist was too great a man to spend his days in a printing office, he procured for him through Sir Thomas More an introduction to the court of Henry VIII, where he won fame and fortune as a portrait painter. I narrate the incident because it illustrates a very attractive and amiable aspect of some of these men of the Renaissance, an uncalculating and generous desire to help gifted men to find their true place in the world where they might do their largest work. This, in an age when competition and jealous rivalry in public and in private life was as common as it is now, may give pause to the cynic and joy to the lover of human kindness.

ANTON KOBERGER

(No printer's mark known)

We are in a different world when we turn to the fourth of our five representative printers, Anton Koberger, of Nuremberg. During the forty years of his career as a publisher, between 1473 and 1513, he issued 236 separate works, most of them in several volumes, and of the whole lot none show any taint of reforming zeal. Koberger was a loyal Catholic, and his published books were largely theological and all strictly orthodox in nature. He is distinguished in two respects from the other German printers of his time, the time between the death of Gutenberg and the rise of Martin Luther. In the first place his work showed great typographical excellence, with many fonts of handsome Gothic type and a lavish use of woodcut illustrations. In the second place, his publishing business was far better organized, far more extensive in its selling and distributing machinery, than that of any other printer in Europe. We learn that he had agents not only in every German city, but in the very headquarters of his greatest competitors at Paris, Venice, and Rome, and in such more distant places as Vienna, Buda-Pesth, and Warsaw. The twenty-four presses in his own Nuremberg establishment were not sufficient for his enormous business, and he let out printing jobs on contract or commission to printers at Strasburg, Basel, and elsewhere. The true German spirit of discipline appears in a contemporary account of his printing plant at Nuremberg. He had more than a hundred workmen there, including not only compositors, pressmen, and proof-readers, but binders, engravers, and illuminators. All these were fed by their employer in a common dining hall apart from the works, and we are told that they marched between the two buildings three times a day with military precision.

Koberger employed for a time the services of Albrecht Dürer, the famous engraver, not only for the illustration of books but also for expert oversight of the typographical form. Typography in its golden age was rightly regarded not as a mere mechanical trade but as an art of design, a design in black upon white, in which the just proportion of columns and margins and titles and initials was quite as important as the illustrations. Perhaps Koberger found Dürer too independent or too expensive for his taste, for we find him in his later illustrated works employing engravers more prolific than expert. Such were Michael Wolgemut and Wilhelm Pleydenwurff, who drew and engraved the 2,000 illustrations in the famous *Nuremberg Chronicle* published by Koberger in 1493. This remarkable work was compiled by Doctor Hartman Schedel, of Nuremberg. It is a history of the world from the creation down to 1493, with a supplement containing a full illustrated account of the end of the world, the Millennium, and the last judgment. This is by no means all. There is combined with this outline of history, not less ambitious though perhaps not more eccentric than H. G. Wells's latest book, a gazetteer of the world in general and of Europe in particular, a portrait gallery of all distinguished men from Adam and Methuselah down to the reigning emperor, kings, and pope of 1493, with many intimate studies of the devil, and a large variety of rather substantial and Teutonic angels. Every city in Europe is shown in a front elevation in which the perspective reminds one of Japanese art, and the castle-towers and bridges and riverboats all bear a strong family resemblance. The book is full of curious material, quite apart from the quaint illustrations. In the midst of grave affairs of state we run across a plague of locusts, an eclipse of the sun, or a pair of lovers who died for love. Scandalous anecdotes of kings and priests jostle the fiercest denunciations of heretics and reformers. A page is devoted to the heresies of Wyclif and Huss. Anti-Semitism runs rampant through its pages. Various detailed accounts are given of the torture and murder of Christian boys by Jews, followed by the capture and burning alive of the conspirators. Superstition and intolerance stand side by side with a naive mystical piety and engaging stories of the saints and martyrs. Of all the vast transformation in human thought that was then taking form in Italy, of all the forward-looking signs of the times, there is little trace. From 1493 to the last dim ages of the expiring world, the downfall of Antichrist and the setting up of the final kingdom of heaven upon earth, seemed but a little way to Hartman Schedel, when he wrote with much complacence the colophon to this strange volume. He left three blank leaves between 1493 and the Day of Judgment whereon the reader might record what remained of human history. It is indeed rather the last voice of the middle ages than the first voice of the Renaissance that speaks to us out of these clear, black, handsome pages that were pulled damp from the press four hundred and twenty-eight years ago on the fourth of last June. At first reading one is moved to mirth, then to wonder, then perhaps to disgust, but last of all to the haunting melancholy of Omar the tent-maker when he sings

> When you and I behind the veil are past,
> Oh, but the long, long while the world shall last.

As to worthy Hartman Schedel, God rest his soul, one wonders whether he has yet learned that Columbus discovered America. He had not yet heard of it when he finished his book, though Columbus had returned to Spain three months before. O most lame and impotent conclusion! But the fifteenth century, though it had an infinite childlike curiosity, had no nose for news. Nuremberg nodded peacefully on while a new world loomed up beyond the seas, and studied Michael Wolgemut's picture of Noah building the ark while Columbus was fitting out the Santa Maria for a second voyage. Such is mankind, blind and deaf to the greatest things. We know not the great hour when it strikes. We are indeed most enthralled by the echoing chimes of the romantic past when the future sounds its faint far-off reveille upon our unheeding ears. The multitude understands noon and night; only the wise man understands the morning.

And now finally, what of William Caxton? The father of English printing had been for many years an English merchant residing in Bruges when his increasing attention to literature led him to acquire the new art of printing. He had already translated from the French the Histories of Troy, and was preparing to undertake other editorial labors when he became associated with Colard Mansion, a Bruges printer. From Mansion he learned the art and presumably purchased his first press and type. Six books bearing Caxton's imprint were published at Bruges between 1474 and 1476, though it is possible that the actual printing was done by Mansion rather than by Caxton himself. In 1476 Caxton set up the first printing shop in England, in a house within the precincts of Westminster Abbey. Between that date and his death in 1491 he printed ninety-three separate works, some of these in several editions. His industry and scholarly zeal as a publisher somewhat exceeded his technical skill as a printer. Caxton's books, which are now much rarer than those of many continental printers of the same period, are not so finely and beautifully done as the best of theirs. But the peculiar interest of his work lies in the striking variety of the works he chose for publication, the conscientious zeal with which he conceived and performed his task, and the quiet humor of his prefaces and notes. Let me illustrate briefly these three points. First, his variety. We have observed that Aldus and Froben published chiefly the Latin and Greek classics, Koberger the Latin scriptures and theological works, and Stephanus a combination of classics and theology. Caxton published a few of the classics and very little theology. His books consist largely of the works of the early

English poets, Chaucer, Gower, and others, of mediaeval romances derived from English, French, and Italian sources, and of chronicles and histories. The two most famous works that came from his press were the first printed editions of Chaucer's *Canterbury Tales* and Malory's *Morte d'Arthur*. His own English translation of the *Golden Legend*, a mediaeval Latin collection of lives of the saints, is scarcely less in importance. Among many other titles the following may serve to show how unusual and unconventional were his selections:

The History of Reynard the Fox.
The History of Godfrey of Boloyne, or the Conquest of Jerusalem.
The Fables of Aesop.
The Book of Good Maners.
The Faytes of Armes and of Chyvalrye.
The Governayle of Helthe.
The Arte and Crafte to Know Well to Dye.

This is indeed humanism, but humanism in a diffrent sense from that of Aldus and Erasmus. Human life from the cradle to the grave, human life in war and peace, human life in its gayer and its graver lights and shadows, human life as embodied equally in famous writers and in anonymous popular legends, was Caxton's field. He accounted nothing human alien to his mind or to his great enterprise.

Again, Caxton was conscientious. He set great store by accuracy, not only typographical accuracy in matters of detail, but also the general accuracy of the texts or sources from which his own translations and his editions of other works were made. For example, in the second edition of the *Canterbury Tales* he explains how the first edition was printed from the best manuscript that he could find in 1478, but how after the appearance of that there came to him a scholar who complained of many errors, and spoke of another and more authentic manuscript in his father's possession. Caxton at once agreed to get out a new edition "whereas before by ignorance I erred in hurting and defaming his book in divers places, in setting in some things that he never said nor made and leaving out many things that are made which are requisite to be set in." A great many other examples of such disinterested carefulness are to be found in the history of those busy fifteen years at Westminster. In view of the fact that he was not only editor, printer, and publisher, but also translated twenty-three books totaling more than 4500 printed pages, this scholarly desire for accuracy deserves the highest praise. Unlike Aldus and Froben, who were likewise editors as well as publishers, he was not surrounded by a capable corps of expert scholars, but worked almost alone. His faithful foreman, Wynkyn de Worde, doubtless took over gradually a large share of the purely mechanical side of the business, but Caxton remained till the end of his life the active head as well as the brains of the concern.

As for his humor, it comes out even in his very selections of books to be printed, but chiefly in little touches all through his prefaces. For example, in his preface to the *Morte d'Arthur* he answers with a certain whimsical gravity the allegations of those who maintain that there was no such person as King Arthur, and that "all such books as been made of him be but feigned and fables." He recounts with assumed sincerity the evidence of the chronicles, the existence of Arthur's seal in red wax at Westminster Abbey, of Sir Gawain's skull at Dover Castle, of the Round Table itself at Winchester, and so on. But he goes on to say, in his own quaint way, which there is not space to quote at large, that in his own opinion the stories are worth while for the intrinsic interest and the moral values in them, whether they are literally true or not. He closes thus:

> Herein may be seen noble chivalry, courtesy, humanity, friendliness, hardiness, love, friendship, cowardice, murder, hate, virture and sin. Do after the good and leave the evil, and it shall bring you to good fame and renommee. And for to pass the time this book shall be pleasant to read in, but for to give faith and belief that all is true that is contained herein, ye be at your liberty.

This wise, sane, gentle apostle of literature in England wrought well in his day, and is justly honored alike by scholars and by printers, who regard him, in England and America, as the father of their craft. Indeed to this day in the printing trade a shop organization is sometimes called a chapel, because according to ancient tradition Caxton's workmen held their meetings in one of the chapels adjoining the abbey of Westminster.

This survey of printing in its relations to the Renaissance is now not finished but concluded. I have shown that the invention and improvement of printing was not the cause but rather the effect of the revival of learning, while on the other hand the wide dissemination of literature made possible by typography of course accelerated enormously the process of popular enlightenment. I have selected five typical printers of that age:

Aldus, with his Homer.
Stephanus, with his Greek Testament.
Froben, with his Plato.
Koberger, with his *Nuremberg Chronicle*.
Caxton, with his *Morte d'Arthur*.

Here we find represented in the Aldus Homer the revival of Greek learning, in the Stephanus Testament the application of this to the free criticism of the scriptures, in the Froben Plato the substitution of Platonic idealism for the scholastic philosophy based on Aristotle, in the Nuremberg book the epitome of mediaeval superstition, credulity, and curiosity on the verge of the new era, and in *Morte d'Arthur* the fond return of the modern mind, facing an unknown future, upon the naive and beautiful legends of Arthurian romance. An age full of contradictions and strange delusions, but an age of great vitality, great eagerness, great industry, patience, foresight, imagination. And in such an age it was the good fortune of these wise craftsmen who handled so deftly their paper and type to be the instruments of more evangels than angels ever sang, more revolutions than gunpowder ever achieved, more victories than ever won the applause of men or the approval of heaven. In the beginning the creative word was *Fiat lux*—let there be light. In the new creation of the human mind it was *Imprimatur*—let it be printed. If printing had never been invented, it is easy to conceive that the enormous learning and intellectual power of a few men in each generation might have gone on increasing so that the world might today possess most of the knowledge that we now enjoy; but it is certain that the masses could never have been enlightened, and that therefore the gulf between the wise few and the ignorant many would have exceeded anything known to the ancient world, and inconceivably dangerous in its appalling social menace. Whoever first printed a page of type is responsible for many crimes committed in the name of literature during the past four centuries; but one great book in a generation or a century, like a grain of radium in a ton of pitchblende, is worth all it has cost; for like the radium it is infinitely powerful to the wise man, deadly to the fool, and its strange, invisible virtue so far as we know may last forever.

Printing and the Mind of Man: An Exhibition of Fine Printing in the King's Library of the British Museum, July - September, 1963.

THE ADVENT OF PRINTING

(c. 1455-1500)

The invention of printing in the Western world was rendered necessary by the growth of the reading public at the close of the Middle Ages, and the inability of the manuscript trade to meet this expanding market. The basic problems were solved by Johann Gutenberg at Strassburg in c. 1436-9, and the technique perfected at Mainz in c. 1450-5, when the great Bible which commonly bears his name was produced. The essential and unique features of his invention were an adjustable hand mould, with punch-stamped matrices, for precision casting of type-sorts in large quantities; a type-metal alloy (probably lead with tin and antimony) with low melting-point and quick, undistorted solidification; a press adapted from those used by, among others, paper-makers and bookbinders; and an oil-based printing-ink. During the next decade this revolutionary invention spread to Bamberg, Strassburg, and Cologne, and was carried by German craftsmen to Italy in 1465, to Switzerland c. 1468, to France in 1470, and to Spain in 1472-3. From early in the 1470's presses were also

SOURCE: Reprinted from *Printing and the Mind of Man: Catalogue of the Exhibitions at the British Museum and at Earls Court, London–16-27 July 1963* (London: Messers. F. W. Bridges and Sons, Ltd., and the Association of British Manufacturers of Printers' Machinery (Proprietary) Ltd., 1963), "Introductory Remarks to the Exhibition of Fine Printing in the King's Library of the British Museum, July - September, 1963," "The Advent of Printing," p. 11; "The Sixteenth Century," p. 21; "The Seventeenth Century," p. 29; "The Eighteenth Century," p. 35; "The Nineteenth Century," p.43, and "The Twentieth Century," p. 51, by permission of British Museum Publications Ltd. Copyright 1963 by Messers. F. W. Bridges and Sons, Ltd., and the Association of British Manufacturers of Printers' Machinery (Proprietary) Ltd.

active in the Netherlands, and it was from Bruges that William Caxton returned in 1476 to establish himself at Westminster as the first printer in his native England.

Printing was originally conceived as a process for the mechanical reproduction of manuscript. Type-design, layout, and decoration tended from the first to evolve autonomously, but were constantly stimulated and newly inspired by manuscript models. By the end of the century the printing houses of Europe had produced nearly 40,000 editions, the best of which remain unsurpassed in the beauty and variety of their craftsmanship.

THE SIXTEENTH CENTURY

The sixteenth century in its typography clearly reflects the spirit of the Renaissance, especially in Italy and France. In the former country, the great figure of Aldus Manutius at Venice opens the century with his stream of first editions of the Greek and Latin classics. His roman, greek, and newly introduced italic types—he never printed in black letter—were of pure Renaissance inspiration and design. The Aldine style was to dominate the typography of Europe for upwards of two centuries. But the publishing impetus of the pocket-size Aldine classics did not inhibit improvements on his italic type on the part of other Italian printers. The formal, less sloped, cursive hand practised in the Vatican Chancery (hence known as *Cancellaresca*) was translated, notably by Lodovico degli Arrighi, writing-master and printer, into a variety of elegant types which found great favour with the new school of printers in Paris: Henri Estienne, first of an illustrious family, Simon de Colines, and Geoffroy Tory, whose taste and enterprise, in tune with the italianate enthusiasms of King François I, made Paris the capital of fine book-making in the second quarter of the century. Paris Books of Hours printed between 1500 and 1550, of which there is an enormous number of editions, are one of the most beautiful class of books ever produced.

The Aldine roman type was refined and improved by a succession of brilliant punchcutters, Garamond and Granjon being the most celebrated names. In these Gallic versions the roman type invaded not only Lyons, where Jean de Tournes was the best printer, but also Rome, Florence, Venice, and the printing houses of the Low Countries, in particular that of Christopher Plantin at Antwerp. The gothic types of Germany and their derivatives meanwhile found most favour in England and Spain.

THE SEVENTEENTH CENTURY

All over Europe this century was marked by a disastrous lowering of standards in everyday printing, the reasons for which were partly political and partly economic. Typographic design was almost at a standstill, presswork was slovenly, and paper of poor quality. The types in use were generally obtained from Holland, but Dutch types and matrices were often derived from sixteenth-century French punches in the possession of a German foundry, that of the Luthers at Frankfurt. Proper consideration was only given to appearance when a special *de luxe* edition—a Bible, an emblem book, or an account of some royal occasion—was put in hand, and even then the presswork was likely to be very indifferent. Yet the printer did sometimes rise to the occasion, and some of the illustrated books of this century are fully up to the level of their more publicized successors of the eighteenth century.

As early as 1640 steps were taken in Paris which were to lead to a revival in printing standards by Richelieu's establishment of the Imprimerie Royale, whose leisurely procession of well-made books culminated in Louis XIV's commission, in 1692, for the design of a wholly new, regal, proprietary type. This, after prolonged and scientific gestation, was brought to birth by Philippe Grandjean; and the 'Romain du Roi' made its first public appearance, to dazzle printers and *cognoscenti* by its brilliance and accuracy of cutting, in a magnificent folio ten years later.

THE EIGHTEENTH CENTURY

The 'Romain du Roi' of 1702, with its short, flat serifs and a sharper contrast between thick and thin strokes than the prevailing types (all variations on the form of letter first evolved by Garamond, which later printers called 'old face') foreshadowed a new fashion in type-design. Yet much that appears as the new fashion has little to do with type, but results from a return to the virtues of black and white from the inexpensive greys of routine printing. More white space in and around the type, more generous margins, fresh white paper set against letters more intensely black and more crisply printed can entirely change the effect of a type-face, as eighteenth-century anecdote reveals.

Typography was often the neglected partner of the engraved illustration and ornament of the early examples of those *éditions de luxe* which have ever since commanded the enthusiasm of French connoisseurship. Fournier's elegance at mid-century and F. A. Didot's glacial perfection in its latter decades raised Paris standards, as Ibarra and de Sancha raised them to a level never before achieved in Madrid; yet it was the productions of an amateur, John Baskerville of Birmingham, with their wide-spread, rather pallid typography and their smooth 'hot-pressed' paper, which 'went forth to astonish the librarians of Europe'. And not librarians only: for it was Baskerville's books which encouraged Bodoni of Parma to shed his French manner and to develop types with an absolute and geometric contrast between thick and thin strokes which, combined with an austere nobility of layout, made him the idol of European taste, the model for later members of the Didot family, and a powerful influence on Baskerville's English successors, Bell, Bulmer, and Bensley. Thus he became spiritual father of—what he would doubtless have disowned—the 'modern face' types of the next century.

THE NINETEENTH CENTURY

The nineteenth century has been regarded as the Cinderella of printing—dull, inartistic, and no match for its predecessors. The first twenty years saw few innovations. Men already in the field, Bulmer, Bensley, and Charles Whittingham the Elder, continued to produce sound, well-printed books in the 'classical' tradition. The appearance of the steam-press, however, and the growth of an industrialized society, clamouring for educative material, was to revolutionize the conception of printing and depress taste. There was an inevitable falling-off in standards all round, although the work of individual printers shows that machine methods were not necessarily a bar to good printing. In England, William Pickering, a publisher of scholarly and antiquarian taste, with a feeling for the fine typography of the old books he reprinted, obtained a consistently high standard both in *pastiches* and in his original works from the printers he used. Notable among these were Charles Whittingham the Younger, whose printing of Lady Willoughby's *Diary* in 1844, set in Caslon's 'old face' types, was an innovation which had an immediate impact, since for several decades only the 'modern face' types made popular by the example of Bodoni had been used. The revolution, though slow in action, had far-reaching results and similar 'revivals' took place in Paris, Lyons, and Basle.

Throughout the century illustration played a dominant role, particularly in France. Restraint was thrown to the winds, and decoration in the form of lithography and wood-engraving, admirable in itself, led to a serious debasement in the design of type. There was a lack of balance between text and design. The illustration was no longer an attractive adjunct, but became the *raison d'être* of the book itself. Instances of this are seen in Delacroix's dramatic lithographs for *Faust* (1828), and Manet's striking illustrations for Poe's *The Raven* (1875). Superb as is Curmer's *Paul et Virginie* (1838), the abundance of woodcuts almost overwhelms the type.

There was a serious need for discipline and a leavening of standards of typography. William Morris came to the fore in the last decade of the century, and sought with Messianic zeal to redeem printing from the slough into which it had sunk. But in his anxiety to avoid the defects of his time, the cramped thin-faced types, poor paper, and slovenly presswork, he went too far in the opposite direction. In praising the standards and techniques of the fifteenth-century printers he accepted their faults as well; and in damning the deterioration that had taken place since, he ignored the value of the real improvements which had accompanied them. But if his views on typography now seem misguided—and much of the blame attached to Morris belongs to his more erratic imitators—his insistence on a proper attention to all the components of the manufacture of books is the fundamental cause of the higher standards which prevail today.

THE TWENTIETH CENTURY

Book typography in the twentieth century reaped the benefit of the Linotype and Monotype systems of mechanical composition. Although these were introduced at the end of the nineteenth century, both systems at first provided only slavish copies of types already made popular by typefounders. The English Private Press Movement encouraged a taste for revivals of the best types from past ages, especially for Jenson's roman. A spur was given by the American Type Founders Company who recut the types of Bodoni and Garamond between 1911 and 1917. During this period the Lanston Monotype Company recut Caslon's types and a Plantin design; but from 1922 it carried out an extensive programme which included many revivals and also several entirely new types by contemporary designers. This programme was supervised by Stanley Morison (b. 1889) whose writings exerted a considerable influence on book typography, and who was responsible for the design of Times New Roman (1931).

The proliferation of type-revivals encouraged the practice of "allusive typography', but this style declined in popularity in the past three decades. To use archaic materials in printing went against the trend of taste in art and architecture. Ideas were propagated at the Bauhaus in Dessau for a "new typography' which eschewed ornaments and which favoured nineteenth-century sanserif types in asymmetrical arrangements. The reading public has not yet accepted sanserif types for general reading, although it accepts them in advertising and other forms of ephemeral printing. More extensive use of sanserif may depend upon the skill with which type-designers can reduce its monotony by introducing greater variety in weight between thick and thin strokes.

The use of photogravure and photolithography in book-production has made possible a much closer integration of text and illustration, and has given the typographer greater freedom in the disposition of his materials. As this freedom becomes better understood and more intelligently exploited, a distinctive twentieth-century style in book typography may gradually emerge.

John Clyde Oswald

From William Caslon to William Morris

Pollard specifies the first half of the seventeenth century as the period when printing in England "was certainly worse than in any other country." There seems, however, no reason why the first half or any particular part of the century should be singled out for that unenviable distinction. Printing was at a low ebb throughout the whole of the hundred years that followed the termination of the Elizabethan era and the accession of James VI of Scotland to the throne of England. The reason may be found in the circumstance that it was a period of incessant religious controversy, led always by the Throne or the powers that nestled close to it. The printing press was not then the tool of an art, but an instrument of propaganda. Privilege to print depended upon considerations other than that of ability to print well.

The eighteenth century brought a beneficial influence with the advent of William Caslon, who was first an engraver upon metals and later and for nearly a half-century the leading and almost the only designer and founder of types used by English printers. Detailed reference to Caslon belongs to later chapters, and there we shall have occasion to refer also to a well-known contemporary in the history of English printing, John Baskerville, born in the sixth year of the eighteenth century, who was not only a printer, but a type-, ink-, and paper-maker as well. Baskerville began his experiments in type-founding in 1750, started to print in 1757, and was appointed Printer to the University of Cambridge in 1758. It was he who first "hot-pressed" paper and who first made wove paper, which, however, did not become popular until Montgolfier put it on the market. He died in 1775. His experiences as a printer brought him no pecuniary return. "The business of printing. . . which I am heartily

SOURCE: Reprinted from John Clyde Oswald, A *History of Printing: Its Development Through Five Hundred Years* (New York: D. Appleton and Company, 1928), Chapter XVI, "From William Caslon to William Morris," pp. 208-219, by permission of Hawthorn Books. Copyright 1928 by D. Appleton and Company.

tired of and repent I ever attempted," is a remark ascribed to Baskerville by Timperley. He did little printing during his last years.

An outstanding name in the annals of printing in English during the eighteenth century is that of the Foulis brothers, Robert and Andrew, who printed not in England, but in Scotland, Both brothers were successful, artistically and commercially, as printers, but neither began his career as a printer, and both failed financially in later years through enterprises other than printing in which they engaged.

Robert Foulis, born in 1707, commenced his wage-earning career as a barber. Later, in company with his brother, who was five years his junior, he became a teacher of languages. The brothers employed a part of their leisure in travel on the Continent, where they followed a pronounced literary inclination, coming into contact with eminent men and extending their knowledge of books. They made collections of books which they took back to Edinburgh and sold at a profit. Robert Foulis eventually went definitely into the bookselling business, later became a publisher, and in 1742 set up as a printer. The next year he was appointed Printer to the University of Glasgow, and Andrew joined the enterprise soon after the Press was established. The work of the Foulis brothers was severely plain typographically, the presswork was good, and great care was taken to avoid errors. As an instance, the proof sheets of an edition of Horace were exposed in the college grounds, and a reward was offered for the detection of typographical errors; six such errors, notwithstanding this precaution, remained undiscovered until too late for correction.

With the money the Foulis brothers made in their printing and publishing they established a school for art students. They persisted in this enterprise for more than twenty years, but evidently the time was not ripe for such an institution, for it ended in disaster. Andrew died in 1775, and the next year Robert decided to dispose at auction of what remained of their property, the most valuable part being a collection of paintings. He took the paintings to London, and when the sale had been completed and all expenses paid, the balance remaining was but fifteen shillings. The disappointment was so great that it resulted in his death at Edinburgh, on his way back to Glasgow from London.

William Bowyer, whom Timperley extravagantly characterizes as "the most learned and distinguished printer of modern times," was born in London in 1699. His father was a printer of some distinction, and the son, who succeeded to the business in 1737, received a university education. The younger Bowyer was a publisher and a writer and the constant companion of many of the literary personages of his time. He died in 1777.

William Bowyer was succeeded by John Nichols, born in 1744, who had been his apprentice and who is credited with ability and distinction equal to that of his former employer. In 1804 Nichols was elected Master of the Stationers Company, which he termed the summit of his ambition. He published a memoir entitled *Literary Anecdotes of the Eighteenth Century* which presents an entertaining picture of the literary life of the time.

Britain was again indebted to Scotland, but from the point of view of nativity only, for another great printer of the eighteenth century. This was William Strahan, born at

HIS
MAIESTIES
SPEECH TO BOTH
the Houſes of Parliament, in
his Highneße great Cham-
ber at *Whitehall,* the day of
the Adiournement of the
laſt Seſſion,

Which was the laſt day of
March 1607.

¶IMPRINTED AT
London by *Robert Barker,*
Printer to the Kings moſt Ex-
cellent Maieſtie.

Title page of *His Maiesties Speech.* Printed by Robert Barker,
London, 1607.

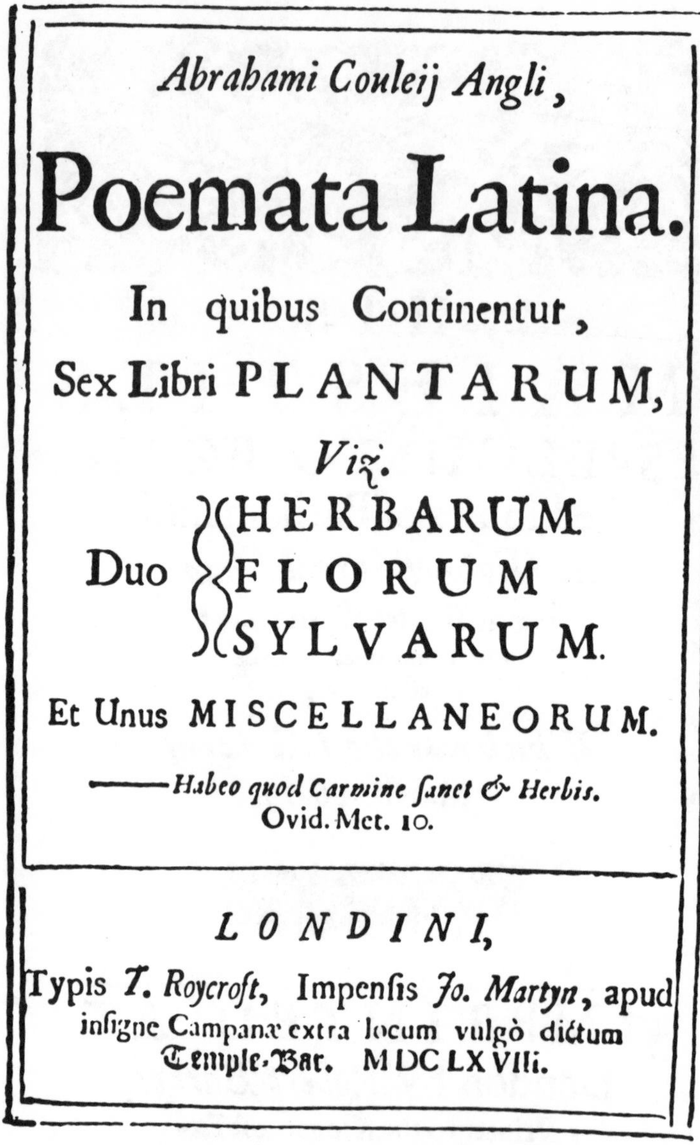

Abrahami Couleij Angli,

Poemata Latina.

In quibus Continentur,

Sex Libri PLANTARUM,

Viȝ.

Duo { HERBARUM
FLORUM
SYLVARUM.

Et Unus MISCELLANEORUM.

———*Habeo quod Carmine sanct & Herbis.*
Ovid. Met. 10.

LONDINI,

Typis *T. Roycrost,* Impensis *Jo. Martyn,* apud
insigne Campanæ extra locum vulgò dictum
𝕮𝖊𝖒𝖕𝖑𝖊-𝕭𝖆𝖗. MDCLXVIII.

Title page of a book of Latin poems. Printed by Thomas Roycroft, London, 1668.

Edinburgh in 1715. At an early age Strahan went to London and in time became associated with the great printing firm that later came to be known as Eyre and Spottiswoode, King's Printers, which is still in existence as one of the leading printing establishments of England. Strahan was a publisher as well as a printer. Many of the great works of English literature first saw the light of day in his establishment, among them those of Samuel Johnson and the historians Hume and Gibbon. Johnson spoke of Strahan's as "the greatest printing house in London."

But it is to his friendship for and close association with a great American printer, Benjamin Franklin, that William Strahan owes his principal renown. Strahan was elected to Parliament in 1775, with an illustrious colleague, Charles James Fox, and as a member of His Majesty's Government found much interest in common, aside from the fact that both were printers, with the representative in London of the American Colonies. When they were separated they exchanged frequent letters, and Franklin's missives to Strahan are by no means the least entertaining of his literary remains. The "You are now my enemy" letter is probably the most famous. It was the desire of both Franklin and Strahan that two of their children should marry, but evidently the young people thought differently, for the match never came off. Strahan was Master of the Stationers Company in 1774. He died in 1785, leaving a fortune of 95,000 pounds.

William Bulmer established the Shakespeare Press in the last decade of the eighteenth century in order, to use a slang expression, to put England from the printing point of view "on the map." "While other nations were publishing splendid editions of their favorite authors," he said, "we in this country contented ourselves with such editions of ours as were merely useful," and he proposed to issue works that could make a successful claim to beauty. An edition of Shakespeare's works was the first production of Bulmer and Company, the initial volume appearing in 1791. Dibdin says that it "at once established Mr. Bulmer's fame as the first practical printer of the day." Other fine editions of leading English authors followed in steady succession. The works of Thomas Frognall Dibdin, probably the most prolific, if not always the most trustworthy, writer on bibliography who ever lived, came mainly from the Shakespeare Press and are prized by collectors because of that fact.

Thomas Bewick, who was the greatest of English wood-engravers, was a boyhood companion and later a business associate of Bulmer. Bewick engraved the ornaments for the Shakespeare Press edition of the *Poems of Goldsmith and Parnell* with such success that George III, who was a book collector and was possessed of some knowledge of printing processes, would not believe that the effects were obtained from wood until the actual blocks were exhibited to him. Bulmer cooperated with Robert Martin, Baskerville's journeyman and successor, in the making of types and ink, and with Whatman, the paper-maker, in the manufacture of paper. Bulmer retired from business in 1819 and died in 1830 in his seventy-fourth year.

Two Whittinghams, uncle and nephew, received the name of Charles. The elder was born near Coventry in 1767. After serving an apprenticeship in printing in that city he went to London in his early twenties. He set up as a printer there, later taking into partnership his foreman, Robert Rowland, to whom he transferred the management of the concern. Whittingham thenceforth gave his personal attention to a new business he established at Chiswick under the name of the Chiswick Press, which he continued to conduct until his death in 1840.

Charles Whittingham the younger, born in 1795, became connected with the Chiswick Press in 1824, and its best work was done under his direction, particularly in association with the celebrated English publisher, William Pickering. Both were ardent lovers of good literature, and they combined their talents to a common end, the production of beautiful books. Warren records: "The two men met frequently for consultation. . . . They made it a point, moreover, to pass their Sundays together, either at the printer's house, or at Pickering's." It was at Whittingham's request that the Caslon Old Face type was resurrected from the vaults of the Caslon foundry, an edition of The Diary of Lady Willoughby, published in 1844, being one of the first for which it was used. Pickering died in 1854 and Whittingham in 1876.

William Morris influenced the art of printing as no other man in modern times influenced it. Pollard calls attention to the fact that by the end of the seventeenth century the printer, with a few notable exceptions, had disappeared behind the publisher. "Printing," he says, "as an art had ceased to exist." Morris was both printer and publisher. He was indeed much more—decorator, poet, weaver of tapestries and rugs, dyer, and designer. But so far as books were concerned, it was their production rather than their distribution that engaged his interest. And he approached each printing project not so much from the standpoint of the typographer, the worker with types, as from that of the designer and decorator, the worker with pencil and brush.

Morris went back to the fifteenth-century printers for his models. His first type face, which he called the Golden type because it was first used for a reprint of Caxton's *Golden Legend*, was modeled upon the types of Nicolaus Jenson. He used only one other type face, which might be called a romanized Gothic, cut in two sizes corresponding to twelve and eighteen point, which he named respectively Chaucer and Troy, after books in which they were first used.

Morris called his printing establishment the Kelmscott Press, Kelmscott being the name of the village near Oxford where Morris in 1871 had established his residence. The Press, however, was located in Hammersmith, a part of the London Metropolitan District. Morris' first book, *The Story of the Glittering Plain*, was issued in 1891, and between that date and the year of his death, 1896, including the work begun by him but finished by the executors of his estate, the product of the Kelmscott Press comprised 53 titles and 65 volumes. "No other printer since printing began," says Pollard, "has ever produced such a series of books as the 53 which poured from the Kelmscott Press during those wonderful seven years, and no book that has ever been printed can be compared for richness of effect with the Chaucer which was the crowning achievement of the Press."

Characteristic pages from a Kelmscott Press book.

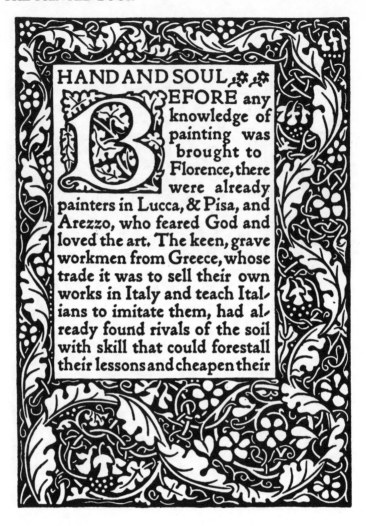

HAND AND SOUL

BEFORE any knowledge of painting was brought to Florence, there were already painters in Lucca, & Pisa, and Arezzo, who feared God and loved the art. The keen, grave workmen from Greece, whose trade it was to sell their own works in Italy and teach Italians to imitate them, had already found rivals of the soil with skill that could forestall their lessons and cheapen their

Printed by William Morris, London, 1895.

Holbrook Jackson

Printing
and
Fine Printing

Printing being human can be good or bad; but the victory and its rewards do not always go to the best, or to the worst, but to the middling sort. Yet the best printing, even when it seems to be ineffectual, is a preservative. Even the worst printing is ultimately innocuous because if let alone it cures by killing itself. Decadence is disintegration. The trouble is with the smug average, the pervasive So-So! 'So-so is good, very excellent good, and yet 'tis not, 'tis but so-so!' A creaking gate hangs longest, and mediocrity in printing is a long time dying, if it ever dies. There is always an uncritical demand, and to those who profit by that demand so-so is good, very excellent good; and there are plenty of business reasons for leaving well alone. Yet it is dangerous to leave well alone. Dangerous to the condition called 'well', because if it is left alone it becomes ill. For ultimate well-being it does not matter because, in the lag between bad and good, cells or nuclei of discontent are developed among people of taste or goodwill. Dissatisfaction with bad conditions may take the form of an exaggerated desire for perfection. Aesthetic starvation, for instance, produces beauty-worship as surely as a starved social consciousness produces utopianism. In printing, an undernourished typographical system provokes visions of Fine Printing, Ideal Books, and Books Beautiful. The private presses of the eighteen-nineties were protests against bad printing. But although idealism may be a malady, utopian dreams have their advantages, even in printing. The example of the utopist has more than once saved printing from complete degradation. On the other hand, Fine Printing

SOURCE: Reprinted from Holbrook Jackson, *The Printing of Books*, Second edition (London: Cassell and Company Ltd., 1947), Chapter III, "Printing and Fine Printing," pp. 25-40.

can be misleading, wasteful, and finally useless, especially in the hands of the commercially minded, and more particularly when the commercial mind is tainted with a sentimental passion for handicraft. Thus the Kelmscott Press found its nemesis in Elbert Hubbard's Roycroft Books.

How far the typographical idealist should be allowed to go is a matter of opinion—and demand. There is, indeed, much to be said for idealism as experimentation and, so long as the principles of typography are understood and respected, there can be no ultimate harm in *éditions de luxe* and when a book is a work of art the appreciation of it cannot go too far. The statement that it may be a work of art will not pass unchallenged, nor should it, for a book is on the borderline. Experts, as usual, disagree, and opinions are further confused by interests and sentiments, both notorious trespassers upon good judgement.

A book, or rather a 'fine book', according to Paul Valéry, is both a 'perfect reading device' and a 'work of art'. It is a work of art because it has a personality of its own, bearing the marks of special thought and suggesting 'the noble intention of a happy and free arrangement'. But the path of creative printing is not smooth, for 'typography excludes improvization', yet personality will have its way.

'The mind of the writer', he says, 'is seen as in a mirror which the printing press provides. If the paper and the ink are in accord, if the type is clear, if the composition is well looked after, the adjustment of line perfect, and the sheet well printed, the author feels his language and his style anew. He thinks he hears a clearer, firmer voice than his own, a voice faultlessly pure, articulating his words, dangerously detaching all his words. Everything feeble, effeminate, arbitrary, and inelegant which he wrote, speaks too clearly and too loud. To be magnificently printed is a very precious and important tribute.'[1]

When Charles Lamb, having, it is said, done all he could to the manuscript of an essay, sent it to press with the exclamation: 'It's the print that does it!' he was thinking of printing as an aid to his own expression and not as an art in itself, and it is conceivable that he would have resented any attempt on the part of the printer or typographer to represent Elia other than as he was in the eyes of Elia's creator, namely, himself. But, on the other hand, we can imagine a writer of feeble, effeminate, or inelegant stuff enjoying, without of course admitting, the sublimation of his work by printer or typographer. That, however, is not the aim or the basis of the art of printing, in so far as printing is an art, although it is one of the risks. The words 'fine' and 'printing' are dangerous bedfellows, for they are apt to beget monstrosities. Good printing, like poetry in Keats's opinion, should be unobtrusive, 'a thing which enters into one's soul, and does not startle or amaze it with itself, but with its subject'.

Printing and writing have more than the obvious relationship of lines of communication. They are both allied with talking. The printer multiplies or extends the talk of the writer, and since writing, whether prose or poetry, has sound as well as sense, the preservation of its cadences is essential. If, therefore, the human voice sounds through the written word it should carry also through the printed word. It is the writer who sets the pace because without him there would be nothing to print, and as writing is the first substitute for talking it is necessary to unequivocal expression that the voice of the writer should not be obliterated. The voice is in the words. Printing transmits them. Transmission is a delicate and responsible art, for it translates into a new medium something that has already been translated from the brain of an author into writing. The reader does not want to see the printer but to hear the writer. Fine, fancy, or ostentatious printing may thus be something more than bad taste: it may be disrespectful to the author and offensive to the reader.

Whether printing has an independent art-life is not an easy problem to solve since there is no generally acceptable definition of a work of art. We all, whether critics or laymen, think we know a work of art when we see one; but even after making allowances for differences of taste, prejudice, and whim, which do not affect the general proposition, the right of admission into the palace of art is subject to fantastic fluctuations. Poetry is an art, but literary history reveals that a poet may please some critics all the time and all critics some of the time, but not all critics all the time. Pope at one time was believed to be a poet and an artist. Later critics (some of them poets as well) called him an artist, but refused to admit him into the hierarchy of the poets. Contemporary criticism would seem to swing him back on to his poetic pedestal. The only one who is indifferent to these mutations is the poet himself. Labels and arguments do not in the long run affect him. He may look on and smile 'from his abode where the eternal are,' or, if he is still living, he goes on writing what he believes to be poetry and the common reader goes on reading it regardless, or amusedly regardful, of critics and criticism. It is the same with printing; whether it is an art or not is a secondary affair, so long as it is good printing. 'Art happens', says Whistler, and the printer who sets out to be an artist is liable to make a mess of both art and print.

There are those who argue that printing is sometimes an art and sometimes something else: a craft, for instance, craftsmanship being the snobbism for something supposed to be superior to a piece of machine made merchandise. A brief examination of the problem from this aspect may prove more fruitful for, although the status of a work of art may be higher or lower in the scale of critical opinion, merchandise can be measured for its utility. But although some, like Eric Gill, argue that there is no fundamental difference between a work of art and a useful piece of goods, an uneasy division exists between the useful arts and the fine arts. Their frontiers are still loosely defined. The wits of the eighteen-nineties would not allow the fine arts (which for them were the only arts) to be useful and beautiful at one and the same time. They believed that the business of art was to be beautiful. We now suspect that to be nonsense, just as we no longer believe that it is the business of art to hold the mirror up to nature. Art can be beautiful and it does, on occasion, reflect nature, even as that term is popularly understood. But, on the other hand, it can be ugly and it can and does distort and defy nature, whilst at the same time and in its own way remaining a part of that nature it is supposed to reflect.

Printing has the same peculiarities. A printed page can be so beautiful that you would rather frame it than read it, and it can be so ugly that it is not only difficult but nauseating to read. Yet the object of a book is to be read, not merely looked at, and any printing which directly or indirectly, deliberately or accidentally, detracts from the primary and fundamental purpose is bad printing. Bad printing is not always mediocre or incompetent printing, it is often what is called 'fine printing'. The phrase is unfortunate because it is inexact and can, therefore, be twisted by the mercenary as well as by the aesthetical to accommodate their own wishes. But when we speak of the 'fine arts', although we are using an inexact term, we know what we are talking about and everybody else knows what we are talking about. We mean the useless as distinct from the useful arts. We mean poems, statues, pictures, symphonies, not pots and pans, frocks, gardens, houses, ships, and bridges. We do not generally mean printing, although the 'fine book', especially when it is superfine, a masterpiece by say Didot bound by Dérome, or the Kelmscott *Chaucer* in pigskin by Cobden-Sanderson, or Baskerville's *Shaftesbury* in the red morocco of Roger Payne, has been raised to the peerage of the fine arts. The 'fine arts' are definite: they are the patrician arts. The term is a survival from a period when one small class was content to surround itself with beautiful things as a means of escape from a distasteful environment, without any desire to impose its tastes or standards upon outsiders. The 'fine book' belongs to that period, and has nothing to do with the cradle-days of printing. It became an anachronism after 1789. The 'fine books' of our time, however modern, are equally anachronistic. [2]

The chief fault of the amateur printers of the eighteen-nineties was that they were not content to be printers. They wished to be artistic printers, and the situation was complicated by the belief that art was mainly concerned with the creation of beauty, and beauty in turn was largely a matter of decoration. They had a morbid suspicion of monotony and avoided simple patterns and plain textures, never realizing that whatever happens to printing the alternatives to most of its operations make for adequate variety. Thus when they came to make a book they insisted upon making it beautiful and they succeeded so well that what after all is a tool for reading was often sacrificed to its looks. It was as though a modern armament manufacturer suddenly threw back to decorated muskets and swords, or a tool maker began to ornament his hammers and chisels. Such results are surprising because the artist-printers revived, perhaps even invented, the idea that a book was not merely a device for holding together a number of printed pages but, as Charles Ricketts defined it, 'an aggregate of living parts harmoniously controlled', [3] or, in matter-of-fact language, an assembly of paper, ink, binding, and type in an agreeable as well as a convenient design.

This respect for coordination was deep-rooted in the men of the period. It was their faith. Even so earnest an advocate of the Book Beautiful as T. J. Cobden-Sanderson, who in association with Emery Walker took the first steps towards lifting the designing of books out of the medieval convention revived by Morris, makes a distinction between typography and beautiful typography. 'The whole duty of Typography, as of Calligraphy', he says, 'is to communicate to the imagination, without loss by the way, the thought or image intended to be communicated by the Author.' That definition may well have inspired recent good printing as well as the self-conscious books of the Doves Press. Cobden-Sanderson went on to say that:

> The whole duty of beautiful typography is not to substitute for the beauty or interest of
> the thing thought and intended to be conveyed by the symbol, a beauty or interest of its

own, but, on the one hand, to win access for that communication by the clearness and beauty of the vehicle, and on the other hand, to take advantage of every pause or stage in that communication to interpose some characteristic and restful beauty in its own art. We thus have a reason for the clearness and beauty of the text as a whole, for the especial beauty of the first or introductory page and of the title, and for the especial beauty of the headings of chapters, capital or initial letters, and so on, and an opening for the illustrator. . . .[4]

And he concludes by charging with treason those who depart from the true faith by permitting 'the self-assertion of any Art beyond the limits imposed by the conditions of its service'.

It was not, however, the typography but the building of the book which was the real contribution to what has been called the 'Revival of Printing'. And it was appropriate and perhaps inevitable that a new attitude towards the designing of books should have come out of the Arts and Crafts Movement, for that movement sought to abolish the division of labour and to restore the organic character of the useful arts.

The complete abolition of the division of labour was not achieved, for although William Morris became a printer he was never a binder and was forced to delegate most of the operations in the construction of the Kelmscott books. But he retained control of the whole job and thus prepared the way for the modern typographer who stands in the same relation to a book as the architect stands towards a building. 'No art is nearer to architecture than typography', says Henri Focillon, Director of the Musée de Lyon;

> like architecture, its first principle is the discriminative and proper adaptation of materials. Like architecture, it rests upon a system of definite conclusions. Its economies are fixed, it repudiates contorted eccentricities. As the designer of a palace cunningly distributes shadows and light on his façade and, in the plans of interiors, adjusts light and shade to living needs, so the designer of a book employs two contrasting qualities, the white of the paper and the black of the ink, assigns to each its part and attains a harmonious whole. There are in architecture great calm planes that are comparable to the margins of a page. There are in a book symmetries and modulations like those of a building. Indeed, is it not true that these two great works of man, a book and a house, should aim at the same fundamental virtue—style? I mean rightness, soberness without sadness, majesty without exaggeration, combined with a personal touch and a noble charm which completely satisfy the spirit.[5]

The modern typographer may have as little practical experience of printing as the architect of masonry, but he has done more for the craft of printing in the last twenty years than the best of the practical printers in the preceding three hundred years. Morris might have been shocked but he would have approved, for in spite of mechanization the 'human element' in printing has not been entirely eliminated. It has survived even mechanical composing. The compositor remains the mason of typography, and type-setting in its mechanical form is still a craft like bricklaying; for the printer, as William Morris and Emery Walker pointed out in the first collection of *Arts and Crafts Essays* (1893), is engaged not only in laying the type in a workmanlike manner, but in giving it a balanced appearance by breaking up lines and 'rivers' 'as in bonding masonry or brick work'. Neither types nor bricks can be well and truly laid unless they achieve these aims.

Charles Ricketts, who helped to restore a 'sense of design' to book production, rightly claimed novelty for the Kelmscott and Vale books because by reviving that sense, in addition to restoring the 'element of personal control', it became possible, 'for the first time in the history of printing', to master all the operations which go to the making of a book. There can be little doubt, as Ricketts continues, 'that the invention of the type and the original woodcut pictures and decorations form an aggregate for which we will hardly find a precedent in the past', and that 'the control of the pagination and press-work has very rarely been due in the past to the designer of the type and the rest'. Of all the lessons of the 'private presses' there can now be little doubt that the control of the whole book in a consistent design is the most important, and has had the greatest influence on modern typography and book production.

Theories, however logical, may conflict with practice, however sincere. This conflict is obvious in the Vale Press books. Ricketts, striving for the coordination of exquisite parts, ends by exploiting the exquisite. He believes in packing a book with beauty inside and out. A book should not only be 'alive in every part' but 'definite' and even 'emphatic' in design. In the past, however, the parts of a book were not expected to show off; they were expected to be of good report, and not to brag about it. During the greater part of last century a well-designed book was so rare that self-consciousness in the early days of the revival was inevitable and even excusable. All would have been well if the precursors of a new typography had been inimitable. But they were far from that, and they increased and multiplied, legitimately and illegitimately. A craftsman's dream, splendid in itself, became a racket. There is an ostentation about many of the fine books of the nineties and those of our own time which makes them more attractive to collectors than to readers or scholars. They are so obviously well-dressed that even their creators sometimes resort to explaining or defending them. The admission that such books are not for everyday use is sufficient condemnation.

> 'The aim of the revival of printing', says Ricketts, 'is. . . merely due to a wish to give a permanent and beautiful form to that portion of our literature which is secure of permanence. By a permanent form I do not mean merely sound as to paper and ink, etc.; I mean permanent in the sense that the work reflects that conscious aim towards beauty and order which are ever interesting elements in themselves'.[6]

The curious thing is that both Ricketts and Morris in addition to the work of their presses produced or designed good books by ordinary trade and mechanical methods, but so obsessed were they with art and handicraft that neither of them seems to have realized the possibilities of the beneficent example they had thus set before all printers. Yet printing as we know it today, although indirectly stimulated by the example of the Kelmscott and Vale books, follows the 'trade' productions and not the 'artistic' books of the private presses. The progenitors of modern printing are the *Roots of the Mountains* and *Daphnis and Chloe* rather than the Vale *Shakespeare* and the Kelmscott *Chaucer*.[7] The creations of the private presses of the nineties have come to occupy the ironical position of being little more than sublimations of what John

Johnson calls the 'lively, if ill-defined, archaism which swept over the country in the second half of Victoria's reign'.[8]

There must always be room for the hand-made book, and that room may possibly expand as standardization increases its grip upon our works and lives. But beautiful books are no longer dependent upon the handicraftsman. Books of fine quality and individual distinction are now produced by mechanical methods and, although they differ from the hand-made books, they have a character and charm of their own and they serve the purposes of a book as well as their predecessors did and much better than many of the hand-made books of yesterday and today. The contemporary range of well-designed books of the common kind is also wider and more varied, and the non-critical reader gets better printing today whether he wants it or not. It is wrong to assume, as some do, that the rank and file of readers for whom standardized and mass-produced books exist have been seduced by traders from appreciating 'quality'. The casual reader has no recognizable taste for quality in printing, and when all books were hand made the proletariat could not read and the middle class as we know it did not exist:

> *Book-larning* hereabouts is rarish:
> I'm thought a *schollard* in my parish.
> For in the village where I dwell,
> Not one can read, and few can spell.[9]

Ruskin was the first English author to offer working men good printing—at a price beyond their reach—and up to his death only those few who became Socialists or who came under the influence of the University Settlement Movement paid any attention to him. Then his greatest disciple Morris had another shot and produced the Kelmscott masterpieces for millionaires. It is the commercial typographer of today who has broken through the ring of badness and is forcing traders and machines to do their best rather than their worst. For proof of this it is only necessary to turn to the excellent design of contemporary series of popular reprints.[10]

Few things are so misleading as historical analogy. To argue that the people of this or that period did so and so and that therefore the people of this should do the same is nonsense. It is a kind of nonsense favoured by those who advocate a return to handicraft. There is little or no resemblance between the people of the handicraft age and those of the machine age. The people of today who have no interest in how a thing is made but a great deal in how to get enough of it are so different from their predecessors that they might be an entirely new race. They and the conditions under which they live exist now for the first time. Machines are their gods and the product of machines their treasure. Indeed, they themselves are products of mechanization, and they not only prefer, but, in the circumstances, it is perhaps natural that they should prefer, to be led by gadgets rather than by ideas.

Hand-press work is not excellent in itself, as anybody knows who has studied the publications of the seventeenth and late eighteenth centuries. There are black sheep also among black letters. Bad printing is bad whether it has been set and printed by hand or set and printed by machine. Most of the characteristics of the two methods are the same. The few differences, such for instance as texture, are accidental. Worship of the irregularities of hand work is sentimental. There would have been fewer irregularities if the printer could have avoided them. What makes printing good is neither the ritualism of handicraft nor the methodism of the machine, but the accordance of the design with the wishes of the reader who wants to get down to the business of reading. Good printing is readable printing, and no print is readable that is not simple, direct, plain, and inclining towards austerity. Printing is not a thing in itself like a picture, admitting the maximum of personal expression, but part of a tool called a book: a bridge between writer and reader. It should contain nothing to impede that traffic. Graciousness, friendliness, even dignity should be there, but always unobtrusively. Self-effacement is the etiquette of the good printer.

NOTES

[1] Trans. Theodore W. Koch, Quoted in *The Ideal Book*, ed. Peter Garnett, The Laboratory Press, Pittsburg (1934).

[2] I know that an anachronism in art or craft may be interesting, or in modern jargon, amusing—but that is another story.

[3] *A Bibliography of the Books by Hacon and Ricketts* (1904), by Charles Ricketts, Introd. 7-9.

[4] *Ecce Mundus: Industrial Ideals and the Book Beautiful* (1902).

[5] Quoted from Introd. to *Le Livre, son architecture, sa technique*, by Marius Audin (Lyons, 1924), in *The Fine Book* (1914), 56-7.

[6] *A Bibliography of Books issued by Hacon and Ricketts* (1904), by Charles Ricketts, Introd. 16. [sic.]

[7] I have touched upon this theme in the chapter on "The Revival of Printing" in *The Eighteen Nineties* (1913), now published in Cape's "Life and Letters Series", and A. J. A. Symons has dealt more fully with it in his essay on 'The Typography of the 'Nineties', *The Fleuron*, vii (1930).

[8] *The Printer, his Customers, and his Men*, by John Johnson (1933), 31.

[9] Rev. John Horseman, Rector of Heydon, 1811. Quoted T. F. Dibdin, *Literary Reminiscences* (1836), i, 301.

[10] Pocketable reprints have generally shown a typographical taste and ingenuity. It began with the smaller Elzevirs and Plantins and has not yet ended: on the contrary, the publication of such admirably designed series as the *Temple Classics*, *Temple Shakespeare*, *Temple Bible*, the *Phoenix*, the *Travellers Library*, the *Florin Books*, Constable's *Miscellany*, and the *Penguin Books*, to name but a few in England, and the *Albatross* (a masterpiece of typography, more satisfying to my taste than any *édition de luxe*), the new *Tauchnitz*, and the so-called Inselbücherei, a series produced by the Insel-Verlag, in Leipzig, at a price of 0.700 RM. = about 9d, most beautifully printed, often illustrated, and widely circulated in Germany, shows that good printing is no handicap to circulation.

J. M. Kerby

Caxton to Computers

In addressing an audience of varied interests in the city of Leeds, an important printing centre with printers of international fame, I realize that in attempting to cover 500 years of development in the printing industry I have set myself a most difficult task, especially as I am not an historian but merely a person who has always found the history of printing a most fascinating topic. Moreover the scope of this task may be gauged from the opening paragraph of an article which I read recently:

> Few technical developments have been more significant for the human race than the invention of printing by movable type [in Europe] in the fifteenth century and the introduction of the electronic computer in the twentieth.

The printing industry is the sixth largest in Britain today, having an annual sales turnover of about £ 800,000,000; a quarter of a million employees are involved in 7,500 establishments, 80% of which have less than 25 on the payroll. The other 20% comprising much larger firms are, however, responsible for 89% of the total sales. Annually some £70,000,000 of print and printing machinery is exported, with imports currently running at about £38,000,000. Such figures show that we have a large and complex printing industry but its importance in the social scene cannot be evaluated by simple statistics. When we pause to consider the involvement of printing in everyday life we see that wherever we go, whatever we do, and whatever article we buy, print in some form or other is always involved, Thus, for example, ½ lb. of printed matter is needed in producing, distributing and selling one motor car whilst in the case of a modern computer about 60 lb. is necessary. Gutenberg, I am sure, never envisaged his child growing to such proportions.

As regards the development of printing, in Europe the earliest attempts to produce multiple copies involved the use of woodcuts which were inked and impressed on damp paper. (Clay cylinders and tablets were used for the same purpose by the ancient

SOURCE: Reprinted from R. Reed, Editor, *Symposium on Printing* (Leeds: Leeds Philosophical and Literary Society, 1971), J. M. Kerby, "Caxton to Computers," pp. 1-7, by permission of the publisher. Copyright 1971 Leeds Philosophical and Literary Society.

civilizations of Mesopotamia and the developments in China were even more remarkable.) Thus in medieval Europe religious tracts and playing cards were produced in this way. Although woodcuts obviously took some time to make, they clearly represented an advance over contemporary methods where books were written by hand. There are rival claimants for the title of the inventor of printing from movable type. Most authorities ascribe the invention (in Europe) to Johann Gutenberg of Mainz, Germany, around 1441; some, however, claim that Lourens Janszoon Coster of Haarlem, in the Netherlands, printed with movable type as early as 1430, whilst doubtless the Russians would insist that it was their countrymen! Because Coster's process of casting type in sand, with wooden hand-cut originals as patterns, was incapable of development into a practicable method, the real honour of inventing the process which led to printing as we know it must probably go to Gutenberg. Yet the fact that there are two claimants to the invention suggests that the process was being mooted generally, a situation which has often led to simultaneous yet independent discoveries of the same device. Apart from movable type several other elements were involved, namely paper, ink and a press of some kind. Paper, apparently first known in China in the second century A.D., moved very slowly westwards, reaching centres of Islamic culture such as Baghdad by the end of the eighth century A.D., and Alexandria by the beginning of the tenth century. By the middle of the twelfth century paper had found its way via Greece to the European continent where it gradually assumed dominance over skin-based writing materials such as parchment and leather. Thus Gutenberg had paper at his disposal. The press was also well known by this time, having been used in Europe for pressing wine grapes over many centuries, so that Gutenberg had only to adapt it for printing on paper. At first the ink presented some problems: ink formerly used for printing from wooden blocks had a water-soluble base, which ran when used with metal type and gave unsatisfactory registration. The medieval painters, however, were developing the use of finely ground pigments mixed with linseed oil and Gutenberg adapted this medium to provide a suitable ink for printing.

It is clear that printing from movable type began to assume importance in the Europe of 1450. The earliest examples of books printed in the new manner appear to be bibles which are attributed to Gutenberg; one cannot be absolutely certain on this point for they were not dated, neither did they bear the printer's name. The records of Mainz for 1450 show that a goldsmith named Fust advanced 800 guilders to Gutenberg against a mortgage on his equipment and later followed this with a similiar amount. In 1455, as a result of a lawsuit, Fust actually took over the business, but by that time Gutenberg is thought to have produced an Indulgence, a 36-line Bible and a 42-line Bible. It is interesting to note that from the outset variable width spaces were used to produce what are known as justified lines, justification being the even spacing of words within lines to a given measure. It has been estimated that the edition of the 42-line Bible ran to 210 copies, 180 on paper and 30 on the more durable material known as vellum, a thin yet very strong form of parchment produced from calfskin. For its production six presses were used and almost certainly these were converted wine presses such as the Romans had used in Mainz and other parts of Germany a thousand years before. One can imagine the impact made by this activity which produced an edition of 210 copies in about 12 months, whereas previously one man might have spent several years to write one copy. Thus it is not surprising that the art of printing spread rapidly throughout Europe and soon presses were established in Basle (1466), Rome (1467), Venice (1469), Paris, Nuremberg and Utrecht (1470), Milan, Naples and Florence (1471), Cologne (1472), London (1480), Antwerp and Leipzig (1481) and Stockholm (1483) as well as in other European cities. Intellectual forces alone were insufficient to attract the businessmen of the printing trade. University towns as such had no overwhelming attraction for printers, who preferred to follow the main streams of commerce and in Italy these led to Venice, the Queen of the Adriatic and the trade centre of the known world during the fifteenth century. At this time there were 268 printers in Venice, more than in the remainder of Italy and prior to 1500 at least two million copies of books appear to have been produced. Aldus Manutius, the most famous name in Venetian printing, was probably the greatest of the early printers, being important not so much as a craftsman but rather as an organizer of book production. He used his business acumen to produce a series of books, mainly Greek and Latin texts, which would be scholarly, compact and cheap. He succeeded in placing as much text as possible on the sextodecimo format which he chose for his pocket-size editions; to achieve this end and to satisfy his liking for cursive letters he used a closely set italic type by Francesco Griffo. In this work, to produce the so-called Aldine editions, he was most successful. The price of books was reduced and thus they became widely available, not only to scholars and professional men but also to merchants and gentlemen of leisure.

Venice is also important in that it was the home of the first really successful Roman or upright typeface, that cut by the Frenchman Nicolas Jenson in 1470.

Caxton, born in the Weald of Kent, c. 1420, is remembered as the man who brought printing to England, having learned the craft in Cologne during 1471-72. After setting up a press in Bruges he returned to England in 1476 and at the Sign of the Red Pale in Westminster he established printing in this country. Although he lived in a turbulent period, for the Wars of the Roses were far from being finished, he persisted in his enterprise and his work prospered. In the growing thirst for knowledge printing had reached that stage of development which was to make it a major factor in education and commerce. It may be noted that his press was set up not in the City but in the precinct of Westminster Abbey, at a rent of ten shilling per annum. A printing establishment on Church property lent an air of sanctity and respectability to an art which many people through ignorance associated with the forces of evil. Apprentices to the craft of printing have long been known as 'printers' devils'. Short popular stories and pamphlets formed the main output of Caxton's press, an Indulgence printed in December 1476, probably being the first example of printing in England. The first book to bear a date, *Dictes or Sayings of the Philosophres*, came from his press on 18 November 1477, whilst in 1478 he produced his first edition of the *Canterbury Tales* of Chaucer. Apart from being a printer Caxton was an accomplished linguist and he spoke several European languages. Although he is remembered as a printer his productions were not notable examples of the printer's art and craft; possibly his greater contribution to the progress of general education lay in translating foreign texts into English. Thus in 1475 on his press at Bruges he printed the first books ever in

English, namely a translation of Lefevre's *Recueil des histoires de Troye* and the popular *Game and Playe of the Chesse* from the Latin of Jacobus de Cessolis.

We may now turn our attention to the eighteenth century for during the sixteenth and seventeenth centuries there was little change in the fundamentals of printing, although the craft had been refined in certain ways. In the main printing was still carried out using wooden presses operated by hand, little different from the adapted wine presses used by Gutenberg. The market for printed material remained virtually unchanged; books were still the main product to come from the presses but by the eighteenth century they had generally become smaller, the octavo format gradually replacing the larger quarto and folio forms, due mainly to the skill of the typefounders in making smaller type. Type proved to be an extremely expensive commodity, far too costly to be kept standing idle against the time when reprint editions were needed. Hence serious attempts were made to produce facsimile copies of a page of made-up type matter for use as a printing medium and for storage purposes. Thus early in the eighteenth century the Dutchman Johan Muller first produced the copies of type matter in plate form, now known as stereotypes. By all accounts the eighteenth century was a remarkable one. It was the age of elegance, the beau and the dandy, the coffeehouse and the tavern, where the poor were invited by means of printed notices to become intoxicated for a penny and hopelessly drunk for twopence. It was also the age of pugilism, cockfighting and highwaymen. The novel, *Tom Jones*, written in 1750, provides a vivid picture of these remarkable times. By the printer, however, the eighteenth century is best remembered for the introduction of the newspaper. The *Daily Courant* was the first, being published two days after the accession of Queen Anne in 1702. The year 1709 saw the appearance of *The Tatler*, and 1785 *The Daily and Universal Register*, which in 1788 changed its name to *The Times*. It was, however, the ninteenth century which proved to be more important for the expansion of printing and the industrial revolution introduced new technical methods into print production whilst simultaneously creating huge new markets. The main product, books, had been greatly supplemented by newspapers and now a new market was brought into being, that of advertising, the demand for the latter being due to increased commercial activity. To provide the printing capacity to cope with the new demand, new equipment appeared: in place of the hand-operated wooden presses fresh designs in metal were constructed and driven by steam power. Thus, in contrast to the 250 single sheets per hour possible with a well-run hand press, the König steam press could easily produce 1,000 sheets per hour and these were 'perfected' or printed on both sides. The installation of the first reel-fed rotary press in the printing office of *The Times* in 1866 was the start of far-reaching changes in newspaper production. Simultaneously paper-making made large advances and the Fourdrinier machine, capable of making long continous rolls, was first seen in England in 1802 and by 1851 there were 413 of these high-output systems in operation.

Increases in printing speed also led to changes in bookbinding practices: by 1820 cloth has begun to replace parchment and leather as the cover or casing material, and machinery for casing books at high speed was introduced by about 1830. The development of photography early in the nineteenth century also had a big impact on printing, particularly where illustrations were concerned. Thus hand-engraving gradually gave way to photo-engraving. The first line block produced by photographic techniques appeared in 1870 and in 1891 the *Daily Graphic* published the first half-tone illustration. Until the nineteenth century all type was set by hand for printing by the letterpress process, but towards the end of this century all three printing processes which are now in wide use, letterpress, lithography and gravure, were established and type was being set by machines.

Lithography, the art of printing or reproducing from a plane surface, was first developed late in the eighteenth century by Senefelder and for many years was regarded as no more than a fashionable hobby. However, late in the nineteenth century photography was allied to the principle of lithography and the new and versatile technique of photolithography found rapid commercial acceptance. About the same time Klietsch introduced the process of photogravure and set up a company to exploit his discovery. Of the many typesetting machines introduced during the nineteenth century, only two survived to prosper as viable commercial propositions—Linotype and Monotype. The Linotype machine produces justified type matter in one linear unit which is easily handled, thus being eminently suitable for newspaper work. The Monotype, on the other hand, produces separate characters and spaces which may be easily removed and exchanged for others, as for example, when correcting work after the proof has been read. The first Linotype casting machine was installed at the press of the *New York Times* in 1886 but it was some time later, in 1897, that the Monotype machine was first used in normal print production. Today, almost a century later, both these typesetting machines still provide the major portion of composing capacity in the western world.

Coming to the present century it is by no means easy to comment on recent trends for they are numerous and change at a rapid pace. One could reasonably say that up to the end of the Second World War developments in printing were mostly confined to refinements in established techniques and equipment. The last twenty years, however, have seen considerable changes, both in the market for print of all kinds and in the methods used for its production. There has been a marked growth in the use of offset lithography as compared with the letterpress technique. This is shown in the following table giving the percentages of total print production by the three major processes:

	Britain	U.S.A.
Lithography	35	55
Letterpress	55	39
Gravure	10	6

In Britain the use of letterpress over the last ten years has dropped from 70% to 55% of the total production whilst gravure has steadily managed to retain some 10% of the market. In the United States of America printers had the advantage during the war years of being able to develop lithographic techniques which are used on a wide scale and have now ousted letterpress as the main producer of print.

To cope with the rapid growth of high volume markets such as paper-back books, directories, magazines, and catalogues of all kinds, bindery techniques have needed to be re-assessed and here the introduction of automated equipment at certain stages of the work has led to tremendous improvements in output.

Some automation techniques have been applied in the more difficult field of type composition; these include:

1. Tape operation of line casters.
2. Use of special purpose computers with typesetting function.
3. Photocomposition.
4. Composition systems based on general purpose computers.

Tape operation is advantageous in that it permits the operator to be separated from the machine, an important point because as machine speeds increase the man becomes the limiting factor. One might also expect higher productivity in the keyboarding operation to arise from the use of special purpose computers equipped to carry out the basic tasks of justification and hyphenation; so far, however, this has not been realized because the overall rate of output is determined by later stages which follow that of keyboarding. In any case, over the last six years or so, potentially greater advances have been made in the field of photocomposition where machines directly expose characters on to photographic material, thereby eliminating the need for metal type. Moreover, it has now been recognized that the general purpose computer can better exploit the potential of photocomposing machines and since 1968, in the composition field, there have been more general purpose computers in use than the single purpose type. Clearly computer composition has gone forward at a tremendous pace, as may be seen from the following Table showing the world use of computer controlled installations.

	Number of firms using computer-controlled composition systems
1964	77
1965	200
1966	300
1967	550
1968	850
1970	1,200 (in 30 countries; 90 of these installations are in Britain)

Apart from the field of composition, the general purpose computer is now being applied at various points in the printing and publishing industries, e.g. costing, accounting, advertising control, stock control, press control, circulation systems, forecasting systems, production scheduling and payroll duty, whilst in the next five years its use will extend even more widely.

The latest forms of photocomposing machines now entering the printing industry are entirely computer dependent and thus will be installed as peripherals to the main computer. Such machines use cathode ray tube character generation techniques which permit half-tone illustrations to be exposed with the text matter—a distinct improvement over the present position where only line drawings may be satisfactorily dealt with. Already results with half-tone illustrations have proved most satisfactory and in the near future we may expect even greater developments in technique. So powerful is the impact of the computer that it is certain that within the next five years newspapers in this country will use a system whereby all text correction, editing, page planning and make-up will be handled by the computer. The final output, via a high-speed photocomposing machine, will be a complete page of the newspaper.

It is important to note that the printers' markets are also changing rapidly as both information and its mode of dissemination are radically altering. No longer does information necessarily imply words printed on paper. The use of microdot and microfilm for storing information is rapidly increasing whilst more and more organizations are making use of on-line T.V. type computer terminals to receive information, channel it, or store it. The computer is undoubtedly the most sophisticated information engine ever devised by man and its impact on the information industry is already profound. As mentioned, the need for the printed word can in many cases be dispensed with, for machine can converse directly with machine and request the retrieval and display of particular portions of the vast amount of information stored. Some typical examples of modern computer-based activities include:

Institute of Electrical Engineers—The Databank, forming the basis of its enquiry service and its list of Abstracts published monthly.

Excerpta Medicus—Databank, storing abstracts of all papers on medical matters.

Telephone Directories—The time taken to amend and produce a telephone page has been cut from forty-five minutes to four minutes by using a computer and photocomposing machines.

Parts Lists—Many organizations store their parts lists and inventories in microdot form.

Newspapers—Advertisements are formatted, scheduled, charged, customers' accounts printed, sales information obtained, credit controlled, etc.

Oxford University Press—The on-line computer terminals handle all enquiries and orders for books.

Thus clearly we are on the threshold of immense technical advances and the printer must move with the times to keep in touch with these new markets. The new technologies must be accepted and fully utilized. This will present both labour and management with many new problems and mutually acceptable solutions must be negotiated. Modern printing has aptly been termed the game of Printers' Poker: to stay in the game money must be put into the kitty. There seems, however, little basis for pessimism. It is certain that printing will survive all these changes as it has survived the changes of the past 500 years because it is more convenient and attractive, for many purposes, than any of the new techniques of communication. The seventies will see far-reaching developments in printing and I am pleased to be associated with them.

Robert Escarpit

Historical Survey— The Book Revolution

WHAT IS A BOOK?

Like anything that lives, the book is not to be defined. At least, no one has yet been able to provide a complete and final definition of it, because a book is not a thing like other things. When we hold it in our hands, all we hold is the paper: the *book* is elsewhere. And yet it is in the pages as well, and the thought alone without the support of the printed words could not make a book. A book is a reading-machine, but it can never be used mechanically. A book is sold, bought, passed from hand to hand, but it cannot be treated like an ordinary commercial commodity, because it is, at once, multiple and unique, in ample supply yet precious.

It is the product of certain techniques, serving certain intentions, which may be put to certain uses. As much could be said of most of the products of human industry, but the peculiarity of the book is that the intentions, the uses and the techniques which combine to define it, far from being crystalized in the phenomenon, go well beyond it, preserving, as it were, their independence, evolving with the circumstances of history, and reacting on one another so that they mutually modify their content and lead to infinite variation not only in the book itself but in its position and its role in the life of every man and of society.

At several points in the course of this development the book has crossed dividing lines beyond which the definitions previously acceptable no longer applied, because actual mutations had taken place. One such mutation is now coming about, in this second half of the twentieth century.

The book as such seems to have appeared in its first form at the beginning of the first

SOURCE: Reprinted from Robert Escarpit, *The Book Revolution* (London: George G. Harrap and Company, Ltd., and Paris: UNESCO, 1966), Chapter I, "Historical Survey," pp. 17-30, by permission of UNESCO. Copyright 1966 by UNESCO. All rights reserved.

millennium B.C. Its appearance was probably associated with the use of various types of light, pliant supports for writing: bark, plant fibers or cloth. *Biblos* in Greek means the inner bark of certain reeds, including papyrus; *liber* in Latin means the fibrous layer beneath the outer bark of trees; *book* in English and *Buch* in German derive from the same Indo-European root as *bois* (wood) in French; *kniga* in Russian probably comes, through Turkish and Mongolian, from the Chinese *king*, which means "a classic" but which originally designated the woof of silk.[1]

Why this almost universal preoccupation with a technical point? And why this insistence upon a certain type of material? Before the discovery of papyrus and silk, were there no books? The bounds of history are continually moving farther back as older and older carved monuments are found. Excavations in the Middle East have led to the discovery of real "libraries", several thousands of years old, composed of baked clay tablets. The very roots of such words as *gramma*, *littera* and *scribere* go back to the time when words were recorded by scratching on some hard material, and many literary works have been handed down to us by such means. At the time when the stone-cutter alone handled writing, literatures existed, but not books; for the written record still lacked one essential quality: mobility.

Verba volant, scripta manent. Writing enabled the word to conquer time, but the book enabled it to conquer space. The pliant, lightweight supports which, thirty centuries ago, gave the book its various names opened the way to two decisive developments: first, it became possible to copy a long text rapidly and easily; and second, it became possible to transport a considerable number of copies of the text rapidly and easily to any destination.

As long as the poet was an oral story-teller, he could rely only on transmission by word of mouth to reach an audience beyond the immediate circle of his hearers. Writing enabled him to speak to posterity. Thanks to the book he can now hope, at least theoretically, to speak to all mankind. The technical revolution which created the book and made the peoples aware of it is thus closely related to the idea of diffusion.

The idea of diffusion is the clue to guide us in following the book through its successive mutations. This is most important, because it is absolutely impossible to understand twentieth-century problems in the field of literary creation, publishing, bookselling and reading if the book is to be considered only as a record, as a repository of intellectual notions or verbal patterns to be drawn on as required, or even as a one-way means of communication. Being a written document, a book is in fact all these things, but being a book it is something else again. Since, in a little space, it has a high density of intellectual and formal content, since it can be easily passed from hand to hand, since it can be copied and reproduced at will, the book is the simplest instrument which, from a given point, can liberate a multitude of sounds, images, feelings, ideas, facts, by opening the gates of time and space to them—and then, joined with other books, can reconcentrate those diffused data in countless other points scattered through the centuries and the continents in an infinity of combinations, each different from any other.

Details may vary greatly from case to case but the scheme is found unchanged regardless of the quality of the literary material which the book contains, regardless of the geographical, historical or social extent of the phenomenon. The book is neither more nor less than its diffusion, and for that reason its mutations are intimately related to the technical innovations that adapt it to the successive requirements of the writers whose words it records, and of the societies to which it diffuses those words.

THE MUTATIONS OF THE BOOK

The first stage was probably that of the *volumen*, a roll of papyrus sheets pasted together, making it possible to handle an entire work, as required by the type of literary life which existed in Athens, and later in Rome in the classical period, with its copyists' workshops (which were true publishing houses), its bookshops, and the compulsory deposit of copies in the great libraries.[2]

But diffusion here was on a relatively small scale, restricted to rich amateurs, scholars in the orbit of a patron of the arts and, later, students and clerks. In the small society of the ancient city, public reading was the most usual means of publication. Shorter documents were written on wax tablets while, for everyday writings, parchment, a cruder but also less fragile and less costly material than papyrus, had been available since the third century B.C.

Just because of its cheapness and its strength, parchment was the instrument which brought about the next mutation: cut into sheets which were then stitched together, it produced the *codex*, with the page arrangement characteristic of the modern book. This arrangement is much better suited, functionally, for reference and scholarly research than was the *volumen*. It is the ideal form for legal records (*code*, incidentally, is derived from *codex*), for sacred texts and for scholarly writings. It is suited to a civilization less interested in literature than in political security, theology and the preservation of ancient learning. From the fourth century of our era, for more than a thousand years, the manuscript of bound sheets of vellum, in the hands of the clerks, was to be the universal means of preserving, communicating and disseminating thought, not only throughout the Christian world but throughout the Arab and Jewish worlds as well.

So vitally important was the book that during the Middle Ages there was no more meritorious labour than to copy or illuminate a manuscript. The transport of books from monastery to monastery, from town to town, sometimes over very great distances, was organized with care.[3]

Because their artistic merits ensured their survival, we are most familiar with the beautiful illuminated manuscripts of the late Middle Ages, but there were also less costly books, especially books of hours, for daily use. As soon as they came into being, the universities organized the copying of classical texts for their students, so that a thirteenth-century scholars' textbook budget was not much greater, in proportion, than that of his successors in the twentieth century.[4]

No matter how ingeniously it was organized, however, hand copying had its limits. From the fourteenth century onwards, new strata of society took up reading, which until then had been the clerks' preserve. These new readers—nobles and bourgeois, merchants and magistrates—had little use for latinizing in everyday life: they wanted technical works, it is true, but also books to entertain them, works of imagination, written in the vulgar tongue. Thus in the Romance dialects was born the "romance", the ancestor of the novel, whose popularity hastened the next, decisive mutation of the book: printing.

FROM THE PRINTED BOOK TO THE BEST-SELLER

Printing had an immediate and spectacular effect, but it appeared only when the time was ripe—which shows that a technical innovation can prosper only if it meets a social need. Paper, which was as indispensable to the development of printing as the tyre and macadam were, later, to the development of the motor-car, had been known in China for more than a thousand years when it reached Europe in the middle of the twelfth century—and even then it was coldly received by the authorities, who were worried about its frailty.[5] Printing from movable type took much less time—two or three years—to cover the same ground. The times had changed, and the new conditions required that printing be discovered, invented or imported.

True, printing prospered because in Europe it encountered languages employing alphabetical script with twenty-six characters, the form best suited for its use, but it prospered even more because it encountered civilizations in the midst of rapid economic and cultural development, where the diffusion of the written word was beginning to create insuperable problems.

What was perhaps the most decisive discovery in history appeared, prosaically enough, to the first printers simply as a convenient way of speeding up the copying of books, improving their appearance and reducing their cost. Everything about the typography, manufacture and publishing of books at this time shows that the printers were mainly concerned with commercial returns. The same concern can be seen in the choice of the first texts printed, all of which were likely to sell well; religious works, novels, collections of anecdotes, technical manuals and recipe-books formed the backbone of the catalogues of these practical businessmen.[6]

The success of the operation exceeded their best hopes. Some authorities estimate the number of *incunabula*—books printed before A.D. 1500—at 20,000,000 in a Europe whose population numbered less than 100,000,000, most of whom were illiterate.[7]

This gave the book a new dimension and no time was lost in exploring its possibilities. Only a few hundred copies of the first *incunabula* were printed; the average printing of a book did not go beyond 1,000 copies until the middle of the sixteenth century. In the seventeenth century it was between 2,000 and 3,000 copies, and continued at that level until the end of the eighteenth century. It was usually difficult to do better with hand presses, and, what is more, the printers, who by now were distinct from the booksellers who handled distribution, would have been afraid of cheapening their wares by making them too common. Guild ordinances restricted both the number of printing-presses and the size of printings. As a result, despite a steady downward trend, book prices in Western Europe remained at a level which made the book available to the well-to-do burgesses, but not to the middle classes in general, let alone to the workers. The latter, if not illiterate, had to satisfy their needs for reading material from the more ephemeral publications to be found in the pedlar's pack: broadsheets, ballads and almanacs.[8]

It can therefore be said that the printed book, which was the support and vehicle of the great European literature of the sixteenth, seventeenth and eighteenth centuries, took it only to a very small circle of society.

In the eighteenth century, England was the least illiterate country in Europe, and the country in which publishing was the most prosperous, but even the most popular books—*Pamela* or *Joseph Andrews*—never had a sale of more than a few thousand copies.[9] In France, printings were decidedly smaller, and though Voltaire's witticism—fifty readers for a serious book and five hundred for an entertaining one—was surely an exaggeration, the fact remains that the readers of books represented a small aristocracy of written culture, or of "literature", as it was then called.

It was an international aristocracy. The absence of any kind of copyright agreement gave a stimulus to piracy in publishing which was morally questionable but culturally beneficial. American publishing, for instance, developed magnificently, after the United States became independent, by establishing itself as a parasite upon the British publishing trade. Owing to their mercantile traditions or their political situation, such cities as Amsterdam and Lyons were, for centuries, international centres of diffusion for the reading public. The *Divine Comedy* took more than four centuries to make its way throughout Europe; twenty years were enough for *Don Quixote*, and five for *Werther*. Five or six major languages shared the literary universe; never has the sense of a world community of the literati been keener than during the eighteenth century.

But this aristocratic cosmopolitanism was directly threatened; the book had long been working up to a fourth mutation, mechanization, which was to destroy it. The premonitory signs were visible from the days of the Encyclopaedists on. As in the fifteenth century, new social strata, including the lower middle classes, took up reading and demanded books of a system which had not been designed for them, which by definition excluded them. This new need for reading matter was one of the causes of the development of the press, whose circulation figures were still, however, very small.

Faced with a developing market, printing and bookselling underwent a major change, as nascent capitalist industry took charge of the book. The publisher appeared as the responsible entrepreneur relegating the printer and bookseller to a minor role. As a side effect, the literary profession began to organize; until then literature had been left to the rich amateur or relied on the support of the art patron, but now the writer began to claim a livelihood from his works. From Dr. Johnson to Diderot, men of letters raised the question of copyright and literary property.

In the last third of the eighteenth century, trends of thought which, though at variance with one another, all converged in the direction of spreading books among what was then called "the people"—Methodism in England, Encyclopaedism and later the revolutionary spirit in France, and, to a lesser extent, *Aufklärung* in Germany—suddenly made the need for reading matter an urgent problem.

Then, in a few years—between 1800 and 1820—a series of inventions revolutionized printing techniques: the metal press, the foot-operated cylinder press, the mechanical steam-press. Before the end of Napoleon's reign, more sheets could be printed in an hour than had been possible in a day fifteen years earlier. The period of large printings could begin.

It began in Britain, for most of the improvements in printing were of British origin. Walter Scott's novels heralded this development, but it really opened with Byron's well-known experience in 1814, when 10,000 copies of *The Corsair* were sold on the day of publication. The wave reached France about 1830,[10] together with the heavy-duty press, and by 1848 it had swept over the rest of Europe and America.

This change in scale produced far-reaching effects. First of all, the writer lost contact with the vast majority of his readers: only the "cultured" stratum of the population continued to participate, either directly or through the critics, in the formation of influential literary opinion, while the anonymous multitude of other readers now figured in the mythology of letters only as a boundless sea into whose waves the poet tossed at random the bottle bearing his message.[11]

But it was no longer possible to ignore the existence of the mass of readers who thenceforth were to support the book amd make it an economic proposition. Just as the fourteenth- and fifteenth-century bourgeois had made the clerkly Latin book give place to the use of the vulgar tongue, so the new readers of the nineteenth century made the cosmopolitan book of the literati give place to the use of national languages. Large printings thus both required and facilitated the splintering of literary languages, leading to independent national literatures. As nationalism awakened, the book kept step with the times.

And it kept in step with the times in the awakening of class consciousness as well. One after another, the circulating library, the serial novel and the public library spread the book ever more widely among the social strata, which the progress of education had opened to reading. In the revolutionary thinking of 1848, the book became a basic symbol. It was realized that the way to freedom lies through cultural conquest. As was to be expected in Britain and in the United States the popular book had a strong puritanical bias, and the stress lay more on its moral role than on its revolutionary value. Its efficiency as a social determinant was nevertheless very great, especially in the United States where, as Richard D. Altick phrases it, "the American author had learned more quickly than his English cousin how to write for a democratic audience".[12] The pirate-market having reversed its pre-Dickensian East-West trend, the American book was read all through the English-speaking world, including Britain and its colonies. By mid-century *Uncle Tom's Cabin* sold a million and a half copies in one year and played a part in the building of a progressive opinion in Anglo-Saxon countries comparable to that of *Les Misérables* ten years later in France.

But the first signs of a new, fifth, mutation of the book were appearing in Britain, where the inevitable consequences of capitalist industrialization developed earlier than elsewhere. While the newly-published book was already being sold at the price of ten shillings and sixpence (half a guinea, the luxury trades' status symbol), which was to remain current up to World War II, from 1885 onwards popular reprints of good books began to appear, selling at about sixpence and in printings of tens of thousands of copies. By the end of the century, abridged novels and poems were being sold for a penny, and from 1896 on, one publisher was even to offer penny editions of unabridged texts by Goldsmith, Poe, Scott, Dickens, Dumas, Eugène Sue and Mérimée. [13]

But it was still too early for such undertakings. In a society where there was no internal mobility, the "masses" interested in this kind of reading matter were still only a privileged minority. Although Britain was rather ahead of the rest of the world in this respect, because of the rapid growth of its urban centres, the majority of the population of the other civilized countries still depended for their reading material on the bookstall and the pedlar: mutilated editions of old classics, sentimental novels, folk-tales, joke-books, ballads, almanacs, etc. [14] In some parts of the world this situation was to last until after the Great War, and even until the second half of the twentieth century.

MASS COMMUNICATION

But even before the turn of the century, the first of the mass-communication media had appeared, to some extent replacing the pedlar in many places throughout the world. By 1900, the popular newspaper, born of the cheap press of the 1830's, had passed the figure of a million copies. Half a century later, the British press was breaking all circulation records with the never-equalled figure of 600 copies a day per thousand inhabitants. Behind the United Kingdom, in the 400-copies category, came the Scandinavian countries, Australia and Luxembourg; New Zealand, the United States and Belgium were in the 300-copies category, while in the 100-copies and 200-copies categories came the main body of the twenty or so economically and technically developed nations which, to all intents and purposes, shared among them the rest of the newsprint consumed throughout the world.

The peak was reached about 1955. Since that time, while the newspaper has continued to develop (although at a slower rate) in those countries which had a cultural lag to make good, elsewhere it is dropping back in the face of keen competition from films, radio and television. [15]

These new mass-communication media have possibilities which the newspaper cannot share. They are suitable not only for the circulation of information, but also for artistic expression. True, the nineteenth-century newspaper attempted to second the book in respect of its literary function, but the serial novel has never had a good press among the "cultured class". Even when it is of good quality, it is incomparably less efficacious than a film, a radio broadcast or a television programme.

From the end of the Great War, and with no interruption other than the five years of World War II, the audio-visual mass-communication media have distributed ever-increasing quantities of information and artistic material (both, it is true, varying greatly in quality) to sectors of society which had previously been totally neglected culturally. In the extreme case, television can bring the highest manifestations of art right into homes in which illiteracy, ignorance and poverty have barred the door to the book.

Besides their virtuosity and their omnipresence, these mass-communication media have two advantages over the book: their cost is relatively low and their "consumption" is agreeable. A fine book, on the other hand, is expensive, and a cheap one, with its dull cover, greyish paper and cramped printing, is horribly ugly and depressing. For this reason the cinema, radio and television exercise both an economic and an aesthetic pressure upon the book. When, for the price of one hour's work, it is possible to go to any neighbourhood cinema and spend two hours watching a pleasant story in elegant, comfortable surroundings, why should anyone spend three or four hours' wages, or even more, to read the same story in a book which becomes steadily less prepossessing as its cost decreases?

Of all these considerations, that of beauty is perhaps the most important. Since World War II, the use of synthetic plastics and the development of industrial design have, generally speaking, freed the outward everyday life of the common man from ugliness. In the commercial field, this evolution had begun before the War, with the one-price store, a beautified version of the Anglo-American Woolworth's. Suddenly finding himself served by shop-girls with well-kept hands and hair, in a brightly-lit shop, perhaps to the strains of soft music, gave the average consumer a strange sense of unreality. In many countries, 1935 was the year of the "chain store", during which a certain kind of beauty came into community life as a sort of public service. It may perhaps be of interest that the Moscow "metro", whose gilt and rococo, in a different social structure, fulfilled the same function of beautifying daily life, also dates from 1935. At about the same time in the mid-thirties Raymond Loewy began popularizing the theories on industrial design which he embodied in his 1937 book, *The Locomotive, Its Aesthetics*, and developed later in his famous work *Never Let Well Enough Alone*.

And 1935 was also the year in which, in England, Sir Allen Lane founded Penguin Books. The early Penguins may not have been objects of great beauty, but the red-and-white jackets of these six-penny paperbacks were unusually cheerful-looking for books of that class. In Germany, the old Tauchnitz[16] editions were soon obliged to modernize themselves to keep up with their young competitor, and to exchange their grim typographical covers for softly-tinted jackets, with a different colour for each type of work.

The Penguin did not set out to be a book for the masses. Somewhat snobbishly, those in charge of it persisted for a long while in disclaiming this role; perhaps in fact they did not intend to play it.[17] But man proposes and history disposes. Once again, a mutation had occured at exactly the right time, the appearance of the Penguins coinciding with a concatenation of circumstances favourable to the book for the masses. A few years earlier, in France, experiments such as those of Fayard or Ferenczi, carried out in a similar spirit and probably under better financial conditions, had not yielded the hoped-for results. J. Ferenczi's *Livre Moderne Illustré* series, which reprinted the best-sellers of Colette, Mauriac and Giono, was already selling at 3.50 francs—about a shilling—when the Penguins appeared; it managed to survive somehow, but only at the price of abandoning its ideas of popularization.

The Penguin series, on the contrary, prospered, and developed in a direction which the founder had perhaps not foreseen. In any case, whether deliberately or not, by launching his venture at the precise moment when the times were ripe for it, Sir Allen Lane opened the door to the mass-circulation book.

So true is this that Penguin books are now partly financing at the University of Birmingham the Centre for Contemporary Cultural Studies, which is working under the supervision of Professor Hoggart on the problems of the ordinary man's reading. Throughout the world—in France, Germany, Belgium, the United States, Japan and the socialist countries—these problems are of the greatest interest not only to publishers and booksellers (which is not surprising), but also to sociologists studying questions of culture and the use of leisure and, even more important, to specialists in literary history and criticism. Therein, in the second half of the twentieth century, lies the new significance of the book.

The mutation occurred rapidly, under the pressure of powerful acceleration factors, of which the War, the establishment of socialist régimes in many book-producing nations, and decolonization and its cultural consequences, were the most important.

The need to furnish abundant cheap reading matter for millions of American soldiers scattered throughout the world was probably what caused the American publisher to become seriously interested in the paperback. Whatever the ideological orientation of a country, the desire to make its national views known abroad stimu-lated large printings and low prices. Overseas cultural centres of the major powers distributed their books in hundreds of thousands of copies. And in the countries where educational advancement was outstripping economic development, only the book for the masses could meet the demand created by the new reading public.

Thus was born the new book which, since 1950, has practically conquered the world—even France, for years set in the firm conviction that, so far as the paper-bound book was concerned, she had nothing to learn from anyone.

The paperback is printed on ordinary, but agreeable, paper, strongly bound in a coloured jacket which is very often illustrated. It is never printed in less than some tens of thousands of copies, and it is seldom sold at more than the equivalent of an hour's wage per volume. It is wide-ranging in its choice of titles: it reprints bestsellers but also publishes original work; it includes the classics, new novels, technical handbooks, scientific works and even reference books, dictionaries and guides. Its intellectual mobility is enormous: while in 1961 it accounted for 14% of the total output of books in the United States, in 1962 it accounted for 31%, and the ratio keeps increasing. It accounts for 25% of books on biography, history, religion, science and technology, for 30% of books on art, business, education, general works, sociology and economics, language, law, medicine and philosophy, and for 46% of all fiction titles.[18] In 1964 there were 30,700 titles available in paperbacks in the United States out of an estimated total of 120,000.

As early as 1960, an exhibition sponsored by the National Book League in London showed 1,000 paperbacks in thirty languages, coming from countries as diverse as Canada, France, the Federal Republic of Germany, Eastern Germany, India, Indonesia, Iran, the Netherlands, Pakistan, Sweden, the Union of Soviet Socialist Republics, the United Kingdom and the United States of America.[19] But this was only a sample, and a few months later it was outdated. A revolution was in progress.

NOTES

[1] One important exception, however, is that of the Semitic languages, in which the root *ktb*, meaning *book*, seems quite unrelated to the material of which the book is made.

[2] For books in ancient times, see the nineteenth-century study by Th. Birt, *Das antike Buchwesen*, 1882, or the standard manual by S. Dahl, *Histoire du livre de l'antiquité à nos jours*, 1933.

[3] *The Mélanges d'histoire économique et sociale* offered as a tribute to Professor Antony Babel, Geneva, 1963, contain (pp. 96-127) an interesting article by M. Stelling Michaud on the international transport of Bolognese legal manuscripts from 1265 to 1320.

[4] The machinery for the publication of university texts is described in the Introduction (pp. 9-13) to the book by L. Febvre and Henri-Jean Martin, *L'Apparition du Livre*, Paris, 1958. Authentic, reliable manuscripts were hired out, under University guarantee, by the 'stationarii' or sworn university booksellers, to students desiring to copy them, or to professional copyists under contract.

[5] Italy began to import paper brought from the Orient by the Arabs in the twelfth century. Paper manufacture in Italy began early in the fourteenth century, but even in the thirteenth century, despite its prohibition by certain chancelleries, paper was already currently used in France and Switzerland.

[6] On the whole of this period of the history of the book, see A. Flocon, *L'Univers des livres*, Paris, 1961, especially Part III: *Les Livres imprimés anciens*.

[7] The perhaps somewhat optimistic estimate of L. Febvre and H.-J. Martin, *op. cit.*, p. 377.

[8] On this question, see David T. Pottinger, *The French Book-trade in the Ancien Régime, 1500-1791*, Harvard, 1958.

[9] According to Richard D. Altick, *The English Common Reader*, Chicago, 1957, pp. 49-50, the printings of these 'best-sellers' never exceeded 4,000 copies, and the average printing was 500 or 1,000. If it was successful, a book had between three and five printings.

[10] To be precise, in 1836, with Emile de Girardin's *La Presse*. In one year, subscriptions to Paris newspapers rose from 70,000 to 200,000 (E. Boivin, *Histoire du journalisme*, Paris, 1949). In the literary field, the effects of large printings were not felt until a little later, between 1840 and 1848.

[11] This is certainly one of the origins of the romantic myth represented by Alfred de Vigny's *La Bouteille à la mer*.

[12] Richard D. Altick, *op. cit.*, p. 301.

[13] George Newnes' Penny Library of Famous Books. See R. D. Altick, *op. cit.*, pp. 314-15.

[14] On the position in France in the mid-nineteenth century, see the invaluable, because unique, work of Charles Nisard, *Histoire des livres populaires ou de la littérature de colportage*, Paris, 1964.

[15] In 1962, printings of British newspapers dropped to 506 per 1,000 inhabitants, Norway and Denmark were at about 350, while Sweden held firm at 462 and Luxembourg at 445.

Among the increases, Japan reached 416 (as against 224 in 1952), and New Zealand climbed slightly, from 365 to 406.

[16] Christian Bernhard Tauchnitz, the nephew of a Leipzig publisher, founded his famous 'Collection of British and American Authors' in 1841; in 100 years, the collection published nearly 6,000 titles. For this story and the history of paperbacks in general, see Part I of Frank L Schick, *The Paperbound Book in America*, New York, 1958.

[17] A 1964 Penguin Books prospectus states, with characteristic smugness, "They are not a product for the masses. Eleven million Penguins sold in the United Kingdom in one year represent only one Penguin bought by one Englishman out of five. The Penguins are made for a (relatively large) minority, a select minority."

[18] *Publishers Weekly* (Philadelphia), vol. 183, No. 3, 21 January 1963, pp. 42-43.

[19] See the article by Desmond Flower, *A Revolution in Publishing*, in *The Times* Supplement on Paperbacks, 19 May 1960, and the article by J. E. Morpurgo, *Paperbacks Across Frontiers*, in *The Library Journal* (New York), 15 January 1961.

Marshall McLuhan

"Remarks" from
Do Books Matter?

Much confusion about the *figure* of the book, past, present and future results from the new *ground* which environs both book and reader today. The printed book is a definitive package that can encode ancient times and be sent to remote destinations. More than electronic information, it submits to the whims of the user. It can be read and re-read in large or small portions, but it always recalls the user to patterns of precision and attention. Unlike radio and phonograph, the book does not provide an environment of information that merges with social scenes and dialogue. As the levels of sound and video images envelop the user, he 'turns off' in order to retain his identity. The first video age presents the example of a generation of literate people who, in various ways, have 'turned off' or gone numb as an involuntary tactic to preserve private individuality. In contrast, the merely tribal man, or pre-literate, would seem to feel no threat to his personal life from the new electronic surround.

If the book can be sent anywhere, as a gift or as a service environment, the paradoxical electric reversal is that it is *the sender who is sent*. This flip, or *chiasmus* of form and function occurs at the level of instant speed, and is characteristic of telephone and radio and video alike. When the *ground* or surround of a service assumes this instant character, the *figure* or the user is transformed. Thus the book does not have its meaning alone. The book in the pre-literate world appears as a magical form of miraculously repeated symbols. To the literate world the book serves a myriad of roles, ornamental and recreative and utilitarian. What is to be the new nature and form of the book against the new electronic surround? What will be the effect of the micro-dot library on books past, present and future? When millions of

SOURCE: Reprinted from Brian Baumfield, Editor, *Do Books Matter?* (Leeds: Morely Books, 1973), "Remarks—Marshall McLuhan," pp. 31-41, by permission of Dunn and Wilson (Leeds) Ltd. Copyright 1973 by the Working Party on Library and Book Trade Relations, H.R.H. The Duke of Edinburgh, McLuhan Associates Ltd., Dr. George Steiner, Professor Asa Briggs, Arthur Garratt, and the Rt. Hon. Richard Crossman.

volumes can be compressed in a match-box space, it is not the book merely, but the library that becomes portable. .

There are many ways in which the book and literate values are, of course, threatened by the mere fact of the electric service environment. The extreme distraction presented by the acoustic and cinematic rivals of the book brings decreasing opportunities for attentive and uninterrupted reading. Beginning with the typewriter, and then the mimeograph, the nature of the book underwent immense change of pattern and use. The typewriter changed the forms of English expression by opening up once more the oral world to the writer of books. Whether it was Henry James dictating interminable sentences to Theodora Bosanquet, or the semi-literate executive giving abrupt letters to a secretary who can spell and compose grammatically, the new services of typing and mimeographing transformed the uses and the character of the printed word. In tracing some of the effects of the printed word on liturgy, James F. White points to a result of the mimeograph:

> A further development considerably affected Protestant worship though not mentioned in any liturgical textbooks. In 1884 a Chicago businessman, A. B. Dick, solved a business need for rapid duplication by inventing a process for stencil duplication. It proved so efficient that he marketed it under the name of "Mimeograph". Gutenberg made it possible to put prayer books in the hands of people; Dick made prayer books obsolete. Prayer books are mostly propers which are hard to locate and confusing to most people. Dick gave each minister his own printing press and a new possibility of printing only what was needed on any specific occasion. Xerox and other processes promise to do the same for hymnals. These developments have simply completed what Gutenberg began, and in worship as elsewhere we are now flooded with printed paper.

> White, New Forms of Worship, p. 28

It would seem clear from this passage that the advantage of always studying any *figure* in relation to its *ground* is that unexpected and unheeded features of both are revealed. It is in Ray Bradbury's 'fantasy' fiction *Fahrenheit 451* that the world ahead is shown to fear the book as the cause of dissension and diversity of opinion and attitude. As such, the book is the enemy of unanimity and happiness, therefore it must be destroyed. To save the book from the furious fireman and the incinerator, numerous individuals volunteer to memorize separate works as a means of perpetuating them to a life beyond the flames. Today there arises the possibility of direct 'brain-printing' of books and data, so that the individual can be equipped instantly with all he need ever know. Such a by-passing of all reading raises many questions about the function of books.

The future of the book raises the question of whether men can ever programme their corporate social lives, in accordance with any civilized pattern, by any other means than that of the printed book? There is no question that people can associate in large numbers without books or training in literary perception. At present, even computers depend on their programming for literate people. The entire use of yes-no 'bit' programming is from the alphabetic modes of Western civilization. But many people look to the computer to by-pass present forms of human action and limitation.

Yet, even the written and printed word, it might be argued, has helped us to surpass ordinary human scale. Eric Havelock's *Preface to Plato* and *Empire and Communication* by Harold Innis have shown us how Western man has shaped himself by the phonetic alphabet and the printing press. Paradoxically, the very individuality achieved by these means has inhibited the study of the effects of technology in the Western world. Having fostered a high degree of private self-awareness by literacy, Western man, unlike Oriental man, has shunned the study of technological impact on his psyche. No Western philosopher has evolved an epistemology of experience or looked into the relation between social and psychic change in regard to man's own artefacts. So, it is only fitting that Western man should be excluded from awareness of the effects of his own actions by the principal effect, namely his own private psyche. That prime product of our own phonetic literacy is the shaping awareness of individual interiority and privacy. Before our time, any approach to study the breaching of this interior life by external technological action has been repulsed by Western man. Since the fifth century B.C., neither Plato nor Aristotle nor any subsequent investigator has regarded the creation of Western individuality by the action of phonetic literacy. Likewise, the effects of any outer technology whatever on the inner life of man have been avoided until the electric age.

But today the electronic effects are so massive that they cannot be ignored. Students such as Eric Havelock and Harold Innis have looked into the matter and found the personal transformations by technology to be quite demonstrable. Writing or printing or broadcasting constitute new service environments that transform entire populations. And whereas private, Western man shuns and deplores the invasion of his privacy by the historian or by the psychologist, the tribal or corporate man feels no such reluctance in checking the psychic and social effects of technology. He feels no such 'compunctious workings of nature' as does the civilized man. The Oriental societies have always been eager to know the effects of any technical innovation on their psychic lives, if only in order to suppress such innovation. Western private man prefers to say 'Let's try it and see what happens'.

The future of the book is inclusive. The book is not moving towards an Omega point but is actually in the process of rehearsing and re-enacting all the roles it has ever played; for new graphics and new printing processes invite the simultaneous use of a great diversity of effects. *Poésie concrète* has inspired many new uses of older printing methods and has called for the invention of new print and paper surfaces. Photoprinting permits the imposition of letters on and through many materials. Print can be moved through liquids and impressed upon fabrics, or it can be broadcast by TV and printed out on plastic sheets in the home or study or office. Thus the current range of book production varies from the cultivation of the art of the illumination of manuscripts, and the revival of hand-presses, to the full restoration of ancient manuscripts by papyrologists and photographic reproduction. Taking Xerography alone, we find the book world confronted with an image of itself that is completely revolutionary. The age of electric technology is the obverse of industrial and mechanical procedure in being primarily concerned with process rather than product, with effects rather than 'content'.

In the present age of ecology it is not easy to write of the future of the book apart from the effects of the book, for ecology is concerned with anticipating effects with causes. In order to programme any situation it is necessary to know exactly what components are congruous and which ones are incongruous with the intended effect. The printed book has a very different meaning and effect even for different age groups in our Western world. It certainly has a very different effect in the Orient from its effect in the West. Today, for example, the meaning of the book for young people in their TV environment is exotic indeed. The printed book, by its stress on intense visual culture, is the means of detachment and civilized objectivity in a world of profound sensuous involvement. The printed book is thus the only available means of developing habits of private initiative and private goals and objectives in the electric age. These characteristics do not develop in the cultural milieu of electric sound and information, for the acoustic world, like the 'auditory imagination' defined by T. S. Eliot, is not private nor civilized but tribal and collective.

The book has always been the vortex of many arts and technologies, including speech and mime and pictorial elaboration. At first, the printed book seemed to have excluded much of the richness of the manuscript. At first, many buyers of printed books took them to the scriptorium to have them copied out by hand. For one thing, the printed or mass-produced book discouraged reading aloud, and reading aloud had been the practice of many centuries. Swift, silent scanning is a very different experience from manuscript perusal with its acoustic invitation to savour words and phrases in many-levelled resonance. Silent reading has had many consequences for readers and writers alike, and it is a phase of print technology which may be disappearing.

Gutenberg had, in effect, made every man a reader. Today, Xerox and other forms of reprography tend to make every man a publisher. This massive reversal has, for one of its consequences, elitism. The nature of the mass-production of uniform volumes certainly did not foster elites but, rather habits of universal reading. Paradoxically, when there are many readers, the author can wield great private power, whereas small reading elites may exert large corporate power.

Today Xerox has brought about many reversals in the relation of publics and writers, and these changes help not only to see the past and present, but also the future of the book. For example, Xerox extends the function of the typewriter almost to the point where the secret, personal memo is moved into the public domain, as with the Pentagon Papers. When notes for briefing individuals or groups are first typed and then Xeroxed, it is as if a private manuscript were put in the hands of the general reader. The typewriter plus photocopying thus, unexpectedly, restore many of the features of confidential hand-written records. Contemporary dialogue in committees depends very much on this new Xerox service; but the very public character of the service is difficult to restrict. The result is that confidential briefing is now beginning to take an oral rather than a written form. It seems useful to consider the impact of Xerox if only because it illustrates how profoundly one technology can alter traditional patterns of relation between writing and speaking.

To write about the present of the book, with a keen eye on the changing *ground* for the book as *figure*, is to realize how many new forms the book has assumed even in our time. In all patterns, when the *ground* changes, the *figure* too is altered by the new interface. When the cinema, and gramophone, and radio, and TV became new environmental services, the traditional book began to be read by a completely different kind of public. If Gutenberg created a new kind of human being with new perception and new outlook and new goals, the electric age of radio and video has perhaps restored a public with many of the oral habits of the pre-Gutenberg time.

Had anyone asked about the future of the book in the fifth century B.C., when Plato was beginning his war against the poetic establishment and its rigorously trained rhapsodes, there would have been as much confusion and uncertainty as now. The time when the world of Nature would appear as an extension of the glorified art of the scribe lay ahead. For Plotinus the stars are 'Like letters forever being written in the sky, or like letters written once and for all and forever moving'. Concerning the seer, Plotinus says that his art is 'to read the written characters of Nature, which reveal order and law'. Yet, strangely, in ancient Greece 'there is hardly any idea of the sacredness of the book, as there is no privileged priestly caste of scribes'. (Curtius, *European Literature and the Latin Middle Ages*, p. 304)

Reading and writing were assigned to slaves in ancient Greece, and it was the Romans who promoted the book to a place of dignity. But essentially:

> It was through Christianity that the book received its highest consecration. . . . Not only at its first appearance but also through its entire early period, Christianity kept producing new sacred writings. . .
>
> (Curtius, p. 310)

It was the elucidation of these writings that called forth encyclopaedic programmes of learning and scholarship which drew as freely on the page of Nature as on the *sacra pagina* of Revelation.

Throughout the middle ages the metaphor of the Book of Nature dominated science. The business of the scientist was to establish the text and its interpretation by intensive contemplation, even as Adam had done in the Garden where his work had been the naming of creatures. Unexpectedly, the massive and ancient trope of the Book of Creatures ended with printing. It became old cliché. What would a sage have said in the early Gutenberg time if asked to predict the future of the book? How would Erasmus or Cervantes have answered this question just at a time when the printed book was opening new vistas of reputation and influence to writers? A century later, Francis Quarles (1592-1644) could still play with the idea of the book of nature in a merely decorative way:

> The world's a book in folio, printed all
> With God's great works in letters capital:
> Each creature is a page; and each effect
> A fair character, void of all defect.
>
> (Curtius, p. 323)

Shakespeare had still found vitality in the trope of *The Book of Nature* as in *As You*

Like It (II, i) where the banished Duke finds the voices of nature:

> And this our life except from public haunt,
> Finds tongues in trees, books in the running brooks,
> Sermons in stones, and good in everything.

It was Mallarmé, the symbolist, who proclaimed that 'the world exists to end in a book'. His perception complements and also reverses the ancient and medieval tropes of the Book of Nature by assuming that in both the industrial and electric ages Nature is superseded by art. Thus the future of the book is nothing less than to be the means of surpassing Nature itself. The material world, as it were, is to be etherealized and encapsulated in a book whose characters will possess all the formulas for the knowledge and recreation of Being. Such was the ambition of James Joyce whose *Finnegans Wake* is a symbolist *Summa* involving all creatures whatever. Joyce embraces both art and artefact in his encyclopedia of creatures, encompassing his task by means of language alone.

Taking the book in the more mundane sense of a printed package, it can have as many incarnations as it can find new techniques to wed. I have already alluded to the power of Xerox to transform the reader into publisher. Indeed, a prominent American publisher, William Jovanovich, has written about the subject of how reader and writer and publisher switch roles today:

> William Saroyan wrote me from Paris: "I seem to have the notion that anything anybody writes has got to be published—so that the writer can begin to feel better, I suppose. . .".
> I replied: "Your idea that anybody who writes should be able to be published may, in fact, come true, Xerography is a process that can make this possible, but whether it will make people feel better I cannot surmise, unless they happen also to be Xerox shareholders. Certainly, if publishing becomes universal, and if it is regarded as a kind of civil right, or a kind of public requital, then our concept of literary property must change. Everything will be published and it will belong to everybody—power to the people. There is nothing illogical in your idea. If everyone finds a publisher, he will then find a reader, maybe just one reader—the publisher himself. Of course, writers want lots of readers, but this desire will be less and less fulfilled as there are more and more writers. Quantity declines as specialization declines. Eventually, every man will become at once a writer, publisher, librarian, and critic—the literary professions will disappear as a single man undertakes all the literary roles."
>
> W. Jovanovich,
> 'The Universal Xerox Life Compiler Machine' in
> *American Scholar* (p. 249)

In the light of this new publishing technology, it is less surprising to hear the alarm in the voice of Jean-Paul Sartre who had already anticipated the Jovanovich report in *What is Literature?*

> From this point of view, the situation of the writer has never been so paradoxical. It seems to be made up of the most contradictory characteristics. On the asset side, brilliant appearances, vast possibilities; on the whole, an enviable way of life. On the debit side, only this: that literature is dying. Not that talent or good will is lacking, but it has no longer anything to do in contemporary society. At the very moment that we are

discovering the importance of *praxis*, at the moment that we are beginning to have some notion of what a *total* literature might be, our public collapses and disappears. We no longer know—literally—for whom to write.

(p. 241)

With Xerox, publishing enters on new courses in a way that is reminiscent of the fantasies entertained by early printed writers such as Cervantes, Rabelais and Montaigne. I would like to conclude this essay with some observations that the printed book inspired in Montaigne in the sixteenth century. From his wonder and aspirations in that early printing time, we may well derive some assurance to begin anew the exploration of the present when the tape-recorder and the video cassette afford the writer new roles and new publics for the published word. When the book and its author can mount the back of another medium like radio or TV or satellite, the scale of the operation both in time and in space, seems to abolish the difference between the microscopic and the macroscopic:

> Amusing notion: many things that I would not want to tell anyone, I tell the public; and for my most secret knowledge and thoughts I send my most faithful friends to a bookseller's shop. . .
>
> *Montaigne:* A *Biography*
> Donald M. Frame—p. 82

If Erasmus, or More, or Tyndale had been asked about the future of the book, could they possibly have imagined that it was to become the means of intense inward investigation of the private psyche on one hand, and the creation of huge reading publics on the other hand? The interplay of these two factors created in the mind of Montaigne a new feeling of moral obligation:

> I owe a complete portrait of myself to the public. The wisdom of my lesson is wholly in truth, in freedom, in reality. . . of which propriety and ceremony are daughters, but bastard daughters.
>
> (Frame—p. 291)

He is saying here that the 'self' demanded by the relevation of the printed form throws into the discard all traditional decorum and propriety. What is called for is the minute realism of self-study:

> He studies himself more than any other subject; that is his metaphysics and his physics. "I would rather be an authority on myself than on Cicero. In the experience I have of myself I find enough to make me wise, if I were a good scholar." Fortune has placed him too low to keep a record of his life by his actions, he keeps it by his thoughts. He makes no claim to be learning: "I speak ignorance pompously and opulently, and speak knowledge meagrely and piteously."
>
> (Frame—p. 253)

By the same token, if print drove Montaigne to minute self-investigation and self-portrayal, may we not expect the book of the electric age to turn this perspective on patterns to corporate human energy and association? The video cassette offers an immediate opportunity for the reader and the author to enter into a totally new relationship. The reader will be given an opportunity to share the creative process in a new way, indicating that the book is on the verge of totally new developments.

Douglas C. McMurtrie

The Spread of Printing in America

The spread of printing throughout the enormous areas of the two Americas presents a picture altogether different from that of the propagation of the art in Europe. In the Old World, printing developed and spread in communities which had each its background of centuries of culture. Across the Atlantic, on the other hand, printing became one of the implements of implanting and fostering the cultural heritage of European civilization in environments that were utterly new and strange. In the Americas the press accompanied the cross and the sword, the ax and the plow, in the world's most magnificent pioneering adventure.

Something has already been said about the first coming of the press in America and its establishment in Mexico and later in Peru before the close of the sixteenth century. And we have also noted the first appearance of printing in English-speaking America a full century after Juan Pablos began work as a printer in New Spain. Of the further spread of printing in North America no more than a brief survey can be offered here.

Nearly fifty years after the first establishment of the press in Massachusetts, William Bradford, a printer from London, came to Philadelphia and there began to print in 1685 under the auspices of the Society of Friends, or Quakers, headed by William Penn. In the same year another English printer, William Nuthead, set up his press at Saint Mary's City, in Maryland, after a futile attempt three years earlier to work at his craft in Virginia. At the time, the governmental authorities in Virginia resolutely forbade printing of any kind in that dominion. In Pennsylvania there was no ban against printing, but its use was so hedged about with official regulations and limitations that William Bradford was often in trouble with the authorities. The first

SOURCE: Reprinted from Douglas C. McMurtrie, *The Book: The Story of Printing and Bookmaking*, Third revised edition (New York: Oxford University Press, 1943), Chapter XXXI, "The Spread of Printing in America," pp. 435-450, by permission of the publisher. Copyright 1943 by Douglas C. McMurtrie, renewed 1971 by Helen M. Hogsdon.

product of his press was a humble almanac for the year 1686, but in it occurred the term "Lord Penn," which the provincial council found so offensive that it reprimanded the printer and gave him strict instructions as to what he might or might not print.

After recurring conflicts with the authorities Bradford in 1692 printed a pamphlet for George Keith, a Quaker who at the time had come under the disapproval of the Society of Friends. The printer was arrested and imprisoned, together with several others involved in producing and distributing the offending pamphlet. Bradford appealed to Governor Benjamin Fletcher, who held the dual position of governor of New York and also of Pennsylvania. Fletcher disposed of the case quite simply by appointing Bradford the royal printer at New York. William Bradford, therefore, hurriedly departing from Philadelphia, became the first printer in the province of New York in 1693.

Philadelphia's outstanding claim to fame in the history of printing in colonial America is that that city was the home for nearly seventy years of the immortal Benjamin Franklin. Philadelphia was also the focal point of the American Revolution, and the printers of that city, on both sides of the controversy, made important contributions to the history of the momentous struggle between the colonists and the mother country. Among Philadelphia's typographic distinctions is also the fact that in that city was printed the first American edition of the Bible in English, produced in 1782 from the press of Robert Aitken. It might further be noted that the large German immigration to Pennsylvania resulted in the development, near Philadelphia, of an important German-language press in that colony, beginning in 1738.

In Maryland the printing career of William Nuthead was brief and unimportant except for the fact that he was the first to set up a press in that colony. He died in 1695 and was succeeded by his widow, Dinah—the first instance in America of a woman being in complete charge of a printing office. She was almost completely illiterate, however, and had little success with the printing business, which she relinquished in 1696. The first really successful printer to work in Maryland was William Parks, from Ludlow, in England, who printed at Annapolis for ten or eleven years beginning in 1726. In 1730 he set up a branch office at Williamsburg, Virginia, thus becoming the first printer actually to operate a printing plant in the Old Dominion. In 1737 he gave up his Annapolis office entirely and printed in Virginia until his death in 1750.

Parks was succeeded at Annapolis by Jonas Green, a grandson of that Samuel Green of Cambridge, Massachusetts, whose descendants appear in American printing history throughout two centuries. Green began to print in Maryland in 1739 and died there in 1767. His widow, three of his sons, and a grandson continued until 1839 the business which he had founded.

Another outstanding figure in the history of the American press was William Goddard, who set up a press in Baltimore in 1773 after a number of years of experience as a printer in Providence, Rhode Island, and in Philadelphia. Goddard was an ardent patriot and sensed the inevitably approaching conflict between the American colonies and Great Britain. In 1774 he put his Baltimore printing enterprise into the competent hands of his sister, Mary Katherine Goddard, and devoted all

THE

HOLY BIBLE,

Containing the OLD and NEW

TESTAMENTS:

Newly tranflated out of the

ORIGINAL TONGUES;

And with the former

TRANSLATIONS

Diligently compared and revifed.

PHILADELPHIA:

PRINTED AND SOLD BY R. AITKEN, AT POPE'S
HEAD, THREE DOORS ABOVE THE COFFEE
HOUSE, IN MARKET STREET.
M.DCC.LXXXII.

TITLE PAGE OF THE FIRST AMERICAN
EDITION OF THE BIBLE IN ENGLISH.

his time and energy to the creation of an American postal system which should take the place of the inefficient British colonial postal service. Though his "American Post Office on constitutional principles" was adopted by the Continental Congress in 1775 as the official postal system of the new government, Goddard's two years of intensive work and the "Goddard post offices" in operation from Maine to Georgia brought almost no further official recognition to the creator of what has since become the United States postal service.

In New York, William Bradford from 1693 until his retirement from active work in 1744 made for himself an enviable reputation as a printer and as a citizen. In 1725 he began the printing and publication of the *New-York Gazette*. Andrew Bradford, one of his two sons, went to Philadelphia and established a successful printing business which was continued by his nephew and foster son, William Bradford. William's son and grandson maintained the tradition of the Bradfords as printers in Philadelphia until 1813.

The outstanding event in the history of the press in colonial New York was the famous trial of John Peter Zenger which established the principle of the freedom of the press in British North America. Zenger, an apprentice and later a partner of the pioneer William Bradford, was the printer and nominally the publisher in 1733 of the *New-York Weekly Journal*, which published some covert attacks on the administration of the province and particularly on William Cosby, the highly unpopular governor. For one of these publications the governor commanded that Zenger be imprisoned, although the grand jury had refused to return an indictment against the printer for libel. At the trial of the prisoner, in August, 1735, the defense was conducted by Andrew Hamilton, a venerable attorney of high reputation from Philadelphia. In spite of a packed court, the defendant was acquitted with a verdict which established for the first time the legal principle that in cases of libel the jury should be the judges of both the law and the facts. This marked an important step forward in the fight for the complete freedom of the press, which almost since the first introduction of printing had been sternly limited in England and elsewhere.

In Connecticut the printing press first made its appearance in 1709, when Thomas Short arrived in New London from Boston and began to print the official documents of the Connecticut colonial government. For thirty years the laws, proclamations, and other official matters had been printed for Connecticut by Samuel Green in Cambridge or by Samuel's son Bartholomew in Boston. Short was a connection by marriage with the Green family and probably a member of Bartholomew's household. But the first Connecticut printer died in 1712, and the colony again applied to the Greens for help. This time Timothy Green, the younger brother of Bartholomew, answered the call in 1714. He and at least ten of his direct descendants printed in Connecticut for over a century.

William Bradford, who introduced printing in Pennsylvania and later in New York, was also the first to operate a press in New Jersey, where he printed a quantity of the colony's paper money and also an issue of the New Jersey laws at Perth Amboy in 1723. For some time before and after this date, Bradford printed for New Jersey in his New York shop. About 1728 Samuel Keimer, of Philadelphia, with a young man named Benjamin Franklin in his employ, set up a press in Burlington to print New Jersey's currency and also the current laws of the colony. But the first permanent press in New Jersey was not put in operation until about 1754, when James Parker began to print at Woodbridge, his birthplace, after having worked for ten years or so in the city of New York.

After New Jersey, the next of the American colonies to welcome the press was Rhode Island, where the first printer was James Franklin, older brother and one-time master in the printing trade of Benjamin Franklin. James was possibly influenced by the unfriendly attitude of the Boston authorities in his removal from that city to Newport, where he set up shop in 1727. He died there in 1735, leaving his business to his widow, Ann Smith Franklin, who carried it on successfully for nearly thirty years. In her conduct of the printing office Ann Franklin was assisted by her son and two daughters, all of whom had been trained as printers. The son, James Franklin, Jr., after an apprenticeship in Philadelphia under his distinguished uncle Benjamin, returned to Newport when he came of age and became his mother's partner.

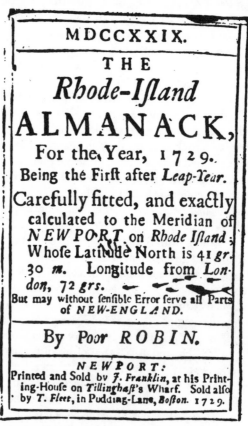

TITLE PAGE OF AN ALMANAC
PRINTED BY JAMES FRANKLIN, 1729.

Historically important among the early printers of Rhode Island was William Goddard. After an apprenticeship under James Parker in New Haven and New York, Goddard set up the first press in the town of Providence in 1762. In this enterprise he was assisted as a business partner by his mother, Sarah Updike Goddard. His career took him later to Philadelphia and finally to Baltimore. His part in the creation of the American postal system has already been mentioned, but it should also be noted that as a craftsman he was distinguished by the quality of his work, his typographic taste and skill being markedly superior to the then prevailing standards of American printing.

The resolute opposition of Virginia's government to the establishment of printing in that colony was not overcome until 1730, when William Parks began to print at Williamsburg. Parks was a good printer, with an intelligent interest not only in typography but also in literature. It is interesting to note that one of the very first things he printed at Williamsburg was a sixteen-page pamphlet containing *Typographia. An Ode, on Printing*, written by a local scholar and "occasion'd by the setting up a Printing Press in Williamsburg"—the earliest American appreciation of the press.

As early as 1722 the province of South Carolina began to make efforts to procure a printer to print its laws, but without success until 1731, when a bonus of £1,000—albeit in colonial currency—induced not one printer but three to move to Charleston and compete for the promised position of official printer. The three were George Webb, Thomas Whitmarsh, and Eleazer Phillips, Jr. Until recent years it was impossible to say which of the three was actually the first to print in South Carolina. But in 1932 the writer was fortunate enough to locate in the Public Record Office, London, the evidence which seems to settle the question. It is a printed document dated November 4, 1731, and bearing the imprint "Charles Town, Printed by George Webb." At the same time and place was also located another document with the imprint of Whitmarsh, but dated November 27, 1731.

Webb and Phillips, however, left but little trace in the records of South Carolina printing. Phillips is thought to have died in an epidemic which ravaged Charleston in 1732, and Webb may have died at the same time. Whitmarsh was left in command of the field. He had gone to Charleston as a partner of Benjamin Franklin, for whom he had worked in Philadelphia. When he died in 1733, he was succeeded as Franklin's Charleston partner by Lewis Timothy. Timothy, with his widow Elizabeth, his son Peter, his daughter-in-law Ann, and his grandson Benjamin Franklin Timothy, formed an influential dynasty of printers which continued until 1802.

South Carolina was predominantly an agricultural province with few centers which could be called in any sense urban. In that region, therefore, the press developed but slowly, and hardly at all outside of Charleston before the end of the century. For the same reasons printing was late in finding a foothold in the neighboring province of North Carolina. Not until 1749 did James Davis move to New Bern, probably from Virginia, and set up his press in response to the government's urgent need of someone to print its laws. He continued to work there until his death in 1785. Printing in this slowly developing province was uneventful and was confined for many years to a few small towns on or near the seacoast.

THE

R I G H T S

OF

COLONIES

EXAMINED.

PUBLISHED BY AUTHORITY.

PROVIDENCE:

PRINTED BY *WILLIAM GODDARD.*

M.DCC.LXV.

A TITLE PAGE BY WILLIAM GODDARD, PROVIDENCE, 1765.

Outside the present borders of the United States, British North America had no press until 1752. In that year John Bushell, from Boston, moved his printing shop to Halifax, Nova Scotia, a town which had just been founded. The prime mover of the Halifax printing venture was Bartholomew Green, grandson of the Cambridge printer, who had the daring to try his fortunes in the Nova Scotian wilderness at the age of fifty. But he died in 1751, a few weeks after his arrival in Halifax, and his mantle of pioneering fell on the shoulders of Bushell, a Boston associate, whose principal claim to fame is that he thus became the first printer in Canada.

New Hampshire had no press until 1756, when Daniel Fowle, disgusted with the repressions of the authorities in Boston, departed from that city and set up shop in Portsmouth. In little Delaware, which was economically hardly more than a dependency of Pennsylvania, James Adams, at Wilmington in 1761, was the first to establish a press. And in far-off Georgia, the last of the colonies to be established, no printing was done until 1763—more than a hundred years after the introduction of printing in Massachusetts. James Johnston, a recent immigrant from Scotland, was induced to procure the necessary equipment with which, in 1763, he set up a press at Savannah, primarily to serve the provincial government.

In 1764 William Brown and Thomas Gilmore, both from Philadelphia, ventured to seek their fortunes far to the north and became the first fully authenticated printers in Quebec. There is some reason to suspect, however, that Bishop Pontbriand, the last ecclesiastical head of the Quebec diocese under the French regime, may have had a small private press there as early as 1759. It was under distinctly French auspices that printing began in Louisiana in 1764 with Denis Braud as the pioneer craftsman. One of the very first things which Braud printed was a proclamation of the French king giving notice that Louisiana had been ceded to Spain.

The struggle of the American Revolution interrupted the spread of printing to new regions, but in 1780, as the war was drawing to its close, Judah Padock Spooner, a connection by marriage with the famous Green family, took the press to the new state of Vermont, where he set up shop at Westminster. The Revolution was over before Benjamin Titcomb, at Falmouth (now Portland) in 1785, became the first printer in Maine, which was then a "district" under the jurisdiction of Massachusetts.

Characteristic of the development of printing in the British American colonies is the fact that the pioneer printers, with very few exceptions, sought to support themselves by the printing of newspapers. In practically every case, too, the compelling motive for the introduction of printing into the different provinces was the urgent necessity of having the laws available in printed form. There was naturally much competition for the appointment as "royal printer," or "king's printer," or "printer of the crown," as such appointment gave the printer a certain official status as well as assuring him a fairly definite income. At centers such as Boston, New York, and Philadelphia, the printing industry at the onset of the Revolution had developed into considerable importance, and the local presses were supplying a consequential part of their communities' cultural needs for reading matter.

The printers for the most part were their own publishers, although the trade of the publisher, whose books were printed for him, was beginning to appear. The printing office in many a town was also the local bookstore, and printers in many places regularly advertised the books which they had imported, from England or from the larger American centers, as well as the books and pamphlets which they themselves had printed.

Under British rule the colonial governments held the press under rather strict control and were quick to "crack down" on any printer who transgressed the limits of the freedom allowed him. The records contain innumerable instances of printers who were reprimanded, fined, or even imprisoned for daring to print something of which the authorities did not approve or for which the requisite permission had not been obtained. The colonial newspapers, therefore, were rather colorless affairs, their columns containing mostly "intelligence" from abroad, with almost no local news and (before the dissension with the mother country became acute) with barely a trace of real editorial opinion—particularly of opinion critical of the government.

But after independence had been achieved, restrictions upon the press were almost entirely removed. Furthermore, the establishment of the new government of the United States opened up for settlement a vast area of land in the "western country," and a new era of American pioneering began. A mass migration was soon under way, and the press was swept with it into almost uncharted regions beyond the Alleghanies.

Hugh Henry Breckenridge stood in the little settlement at the confluence of the Monongahela and Alleghany rivers and prophetically said of the site, "Nevertheless, it appeared to me as what would one day be a town of note." He procured two young craftsmen from Philadelphia, John Scull and Joseph Boyd, and backed them in establishing the *Pittsburgh Gazette*. Its first issue appeared on July 29, 1786—a memorable date because it marked the first issue of a press which definitely looked westward for its destiny.

The following year John Bradford, from Virginia, a surveyor by profession, began the *Kentucky Gazette* at Lexington. Bradford's brother, Fielding Bradford, learned what he could of the printing craft in a few months' apprenticeship with John Scull in Pittsburgh, procured a simple printing equipment, and brought it down the Ohio. With such technical aid and advice as they could get from Thomas Parvin, an aged and broken-down craftsman from Philadelphia, the Bradfords launched the press in Kentucky, where for a generation it was to be the principal source of cultural material for the whole western country. In 1791 George Roulstone, a printer from Salem, Massachusetts, who had been working at Fayetteville, North Carolina, with Robert Ferguson as partner, crossed the mountains with his equipment and set up a press at Rogersville, the first in Tennessee. In 1793 William Maxwell, printer and former Revolutionary soldier, after working at his trade for a short time at Lexington, moved across the Ohio and established the first press in Ohio at Cincinnati, publishing on November 9 of that year the initial issue of the *Centinel of the North-Western Territory*.

Growth of the western country was rapid as population poured into it at an amazing rate. By 1804 there was sufficient settlement in the wilds of Indiana to require the service of the press, and Elihu Stout, formerly an employee under John Bradford in Kentucky, introduced printing into that territory at Vincennes, then the seat of territorial government. In 1808 the press crossed the Mississippi River for the first time when Joseph Charless, an Irish printer who had worked in Philadelphia and later in Kentucky at Lexington and Louisville, established the *Missouri Gazette* at the old French settlement of Saint Louis. Printing took root in Michigan in 1809, under the direction of Rev. Gabriel Richard, a courageous and enterprising Catholic missionary priest, who brought James Miller from Utica, New York state, to print textbooks and religious works for him at Detroit. There had been some earlier printing at Detroit, however, the evidence showing that a printer named John McCall had worked there from 1796 to 1805.

Meanwhile, far to the south, the press had been introduced into Florida in 1783 by John Wells and William Charles Wells, loyalist refugees from revolutionary Charleston, who continued at Saint Augustine a newspaper which had earlier been published in the South Carolina town. It cannot be said, however, that the press became an established factor in Florida until 1821, two years after the United States had purchased that territory from Spain. In Mississippi, Andrew Marschalk, a printer who was also an army officer, introduced printing by the operation of a small printing shop at Walnut Hills, near Natchez, about 1798. Marschalk continued his career as a printer in Mississippi for about forty years. In Alabama, in 1807, an unidentified craftsman did the first printing, with types that were "old and much worn" at Wakefield, a site which has since vanished. The earliest Alabama printer whose name is known was P. J. Forster, whose imprint appeared at St. Stephens early in 1811. Later in the same year, Samuel Miller and John B. Hood began a newspaper at Fort Stoddert, a temporary military establishment a few miles above Mobile.

Illinois Territory, set off from Indiana in 1809, had its first capital at Kaskaskia, a settlement on the Mississippi River which has long since disappeared. As no press had as yet been set up in the new territory, the first book of Illinois laws was printed in 1813 by Matthew Duncan at Russellville, Kentucky, the town from which had come Ninian Edwards, territorial governor of Illinois. But in the spring of 1814 the need for a printer in the territory had become so acute that Duncan was induced to remove his shop from Russellville to Kaskaskia and thus became the first printer in Illinois.

By 1830, five new states had been created out of the western wilderness and added to the Union. The population of these states was then served by some two hundred newspapers, while it also provided many other activities for the press in the varied demands of its political, economic, social, and religious life. Up to about this time, most of the migration into the western country had followed the Ohio River or had crossed the mountain passes from Virginia and North Carolina into Tennessee. But there then set in a second wave of migration, mostly from New England and New York, which followed the Mohawk Valley and passed over to the Great Lakes. This northern stream populated Michigan, the northern parts of Ohio, Indiana, and Illinois, and also reached into Wisconsin.

A birdseye view of the spread of the press throughout the region west of the Mississippi is presented in the following dates of the advent of printing in a number of the present states of the Union: Texas, 1817; Iowa, 1836; Minnesota, 1849; Nevada, 1858; Colorado, 1859. The Mormons operated a press at Salt Lake City, Utah, beginning in 1849. In California and in New Mexico, printing began in 1834, in both cases under Mexican auspices. Some crude, amateurish printing has been recorded in California two years or so before the regular establishment of the press there. Oregon had its first press in 1846, Washington in 1852, Arizona in 1859. The zeal of Christian missionaries to the Indians had taken printers, in advance of commercial need for the press, into the present areas of Kansas in 1834, Oklahoma in 1835, and Idaho in 1839. Last of the states to receive the benefits of the press were Montana and Wyoming, in both of which printing began in 1863, and North Dakota, in which the first authenticated printing was done in 1864.

Wherever the settlers went, there too went the pioneer printers, with the materials for publishing their little newspapers, in raw, frontier settlements, far from sources of supplies and beset with all the difficulties and dangers of life at the edge of the wilderness. Truly, these adventurous craftsmen played a notable part in the winning of the West and the making of America!

Joseph Blumenthal

The Printed Book
in the United States

A frontier and colonial society concerned with survival does not produce fine printing. The great printed books which appeared in Europe during the first hundred years after the invention of printing were patterned on magnificent manuscript volumes. Thereafter consciously elegant books were made during periods of civilized leisure, when designers and printers were free to plan them and when buyers existed who had the financial resources and personal inclination to acquire them. It is hardly surprising, therefore, that no American practitioner of international stature appeared in the United States until the last decade of the nineteenth century.

Benjamin Franklin (1706-1790)

The printing done in England and on the Continent during the eighteenth century rubbed off on a few Americans. Benjamin Franklin was an apprenticed journeyman who spent two years in London workshops as a trade compositor. In 1730 at twenty-four years of age he established his own plant in Philadelphia. His financial success during the next twenty years enabled him to retire from active business in his early forties and to devote his wide-ranging mind to a variety of other interests. We know that later he would be enamored of the books of Baskerville, Bodoni, and Didot, but the minutiae of fine bookmaking were not for him. Probably his best volume, said

SOURCE: Reprinted from *Art of the Printed Book, 1455-1955: Masterpieces of Typography Through Five Centuries from the Collections of the Pierpont Morgan Library, New York* With an Essay by Joseph Blumenthal (New York: The Pierpont Morgan Library, 1973), "The Printed Book in the United States," pp. 44-51, by permission of the publisher. Copyright 1973 by The Pierpont Morgan Library.

to be his own favorite, is Cicero's *Cato Major,* Philadelphia, 1744, in Caslon type he had imported and with a two-color title page. It is not more than a workmanlike job, of special interest, too, because the translation was made by the Chief Justice of the State of Pennsylvania. In his foreword, "Printer to the Reader," Franklin concludes with, ". . . my hearty Wish that this first Translation of a *Classic* in this *Western World*, may be followed with many others, performed with equal Judgment and Success; and be a happy Omen that *Philadelphia* shall become the Seat of the *American* muses."

Isaiah Thomas (1749-1831)

Isaiah Thomas, another successful colonial printer and publisher, established a workshop in Massachusetts in 1770 which grew into twelve presses, branch offices, a bindery, and a paper mill. His extensive publishing included the first American illustrated folio Bible in 1791, the first Greek grammar, the first American dictionary, a type specimen book, as well as newspapers and miscellaneous printing. Most remarkable, he spent the later years of his life writing a scholarly book in two volumes, *The History of Printing in America* (1810), which also included the European scene from the Gutenberg invention. If he was not an innovative craftsman, he does have the distinction of being the first of several scholar-printers in the United States. He founded the American Antiquarian Society in Worcester, Massachusetts, which still thrives.

In 1807 Fry and Kammerer in Philadelphia printed a deluxe quarto volume, *The Columbiad,* a long epic poem by Joel Barlow. The typographic arrangement and the type cast by Binny and Ronaldson, the first successful typefounders in America, were closely patterned on the work of Bulmer in London. *The Columbiad* is an isolated accomplishment, worthy of some notice in view of the limited resources then available on this continent. As the nineteenth century advanced, the separation of printers and publishers grew quite complete. New York had become the new center of the book trade with Harper, Scribner, Putnam, Appleton, and other publishers.

Theodore Low De Vinne (1828-1914)

Theodore Low De Vinne, the cultivated son of a Methodist minister, entered the printing trade as an apprentice compositor in 1843, at fourteen years of age, when books and magazines were still set by hand. In his long career as a highly successful entrepreneur, he welcomed the great changes involved in the new technological improvements. At his death in 1914, his six-story building in New York housed his modern, mechanized plant. De Vinne printed the *Century* magazine with its own type series, the *Century Dictionary, Harper's,* and *Scribner's* magazines, to all of which he gave clean, conservative, and workmanlike typographic dress. De Vinne was not a memorable designer, but he maintained high standards in his undertakings and had profound respect for the best traditions of his calling. He accumulated a library of six thousand volumes, including almost a hundred incunabula which he used in the writing of his highly respected *The Invention of Printing*, published in 1876. Stanley Morison wrote of this book as recently as 1963 that "De Vinne's original scholarship has still to be superseded." Among other books, De Vinne completed a four-volume manual, *The Practice of Typography*, which reflects his own thorough research and experience. De Vinne, a man of affairs who paid homage to the civilizing influence of the printed book, received honorary degrees from Columbia and Yale universities. He was a founder in 1884 and an early president of The Grolier Club whose purpose was "the literary study and promotion of the arts entering into the production of books."

Ground swells in the last quarter of the nineteenth century could not be seen for their true worth until much later. In 1870 the great museums of art were founded in New York and Boston. A fresh awareness of the arts and crafts cracked the heavy crust of pervasive industrialism. Soon after a group of prominent New Yorkers formed The Grolier Club in New York, The Club of Odd Volumes was established in Boston. That center of American culture drew together in the 1890's an extraordinary confluence of young men: printers, designers, and publishers with typographic convictions and talents. Out of this group came Daniel Berkeley Updike, a scholar-printer, and Bruce Rogers, a designer, both of whom would for the first time exert an important American influence on the history and development of the printed book.

Thomas Bird Mosher (1852-1923)

Thomas Bird Mosher of Portland, Maine, starting in 1891 and continuing until 1923, published some four hundred titles, modest in format, price, and design, with forthright charm—the first American to sustain a consistent program of fine book-making. He designed his books, then supervised production in local printing shops. Mosher early expressed the wish that someday he would publish books "that would be truly beautiful as well as within the reach of those who appreciate beauty but who cannot possess it at exorbitant rates." He took advantage of the lack of copyright laws to publish without royalties English authors whose work, he claimed, would not otherwise have become available in the United States. He was accused of piracy, but some of his authors did not object. In 1892 George Meredith wrote to Mosher: "Sir, a handsome pirate is always half pardoned, and in this case he has broken only the upper laws. I shall receive with pleasure the copy of 'Modern Love' which you propose to send. I have it much at heart that works of mine should be read by Americans."

Daniel Berkeley Updike (1860-1941)

Daniel Berkeley Updike, son of a prominent New England family, started as an errand boy in 1880 at Houghton, Mifflin & Company, publishers of Emerson,

Thoreau, and Hawthorne. The publishers were the owners of The Riverside Press, a book printing plant with high standards. After a dozen years at the Press, the young Updike decided rather reluctantly, as he tells in his own Notes on the Press and Its Work, to set out for himself. At first he tried to place work he had designed with established printers. Because this lack of direct control over production did not satisfy him, he established his own plant, The Merrymount Press, in 1893. As a printer he succeeded with great style. In his Notes he wrote with classic understatement: "Perhaps the reason that I survived, in spite of mistakes, was that a simple idea had got hold of me—to make work better for its purpose than was commonly thought worthwhile, and by having one's own establishment, to be free to do so."

Updike gave stature, dignity, scholarship, and a lofty excellence to the printing shop. He came from an exceptional background. His plant, his large library, his customers, his work, reflected his inheritance. His early work showed some Kelmscott influence, but Updike soon developed his own style, with deference to the clarity of the English eighteenth century. His work had structure and depth. Updike chose his type and ornament with discrimination at a time when sources were few and scattered. He commissioned Bertram Grosvenor Goodhue, an architect (who later designed "Cheltenham") to design the "Merrymount" type, which was not too successful. Updike's customers were universities, publishing houses, collectors, book clubs, cultural institutions, and the church. His most famous book is The Book of Common Prayer, 1930, to which he brought mature typographic judgment, an intense personal theology, and a profound knowledge of liturgical printing.

Updike's greatest contribution is to the scholarship of printing. His most lasting monument is his enormously important, two-volume work, Printing Types, Their History, Forms, and Use, which grew out of a series of lectures at Harvard University, published by the Harvard University Press in 1922 and since reprinted. It is the keystone to any study in the history of printing.

John Henry Nash (1871-1947); Grabhorn Press (fl. 1919-1965)

A regional and cosmopolitan culture on the American Pacific Coast during the first half of the twentieth century produced a group of literate, skillful printers, loyally supported by book clubs in San Francisco and Los Angeles, by the Huntington Library in San Marino, and by collectors. The earliest designer-printer of note was the flamboyant John Henry Nash whose impressive folios had a large following and who printed elaborate catalogues for some of the wealthiest collectors then resident in California. Nash's four-volume Dante, 1929, is his most respected work. The books of Edwin and Robert Grabhorn at their Grabhorn Press in San Francisco were widely collected over a forty-year career of high-spirited, colorful workmanship. Their folio John Maundevile, 1928, with woodcuts by Valenti Angelo, was printed in Rudolf Koch's "Jessen" type, and published by Random House, New York. The Grabhorn Leaves of Grass, 1930, in Goudy's "Newstyle" type is no doubt their best-known work, but the Maundevile is probably more interesting and more "bookish."

Elmer Adler (1884-1961)

Elmer Adler as a young man was the advertising manager for a large family clothing business in Rochester, New York. His contact with promotional printing provoked an intellectual curiosity in the important typographic work of the past, and led to the acquisition of a fine collection of old and contemporary books and prints. The collector then put his interests to a hard test by setting up a press in New York City in 1922—The Pynson Printers—for the production of fine books and ephemera for publishers, collectors, and at least one New York men's furnishing store. During the eighteen years of its existence The Pynson Printers became a meeting place for the makers and collectors of fine books, where, too, Adler became the chief editor, printer, and publisher of *The Colophon*, a lively magazine for book collectors. Adler's favorite book, certainly his most original work, is Voltaire's *Candide*, 1928, profusely illustrated by Rockwell Kent, set in type designed by Lucien Bernhard.

Dard Hunter (1883-1966)

Dard Hunter, son of a prosperous newspaper publisher in Chillicothe, Ohio, was an American phenomenon. The young Dard was fascinated by paper, pursued its history, and put study into practice by making paper himself, expertly, by hand, on his own equipment. He traveled over the world on visits to surviving handmade paper mills, many in remote corners of the Orient where ancient methods were still practiced, and where he gathered samples which he mounted in his books. Altogether he wrote ten volumes on the history of paper from original research in unexplored areas. His first book, *Old Papermaking*, appeared in 1923. Hunter printed this and subsequent volumes on his own hand press from type he had himself designed and cut, on his own handmade paper. The formats were large, issued in editions of less than two hundred copies. His last personally produced book, and his magnum opus, is *Papermaking by Hand in America*, 1950. Hunter also wrote two books published in trade editions by Alfred A. Knopf, New York: *Papermaking, The History and Technique of an Ancient Craft* in 1947, and a very readable autobiography in 1958, *My Life with Paper*.

Victor Hammer (1882-1967)

Victor Hammer, a man of many gifts—painter, sculptor, architect, typographer, printer—lived and worked in the spirit of the Italian Renaissance. He was born in Vienna where he became a prominent portraitist. He established his press (Stamperia del Santuccio) in Florence and there cut two uncial types, and produced books of a pure, personal craftsmanship, "Ad Maiorem Dei Gloriam." He came to the United States in 1939, to Wells College in Aurora, New York, in the art department. A number of dintinguished hand-press books in "Emerson" type appeared during his nine years in Aurora. Meanwhile he had begun to cut the punches for his new uncial type. In 1948 he joined the faculty of Transylvania College in Lexington, Kentucky, as Professor in Art. Here Hammer's American career continued and blossomed, sustained by devoted associates, and here in 1949 he completed his masterpiece, the Hölderlin poems on his hand press, beautifully set and impeccably printed in his new American Uncial type in an edition of fifty-one copies.

Limitations imposed on this essay have allowed only brief discussion of major historical trends and their makers. Regretfully we must pass over many designers and printers whose work would deserve discussion in a longer review. Chief among these in the East are Will Bradley, Frederic W. Goudy, Carl Purington Rollins, Walter Gillis, Henry W. Kent, William Edwin Rudge, T. M. Cleland, Rudolph Ruzicka, W. A. Dwiggins, and the publisher Alfred A. Knopf. Time is arbitrary, and selections by anthology are inevitably inadequate. Many younger men and women came along during and since the 1920's, and are still at work here and in Europe, but they must be dealt with by other hands when perspectives have become longer and judgments less personal.

Bruce Rogers (1870-1957)

We now approach the end of our historical panorama with Bruce Rogers, born in the American Middle West in 1870, later said by Francis Meynell (and confirmed in a letter to this writer) to have been "the greatest artificer of the book who ever lived." If an artificer employs artful devices, subtle stratagems, and delicate maneuvers, and if these are absorbed into skillful arrangements of type for book design, we will be aware of some of the ingredients that entered into the charm and finish of the Bruce Rogers books.

Soon after graduation from Purdue University, Rogers came to Boston as a free-lance designer for the magazine *Modern Art*. Here he saw Kelmscott books and is quoted by Frederic Warde that "upon seeing Morris's printing, his whole interest in book production became rationalized and intensified. He abandoned the prevalent idea that a book could be made beautiful through the work of an illustrator alone, and determined instead to use that curiosity he had always felt as to type and paper, toward a study of the physical form of printed books." In 1896 Rogers joined The Riverside Press where he designed trade books and book advertisements for the next four years. Then, in the late 'nineties he induced George H. Mifflin, a senior partner at the Press, to establish a special department for the production of limited editions. What a happy combination of personalities and potentialities this was: the proprietor of a solid, conservative business in Cambridge, Massachusetts, who gave full scope to the young designer out of the American cornbelt at the beginning of a new century.

During the next dozen years (1900-1912) Rogers completed sixty editions which set a wholly new approach to book design. Books were done with rare but somehow lighthearted discrimination. Each new title was an adventure down new paths for the designer, as it was for his collectors. Each book was different in design, format, type, paper, printing, and binding. Some were inventive and experimental, some derivative and allusive. Neither Rogers nor Updike had an American tradition on which to build. With scholarly logic they looked to historical sources for their criteria. Updike, a New Englander, naturally found antecedents in English workmanship. Rogers' blithe spirit was more in sympathy with the eloquence of fifteenth-century Venice and the grace and sophistication of sixteenth-century France. But along with tradition, Rogers had developed a style of his own. Here were the beautiful Riverside Press limited editions made in a commercial printing plant, at least a dozen of which were small masterpieces—the work of an "artist-typographer." In his wide-ranging eclecticism Rogers might well be called the first modern book designer, the progenitor of the typographers who have made books since his time.

After sixteen years at The Riverside Press, Rogers became restive. In a letter he said he had "always looked forward to living, for a term of years at least, either in England or the Continent. . . . My present agreement with the Riverside Press expires next year. . . . They pay very well. . . but they give me no leisure except two weeks' vacation yearly. And now leisure for my own pursuits has come to mean more than money to me." A summer in England in 1912 did not provide working opportunities. He then returned to the United States for five rather lean years, with, however, his newly designed and cut "Centaur" type a conspicuous achievement. It was first used in one of his superb books, Maurice de Guérin's *The Centaur*, printed in 1915 in an edition of one hundred and thirty-five copies at the Montague Press, the idealistic printing shop at the Dyke Mill in Massachusetts owned by Carl Purington Rollins, later the influential printer to Yale University.

In 1916 Emery Walker invited Rogers to come to England to form a partnership for the production of fine printing somewhat in the spirit of the Kelmscott and Doves presses. Rogers accepted with keen anticipation and with a commission in his pocket from The Grolier Club to reprint that part of Dürer's *Geometry* which deals with the design of letters for inscriptions. Entitled *On the Just Shaping of Letters*, the edition was completed late in 1917 under formidably trying working conditions in wartime London which B. R., as he came to be known, described in remarkable letters to his friend Henry W. Kent, then Secretary of the Metropolitan Museum of Art in New York. The partnership with Emery Walker soon foundered. There followed, to quote B. R., "a month of starvation in a miserable boarding house on Trumpington Street." He was about to return to the United States when Sydney Cockerell, Director of the Fitzwilliam Museum, formerly secretary to William Morris at the Kelmscott Press, determined to secure Rogers' services for the Cambridge University Press. Despite the gravity of the war, the Syndics appointed Rogers to be Adviser to the Press and to make recommendations for improvement of their books. Rogers soon delivered a lengthy statement which included the frank comment: "I cannot believe that any other printing-house of equal standing can have gone on for so many years with such an inferior equipment of types. . . . They are, in my opinion, bad beyond belief." To the credit of the Syndics the report was adopted and implemented as war and postwar conditions allowed. In 1950, in an official publication, Brooke Crutchley, the eminent University Printer, wrote: "It was the example of Bruce Rogers' painstaking quest for perfection as much as the report itself that was to put new life into the University Press, and it is a pleasure, thirty-three years later, to acknowledge once more the debt that Cambridge, as indeed the whole world, owes to a great craftsman and artist."

Many years had slipped by since Rogers had done the kind of work that could nourish his soul. He returned to the United States in 1919 and assumed duties as an active adviser to the Harvard University Press. Then, fortunately, he met William Edwin Rudge whose new building in Mount Vernon, outside New York City, housed a fine and well-equipped printing establishment. This became Rogers' haven during the prosperous and expansive 'twenties. In B. R.'s own words: "All in all, I spent eight productive years working with Rudge, and no collaboration could have been happier for me. He left me an entirely free hand and unhesitatingly backed up nobly even my most unpromising projects, with new types, papers, equipment—everything— whether they were likely to prove profitable or the reverse." Rogers was fifty years of age when he started with Rudge. During the ensuing eight fruitful years he made about a hundred books, many of which have become part of American typographic history. In 1927 B. R. began to stir the ingredients that became one of his master- pieces. He induced T. E. Lawrence to translate the Odyssey of Homer, but the scholar who had made a reputation for boldness and courage as Lawrence of Arabia expressed fear that his words would not be worthy of Rogers' bookmaking. With this translation under way, the urge came over Rogers to see his English friends again and to roam the English countryside. Besides, the Monotype people wished to cut his Centaur type under his immediate supervision. In 1928 he sailed for England where, during the next four years, he would produce his finest work.

In the First World War many Canadians lost their lives in the Belgian town of Ypres—pronounced "Wipers" by the soldiers. Ten years later the Canadian govern- ment built a memorial chapel where their young had died. The King of England wished to present a lectern Bible worthy of the occasion. But no Bible had been printed in Britain comparable to the Baskerville volume of 1763. The Oxford University Press immediately set out to repair the omission. Bruce Rogers, then resident in London (1928) and recognized as the foremost typographer of his time, was commissioned to design a new folio Bible in the King James Version, in a volume not to exceed twelve hundred and fifty pages. John Johnson, then printer to Oxford University, suggested the Centaur type which was modified to fit. The story of the making of the Bible during its four years in production at the Oxford University Press was told by Rogers in a pamphlet issued by the Monotype Corporation in 1936.

These years in England saw the ultimate flowering of Bruce Rogers' genius. Three books can be chosen from this sojourn as among his best works. They are The Odyssey of Homer, 1932, printed with Emery Walker; Fra Luca de Pacioli, 1933, printed at the Cambridge University Press for The Grolier Club; and that crowning achieve- ment, the Oxford Lectern Bible published in 1935. This writer has yet to be contradicted in having stated that the Oxford Lectern Bible is the most important printed book of the twentieth century.

After returning to his home in New Fairfield, Connecticut, in 1932, a quarter century of life remained to Bruce Rogers. He clung to his *métier* and was responsible for a few fine volumes, especially for the Limited Editions Club of New York. Bruce Rogers' long life spanned great years in the history of the printed book. He began when printing was still within the province of the hand. It is a mark of his genius that he was able to cross the frontier to the area of the machine and to retain artistry and finesse in the transition. In Rogers' command of this fundamental change he showed himself to be a man of his time.

Having looked back to the impressive monuments of five hundred years of book-making, let us glance briefly at our own time and hazard some prophecy for the future. The great and noble folios which graced the libraries of ancestral homes are not relevant to the present way of life. Vast technological changes have already affected the production of books, including those made with esthetic devotion. However, the preservation of human thought has taken many forms since pictures were made on the walls of prehistoric caves and cuneiform strokes were baked into Sumerian clay tablets. A thousand years of the book as we have known it, first written, then printed, are links in the long historic chain of the dissemination of accumulated knowledge. Staggering problems of storage and preservation are dictating great changes. The book in its present form may well continue far into the future. But if not, we can be sure that language and the alphabet will remain the fundamental means of communication; that literature, philosophy, and science will never fail man's restless search; neither will the urge for beauty fade. Whatever its name, whatever its form, something will always exist to uphold the civilized word. "In the beginning was the word." So it will be at the end.

THE PRINTED BOOK
Additional Readings

INVENTION OF PRINTING WITH MOVABLE TYPE

Bühler, Curt; *The Fifteenth Century Book*. Philadelphia: University of Pennsylvania Press, 1960.

Butler, Pierce. *The Origin of Printing in Europe*. Chicago: University of Chicago Press, 1940.

De Vinne, Theodore L. *The Invention of Printing*. New York: Francis Hart, 1877.

Febvre, Lucien, and Martin, Henri-Jean. *The Coming of the Book: The Impact of Printing, 1450-1800*. Atlantic Highlands: Humanities Press, 1976.

Gerulaitis, Leonardas V. *Printing and Publishing in Fifteenth Century Venice*. Chicago: American Library Association, 1976.

Goldschmidt, E. P. *Medieval Texts and Their First Appearance in Print*. London: Bibliographical Society Transactions No. 16, 1943. Reprint. New York: Biblo and Tannen, 1969.

Haebler, Konrad. *Study of Incunabula*. New York: Grolier Club, 1933. Reprint, New York: Kraus Reprints, 1967.

Stillwell, M. B. *The Beginning of the World of Books 1450 to 1470*. New York: Bibliographical Society of America, 1972.

Wilson, Adrian. *The Making of the Nuremberg Chronicle*. Amsterdam: Nico Israel, 1976.

Winship, George Parker. *Gutenberg to Plantin: An Outline of the Early History of Printing*. Cambridge: Harvard University Press, 1926. Reprint. New York: Burt Franklin, 1968.

————. *Printing in the Fifteenth Century*. Philadelphia: University of Pennsylvania Press, 1940.

BOOKS AND PRINTING IN THE RENAISSANCE

Goldschmidt. E. P. *The Printed Book of the Renaissance*. 2d ed. Amsterdam: van Heusden, 1966.

Proctor, Robert. *The Printing of Greek in the Fifteenth Century*. Oxford: Oxford University Press, 1900.

Scholderer, Victor. *Printers and Readers in Italy in the Fifteenth Century*. London: G. Cumberlege, 1949.

BOOKS AND PRINTING IN THE MODERN WORLD

Brown, H. *The Venetian Printing Press, 1469-1800*. New York: G. P. Putnam's Sons, 1891. Reprint, Amsterdam: van Heusden, 1969.

Cave, Roderick. *The Private Press*. London: Faber and Faber, 1971.

Clair, Colin, A *History of European Printing*. New York: Academic Press, 1976.

————. A *History of Printing in Britain*. New York: Oxford University Press, 1966.

Clair, Colin, ed. *The Spread of Printing: A History of Printing Outside Europe in Monographs*. Amsterdam: Vangendt and Company, 1969-1973. [Distributed by Abner Schram.]

Day, Kenneth, ed. *Book Typography, 1815-1965 in Europe and the United States of America*. Chicago: University of Chicago Press, 1966.

Franklin, Colin. *The Private Presses*. Chester Springs: Dufour, 1969.

Jennett, Sean. *Pioneers in Printing*. London: Routledge and Kegan Paul, 1958.

Lewis, John. *Anatomy of Printing: The Influences of Art and History on Design*. New York: Watson-Guptill, 1970.

McLuhan, Marshall. *The Gutenberg Galaxy: The Making of Typographic Man*. Toronto: University of Toronto Press, 1962.

Macrobert, T. M. *Printed Books: A Short Introduction to Fine Typography*. 2d ed. London: Her Majesty's Stationery Office, 1971.

Moran, James, ed. *Printing in the 20th Century–A Penrose Anthology*. New York: Hastings House, 1974.

Morison, Stanley. *Four Centuries of Fine Printing*. 4th ed. New York: Barnes and Noble, 1960.

Ransom, Will. *Private Presses and Their Books*. New York: R. R. Bowker, 1929.

Steinberg, S. H. *Five Hundred Years of Printing*. 3d rev. ed. Baltimore: Penguin, 1974.

Twyman, Michael. *Printing 1770-1970: An Illustrated History of Its Development and Uses in England*. London: Eyre and Spottiswoode, 1970.

BOOKS AND PRINTING IN AMERICA

Blumenthal, Joseph. *The Printed Book in America*. Boston: David Godine, 1977.

Lehmann-Haupt, Hellmut. *The Book in America*. 2d rev. ed. New York: R. R. Bowker, 1951.

McMurtrie, Douglas C. *A History of Printing in the United States*. New York: R. R. Bowker, 1936. Reprint. New York: Burt Franklin, 1969. (Only vol. 2 was published.)

"The New and the Old: Perspective in Printing History" Part Two: *The 1976 Bookman's Yearbook*. First Annual Conference of the American Printing History Association.

Oswald, John C. *Printing in the Americas*. New York: Gregg Publishing Company, 1937.

Silver, Rollo. *The American Printer, 1787-1825*. Charlottesville: University Press of Virginia, 1967.

_____. *Typefounding in America, 1787-1825*. Charlottesville: University Press of Virginia, 1965.

Thomas, Isaiah. *The History of Printing in America*. 2 vols. 2d ed. Albany: J. Munsell, 1874. Reprint. New York: Burt Franklin, 1976.

Thompson, Susan O. *American Book Design and William Morris*. New York: R. R. Bowker, 1977.

Winterich, John T. *Early American Books and Printing*. Boston: Houghton Mifflin, 1935. Reprint. Detroit: Gale Research, 1974.

Woodbridge, Hensley, and Thompson, Lawrence S. *Printing in Colonial Spanish America*. Troy: Whitson Publishing Company, 1976.

Wroth, Lawrence C. *The Colonial Printer*. 2d rev. ed. Portland: Southworth-Anthoensen Press, 1938. Reprint. Charlottesville: Dominion Books, 1964.

Index